CBEST: CALIFORNIA BASIC EDUCATIONAL SKILLS TEST

American River College Library
4700 College Oak Drive
Sacramento, CA 95841

CBEST: CALIFORNIA BASIC EDUCATIONAL SKILLS TEST

5th Edition

New York

Copyright © 2011 LearningExpress, LLC.

All rights reserved under International and Pan-American Copyright Conventions.
Published in the United States by LearningExpress, LLC, New York.

Library of Congress Cataloging-in-Publication Data:
CBEST : California Basic Educational Skills Test.—5th ed.
   p. cm.
  Includes bibliographical references and index.
  ISBN-13: 978-1-57685-759-5 (alk. paper)
  ISBN-10: 1-57685-7599-X (alk. paper)
 1. California Basic Educational Skills Test—Study guides. I. Learning Express (Organization)

  LB3060.33.c34c24 2011
  370.76—dc22
                              2010027964

Printed in the United States of America

9 8 7 6 5 4 3 2 1

For more information or to place an order, contact LearningExpress at:
  2 Rector Street
  26th Floor
  New York, NY 10006

Or visit us at:
  www.learnatest.com

CONTENTS

INTRODUCTION	How to Use This Book	vii
CHAPTER 1:	What is the CBEST?	1
CHAPTER 2:	The LearningExpress Test Preparation System	9
CHAPTER 3:	Diagnostic CBEST Exam	27
CHAPTER 4:	CBEST Mini-Course	69
CHAPTER 5:	CBEST Practice Exam 1	159
CHAPTER 6:	CBEST Practice Exam 2	201
CHAPTER 7:	CBEST Practice Exam 3	247
GLOSSARY		287
ADDITIONAL ONLINE PRACTICE		293

HOW TO USE THIS BOOK

CHAPTER SUMMARY
So you have to take the CBEST, and you're wondering if this book can help you. The answer is YES! Read on to see how.

This book is designed to help you pass the California Basic Educational Skills Test (CBEST®). It contains all the information you'll need to help you improve your chances of achieving a good score—in the shortest amount of time possible.

The Book

As you will discover in subsequent chapters, one of the most important skills for a test taker to have is a good reading ability. Good readers often begin with an overview of the text they are about to take. So, if you haven't done so yet, you may want to look at the Table of Contents. By doing this, you will know what to expect. Knowing what to expect offers you the freedom and opportunity to focus on what is most relevant to your goals. This also allows you to maximize your time if you are in a hurry.

HOW TO USE THIS BOOK

After taking a look at the Table of Contents, turn to **Chapter 1**, "What is the CBEST?" This chapter provides you with the *Who, What, When, Where,* and *How,* those all-important details such as who must take the test, what's on it, when and where it's given, how it's scored, and how to register.

Once you know this information, move on to **Chapter 2**, which explains our innovative Learning-Express Test Preparation System. It is packed full of test-taking tips and advice developed exclusively for LearningExpress by leading test experts. This chapter shows you how to get prepared—physically, emotionally, and mentally—to take the CBEST. It also shows you how to use this book to set up an individualized study plan.

Chapter 3 is the first of four sample CBEST exams in this book. You can take this first exam as a diagnostic exercise to see where your strong and weak points are.

Next is **Chapter 4**, the "CBEST Mini-Course." This Mini-Course—successfully used for CBEST test prep classes in California—reviews everything you need to know to pass the CBEST. Conveniently divided into 24 lessons, the material can be covered effortlessly in half-hour segments. The first pages of Chapter 4 give you an outline of the topics covered in each of the 24 lessons. You can work through the whole Mini-Course from start to finish, or you can pick out the areas that you need to work on most and just concentrate on those. If you're still having trouble after working through the lessons in a given area, check out the last section of Chapter 4, "More Help with Reading, Math, and Writing." This section lists other books you can turn to for more advice.

In **Chapters 5**, **6**, and **7**, you have three complete, three-section, sample CBEST exams to help you practice your test-taking skills. Once finished with your practice tests, you will be able to evaluate your progress with the answer and scoring explanations included at the end of each of these three chapters. Answer explanations are written in an informative, yet conversational tone, so you can quickly diagnose your weakest areas and see where you might need more work.

There's nothing like having a lot of practice under your belt to make you feel confident when you go in to take the real exam!

CBEST Success

The most important factor in your success on the CBEST is you. You can't put this book under your pillow at night and expect to improve your score. But you can use this book to find out where you need to improve and what you need to know. If you carefully follow all the steps in the LearningExpress Test Preparation System, you'll be fully prepared for the CBEST, and you will go into the exam knowing how to conquer it.

CBEST: CALIFORNIA BASIC EDUCATIONAL SKILLS TEST

CHAPTER 1

WHAT IS THE CBEST?

CHAPTER SUMMARY
This chapter provides the *Who, What, When, Where, and How* of the CBEST—those all-important details such as who has to take the exam, what it's used for and what's on it, when and where it's given, how it's scored, and how to register.

California Education Code (Section 44252) requires that teachers, administrators, and other school practitioners demonstrate adequate proficiency, in English, of three basic skills: reading, mathematics, and writing. Administered by the Evaluation Systems group of Pearson, the California Basic Educational Skills Test (CBEST®) was created to assess and verify these skills. The CBEST is not a measurement of teaching abilities or skills; it is a tool for measuring proficiency in the more fundamental, necessary skills. These skills are used by all school practitioners at the elementary, secondary, and adult education levels.

By law, the CBEST provides separate scores in each of these three areas, and acceptable scores must be achieved in each area to meet the requirements of the code relative to credentialing and employment in California and Oregon.

In July 1984, the CBEST guideline was adopted by the Oregon Teacher Standards and Practices Commission (TSPC). Within six months, satisfactory CBEST scores were made mandatory for initial licensure in Oregon as a teacher, personnel specialist, or administrator. The CBEST test requirement is additional to other licensing requirements as set forth in the Oregon Revised Statutes (ORS, Chapter 342) and the Oregon Rules for Licensure of Teachers, Personnel Specialists, and Administrators (OAR, Chapter 584).

WHAT IS THE CBEST?

Who Must Take the CBEST?

California

In California, you are required to take the CBEST if any one of the following provisions applies to you:

- You are applying for a teaching or services credential for the first time.
- You are applying to be a day-to-day substitute.
- You are applying for issuance or renewal of an Emergency Permit (unless you already hold a valid California teaching credential for which a bachelor's degree is required).
- You are seeking employment in California, and satisfying the basic skills requirement is mandatory under ECS 44830. (If you are uncertain whether the CBEST is required in the school district where you are considering employment, contact the district directly.)
- You are applying for admission to either a teacher-preparation or services-credential program approved by the California Commission on Teacher Credentialing (CCTC) (unless you already hold a valid California teaching credential for which a bachelor's degree is required).

Oregon

Oregon requires passing CBEST scores prior to initial credentialing as a teacher, personnel specialist, or administrator, unless one of the following provisions is met:

- You can document completion of a regionally accredited doctoral degree.
- You already hold one type of Oregon license and are a first-time applicant for a license of a different type. For example, an Oregon-licensed teacher who applies for an initial personnel specialist license does not need CBEST scores.
- You give evidence of passing scores on Praxis I or the NTE Core Battery Test of Communication Skills and General Knowledge.

Who Is Exempt from the CBEST?

California

In California, you are exempt from taking the CBEST for the following kinds of employment:

- Instructor of adults in an apprenticeship program
- Teacher in a children's center or a development center
- Teacher in any subject for which a bachelor's degree is not required
- Provider of health services, unless you are also required to teach
- Student teacher status, which requires a Certificate of Clearance
- Educational Specialist in Deaf and Hearing Impaired or School Counseling Services, where the individual seeking employment is prelingually deaf. Service under this option is limited to state special schools or to classes for students who are deaf or hearing impaired. However, those who choose this option are required to complete a job-related assessment in lieu of the CBEST.
- Any position in which a valid, non-emergency California teaching credential is held that requires a bachelor's degree, and for which CBEST is not required for renewal
- Any position that requires the renewal or reissuance of a clear, or professional clear, credential

WHAT IS THE CBEST?

NOTE: CBEST states that candidates wishing to obtain an Exchange Credential, a Sojourn Credential, or a credential based upon the completion of a teacher-preparation program outside of California may obtain an initial teaching credential without meeting the CBEST requirement. All such candidates must pass the CBEST, however, during the first year of validity of the initial credential.

CBEST Details

What Types of Questions Are on the CBEST?

The CBEST is comprised of three separate sections: (1) Reading, which consists of 50 multiple-choice questions; (2) Mathematics, which consists of 50 multiple-choice questions; and (3) Writing, which consists of two essay subjects.

Questions in the Reading section are derived from two important skill areas: critical analysis/evaluation and research/comprehension. Drawn from a variety of fields, such as humanities, the social sciences, consumer affairs, or health, CBEST questions are based on passages that vary in degree of difficulty and complexity, and are designed to assess the test taker's ability to evaluate and comprehend the information presented. Some passages are longer (200 words or more); some are shorter (about 100 words). Some may be statements of one or two sentences, while others may even be tables or graphs. Every question is based on a particular passage, table, or graph. None requires prior knowledge, and all of the questions can be answered on the basis of the information provided.

The Mathematics section is mostly comprised of questions—presented as word problems—that evaluate your ability to solve mathematical problems. The questions are designed to assess three major skill areas: estimation, measurement, and statistical principles; computation and problem solving; and numerical and graphic relationships.

The Writing section is comprised of two essay subjects—both of which you must respond to—that are designed to assess your ability to write coherently, authoritatively, and persuasively. In one of the essays, you will be asked to analyze a situation or statement, while the other requires a written response relating to a personal experience. Your essays must be written in your own words, and you must write only on the topics presented. All points in both essays must address the assigned topic, and should be aimed at a specific audience. Essay responses must support any assertions with specific, relevant details and examples. The key to success here is to stay specific—do not digress! For more detailed information on what it takes to write a high-scoring essay, see the section on Writing in the CBEST Mini-Course (Chapter 4). The criteria for scoring the CBEST essays is found on pages 62–63 and at the end of Chapter 5; many tips for successfully writing an essay that receives a passing score are also found there.

How Long Does the CBEST Take?

When you take the CBEST, you have a total of four hours in which to complete the three sections. You do not need to complete all three sections in one four-hour sitting. However, the essays cannot be split up; both essays in the section must be completed in one sitting. You may choose to concentrate on one or two sections at any given test administration, reregister, and then work solely on a third section at a later date. If you choose this latter option, take note that regardless of the number of sections you are taking at any given sitting—even just *one*—the *entire test fee* is required, and you will be required to reregister each time.

If you choose to do the whole test in one four-hour sitting, know that you don't have to do the sections in any particular order. The test is not timed according to individual sections, so you may want to get the hardest sections out of the way first. You may want to do the essays first, because you can guess on the other sections if you run out of time. This may work to your advantage, because no points are deducted for guessing.

Doing the practice tests in this book, or taking advantage of the practice questions on the CD-ROM—which has the advantage of ease of use, and automatic, immediate test scores—will help you decide what is the best course of action for you on test day.

Paper- or Computer-Based Test?

You can take the CBEST in its traditional format, with a pencil and paper, or you can now take it on a computer at a Pearson Professional Center anywhere in the United States. The computer and paper tests are the same. They cover the same skills and have the same time limits. So why might you choose to take the test on computer instead of on paper?

If it isn't convenient for you to travel to California to take the paper test, the computer version is a good alternative. The test is offered more frequently as a computer version than it is as a paper version. Whether you are in California or not, taking the computer test allows you access to the unofficial test results for the math and reading sections before you leave the testing center. Be aware, however, that the cost of the computer version of the test may be higher than the paper version.

What Should I Bring to the Test Site?

Because of test security, few materials are allowed in the test-taking room. You will need to bring the following materials:

- Your admission ticket
- Several sharpened #2 pencils with erasers
- A current, government-issued photo ID with signature

Materials NOT permitted in the testing room (unless previously authorized or provided by NES) include:

- Scratch paper
- Calculators
- Dictionaries
- Cellular phones or other communication devices
- Alarm watches
- Unauthorized aids
- Food and drink

Bringing any prohibited materials to a test administration may result in your score(s) being voided. If you have questions or require more detailed information, call CBEST at 916-928-4001, from 7:30 A.M. to 3:30 P.M. Pacific Standard Time (PST).

What Is a Passing Score?

To pass the CBEST, you must pass all three sections of the CBEST. Raw scores can range from 1–50, and these are then converted to scaled scores ranging from 20–80. The passing scaled score on each section of the test is 41. You must achieve a minimum total score of 123 for the three sections (the sum of the Reading, Writing, and Mathematics scaled scores).

It is possible to pass the CBEST even if your scaled score in one or two sections is as low as 37, providing your total scaled score is 123 or higher. (Take note that regardless of how high your total scaled score might be, you will *not* pass the CBEST if, in any section, you get a scaled score *lower* than 37.)

WHAT IS THE CBEST?

What Do My Scores Mean?

You should receive your scores four to six weeks after the test date. For each section—Reading, Math, and Writing—your scores will tell whether or not you passed the section and will suggest areas within each section that you may need to improve. The score report will also include the highest score you have obtained so far in that section. A passing score on any part of the test means that you will not have to take that part of the CBEST again.

Retaking the Test

What happens if you fail, or fail to finish, one or more sections of the CBEST? Don't worry. You don't need to pass all three sections at the same time, nor is there a limit to the number of times you can retake any or all sections of the CBEST to achieve a passing score. Once you pass a section, you need never take that section again. However, you may wish to repeat a section already passed to achieve a higher score, if that higher score can help you reach the total score required to pass the entire CBEST.

Once you have passed the entire CBEST, you will never have to take it again. You need to pass the entire CBEST only once to qualify for the initial issuance or renewal of any teaching credential.

When Is the Test Given?

The paper version of the CBEST is offered six times a year, once every two months, at various locations throughout California and Oregon. It is usually given on the first or second Saturday of the months of February, April, June, August, October, and December.

The computer version of the CBEST is available during 12 windows per year, approximately once per month. During each window of testing, the Pearson Professional Center will offer testing on five or six days. The dates are available on a first-come, first-served basis. Check the CBEST website to determine which testing windows and dates are available in your time frame.

How Do I Register?

There are three periods of registration: Regular, Late, and Emergency; and three registration options: by mail, phone, or Internet.

For Regular Registration, you should register at least one month prior to the applicable test date. You can register either by mail or through the Internet; phone registration is not available for this option. If you register by mail, applications must be postmarked by the Regular Registration deadline, or received by the Late Registration deadline. If you register online, applications should be completed by 5:00 P.M. PST on the Regular Registration deadline.

For Late Registration (up to approximately two weeks prior to the test date), a late fee applies, and registration is granted on a space-available basis only. You may complete late registration by mail, phone, or Internet. If you are registering by mail, your completed materials must be received on or before the Late Registration deadline. If you register by phone, you must call before 5:00 P.M. PST on the Late Registration deadline. If you register online, your application must be finished by 5:00 P.M. PST on the Late Registration deadline.

For Emergency Registration (up to four days prior to the test), an additional late fee is charged, and registration is granted on a space-available basis only. You can register either by phone or Internet; mail registration is not available for this option. If you register by phone, you must call before 5:00 P.M. PST on the Emergency Registration deadline. If you are registering online, your application must be submitted by 5:00 P.M. PST on the Emergency Registration deadline. Emergency Registration limits you to ten test sites in California, and one in Oregon.

— WHAT IS THE CBEST? —

Alternative testing arrangements can be made for either religious reasons or for special needs accommodations. All requests for alternative testing arrangements must be postmarked by the Regular Registration deadline for the test date applied for. Be advised that registration deadlines are *strictly enforced*—and there are NO exceptions!

Whom Do I Contact with Questions?

For any questions, or more detailed information regarding registration procedures, test dates, or locations, contact:

CBEST Program
Evaluation Systems Pearson
P.O. Box 340880
Sacramento, CA 95834-0880
916-928-4001
Telephones are open 9:00 A.M.–5:00 P.M. PST,
  Monday–Friday, excluding holidays; Saturday test dates only: 7:00 A.M.–3:00 P.M. PST
Facsimile: 916-928-6110 (Note: Registration forms are not accepted by fax.)
Automated Information System is available 24 hours daily: 800-262-5080
CBEST website: www.cbest.nesinc.com
Teletypewriter (TTY) number
  916-928-4191

For more information about scheduling the computer version of the CBEST, contact:

Pearson Vue
800-989-8532
Telephones are open 7:00 A.M.–5:00 P.M. PST,
  Monday–Friday, excluding holidays.
Website: www.pearsonvue.com

For more detailed information about CBEST policies in general, contact:

California Commission on Teacher Credentialing (CCTC)
Information Services
P.O. Box 944270
Sacramento, CA 94244-2700
916-445-7254; If outside the 916 area code, call toll free:
  888-921-2682.
Telephones are open 1:00 P.M.–4:45 P.M. PST,
  Monday–Friday, excluding holidays.
Automated Information System is available 24 hours daily.
CCTC website: www.ctc.ca.gov
(Please include postal address in any e-mail messages.)

OR

Oregon Teacher Standards and Practices Commission
465 Commercial Street NE
Salem, OR 97310
503-378-3586

For more detailed information about CBEST test requirements in California and Oregon, or other questions:

- For college or university program admission in California, you can contact the department or school of education that you are interested in.
- For employment in California, you can contact the county school district's credentialing department, or office of education.
- For employment, or college or university Commission-approved program admission in Oregon, call the personnel office or the Education Service District, of the school district you are interested in, the Dean of Teacher Education at the university or college you are interested in, or the Oregon Teacher Standards and Practices Commission.

WHAT IS THE CBEST?

Don't Panic

The CBEST probably will not be the hardest test you will be faced with in your life. For many, it will require some careful and thoughtful preparation. If you have completed four years of college, you will be able to pass the CBEST. Some of you may need extensive review first, and some of you may need private tutoring. If you are willing to put forth the effort, passing is possible!

CHAPTER

THE LEARNINGEXPRESS TEST PREPARATION SYSTEM

CHAPTER SUMMARY
Taking the CBEST can be difficult. Achieving a passing score demands a lot of preparation. And you need that passing score if you want to be certified! The LearningExpress Test Preparation System, developed exclusively for LearningExpress by leading test experts, gives you the attitude and discipline you need to be successful.

First, the bad news: Taking the CBEST is no picnic, and neither is getting ready for it. Your future career as a teacher depends on a passing score, and there are all sorts of pitfalls that can keep you from doing your best on this important exam. Here are some of the obstacles that can stand in the way of your success:

- Being unfamiliar with the format of the exam
- Suffering from test anxiety
- Leaving your preparation to the last minute
- Not knowing vital test-taking skills: how to pace yourself through the exam, how to use the process of elimination, and when to guess
- Failing to prepare
- Not being in good mental and physical shape
- Arriving late at the test site, having to work on an empty stomach, or being uncomfortable during the exam because the room is too hot or cold

What's the common denominator of all of these test-taking pitfalls? One word: control. Who's in control, you or the exam?

Now the good news: The LearningExpress Test Preparation System puts *you* in control. You have to pass the CBEST only *once*, and in nine easy-to-follow steps, you will learn everything you need to know to make sure that you do. Why? Because *you* will be in charge of your preparation and and your performance on the exam. Other test takers may let the test get the better of them; other test takers may be unprepared or out of shape, but not you. You will have taken all the steps that you need to take to get a good score on the CBEST.

Here's how the LearningExpress Test Preparation System works: Nine easy steps lead you through everything you need to know and do to master your exam. Each of the steps includes both reading about the step and one or more activities. It's important that you do the activities along with the reading, or you won't be getting the full benefit of the system. Each step tells you approximately how much time that step will take to complete.

We estimate that working through the entire system will take you approximately three hours, though it's perfectly acceptable if you work faster or slower than the time estimates assume. If you can take a whole afternoon or evening, you can work through the LearningExpress Test Preparation System in one sitting. Otherwise, you can break it up, and do just one or two steps a day for the next several days. It's up to you—remember, *you're* in control.

Step 1: Get Information

Time to complete: 60 minutes
Activities: Use the suggestions listed here to find out about the content of your exam

Knowledge is power. The first step in the LearningExpress Test Preparation System is finding out everything you can about the CBEST. Once you have your information, the next steps in the LearningExpress Test Preparation System will show you what to do with it.

Part A: Straight Talk about the CBEST

Why do you have to take this exam? The states of California and Oregon require the CBEST of all applicants for a first-time teaching or service credential. Unless the applicant already has a California teaching credential or is exempted, he or she must take the CBEST in order to be issued—or obtain renewal of—an Emergency Permit. (This latter requirement does not apply to Oregon applicants.) The CBEST might also be required for

Step 1: Get Information	60 minutes
Step 2: Conquer Test Anxiety	20 minutes
Step 3: Make a Plan	25 minutes
Step 4: Learn to Manage Your Time	10 minutes
Step 5: Learn to Use the Process of Elimination	20 minutes
Step 6: Know When to Guess	20 minutes
Step 7: Reach Your Peak Performance Zone	10 minutes
Step 8: Get Your Act Together	10 minutes
Step 9: Do It!	5 minutes
Total	**3 hours**

THE LEARNINGEXPRESS TEST PREPARATION SYSTEM

applicants who have not taught for 39 months or more, and for students applying for admission to a California Commission on Teacher Credentialing (CCTC) approved teacher-preparation program.

But why reading, writing, and math? Why doesn't the CBEST test professional knowledge instead? Simply because the states of California and Oregon want to know that every teacher has the basic skills necessary both to communicate clearly to students, parents, and colleagues and to impart their knowledge of the English language and math to their students. Basically, the states just want to know that you *did* learn what you should have learned in high school and college.

Don't forget that this test covers material you learned in high school. This is not a test of teaching strategies, and it is not a test of what you master in college. The test will not tell you what kind of teacher you will make. Rather, it will simply show the state that you are able to understand basic math, reading, and writing concepts. Passing the CBEST is an important step on your path to certification. And that's why you are reading this book. The LearningExpress Test Preparation System will help you achieve your goal of passing the CBEST.

Part B: What's on the Test

If you haven't already done so, stop here and read the first chapter of this book, which gives you vital information on the CBEST. The CBEST is given six times a year at locations in California and Oregon; you can go to the placement office at your school or check the CBEST website, at the Web address listed in Chapter 1, to find out when and where to take the exam.

The CBEST tests the skills reflected in the practice exams in this book:

- **Reading comprehension:** demonstrating skills in criticism, understanding literal meaning, and making inferences
- **Writing:** demonstrating insight, logical thinking, and the ability to write clearly and coherently for a specific audience
- **Mathematics:** demonstrating skills in arithmetic, algebra, measurement, and geometry

Step 2: Conquer Test Anxiety

Time to complete: 20 minutes
Activity: Take the Test Stress Test

Having complete information about the exam is the first step to mastering the exam. Next, you have to overcome one of the biggest obstacles to test success: test anxiety. Test anxiety can not only impair your perfomance on the exam, but can even keep you from preparing! With the LearningExpress Test Preparation System, you'll learn stress management techniques that will help you succeed on your exam. Learn these strategies now, and practice them as you work through the exams in this book, so they'll be second nature to you by exam day.

Combating Test Anxiety

The first thing you need to know is that a little test anxiety is a good thing. Everyone gets nervous before a big exam—and if that nervousness motivates you to prepare thoroughly, so much the better. It's said that Sir Laurence Olivier, one of the foremost British actors of the twentieth century, felt nauseous before every performance. But his stage fright didn't impair his performance. In fact, it probably gave him a little extra edge—just the kind of edge you'll need to do well on the CBEST.

On page 10 is the Test Stress Test. Stop here and answer the questions to find out whether your level of test anxiety is something you will need to manage.

Test Stress Test

You need to worry about test anxiety only if it is extreme enough to impair your performance. The following questionnaire will provide a diagnosis of your level of test anxiety. In the blank before each statement, write the number that most accurately describes your experience.

0 = Never
1 = Once or twice
2 = Sometimes
3 = Often

___ I have gotten so nervous before an exam that I simply put down the books and didn't study for it.
___ I have experienced disabling physical symptoms such as vomiting and severe headaches because I was nervous about an exam.
___ I have simply not showed up for an exam because I was scared to take it.
___ I have experienced dizziness and disorientation while taking an exam.
___ I have had trouble filling in the little circles because my hands were shaking too hard.
___ I have failed an exam because I was too nervous to complete it.
___ **Total:** Add up the numbers in the blanks.

Your Test Anxiety Score

Here are the steps you should take, depending on your score. If you scored:

- **Below 3**, your level of test anxiety is nothing to worry about; it is probably just enough to give you that little extra edge.
- **Between 3 and 6**, your test anxiety may be enough to impair your performance, and you should practice the stress management techniques listed in this section to try to bring your test anxiety down to manageable levels.
- **Above 6**, your level of test anxiety is a serious concern. In addition to practicing the stress management techniques listed in this section, you may want to seek additional, personal help. Call your local high school or community college and ask for the academic counselor. Tell the counselor that you have a level of test anxiety that sometimes keeps you from being able to take an exam. The counselor may be willing to help you or may suggest someone else you should talk to.

THE LEARNINGEXPRESS TEST PREPARATION SYSTEM

Stress Management before the Test

If you feel your level of anxiety getting the best of you in the weeks before the test, here is what you need to do to bring the level down:

- **Get prepared**. There's nothing like knowing what to expect and being prepared for it to put you in control of test anxiety. That's why you're reading this book. When you start to feel anxious, remind yourself of the time and effort that you have invested in preparing. You have the skills to pass the test.
- **Practice self-confidence**. A positive attitude is a great way to combat test anxiety. This is no time to be humble or shy. Stand in front of the mirror and say to your reflection, "I'm prepared. I'm full of self-confidence. I'm going to ace this test. I know I can do it." Say it into a recorder and play it back once a day. Memorize the words. If you hear it often enough, you'll believe it.
- **Fight negative messages**. Every time someone starts telling you how hard the exam is or how it's almost impossible to get a good score, start telling them the self-confidence messages you have been practicing. If others are speaking negatively, politely ask them to stop. Don't give your time or energy to people that aren't helping you toward your goal.
- **Visualize**. Imagine yourself standing in front of your class or chatting with a student. Think of yourself coming home with your first paycheck as a teacher and taking your family or friends out to celebrate. Visualizing success can help make it happen—and it reminds you of why you're going through all this work in preparing for the exam.
- **Exercise**. Physical activity helps calm your body down and focus your mind. Besides, being in good physical shape can actually help you do well on the exam. Go for a run, lift weights, go swimming—and do it regularly.

Stress Management on Test Day

There are several ways you can bring down your level of test anxiety on test day. Practice them in the weeks before the test; they'll be effective only if you know which ones work best for you.

- **Deep breathing**. Take a deep breath while you count to five. Hold it for a count of one, then let it out on a count of five. Repeat several times.
- **Move your body**. Try rolling your head in a circle. Rotate your shoulders. Shake your hands from the wrist. Many people find these movements very relaxing.
- **Visualize again**. Think of the place where you are most relaxed: perhaps lying on the beach in the sun or walking through the park. Now close your eyes and imagine you're actually there. If you practice in advance, you'll find that you only need a few seconds of this exercise to experience a significant increase in your sense of well-being.

When anxiety threatens to overwhelm you during the exam, there are still things you can do to manage the stress level:

- **Repeat your self-confidence messages**. You should have them memorized by now. Say them silently to yourself, and believe them!
- **Visualize one more time**. This time, visualize yourself moving smoothly and quickly through the test, answering every question right and finishing with time to spare. Like most visualization techniques, this one works best if you've practiced it ahead of time.
- **Find an easy question**. Skim over the test until you find an easy question, and answer it. Getting even one circle filled in gets you into the test-taking groove.
- **Take a mental break**. Everyone loses concentration once in a while, so don't worry about it.

13

THE LEARNINGEXPRESS TEST PREPARATION SYSTEM

Instead, accept what has happened. Say to yourself, "Hey, I lost it there for a minute. My brain is taking a break." Put down your pencil, close your eyes, and do some deep breathing for a few seconds. Then you're ready to go back to work.

Use these tried and true techniques ahead of time, and you'll see how they work for you!

Step 3: Make a Plan

Maybe the most important thing you can do to manage anxiety and get control of your exam is to make a study plan. Too many people fail their test simply because they don't allot enough study time for test preparation. Spending hours cramming on the day before the test and poring over sample test questions only raises the level of your test anxiety. There is simply no substitute for careful preparation and practice over time.

So DON'T fall into the cram trap. Take control of your preparation time by mapping out a study schedule. In fact, all the instructional material you'll need to study for the CBEST is in Chapter 4, the "CBEST Mini-Course." The "Mini-Course" is conveniently divided into 24 half-hour lessons, so a study schedule has already been provided for you, built right into the LearningExpress Test Preparation System. The best way to devise your own personal study plan is to first do the sample CBEST Diagnostic Exam in Chapter 3 of this book. Your study plan will be based on your own personalized scores from each of the individual sections—with this knowledge, you can then concentrate on the areas that give you the most difficulty.

On the following pages, we have provided sample schedules based on how much time you have before you take the exam. If you have months before the exam—lucky you! Remember: You can't improve your reading, writing, and math skills overnight. Choose a plan that fits your schedule and make a committment to yourself to stick to it. Having a plan will help you pass the CBEST.

You will do best if you set aside some time every day for study and practice. Try for at least 30 minutes a day—but even a few minutes a day, with a half-hour or more on weekends, can make a big difference in your score—and your chances of landing that teaching job will dramatically be improved.

Schedule A: The Leisure Plan

If you have six months or more in which to prepare, you're very fortunate! Make the most of your time.

Schedule B: The Just-Enough-Time Plan

If you have three to four months before the exam, you still have enough time to prepare for the written test. This schedule assumes four months; stretch it out or compress it if you have more or less time.

Schedule C: More Study in Less Time

If you have one to three months before the exam, you still have enough time for some concentrated study that will help you improve your score. This schedule is built around a two-month time frame. If you have only one month, spend an extra couple of hours a week to get all these steps in. If you have three months, take some of the steps from Schedule B and fit them in.

Schedule A: The Leisure Plan

Time	Preparation
Exam minus 6 months	Take the CBEST Diagnostic in Chapter 3 and skim the 24 lessons in the Mini-Course. Based on your scores on the individual sections of the diagnostic exam, divide up the next five months into segments of time which you estimate each lesson will take. Be sure to schedule in more time on those skills that give you problems.
Exam minus 6 months to 2 months	Work steadily through each lesson, sticking to your schedule and being sure to do the practice exercises. Besides doing the lessons, be sure to read more during these months than you are accustomed to—novels, nonfiction books, magazines, newspapers; it is very important for the CBEST that you hone your reading skills. Also, look at the "More Help" section of the Mini-Course. Choose one or two books from the area that gives you the most trouble, and use them to help you improve your weak area.
Exam minus 4 months	Take the first practice exam, CBEST Practice Exam 1. Use your score to help you decide where to concentrate your efforts. Review the relevant lessons of the Mini-Course and get the help of a friend or teacher. If necessary, choose additional resources from the "More Help" section of the Mini-Course to help you.
Exam minus 2 months	Take the second practice test, CBEST Practice Exam 2, to see how much you've improved, and then, again, review the areas that give you the most trouble.
Exam minus 2 weeks	Take the third practice test. CBEST Practice Exam 3, to see if there are areas that still need refining. Review the areas that need improvement.
Exam minus 1 day	Relax. Do something unrelated to the exam. Eat a good meal and go to bed at your usual time.

Schedule D: The Short-Term Plan

If you have three weeks or less before the exam, you really have your work cut out for you. Set aside a half-hour out of your day, every day, for study. This schedule assumes you have the whole three weeks to prepare; if you have less time, you'll have to compress the schedule accordingly.

Step 4: Learn to Manage Your Time

Time to complete: 10 minutes to read, many hours of practice!

Activities: Practice these strategies as you take the sample tests in this book

Steps 4, 5, and 6 of the LearningExpress Test Preparation System put you in charge of your exam by showing you test-taking strategies that work. Practice these strategies as you take the sample tests in this book, and then you'll be ready to use them on test day.

First, you'll take control of your time on the exam. The CBEST has a time limit of four hours, which may give you more than enough time to complete all the questions—or may not. It's a terrible feeling to hear the

Schedule B: The Just-Enough-Time Plan

Time	Preparation
Exam minus 4 months	Take the CBEST diagnostic in Chapter 3 and skim the 24 lessons in the Mini-Course. Based on your scores on the individual sections of the diagnostic exam, divide up the next four months into segments of time which you estimate each lesson will take. Be sure to schedule in more time on those skills that give you problems.
Exam minus 4 months to 1 month	Work steadily through each lesson, sticking to your schedule and being sure to do the practice exercises. Besides doing the lessons, schedule in more reading during these months than you're used to doing—novels, nonfiction books, magazines, newspapers; it is very important for the CBEST that your reading skills be in top shape. If you fall behind in your schedule, remember that *you're* in control—it's your schedule. Don't shrug your shoulders and moan, "I'll never make it!" Just take a look at the schedule, see where you went off track, revise the schedule for the time you have left, and continue.
Exam minus 3 months	Take the first practice exam, CBEST Practice Exam 1. Use your score to help you decide where to concentrate your efforts. Review the relevant lessons of the Mini-Course and get the help of a friend or teacher. If you need more help, choose additional resources.
Exam minus 6 weeks	Take the second practice test, CBEST Practice Exam 2, to see how much you've improved, and then, again, review the areas that give you the most trouble.
Exam minus 2 weeks	Take the third practice test, CBEST Practice Exam 3, to see if there are areas that still need refining. Review the areas that need improvement.
Exam minus 1 day	Relax. Do something unrelated to the exam. Eat a good meal and go to bed at your usual time.

examiner say, "Five minutes left," when you're only three-quarters of the way through the test. Here are some tips to keep that from happening to you.

- **Follow directions.** If the directions are given orally, listen to them. If they're written on the exam booklet, read them carefully. Ask questions before the exam begins if there's anything you don't understand. In your exam booklet, write down the beginning time and the ending time of the exam.
- **Pace yourself.** Glance at your watch every 15 minutes, and compare the time to how far you've gotten in the exam. When one-quarter of the time has elapsed, you should be a quarter of the way through the exam, and so on. If you're falling behind, pick up the pace a bit.
- **Keep moving.** Don't waste time on one question. If you don't know the answer, and are taking the paper exam, skip the question and move on. Circle the number of the question in your test booklet in case you have time to come back to it later.
- **Keep track of your place on the answer sheet.** If you are taking the paper exam and you skip a question, make sure you skip the corresponding bubble on the answer sheet too. Check yourself every 5–10 questions to make sure the question number and the answer sheet number are still the same.
- **Don't rush.** Though you should keep moving, rushing won't help. Try to keep calm. Work methodically and quickly.

Schedule C: More Study in Less Time

Time	Preparation
Exam minus 2 months	Take the CBEST diagnostic in Chapter 3 and skim the 24 lessons in the Mini-Course. Based on your scores on the individual sections of the diagnostic exam, divide up the next month into segments of time which you estimate each lesson will take. Be sure to schedule in more time on those skills that give you problems.
Exam minus 2 months to 1 month	Work quickly but steadily through each lesson, sticking to your schedule and being sure to do the practice exercises. Besides doing the lessons, schedule in more reading than you usually do—novels, nonfiction books, magazines, newspapers; it is crucial for the CBEST that you sharpen your reading skills. If you fall behind in your schedule, remember that *you* are the one who devised the schedule, and you're in control. Don't take to your bed lamenting, "I can't, I can't!" Just peruse your schedule, see where you went astray, revise the schedule for the time you have left, and forge ahead.
Exam minus 6 weeks	Take the first practice exam, CBEST Practice Exam 1. Use your score to help you decide where to concentrate your efforts. Review the relevant lessons of the Mini-Course and get the help of a friend or teacher. If necessary, get more help.
Exam minus 2 weeks	Take the second practice test, CBEST Practice Exam 2, to see how much you've improved, and then, again, review the areas that give you the most trouble.
Exam minus 1 week	Take the third practice test, CBEST Practice Exam 3, to see if there are areas that still need refining. Review the areas that need improvement.
Exam minus 1 day	Relax. Do something unrelated to the exam. Eat a good meal and go to bed at your usual time.

Schedule D: The Short-Term Plan

Time	Preparation
Exam minus 3 weeks	Take the CBEST diagnostic in Chapter 3 and skim the 24 lessons in the Mini-Course. Based on your score, choose one area to concentrate on this week: reading, writing, or math. Spend an hour a day working on that area.
Exam minus 2 weeks	First, skim over the CBEST Mini-Course lessons on the areas you didn't study last week. Choose six lessons to do in the first three days of this week. For the rest of the days, go back to the one area you need the most work on, and review the lessons that were most difficult for you.
Exam minus 10 days	Take the first practice exam, CBEST Practice Exam 1. Use your score to help you decide where to concentrate your efforts. Review the relevant lessons and get the help of a friend or teacher on those areas.
Exam minus 1 week	Take the second practice test, CBEST Practice Exam 2, to see how much you've improved, and then, again, review the areas that give you the most trouble.
Exam minus 3 days	Take the third practice test, CBEST Practice Exam 3, to see if there are areas that still need refining. Review the areas that need improvement.
Exam minus 1 day	Relax. Do something unrelated to the exam. Eat a good meal and go to bed at your usual time.

Step 5: Learn to Use the Process of Elimination

Time to complete: 20 minutes
Activity: Complete the worksheet, "Using the Process of Elimination"

After time management, your next most important tool for taking control of your exam is using the process of elimination wisely. It's standard test-taking wisdom that you should always read all the answer choices before choosing your answer. This helps you find the right answer by eliminating wrong answer choices. And, sure enough, that standard wisdom applies to your exam, too.

Let's say you're facing a reading comprehension question like this:

13. According to the passage, "Biology uses a <u>binomial</u> system of classification." In the context of the passage, the word *binomial* most nearly means
    a. understanding the law.
    b. having two names.
    c. scientifically sound.
    d. having a double meaning.

If you happen to know what *binomial* means, of course, you don't need to use the process of elimination, but let's assume that you don't. So you look at the answer choices. "Understanding the law" doesn't sound likely for something having to do with biology. So you eliminate choice **a**—and now you have only three answer choices to deal with. Mark an X next to choice **a** so you never have to read it again.

On to the other answer choices. If you know that the prefix *bi-* means *two*, as in *bicycle*, you'll flag choice **b** as a possible answer. Put a check mark beside it, meaning "good answer, I might use this one."

Choice **c**, "scientifically sound," is a possibility. At least it's about science, not law. It could work here, though when you think about it, having a "scientifically sound" classification system in a scientific field is kind of redundant. You remember the *bi* thing in *binomial*, and probably continue to like choice **b** better. But you're not sure, so you put a question mark next to **c**, meaning "well, maybe."

Now, choice **d**, "having a double meaning." You're still keeping in mind that *bi-* means *two*, so this one looks possible at first. But then you look again at the sentence the word belongs in, and you think, "Why would biology want a system of classification that has two meanings? That wouldn't work very well!" If you're really taken with the idea that *bi* means *two*, you might put a question mark here. But if you're feeling a little more confident, you'll put an **X**. You've already got a better answer picked out.

Now your question looks like this:

13. According to the passage, "Biology uses a <u>binomial</u> system of classification." In the context of the passage, the word *binomial* most nearly means
    X a. understanding the law.
    ✓ b. having two names.
    ? c. scientifically sound.
    ? d. having a double meaning.

You've got just one check mark, for a good answer. If you're pressed for time, you should simply mark choice **b** on your answer sheet. If you've got the time to be extra careful, you could compare your check-mark answer to your question-mark answers to make sure that it's better. (It is: The *binomial* system in biology is the one that gives a two-part genus and species name like *homo sapiens*.)

It's good to have a system for marking good, bad, and maybe answers. We're recommending this one:

X = bad
✓ = good
? = maybe

THE LEARNINGEXPRESS TEST PREPARATION SYSTEM

If you don't like these marks, devise your own system. Just make sure you do it before you're working through the practice exams in this book. This way it will be second nature during the test.

Even when you think you're absolutely clueless about a question, you can often use the process of elimination technique to get rid of one answer choice. If so, you're better prepared to make an educated guess, as you'll see in Step 6. More often, the process of elimination allows you to get down to only two possibly right answers. Then you're in a stronger position to guess. And sometimes, even though you don't know the right answer, you can find it simply by getting rid of the wrong ones, as you did in the previous example.

Try using your reasoning skills on the questions in the Using the Process of Elimination worksheet. The answer explanations there show one possible way you might use the process to arrive at the right answer.

The process of elimination is your tool for the next step, which is knowing when to guess.

Using the Process of Elimination

Use the process of elimination to answer the following questions.

1. Ilsa is as old as Meghan will be in five years. The difference between Ed's age and Meghan's age is twice the difference between Ilsa's age and Meghan's age. Ed is 29. How old is Ilsa?
   a. 4
   b. 10
   c. 19
   d. 24

2. "All drivers of commercial vehicles must carry a valid commercial driver's license whenever operating a commercial vehicle."
   According to this sentence, which of the following people need NOT carry a commercial driver's license?
   a. a truck driver idling his engine while waiting to be directed to a loading dock
   b. a bus operator backing her bus out of the way of another bus in the parking lot
   c. a taxi driver driving his personal car to the grocery store
   d. a limousine driver taking the limousine to her home after dropping off her last passenger of the evening

3. Smoking tobacco has been linked to
   a. increased risk of stroke and heart attack.
   b. all forms of respiratory disease.
   c. increasing mortality rates over the past ten years.
   d. juvenile delinquency.

4. What can gardeners do to cause a gydrangea to produce blue flowers?
   a. Gardeners can add aluminum sulfate to the soil to lower the pH and cause the plant to produce blue flowers.
   b. Gardeners can add lime or high phosphorous fertilizer to the soil to raise the pH and cause the plant to produce blue flowers.
   c. Gardeners can add blue food coloring to the soil to lower the pH and cause the plant to produce blue flowers.
   d. Gardeners cannot change the color of the blossoms of a hydrangea plant.

Using the Process of Elimination (continued)

Answers

Here are the answers, as well as some suggestions as to how you might have used the process of elimination to find them.

1. **d.** You should have eliminated choice **a** immediately. Ilsa can't be four years old if Meghan is going to be Ilsa's age in five years. The best way to eliminate other answer choices is to compare them against the information given in the problem. For instance, for choice **b**, if Ilsa is 10, then Meghan must be 5 years old. The difference in their ages is 5. The difference between Ed's age, 29, and Meghan's age, 5, is 24. Is 24 two times 5? No. Then choice **b** is wrong. You could eliminate choice **c** in the same way and be left with choice **d**.

2. **c.** Note the word *not* in the question, and go through the answers one by one. Is the truck driver in choice **a** "operating a commercial vehicle?" Yes, idling counts as "operating," so he needs to have a commercial driver's license. Likewise, the bus operator in choice **b** is operating a commercial vehicle; the question doesn't say the operator has to be on the street. The limo driver in choice **d** is operating a commercial vehicle, even if it doesn't have a passenger in it. However, the taxi driver in choice **c** is not operating a commercial vehicle, but his own private car.

3. **a.** You could eliminate choice **b** simply because of the presence of the word *all*. Such absolutes hardly ever appear in correct answer choices. Choice **c** looks attractive until you think a little about what you know—aren't fewer people smoking these days, rather than more? So how could smoking be responsible for a higher mortality rate? (If you didn't know that *mortality rate* means the rate at which people die, you might keep this choice as a possibility, but you would still be able to eliminate two answers and have only two to choose from.) It's hard to imagine that smoking could be directly responsible for juvenile delinquency so you could eliminate choice **d**. You are left with the correct choice, **a**.

4. **a.** Even if you don't know much about gardening, you can still use the process of elimination to improve your chances of getting this answer correct. Consider choice **d** first. The question implies that gardeners can change the color of the hydrangea blossoms, but choice **d** contradicts this. Answers that contradict information in the question are usually wrong, so we can eliminate **d**. Choice **c** is a little silly compared to the first two choices. Food coloring isn't something you usually see people use in the garden, so eliminate **c**. This narrows your options down to **a** and **b**. The answers sound similar, so you would either have to know which choice is correct, or you could now make a guess. By narrowing the reasonable choices down to two, your odds of getting the answer right is up to 50%!

THE LEARNINGEXPRESS TEST PREPARATION SYSTEM

Step 6: Know When to Guess

Time to complete: 20 minutes
Activity: Complete the worksheet, "Your Guessing Ability"

Armed with the process of elimination, you're ready to take control of one of the big questions in test taking: Should I guess? The first and main answer is "Yes." The CBEST exam has no "guessing penalty," so you have nothing to lose and everything to gain from guessing. The more complicated answer depends on you—your personality and your "guessing intuition."

Simply go ahead and guess. Try not to guess wildly unless you absolutely have to. Remember to read the question carefully. You may know more about the subject than you think. Use the process of elimination as outlined in Step 5.

"Yes," you might say, "but the whole idea of guessing makes me nervous. I'm not good at guessing." Maybe, maybe not. Maybe you're not much of a risk-taker, so you don't like to guess. But remember, your score won't be lowered if you guess wrong.

Maybe you really think you have lousy intuition. It seems like, when you have to guess, you *always* guess wrong! Test out your assumption about your guessing ability. Complete the Your Guessing Ability worksheet to get an idea of how good or bad your intuition really is.

Step 7: Reach Your Peak Performance Zone

Time to complete: 10 minutes to read; weeks to complete
Activity: Complete the Physical Preparation Checklist

To get ready for a challenge like a big exam, you have to take control of your physical, as well as your mental, state. Exercise, proper diet, and rest will ensure that your body works with, rather than against, your mind on test day, as well as during your preparation.

Exercise

If you don't already have a regular exercise program going, the time during which you're preparing for an exam is actually an excellent time to start one. And if you're already keeping fit—or trying to get that way—don't let the pressure of preparing for an exam fool you into quitting now. Exercise helps reduce stress by pumping good-feeling hormones called endorphins into your system. It also increases the oxygen supply throughout your body, including your brain, so you'll be at peak performance on test day.

A half hour of vigorous activity—enough to raise a sweat—every day should be your aim. If you're really pressed for time, every other day is fine. Choose an activity you like and get out there and do it. Jogging with a friend or listening to music always makes the time go faster.

But don't overdo it. You don't want to exhaust yourself. Moderation is the key.

Diet

First of all, cut out all the junk food. Go easy on caffeine and nicotine, and eliminate alcohol from your system at least two weeks before the exam.

What your body needs for peak performance is simply a balanced diet. Eat plenty of fruits and vegetables, along with protein and carbohydrates. Foods that are high in lecithin (an amino acid), such as fish and beans, are especially good "brain foods." Eating wild salmon, blueberries, walnuts, and even dark chocolate can result in improved thinking and concentrating abilities.

On the night before test day, be aware of what carbohydrates you eat. If you munch on sweet cereal or a donut, you will find yourself running out of steam in a few short hours. Instead, look for complex carbohydrates for energy without the crash. Eat whole

Your Guessing Ability

The following are ten difficult questions. You're not supposed to know the answers. Rather, this is an assessment of your ability to guess when you don't have a clue. Read each question carefully, just as if you expected to be able to answer it. If you have any knowledge at all of the subject of the question, use that knowledge to help you eliminate wrong answer choices.

1. A bench is
   a. an object with four hexagon-shaped legs.
   b. an object which has two surfaces, one 12 inches long.
   c. an object which has a base measuring 48 inches high and a seat measuring 36 inches long.
   d. an object with legs and a seat.
   e. an object with six identical legs.

2. A farce is
   a. a sad story.
   b. a long work of fiction.
   c. a comedic work, especially in which the action is exaggerated or highly improbable.
   d. an epic tale.
   e. the beginning of a story.

3. How many teeth are in an average adult human's mouth?
   a. 17
   b. 32
   c. 56
   d. 9
   e. 60

4. Russia did not sign the Treaty of Versailles because
   a. Tsar Alexander I wanted Napoleon out of Russia.
   b. Russia would not negotiate the distribution of land with representatives of the Allied Powers.
   c. Russia would not discuss terms with the representatives from France, Great Britain, and the United States.
   d. Russia was not offered enough land in the treaty.
   e. Lenin pulled Russia out of World War I earlier.

5. The number 0 is
   a. both prime and composite.
   b. a multiple of all numbers.
   c. divisible by 3.
   d. neither prime nor composite.
   e. the absolute value of 1 and −1.

6. What is a scientist who specializes in the study of ecosystems?
   a. an ecologist
   b. an entomologist
   c. a naturalist
   d. a biologist
   e. an agronomist

7. Which best describes John Steinbeck's *The Grapes of Wrath*?
   a. a tale of the difficult life of a poor sharecropper family who travels to California during the Great Depression
   b. a story about how an Irish immigrant and a wealthy rancher become intertwined
   c. a description of the author's travels across the United States with his dog Charlie
   d. a discussion of the settlement of the western half of the United States in the 1800s
   e. a folktale that describes the activities of a family of farmers in South Africa

Your Guessing Ability (continued)

8. What statement is true about mosquitoes?
   a. Mosquitoes always carry diseases such as the West Nile virus.
   b. Mosquito eggs never survive through the winter.
   c. Heat, light, perspiration, and carbon dioxide attract mosquitoes.
   d. There are about 700 different species of mosquitoes.
   e. Mosquitoes survive only in spring and summer.

9. What statement is true about synthetic motor oil?
   a. Synthetic motor oils always cost more than petroleum-based motor oils.
   b. Synthetic motor oils often use a combination of up to three different base fluids.
   c. Cars uisng synthetic motor oils start more easily than cars with petroleum-based motor oils.
   d. Automobile manufactures never advocate using synthetic motor oil in new cars.
   e. Synthetic motor oil is only available to customers in the United States.

10. What islands became independent as the nation of Kiribati in 1979?
    a. the Gilbert, Phoenix, and most of the Line Islands
    b. the Marshall Islands
    c. Diego Garcia Island and Bikini Atoll Island
    d. Samoa and the Island of Tuvalu
    e. the islands of Tahiti, Fiji, and Vanuatu

Answers

Check your answers against the following correct answers. Read the strategies that follow for making your best guess on these questions.

1. **d.** Look at the answer choices. Some are very specific, one is general. If you must guess, choose the most general choice.
2. **c.** The length of an answer can stand out. If you must guess, look for an answer that is shorter or longer than the rest.
3. **b.** When the answers are numbers, choose a middle value.
4. **e.** In this case, two responses (**b** and **c**) mean the same thing. When that happens, neither is likely to be correct.
5. **d.** When you are given two responses that are opposite, one of them is probably correct. The choice, then, is between **a** and **d**.
6. **a.** In this case, one answer contains a word very similar to a word in the question. Don't disregard an answer that seems obvious.
7. **a.** Look for the response that reflects information in the question. In this example, grapes grow in California, and people looking for work during the Great Depression would naturally feel anger, or wrath.
8. **c.** Watch absolute words, such as *always*, *never*, *only*, *all*, and *none*. These answers are rarely correct.
9. **b.** In this case, the more general word, *often*, is the clue that the answer is correct.
10. **a.** If you have no idea, just guess. You have a 25% chance of being correct. Choose one letter to use as a guess for all questions that you must outright guess on.

Physical Preparation Checklist

During the week before the test, write down (1) what physical exercise you engaged in and for how long and (2) what you ate for each meal. Remember, you're trying for at least a half hour of exercise every other day (preferably every day) and a balanced diet that's light on junk food.

Exam minus 7 days
Exercise: _____ for _____ minutes
Breakfast: _____
Lunch: _____
Dinner: _____
Snacks: _____

Exam minus 6 days
Exercise: _____ for _____ minutes
Breakfast: _____
Lunch: _____
Dinner: _____
Snacks: _____

Exam minus 5 days
Exercise: _____ for _____ minutes
Breakfast: _____
Lunch: _____
Dinner: _____
Snacks: _____

Exam minus 4 days
Exercise: _____ for _____ minutes
Breakfast: _____
Lunch: _____
Dinner: _____
Snacks: _____

Exam minus 3 days
Exercise: _____ for _____ minutes
Breakfast: _____
Lunch: _____
Dinner: _____
Snacks: _____

Exam minus 2 days
Exercise: _____ for _____ minutes
Breakfast: _____
Lunch: _____
Dinner: _____
Snacks: _____

Exam minus 1 day
Exercise: _____ for _____ minutes
Breakfast: _____
Lunch: _____
Dinner: _____
Snacks: _____

grains, beans, nuts, oats, and sweet potatoes. Add some protein for energy that will last through the test.

Rest

You probably know how much sleep you need every night to be at your best, even if you don't always get it. Make sure you do get that much sleep, though, for at least a week before the exam. Moderation is important here, too. Extra sleep will just make you groggy.

If you're not a morning person and your exam will be given in the morning, you should reset your internal clock so that your body doesn't think you're taking an exam at 3 A.M. You have to start this process well before the exam. Try to get up a half hour earlier each morning, and then go to bed half an hour earlier that night. The next morning, get up half an hour earlier, and so on. How long you will have to do this depends on how late you're used to waking.

Step 8: Get Your Act Together

Time to complete: 10 minutes to read; time to complete will vary
Activity: Complete the Final Preparations worksheet

You're in control of your mind and body; you're in charge of test anxiety, your preparation, and your test-taking strategies. Now it's time to take charge of external factors, like the testing site and the materials you need to take the exam.

Find Out Where the Test Is and Make a Trial Run

You'll know ahead of time when and where your exam is being held. But do you know how to get to the testing site? Do you know how long it will take to get there? If not, make a trial run, preferably on the same day of the week at the same time of day. Make note, on the Final Preparations worksheet at the end of this chapter, of the amount of time it will take you to get to the exam site. Plan on arriving 10–15 minutes early so you can get the lay of the land, use the bathroom, and calm down. Then figure out how early you will have to get up that morning, and make sure you get up that early every day for a week before the exam.

Gather Your Materials

The night before the exam, lay out the clothes you will wear and the materials you have to bring with you to the exam. Plan on dressing in layers; you won't have any control over the temperature of the examination room. Have a sweater or jacket you can take off if it's warm. Use the checklist on the Final Preparations worksheet to help you pull together what you'll need.

Don't Skip Breakfast

Even if you don't usually eat breakfast, do so on exam morning. A cup of coffee doesn't count. It's not a good idea to eat doughnuts or other sweet foods, either. A sugar high will leave you with a sugar low in the middle of the exam. A mix of protein and complex carbohydrates is best. Cereal with milk, or eggs with toast, will do your body a world of good.

Step 9: Do It!

Time to complete: 5 minutes, plus test-taking time
Activity: Ace the CBEST!

Fast forward to exam day. You're ready. You made a study plan and followed through. You've practiced your test-taking strategies while working through this book. You're in control of your physical, mental, and emotional state. You know when and where to show up and what to bring with you.

Just one more thing. When you're done with the CBEST, you will have earned a reward. Plan a celebration for exam night. Call up your friends and plan a party, or have a nice dinner for two—whatever your heart desires. Give yourself something to look forward to.

And then do it. Go into the exam full of confidence, armed with test-taking strategies you've practiced until they're second nature. You're in control of yourself, your environment, and your performance on the exam. You're ready to succeed. So do it! Go in there and ace the exam—and look forward to your future career in education!

Final Preparations

Getting to the Exam Site

Location of exam: _____

Date: _____

Time of exam: _____

Do I know how to get to the exam site?   Yes ___   No ___

(If no, make a trial run.)

Time it will take to get to exam site: _____

Things to Lay Out the Night Before

Clothes I will wear   ____

Sweater/jacket   ____

Watch   ____

Admission card   ____

Photo ID   ____

4 #2 pencils   ____

Other   _____

CHAPTER 3 ▶ DIAGNOSTIC CBEST EXAM

CHAPTER SUMMARY
This is the first of the four practice tests in this book based on the California Basic Educational Skills Test (CBEST). Use this test to see how you would do if you were to take the exam today.

This diagnostic practice exam reflects the real California Basic Educational Skills Test you will be taking. Like the actual exam, it is divided into three sections. The Reading Comprehension section consists of 50 multiple-choice questions on reading passages that vary from a few sentences to between 100 and 200 words. The Mathematics section consists of 50 multiple-choice questions. The Essay Writing section consists of two topics on which you are asked to write essays; one essay is based on a situation or statement, the other on a personal experience.

The answer sheet you should use for the multiple-choice questions is on the following page. (Write your essay on a separate piece of paper.) Then comes the exam itself, and after that is the answer key. Each answer on the test is explained in the answer key to help you find out why the correct answers are right and the incorrect answers are wrong. You'll also find scoring criteria for the essay section and sample essays based on the topics in the exam. The answer key is followed by a section on how to score your exam.

LEARNINGEXPRESS ANSWER SHEET

Section 1: Reading Comprehension

1. ⓐ ⓑ ⓒ ⓓ ⓔ
2. ⓐ ⓑ ⓒ ⓓ ⓔ
3. ⓐ ⓑ ⓒ ⓓ ⓔ
4. ⓐ ⓑ ⓒ ⓓ ⓔ
5. ⓐ ⓑ ⓒ ⓓ ⓔ
6. ⓐ ⓑ ⓒ ⓓ ⓔ
7. ⓐ ⓑ ⓒ ⓓ ⓔ
8. ⓐ ⓑ ⓒ ⓓ ⓔ
9. ⓐ ⓑ ⓒ ⓓ ⓔ
10. ⓐ ⓑ ⓒ ⓓ ⓔ
11. ⓐ ⓑ ⓒ ⓓ ⓔ
12. ⓐ ⓑ ⓒ ⓓ ⓔ
13. ⓐ ⓑ ⓒ ⓓ ⓔ
14. ⓐ ⓑ ⓒ ⓓ ⓔ
15. ⓐ ⓑ ⓒ ⓓ ⓔ
16. ⓐ ⓑ ⓒ ⓓ ⓔ
17. ⓐ ⓑ ⓒ ⓓ ⓔ
18. ⓐ ⓑ ⓒ ⓓ ⓔ
19. ⓐ ⓑ ⓒ ⓓ ⓔ
20. ⓐ ⓑ ⓒ ⓓ ⓔ
21. ⓐ ⓑ ⓒ ⓓ ⓔ
22. ⓐ ⓑ ⓒ ⓓ ⓔ
23. ⓐ ⓑ ⓒ ⓓ ⓔ
24. ⓐ ⓑ ⓒ ⓓ ⓔ
25. ⓐ ⓑ ⓒ ⓓ ⓔ
26. ⓐ ⓑ ⓒ ⓓ ⓔ
27. ⓐ ⓑ ⓒ ⓓ ⓔ
28. ⓐ ⓑ ⓒ ⓓ ⓔ
29. ⓐ ⓑ ⓒ ⓓ ⓔ
30. ⓐ ⓑ ⓒ ⓓ ⓔ
31. ⓐ ⓑ ⓒ ⓓ ⓔ
32. ⓐ ⓑ ⓒ ⓓ ⓔ
33. ⓐ ⓑ ⓒ ⓓ ⓔ
34. ⓐ ⓑ ⓒ ⓓ ⓔ
35. ⓐ ⓑ ⓒ ⓓ ⓔ
36. ⓐ ⓑ ⓒ ⓓ ⓔ
37. ⓐ ⓑ ⓒ ⓓ ⓔ
38. ⓐ ⓑ ⓒ ⓓ ⓔ
39. ⓐ ⓑ ⓒ ⓓ ⓔ
40. ⓐ ⓑ ⓒ ⓓ ⓔ
41. ⓐ ⓑ ⓒ ⓓ ⓔ
42. ⓐ ⓑ ⓒ ⓓ ⓔ
43. ⓐ ⓑ ⓒ ⓓ ⓔ
44. ⓐ ⓑ ⓒ ⓓ ⓔ
45. ⓐ ⓑ ⓒ ⓓ ⓔ
46. ⓐ ⓑ ⓒ ⓓ ⓔ
47. ⓐ ⓑ ⓒ ⓓ ⓔ
48. ⓐ ⓑ ⓒ ⓓ ⓔ
49. ⓐ ⓑ ⓒ ⓓ ⓔ
50. ⓐ ⓑ ⓒ ⓓ ⓔ

Section 2: Mathematics

1. ⓐ ⓑ ⓒ ⓓ ⓔ
2. ⓐ ⓑ ⓒ ⓓ ⓔ
3. ⓐ ⓑ ⓒ ⓓ ⓔ
4. ⓐ ⓑ ⓒ ⓓ ⓔ
5. ⓐ ⓑ ⓒ ⓓ ⓔ
6. ⓐ ⓑ ⓒ ⓓ ⓔ
7. ⓐ ⓑ ⓒ ⓓ ⓔ
8. ⓐ ⓑ ⓒ ⓓ ⓔ
9. ⓐ ⓑ ⓒ ⓓ ⓔ
10. ⓐ ⓑ ⓒ ⓓ ⓔ
11. ⓐ ⓑ ⓒ ⓓ ⓔ
12. ⓐ ⓑ ⓒ ⓓ ⓔ
13. ⓐ ⓑ ⓒ ⓓ ⓔ
14. ⓐ ⓑ ⓒ ⓓ ⓔ
15. ⓐ ⓑ ⓒ ⓓ ⓔ
16. ⓐ ⓑ ⓒ ⓓ ⓔ
17. ⓐ ⓑ ⓒ ⓓ ⓔ
18. ⓐ ⓑ ⓒ ⓓ ⓔ
19. ⓐ ⓑ ⓒ ⓓ ⓔ
20. ⓐ ⓑ ⓒ ⓓ ⓔ
21. ⓐ ⓑ ⓒ ⓓ ⓔ
22. ⓐ ⓑ ⓒ ⓓ ⓔ
23. ⓐ ⓑ ⓒ ⓓ ⓔ
24. ⓐ ⓑ ⓒ ⓓ ⓔ
25. ⓐ ⓑ ⓒ ⓓ ⓔ
26. ⓐ ⓑ ⓒ ⓓ ⓔ
27. ⓐ ⓑ ⓒ ⓓ ⓔ
28. ⓐ ⓑ ⓒ ⓓ ⓔ
29. ⓐ ⓑ ⓒ ⓓ ⓔ
30. ⓐ ⓑ ⓒ ⓓ ⓔ
31. ⓐ ⓑ ⓒ ⓓ ⓔ
32. ⓐ ⓑ ⓒ ⓓ ⓔ
33. ⓐ ⓑ ⓒ ⓓ ⓔ
34. ⓐ ⓑ ⓒ ⓓ ⓔ
35. ⓐ ⓑ ⓒ ⓓ ⓔ
36. ⓐ ⓑ ⓒ ⓓ ⓔ
37. ⓐ ⓑ ⓒ ⓓ ⓔ
38. ⓐ ⓑ ⓒ ⓓ ⓔ
39. ⓐ ⓑ ⓒ ⓓ ⓔ
40. ⓐ ⓑ ⓒ ⓓ ⓔ
41. ⓐ ⓑ ⓒ ⓓ ⓔ
42. ⓐ ⓑ ⓒ ⓓ ⓔ
43. ⓐ ⓑ ⓒ ⓓ ⓔ
43. ⓐ ⓑ ⓒ ⓓ ⓔ
44. ⓐ ⓑ ⓒ ⓓ ⓔ
45. ⓐ ⓑ ⓒ ⓓ ⓔ
46. ⓐ ⓑ ⓒ ⓓ ⓔ
47. ⓐ ⓑ ⓒ ⓓ ⓔ
48. ⓐ ⓑ ⓒ ⓓ ⓔ
49. ⓐ ⓑ ⓒ ⓓ ⓔ
50. ⓐ ⓑ ⓒ ⓓ ⓔ

Section 1: Reading Comprehension

Answer questions 1–8 on the basis of the following passage.

(1) The coast of the state of Maine is one of the most irregular in the world. A straight line running from the southernmost city in Maine—Kittery—to the northernmost coastal city, Eastport, would measure about 225 miles. If you followed the coastline between the same two cities, you would travel more than ten times as far. This irregularity is the result of what is called a *drowned coastline*. The term refers to the results of the glacial activity of the Ice Age. At that time, the whole area that is now Maine was part of a mountain range that towered above the sea. As the glacier descended, however, it expended enormous force on those mountains and they sank into the ocean.

(2) As the mountains sank, ocean water charged over the lowest parts of the remaining land, forming a series of twisting inlets and lagoons, of contorted grottos and nooks. Once the glacier receded, the highest parts of the former mountain range that were nearest the shore remained as islands. Although the mountain ranges were never to return, the land rose somewhat over the centuries. On one of the islands that the glacier left behind, marine fossils have been found at 225 feet above today's sea level, indicating that the island was once part of the shoreline.

(3) The 2,500-mile-long rocky and jagged coastline of Maine keeps watch over nearly 2,000 islands. Many of these islands are tiny and uninhabited, but many are home to thriving communities. Mt. Desert Island is one of the largest—16 miles long and nearly 12 miles wide—and one of the most beautiful of Maine's coastal islands. Mt. Desert Island very nearly formed as two distinct islands. It is split almost in half by Somes Sound, a very deep and very narrow stretch of water seven miles long. On the east side of the island, Cadillac Mountain rises 1,532 feet, making it the highest mountain on the Atlantic seaboard.

(4) For years, Mt. Desert Island, particularly its major settlement, Bar Harbor, <u>afforded</u> summer homes for the wealthy. Recently, Bar Harbor has made a name for itself as a burgeoning arts community as well. But there is much more to Mt. Desert Island than a sophisticated and wealthy playground. A majority of the island is unspoiled forestland, which makes up the greatest part of Acadia National Park. Mt. Desert Island sits on the boundary line between the temperate and sub-Arctic zones. The island, therefore, supports the flora and fauna of both zones, as well as beach, inland, and alpine plants. In addition to its geological treasures, Mt. Desert Island lies in a major bird-migration lane; all kinds of migratory birds pass over the island.

(5) The establishment of Acadia National Park in 1916 means that this diversity of nature will be preserved and will be available to all people, not just the wealthy who once had exclusive access to the island's natural beauty. Today, visitors to Acadia may receive nature instruction from the park naturalists, in addition to enjoying the beauty of the island by camping, hiking, cycling, or boating. Or visitors may choose to spend time at the archeological museum, learning about the Stone Age inhabitants of the island. The best view on Mt. Desert Island, though, is from the top of Cadillac Mountain. From the summit, you can gaze back toward the mainland or out over the Atlantic Ocean and contemplate the beauty created by a retreating glacier.

1. Which of the following statements best expresses the main idea of paragraph 4?
   a. The wealthy residents of Mt. Desert Island selfishly kept it to themselves.
   b. Acadia National Park is one of the smallest of the national parks.
   c. On Mt. Desert Island, there is great tension between the year-round residents and the summer tourists.
   d. Due to its location and environment, Mt. Desert Island supports an incredibly diverse animal and plant life.
   e. A variety of activities are available to tourists who visit Mt. Desert Island.

2. According to the passage, the large number of small islands along the coast of Maine is the result of
   a. glaciers.
   b. a temperate climate.
   c. volcanic mountains.
   d. floods.
   e. the irregular coastline.

3. According to paragraph 2, one way to tell whether the top of a mountain was once at sea level is to look for
   a. inlets and lagoons.
   b. grottos and nooks.
   c. marine fossils.
   d. islands.
   e. mountains.

4. In the context of paragraph 4, which of the following words or phrases would most logically be substituted for the underlined word *afforded*?
   a. remembered
   b. discouraged
   c. bought for a higher price
   d. caused to exist
   e. endured

5. Paragraph 5 suggests that the writer believes that
   a. the continued existence of national parks is threatened by budget cuts.
   b. the best way to preserve the environment on Mt. Desert Island is to limit the number of visitors.
   c. national parks allow large numbers of people to visit and learn about interesting wilderness areas.
   d. Mt. Desert Island is the most interesting tourist attraction in Maine.
   e. Acadia National Park should be made into a sanctuary for endangered birds.

6. In the first paragraph, the author compares the straight-line distance (225 miles) from Kittery to Eastport with the driving distance (2,250 miles) to illustrate
   a. just how jagged the Maine coastline is.
   b. that Maine's coastline is very mountainous.
   c. that driving the coast of Maine can be dangerous.
   d. the difference in appearance between the two cities.
   e. that air travel is the best way to reach Maine's coastal cities.

Use the excerpt from an index to answer questions 7–8.

> Division manager, 88
> Docent, 341
> Doctor, 202, 498 (see Medical work, Physician)
> Domestic science, 93, 210, 521
> Drama critic, 348
> Economic research, 551
> Editor, 82, 190, 314, 351, 359, 363
>   feature, 351
>   magazine, 323
>   motion picture, 363–364
> Education, 50, 94, 232, 251, 254, 264, 317, 368–372
> Elementary school teacher, 119–120
>   readings on, 120–121
> Engineering, 280–285
>   architectural, 287–290
>   civil, 290–291
>   electrical, 282–284
>   mechanical, 285
> Engraving, 82

7. On which pages would one look to find information about editing movies?
   a. 120–121
   b. 363–364
   c. 290–291
   d. 368–372
   e. 287–290

8. Which of the following best describes the organizational pattern used in the section of the book dealing with types of engineering?
   a. by area of study
   b. by order of importance
   c. by income opportunities
   d. by physical requirements
   e. by popularity

Answer questions 9–11 on the basis of the following passage.

On the face of it, the idea of travelling by car may not sound appealing. Compared to flying, driving is extremely slow. The cost of gas and hotels can often be more than the cost of a plane ticket as well. Some trips, however, are best made by car.

Highway 1 in California travels from Orange County north past San Francisco. Drivers wanting to enjoy the views should make plans for plenty of stops along the way. The highway passes through the grand redwoods in Big Sur, as well as through Sonoma County's wine country. _____.

9. Which sentence, if inserted into the blank line at the end of the second paragraph, would be most consistent with the writer's purpose and intended audience?
   a. Watch for police who patrol the highway for speeding drivers trying to shorten their drive time.
   b. Travelers should plan to pull over in Monterey Bay to watch sea otters playing in the surf.
   c. Tourists can choose from hundreds of wineries to visit.
   d. Choose a car with a built-in entertainment system to keep children occupied during a long trip.
   e. Be sure to bring plenty of money, as the gas stations charge more for gas than those in the cities.

10. Which of the following is the best meaning of the phrase *On the face of it*, as it is used in the first sentence of the passage?
   a. depending on how you look at it
   b. from the front seat
   c. the look on the face of drivers
   d. from the first impression
   e. on the hood of the car

11. Which of the following best organizes the main topics addressed in this passage?
   a. I. Comparing the cost of flying and driving
      II. California as a tourist destination
   b. I. Top reasons to fly instead of drive on vacation
      II. Reasons to visit California on vacation
   c. I. Choosing to drive even with drawbacks such as cost and time
      II. Various attractions along California's Highway 1
   d. I. Driving as a family-friendly choice for vacation travel
      II. Ways to make a driving vacation in California fun
   e. I. Driving can be cost-effective with careful planning
      II. Areas to drive in California

Answer questions 12–13 on the basis of the following passage.

(1) The city of Humberstone, Chile, developed in the 1860s to support the mines in the desert nearby. (2) The mines yielded saltpeter, an ingredient in fertilizers. (3) Factories that processed the saltpeter soon brought people from nearby villages. (4) The factory workers needed homes, schools, groceries, and more, so Humberstone quickly grew. (5) In the 1930s, scientists developed a cheaper ingredient to take the place of saltpeter, and farmers were happy to spend less money to feed their crops. (6) Slowly, the population of Humberstone declined. (7) In 1961, the last factory closed. (8) Today, Humberstone's homes and businesses sit as its former residents left them. (9) In 1990, the Chilean government declared the ghost town a national monument.

12. Which of the following numbered sentences of the passage best expresses an opinion rather than a fact?
   a. Sentence 1
   b. Sentence 2
   c. Sentence 3
   d. Sentence 4
   e. Sentence 5

13. Which of the following numbered sentences is least relevant to the main idea of the paragraph?
   a. Sentence 9
   b. Sentence 8
   c. Sentence 7
   d. Sentence 6
   e. Sentence 5

Use the graph below to answer the question that follows.

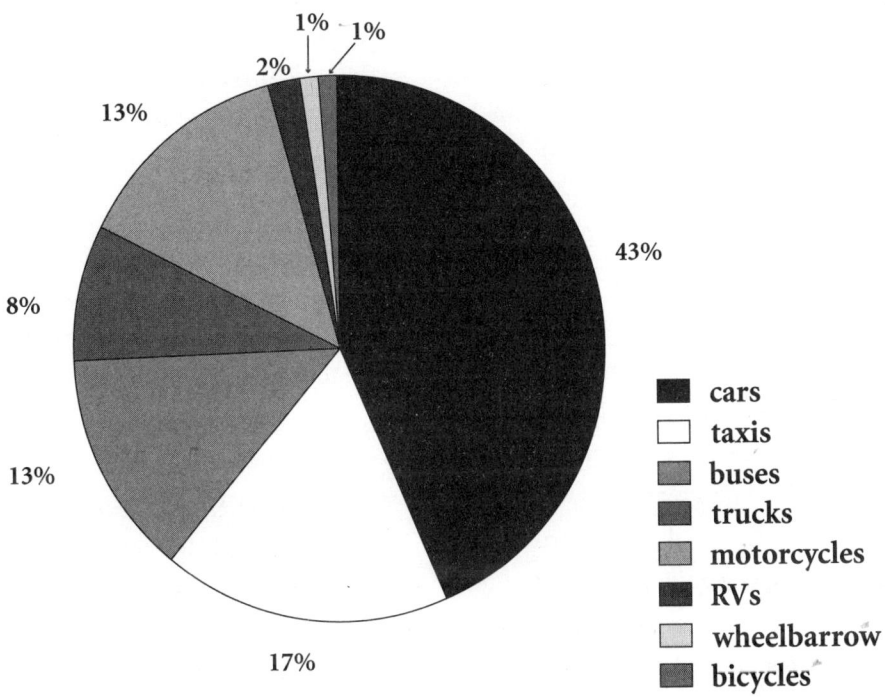

Traffic on County Road 217

14. What form of traffic had the same percentage as buses?
    a. cars
    b. trucks
    c. bicycles
    d. motorcycles
    e. wheelbarrows

Use the passage below to answer question 15.

The installation of red light cameras at intersections can greatly reduce the number of automobile-related crimes. People are less inclined to run red lights, as it is difficult to protest photographic evidence. This, in turn, reduces accidents caused by drivers running red lights. The revenue raised by more tickets can benefit the community as well.

15. Which of the following statements does NOT fit into the pattern of logic developed in the passage?
    a. Red light cameras are constitutional tools that can be used to fight crime.
    b. Red light cameras should be clearly marked so drivers can see them.
    c. Using red light cameras frees up law enforcement officials to respond to more important issues.
    d. Cities spend more money on red light cameras than they generate in ticket revenue.
    e. Red light cameras are used to monitor crime on the streets in the surrounding intersections.

Answer questions 16–19 on the basis of the following passage.

Tennessee Williams' play *The Glass Menagerie* is a highly autobiographical work, portraying Williams as the narrator who comes in and out of the action to describe his memories of his <u>overweening</u>, meddlesome mother and socially challenged sister. *Menagerie* made its premiere in Chicago in December 1944. Before opening night, rehearsals had been going badly, and the show's producers feared the play would be a miserable failure. _____. When the show opened on December 26, however, everything came together. Claudia Cassidy of the *Chicago Daily Review* wrote in her review, "It gripped players and audiences alike, and created one of those evenings in the theater that make 'stagestruck' an honorable word." *Menagerie* became Williams' first hit play and moved to Broadway, where it won the New York Drama Critics' Circle Award for Best Play. A highly revered playwright, Williams is recognized as having brought poetry and imagination back into the theater that was, at the time, in the throes of post–World War II realism. Although two of Williams' subsequent plays won the Pulitzer Prize, many consider *Menagerie* to be his finest work.

16. Which sentence, if inserted in the blank space in the passage, would make the best sense in the context of the passage?
    a. Despite the producers' apprehensions, the cast members continued to believe in the play.
    b. Williams and the cast members had to beg the producers not to close the play immediately but to wait for critics' reviews.
    c. It was becoming apparent that Tennessee Williams was going to be known as the twentieth century's most controversial playwright.
    d. Because there were no advance ticket sales, they prepared a closing notice, and *Menagerie* was in danger of becoming nothing more than a footnote in the history of the theater.
    e. Williams was especially forlorn when he realized that the actors had misinterpreted his entire script.

17. The passage suggests that
    a. Tennessee Williams was a troubled man.
    b. the play's producers were narrow-minded.
    c. the plot and characters were typical of post–World War II plays.
    d. the public wasn't interested in theater during the 1950s.
    e. people were ready to move away from realism.

18. Which of the following provides the best definition of *overweening*?
    a. self-effacing
    b. pushy
    c. maternal
    d. cajoling
    e. protective

19. Judging from the information provided in the paragraph, which of the following statements about *The Glass Menagerie* is accurate?
   a. It was a curiosity in theater history.
   b. It was the most important play of the twentieth century.
   c. It represents a turning point in post–World War II theater.
   d. It was too dark of a theme for post–World War II America.
   e. It had no effect on the public.

Answer questions 20 and 21 on the basis of the following passage.

Every February, people in the United States celebrate Black History Month. Carter G. Woodson, a Harvard scholar and son of former slaves, started this tradition as one way to ensure that black history was accurately portrayed. As part of its ongoing effort to promote diversity awareness, the university, in conjunction with the Cultural Center, is offering half-price campus bus fare to anyone who attends the Black History Month Exhibit at the Cultural Center during the second week of February. In order to receive the half-price fare, each passenger must show the bus driver his or her ticket stub from the exhibit, and deposit the half fare in the coin slot. Drivers will record these fares in the "reduced fares" column of their trip sheets for each route.

20. Passenger A and Passenger B get on the campus bus at 6:00 P.M. at the corner of University Avenue and Main Street. Passenger A shows the driver his exhibit ticket stub and deposits a half fare in the coin slot. Passenger B deposits a half fare in the coin slot. Both passengers move toward their seats. What should the bus driver do?
   a. Continue to the next stop without saying anything.
   b. Tell Passenger B that she needs to exit the bus at the next stop.
   c. Assume that Passenger B has an exhibit ticket stub, too.
   d. Tell Passenger B that she may go see the Black History Month Exhibit at the Cultural Center.
   e. Tell Passenger B that if she doesn't have an exhibit ticket stub, she will have to pay full fare.

21. The passage implies that
   a. university students like to take advantage of half-price fares.
   b. the campus bus is very expensive.
   c. the university and the Cultural Center regularly join forces.
   d. the university regularly encourages diversity awareness.
   e. bus drivers have to work harder during the month of February.

Answer question 22 on the basis of the following passage.

In space flight, there are the obvious hazards of meteors, debris, and radiation; however, astronauts must also deal with two vexing physiological foes—muscle atrophy and bone loss. Space shuttle astronauts, because they spend only about a week in space, undergo minimal wasting of bone and muscle. But when longer stays in microgravity or zero gravity are contemplated, as in the proposed space station or a two-year round-trip voyage to Mars, these problems are of particular concern because they could become acute.

22. The most appropriate audience for the passage would be students in
    a. a physiology class.
    b. an engineering class.
    c. a physics class.
    d. an astronomy class.
    e. a history of science class.

Answer question 23 on the basis of the following passage.

Light pollution is a growing problem worldwide. Like other forms of pollution, light pollution degrades the quality of the environment. Where once it was possible to look up at the night sky and see thousands of twinkling stars in the inky blackness, one now sees little more than the yellow glare of urban sky glow. When we lose the ability to connect visually with the vastness of the universe by looking up at the night sky, we lose our connection with something profoundly important to the human spirit, our sense of wonder.

23. The passage implies that the most serious damage done by light pollution is to our
    a. artistic appreciation.
    b. sense of physical well-being.
    c. cultural advancement.
    d. spiritual selves.
    e. intellectual curiosity.

Answer questions 24–27 on the basis of the following passage.

The Northern Spotted Owl lives primarily in old-growth forests between southern Canada and California. This Pacific-Coast dweller hunts at night and feeds mostly on rodents, flying squirrels, and rabbits.

In 1990, the species was listed as threatened, mostly due to the loss of habitat as a result of logging. In 1991, a court order put a stop to logging in National Forests. This, _____, pit loggers and sawmill owners against environmentalists interested in saving the owl and its habitat. Loggers retaliated against the court order in a vicious manner. For example, it was not uncommon to see bumper stickers on loggers' vehicles that read "I like Spotted Owls—Fried," or "Kill a Spotted Owl, Save a Logger." Loggers saw the protection of the owls as excessive, but their petulant reaction to the situation was not in their best interests.

24. Which word or phrase, if inserted into the blank, would make the most sense in the context of the passage?
    a. in other words
    b. apparently
    c. unexpectedly
    d. in so many words
    e. of course

25. Based on the information in the passage, it can be inferred that court order to stop logging was issued so that
   a. loggers would have to find work elsewhere.
   b. environmentalists would stop lobbying for the owl's protection.
   c. owls would not continue to lose their habitat and become extinct.
   d. sawmills would have an upsurge in potential job applicants.
   e. owls would continue to hunt and kill pests such as rodents.

26. Based on the tone of the passage, which of the following words best describes the author's attitude toward the loggers?
   a. indifferent
   b. neutral
   c. admiring
   d. respectful
   e. disapproving

27. Including the quotes from the bumper stickers serves to
   a. strengthen the author's viewpoint.
   b. support the statement that the loggers reacted in a "vicious manner."
   c. show that loggers band together.
   d. show that loggers were well within their right to be angry.
   e. give the loggers a voice.

Answer questions 28–29 on the basis of the following table.

THE FUJITA–PEARSON TORNADO INTENSITY SCALE

CLASSIFI-CATION	WIND SPEED	DAMAGE
F0	40–72 mph	Mild
F1	73–112 mph	Moderate
F2	113–157 mph	Significant
F3	158–206 mph	Severe
F4	207–260 mph	Devastating
F5	261–318 mph	Cataclysmic

28. A tornado with a wind speed of 173 mph would be assigned which classification?
   a. F0
   b. F1
   c. F2
   d. F3
   e. F4

29. The names of the categories in the third column, labeled "Damage," could best be described as
   a. scientific.
   b. descriptive.
   c. objective.
   d. persuasive.
   e. whimsical.

Answer question 30 on the basis of the following passage.

James Carruthers' recent essays attempt to redefine arts criticism as a <u>play</u> of critical intelligence that can take place free from the bonds of political partisanship. In Carruthers' view, this <u>play</u> of the mind, working itself free from constraints, is the only ethical approach to the arts.

30. What is the best definition of the word *play* as it is used in the passage?
   a. to act or conduct oneself in a specified way
   b. to move or operate freely within a confined space
   c. to pretend to be; mimic the activities of
   d. to behave carelessly or indifferently
   e. to stake or wager in a game

Answer questions 31–36 on the basis of the following passage.

In his famous study of myth, *The Hero With a Thousand Faces*, Joseph Campbell writes about the archetypal hero who has ventured outside the boundaries of the village and, after many trials and adventures, has returned with the <u>boon</u> that will save or enlighten his fellows. Like Carl Jung, Campbell believes that the story of the hero is part of the collective unconscious of all humankind. He likens the returning hero to the sacred or tabooed personage described by James Frazier in *The Golden Bough*. Such an individual must, in many instances of myth, be insulated from the rest of society, "not merely for his own sake but for the sake of others; for since the virtue of holiness is, so to say, a powerful explosive which the smallest touch can detonate, it is necessary in the interest of the general safety to keep it within narrow bounds."

There is _____ between the archetypal hero who has journeyed into the wilderness and the poet who has journeyed into the realm of imagination. Both places are dangerous and full of wonders, and both, at their deepest levels, are journeys that take place into the kingdom of the unconscious mind, a place that, in Campbell's words, "goes down into unsuspected Aladdin caves. There not only jewels but dangerous jinn abide. . . ."

31. Based on the passage, which of the following would best describe the hero's journey?
   a. wonderful
   b. terrifying
   c. awesome
   d. whimsical
   e. mundane

32. The title of Campbell's book, *The Hero With a Thousand Faces*, is meant to convey
   a. the many villagers whose lives are changed by the story the hero has to tell.
   b. the fact that the hero journeys into many different imaginary countries.
   c. the many languages into which the myth of the hero has been translated.
   d. the many adventures the archetypal hero has during the journey into the wilderness.
   e. the universality of the myth of the hero who journeys into the wilderness.

33. Based on the passage, which of the following best describes the story that will likely be told by Campbell's returning hero and Frazier's sacred or tabooed personage?
   a. a radically mind-altering story
   b. a story that will terrify people to no good end
   c. a warning of catastrophe to come
   d. a story based on a dangerous lie
   e. a parable aimed at establishing a religious movement

34. Which of the following is the most accurate definition of *boon* as the word is used in the passage?
   a. gift
   b. blessing
   c. charm
   d. prize
   e. prayer

35. The phrase that would most accurately fit into the blank in the first sentence of the second paragraph is
   a. much similarity.
   b. a wide gulf.
   c. long-standing conflict.
   d. an abiding devotion.
   e. great diversity.

36. As depicted in the last sentence of the passage, "Aladdin caves" are most likely to be found in
   a. holy books.
   b. fairy tales.
   c. the fantasies of the hero.
   d. the hero's preparation for the journey.
   e. the unconscious mind.

Answer questions 37–40 on the basis of the following passage.

The word *schizophrenia* is derived from Greek and means "split mind." The word's translation into English is most likely the source of confusion regarding the disease's symptoms. It is not, as many people believe, a multiple personality disorder. _____, people with schizophrenia experience an impaired perception of reality. Hallucinations, disorganized speech and thinking, and paranoid delusions are common symptoms and are classified as positive, or productive. Negative symptoms, which are classified as such because they are characterized by a loss or absence of normal abilities, include flat emotion and a lack of speech and motivation.

There is no laboratory test that can verify someone is schizophrenic, but an increase in dopaminergic activity in the mesolimbic pathway of the brain is a commonality that exists among most schizophrenics. Approximately 6% of the population is affected with schizophrenia, and symptoms usually appear in young adulthood. Treatment includes administering antipsychotic medication to suppress the production of dopamine.

37. Which word or phrase, if inserted into the blank space in the passage, would make the most sense in the context of the passage?
   a. Although
   b. However
   c. Nonetheless
   d. Instead
   e. In other words

38. According to the information presented in the passage, what is the source of confusion regarding schizophrenic symptoms?
   a. The word *schizophrenia* is of Greek origin.
   b. People believe schizophrenia to be a multiple personality disease.
   c. The English translation of the word *schizophrenia* means "split mind."
   d. There is no laboratory test that can verify if someone has schizophrenia.
   e. The disease can be managed with antipsychotic medications.

39. Which of the following would be the best title for the passage?
   a. Schizophrenia Demystified
   b. Schizophrenia and Its Sufferers
   c. Dealing with Schizophrenia
   d. Recent Discoveries in the Treatment of Schizophrenia
   e. Living with Schizophrenia

40. Given the information in the passage, which of the following statements is true?
   a. Schizophrenia is curable.
   b. The onset of schizophrenia happens only in young adulthood.
   c. All schizophrenics experience a lack of motivation.
   d. Schizophrenics experience an impaired perception of reality.
   e. Symptoms of schizophrenia disappear with the administration of antipsychotic medication.

Answer questions 41 and 42 on the basis of the following passage.

Hepatitis A is a disease of the liver caused by the hepatitis A virus (HAV). The occurrence of hepatitis A is linked to socioeconomic conditions, and it spreads by person-to-person contact. Currently, there is no antiviral course available. There are, however, four highly immunogenic vaccines available. Three of these vaccines are manufactured from cell-culture-adapted HAV propagated in human fibroblasts. The HAV in each is then formalin-inactivated and adsorbed to an aluminum hydroxide adjuvant. The fourth vaccine is made out of HAV that has been purified from infected human diploid cell cultures and also inactivated with formalin. The fourth vaccine's virosomes, which have a protein or lipid from the envelope of the virus attached to their membranes, possess the antigenic, or antibody-stimulating properties of the virus, and in effect, transport the vaccine. These virosomes are thought to target influenza-primed antibody-presenting cells and macrophages. Travelers should be vaccinated before entering countries where HAV is highly endemic.

41. According to the information in the passage, the difference between the three hepatitis A vaccines and the fourth one is that
   a. the HAV in the three vaccines is formalin-inactivated and the HAV in the fourth vaccine is not.
   b. the three vaccines are more immunogenic than the fourth one.
   c. the HAV in the three vaccines is adsorbed to an aluminum hydroxide adjuvant and the fourth vaccine is purified.
   d. the three vaccines are bred in human fibroblasts and the fourth one comes from human diploid cells infected with HAV.
   e. the three vaccines do not target influenza-primed antibody-presenting cells and the fourth one does.

42. Virosomes can best be defined as
   a. vehicles that transport a part of the HAV and stimulate the body to produce antibodies to it.
   b. vehicles that transport influenza-primed antibody-presenting cells and macrophages.
   c. proteins.
   d. transporters of fibroblasts.
   e. lipids.

Answer questions 43–44 based on the following passage.

Obtaining student loans may be more difficult for students, with banks and the government reforming lending practices. Students and their families can look to local community colleges as an alternative to attending more expensive universities. Attending a local school also allows students to live at home and avoid the expense of living in an apartment or dormitory. Students can complete the first two years of classes at a community college. After this, they can transfer the credits to a university. Then students can complete a bachelor's degree.

43. The writer's argument in the passage is based primarily on which of the following assumptions?
   a. College loans are given out to all students who apply.
   b. Students may not be able to afford to attend a university.
   c. Students will have roommates in the dormitory.
   d. A college education is necessary for future success.
   e. All college students need loans to afford tuition.

44. According to information presented in the passage, what can students do after completing two years at a community college?
   a. live at home instead of in a dorm
   b. apply for a student loan from a bank
   c. transfer credits to a four-year college
   d. complete a four-year degree
   e. request that their debt be erased

Answer questions 45 and 46 on the basis of the following passage.

Diabetes mellitus is a group of metabolic diseases that result in abnormally high levels of blood glucose (sugar) due to problems with insulin production or utilization. Insulin is a hormone manufactured in the pancreas, and it is responsible for transporting glucose from the bloodstream into the cells where it is used as fuel.

Type I diabetes, which was previously known as *insulin-dependent* diabetes or *juvenile-onset* diabetes, develops when the body's immune system attacks and destroys pancreatic beta cells—the ones that manufacture insulin. Most people with Type I diabetes have to manage their disease with regular insulin injections.

Type II diabetes, which was previously known as *non-insulin-dependent* diabetes or *adult-onset* diabetes, is usually marked by insulin resistance, a condition in which the cells cannot utilize insulin properly. The pancreas may react to this by producing excessive amounts of insulin. As a result, the pancreas may eventually lose its ability to produce the vital hormone.

45. Pancreatic beta cells are responsible for
   a. bringing glucose from the bloodstream into the cells.
   b. insulin production.
   c. stabilizing the metabolism.
   d. providing fuel for the body.
   e. making glucose.

46. The difference between Type I and Type II diabetes is
   a. Type I can be managed with regular insulin injections and Type II cannot.
   b. Type I is now known as insulin-dependent diabetes and Type II as non-insulin-dependent diabetes.
   c. In Type I, the pancreas produces excessive amounts of insulin.
   d. In Type I, the body destroys its pancreatic beta cells, and in Type II, the body produces insulin but is resistant to its effects.
   e. Type I is marked by abnormally high levels of blood glucose, and Type II always results in high levels of insulin production.

Answer questions 47–50 on the basis of the following passage.

Mental and physical health professionals may consider referring clients and patients to a music therapist for a number of reasons. It seems a particularly good choice for the social worker who is coordinating a client's case. Music therapists use music to establish a relationship with the patient and to improve the patient's health, using highly structured musical interactions. Patients and therapists may sing, play instruments, compose music, dance, or simply listen to music.

The course of training for music therapists is comprehensive. In addition to their formal musical and therapy training, music therapists are taught to discern what kinds of interventions will be most beneficial for each individual patient. Because each patient is different and has different goals, the music therapist must be able to understand the patient's situation and choose the music and activities that will be the most effective, helping the patient achieve his or her goals. The referring social worker can help this process by clearly articulating each client's history.

Although patients may develop their musical skills, that is not the main goal of music therapy. Any client who needs particular work on communication or on academic, emotional, and social skills, and who is not responding to traditional therapy, is an excellent candidate for music therapy.

47. Which of the following would be the most appropriate title for this passage?
   a. The Use of Music in the Treatment of Autism
   b. How to Use Music to Combat Depression
   c. Music Therapy: A Role in Social Work?
   d. Training for a Career in Music Therapy
   e. The Social Worker as Music Therapist

48. According to information presented in the passage, music therapy can be prescribed for social work clients who
   a. need to develop coping skills.
   b. were orphaned as children.
   c. need to resolve family issues.
   d. are under the age of 18.
   e. need to improve social skills.

49. Which of the following inferences can be drawn from the passage?
    a. Music therapy can succeed where traditional therapies have failed.
    b. Music therapy is a relatively new field.
    c. Music therapy is particularly beneficial for young children.
    d. Music therapy probably will not work well for psychotic people.
    e. Music therapy is appropriate only in a limited number of circumstances.

50. Which of the following best organizes the main topics addressed in this passage?
    a. I. The role of music therapy in social work
        II. Locating a music therapist
        III. How to complete a music therapist referral
    b. I. Using music in therapy
        II. A typical music therapy intervention
        III. When to prescribe music therapy
    c. I. Music therapy and social work
        II. Training for music therapists
        III. Skills addressed by music therapy
    d. I. How to choose a music therapist
        II. When to refer to a music therapist
        III. Who benefits the most from music therapy
    e. I. Music therapy as a cost-effective treatment
        II. Curriculum of a music therapy program
        III. Music therapy and physical illness

Section 2: Mathematics

1. Which of the following numbers is NOT between −0.02 and 1.02?
   a. −0.15
   b. −0.015
   c. 0
   d. 0.02
   e. 1.015

Use the following graph to answer question 2.

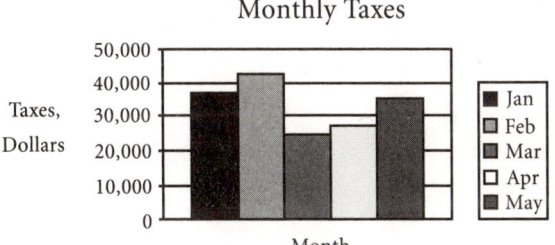

2. What were the total taxes collected for January, February, and April?
   a. $78,000
   b. $98,000
   c. $105,000
   d. $115,000
   e. $132,000

Use the following table to answer question 3.

BLUE ROUTE BUS SCHEDULE

	Depot	Washington St.
Bus 1	6:00	6:53
Bus 2	6:30	7:23
Bus 3	7:00	7:53
Bus 4	7:20	
Bus 5	7:40	8:33

3. What time is Bus 4 scheduled to arrive at Washington St.?
   a. 8:03
   b. 8:10
   c. 8:13
   d. 8:18
   e. 8:23

4. Membership dues at Arnold's Gym are $53 per month this year, but were $50 per month last year. What was the percentage increase in the gym's prices?
   a. 5.5%
   b. 6.0%
   c. 6.5%
   d. 7.0%
   e. 7.5%

5. Mr. Judah teaches at Silverlake Middle School. His last class ends at 2:10 P.M. He then has to supervise the bus zone. It takes 35 minutes to drive from his school to the Central Administration Building. If he has to be at a meeting at the Central Administration Building at 3:15 P.M., what is the most amount of time he can supervise the bus zone and still make it to the meeting on time without speeding?
   a. 10 minutes
   b. 20 minutes
   c. 30 minutes
   d. 40 minutes
   e. 50 minutes

6. Simone took a standardized test to measure her performance in mathematics. She earned a stanine score that showed she performed better than 50% of students who also took the test. Which score could Simone have received?
   a. 3
   b. 4.5
   c. 5.5
   d. 6
   e. 9

7. A weather station in Boca, California, records a temperature of −12°C. Within the next hour, the temperature falls seven degrees. By the next morning, the temperature has dropped another four degrees. What temperature is it in the morning?
   a. −23°C
   b. −19°C
   c. −16°C
   d. −1°C
   e. 7°C

Answer questions 8–10 by referring to the following graph, which shows wildfire trends in a particular region.

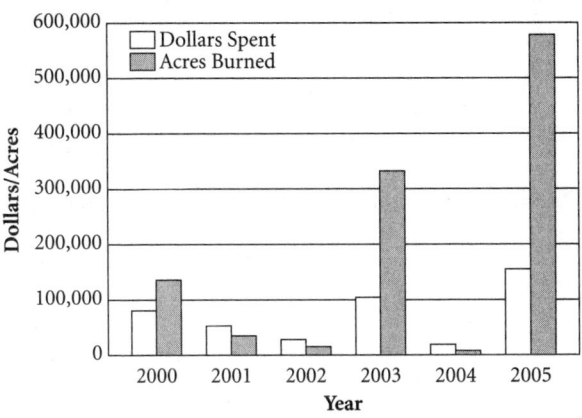

WILDFIRE TRENDS (WESTERN U.S. INTERMOUNTAIN REGION)

8. In which of the following years were the fewest acres burned?
   a. 2000
   b. 2001
   c. 2002
   d. 2003
   e. 2004

9. About how much money was spent fighting wildfires in the Intermountain Region during 2003?
   a. $90,000
   b. $100,000
   c. $110,000
   d. $300,000
   e. $320,000

10. In which of the following years was the cost per acre of fighting wildfires the lowest?
    a. 2000
    b. 2001
    c. 2002
    d. 2003
    e. 2005

Answer questions 11–13 by referring to the following graph, which compares the average annual rainfall with the actual rainfall for one year in a particular city.

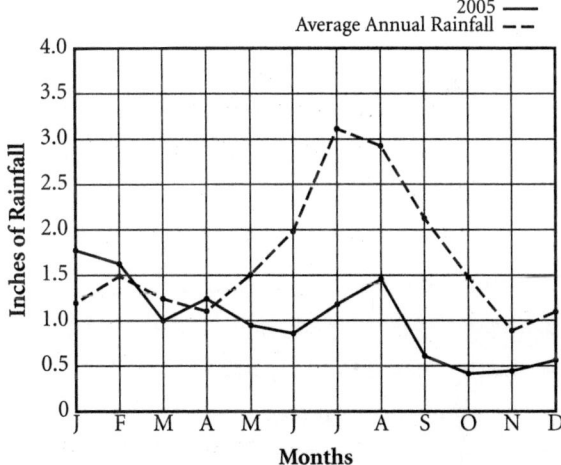

11. In which of the following months during 2005 was the rainfall nearest normal?
    a. April
    b. May
    c. June
    d. July
    e. August

12. What is the average rainfall amount for the month of September?
   a. 0.5 inches
   b. 0.7 inches
   c. 2.0 inches
   d. 2.1 inches
   e. 2.5 inches

13. During 2005, how many months had above-average rainfall amounts?
   a. 2
   b. 3
   c. 6
   d. 9
   e. 10

14. A fencing company charges $45 per hour plus $500 for materials to build a privacy fence for Ms. Dunn. What information is needed to determine the cost of Ms. Dunn's fence?
   a. the materials needed
   b. the number of hours worked
   c. the number of workers
   d. the location of the fence
   e. the price of the fencing

15. Juan earns $15.50 for each hour that he works. If Juan works 7.5 hours per day, 5 days a week, how much does he earn in a week?
   a. $116.25
   b. $135
   c. $581.25
   d. $813.75
   e. $925

16. Melissa can grade five of her students' papers in an hour. Joe can grade four of the same papers in an hour. If Melissa works for three hours grading, and Joe works for two hours, what percentage of the 50 students' papers will be graded?
   a. 44%
   b. 46%
   c. 52%
   d. 54%
   e. 56%

17. James has a length of rope that he measures with a yardstick to be 28 inches long. By laying the yardstick end-to-end with the rope, what is the longest distance that he can measure accurately?
   a. 28 inches
   b. 36 inches
   c. 40 inches
   d. 54 inches
   e. 64 inches

18. Students in a math class are asked to look at the pattern and find the next number in the series. The pattern is:

1, 4, 9, 16, 25, 36, . . .

One student points out that the numbers are all squares, so the next number would be 49. What is another correct way to describe the pattern?
   a. Name the next multiple of 7: 7×6
   b. Double the last number and subtract the previous number: $(2 \times 36) - 25$
   c. Add the previous numbers in the series: $1 + 4 + 9 + 16 + 25 + 36$
   d. Find the sum of sequential odd numbers: $1 + 3 + 5 + 7 + 9 + 11 + 13$
   e. Add 11 to the previous number

19. Des Moines recently experienced a snowstorm that left a total of eight inches of snow. If it snowed at a consistent rate of three inches every two hours, how much snow fell in the first five hours of the storm?
   a. 3 inches
   b. 3.3 inches
   c. 5 inches
   d. 7.5 inches
   e. 8 inches

20. Kira collected $1\frac{3}{4}$ pounds of trash on the Crystal Beach Clean-Up Day. Marcella collected $2\frac{1}{2}$ pounds of trash on the same day. Oscar collected more trash than Kira but less than Marcella. What could be an amount that Oscar collected?
   a. 1.6 pounds
   b. 2.3 pounds
   c. 2.7 pounds
   d. 3.1 pounds
   e. 4.3 pounds

21. The area of a rectangle is 24 square centimeters. If the width of the rectangle is 3 centimeters, find the perimeter.
   a. 10 centimeters
   b. 11 centimeters
   c. 20 centimeters
   d. 22 centimeters
   e. 48 centimeters

22. A piece of ribbon 3 feet 4 inches long was divided into 5 equal parts. How long was each part?
   a. 1 foot 2 inches
   b. 11 inches
   c. 10 inches
   d. 9 inches
   e. 8 inches

23. Sophia harvested 4.29 pounds of strawberries on Monday. On Tuesday, she harvested 4.029 pounds of strawberries. On Wednesday, she harvested 4.209 pounds of strawberries. Which sentence correctly shows the relationship between the numbers?
   a. $4.29 > 4.029 > 4.209$
   b. $4.29 < 4.209 < 4.029$
   c. $4.029 > 4.29 > 4.209$
   d. $4.29 > 4.209 > 4.029$
   e. $4.209 > 4.29 > 4.029$

24. The bands in a school district are traveling to a music festival. They will use buses to get all of the students to the festival. Each bus can hold 62 passengers. If the district has 430 students to take to the festival, how many buses will the district need?
   a. 3
   b. 4
   c. 5
   d. 6
   e. 7

25. A builder uses 27 cubic feet of concrete to pave a sidewalk whose length is 6 times its width. The concrete is poured 6 inches deep. How long is the sidewalk?
   a. 9 feet
   b. 12 feet
   c. 15 feet
   d. 18 feet
   e. 20 feet

26. After three days, a group of hikers discovers that they have used $\frac{2}{5}$ of their supplies. At this rate, how many more days can they go forward before they have to turn around?

   a. 0.75 days
   b. 1.5 days
   c. 3.75 days
   d. 4.5 days
   e. 7.5 days

27. A supply truck can carry 3 tons. A breakfast ration weighs 12 ounces, and the other two daily meals weigh 18 ounces each. On a ten-day trip, how many troops can be supplied by one truck?

   a. 100
   b. 150
   c. 200
   d. 320
   e. 600

28. A clerk can process 26 forms per hour. If 5,600 forms must be processed in an 8-hour day, how many clerks must you hire for that day?

   a. 24
   b. 25
   c. 26
   d. 27
   e. 28

29. On the same latitude, Janice travels east at 35 miles per hour and Harriet travels west at 15 miles per hour. If the two women start out 2,100 miles apart, how long will it take them to meet?

   a. 30 hours
   b. 42 hours
   c. 60 hours
   d. 105 hours
   e. 140 hours

30. In a class, students' grades are determined by taking the average of their best four exam scores. A student had exam scores of 87, 91, 63, 82, 96, 75, and 81. What was the student's final grade?

   a. 82
   b. 85
   c. 87
   d. 89
   e. 91

31. Fifteen less than 3 times a number is 21. What is the number?

   a. 2
   b. 3
   c. 6
   d. 9
   e. 12

Use the following information to answer question 32.

A family eats at Joe's Grill and orders the following items from the menu:

Hamburger	$2.95
Cheeseburger	$3.35
Chicken Sandwich	$3.95
Grilled Cheese	$1.95

32. If the family orders 2 hamburgers, 1 cheeseburger, 2 chicken sandwiches, and 1 grilled cheese, what is the total cost of their order?

   a. $12.20
   b. $15.15
   c. $17.10
   d. $18.05
   e. $19.10

33. If Rachel has worked $26\frac{1}{4}$ hours so far this week, and has to work a total of $37\frac{1}{2}$ hours, how much longer does she have to work?

   a. $10\frac{1}{4}$ hours
   b. $11\frac{1}{4}$ hours
   c. $11\frac{3}{4}$ hours
   d. $13\frac{1}{2}$ hours
   e. $13\frac{3}{4}$ hours

34. If candy bars cost $0.40 and soft drinks cost $0.50, what is the cost of four candy bars and three soft drinks?

   a. $2.10
   b. $2.30
   c. $2.60
   d. $3.10
   e. $4

35. On James's daily jog, he travels a distance of $\frac{3}{4}$ mile to get to the track and $\frac{3}{4}$ mile to get home from the track. One lap around the track is $\frac{1}{4}$ mile. If James runs 7 laps around the track, what is the total distance that he travels?

   a. $1\frac{1}{4}$ miles
   b. $1\frac{1}{2}$ miles
   c. $2\frac{1}{2}$ miles
   d. 3 miles
   e. $3\frac{1}{4}$ miles

36. A teacher spacing desks in a classroom determines that she can have 4 rows of desks if she spaces them 4 feet apart. Each desk is 3 feet wide. If there is 4 feet from the wall to the rows of desks on the edges, how wide is the classroom?

   a. 20 feet
   b. 28 feet
   c. 32 feet
   d. 36 feet
   e. 40 feet

37. Kathy was half the age of her mother 20 years ago. Kathy is 40 now. How old is Kathy's mother?

   a. 50
   b. 60
   c. 70
   d. 80
   e. 100

Use the following information to answer question 38.

A used car dealer has 40 cars on his lot. Fifteen of them are Fords, 9 are Chevrolets, 10 are Dodges, and 6 are foreign models. The dealer sells 2 cars after a day.

38. Which of the following statements can be determined from the information above?

   a. the number of cars remaining on the lot after the day ends
   b. the number of Toyotas on the lot
   c. the cost of a Dodge
   d. the amount the dealer earned in sales
   e. the number of Fords sold

Use the following information to answer question 39.

Ms. Margaret Peabody wishes to insure items of jewelry valued as follows:

- 1 gold watch, valued at $240
- 2 rings, each valued at $150
- 1 ring, valued at $70

39. Ms. Peabody's insurance agent is preparing a report on the jewelry. Which one of the following represents the total value?

   a. $460
   b. $545
   c. $610
   d. $705
   e. $785

Use the following information to answer question 40.

A man turns in a woman's handbag to the Lost and Found Department of a large downtown store. The man informs the clerk in charge that he found the handbag on the floor beside an entranceway. The clerk estimates that the handbag is worth approximately $150. Inside, the clerk finds the following items:

- 1 leather makeup case valued at $65
- 1 vial of perfume, unopened, valued at $75
- 1 pair of earrings valued at $150
- cash $178

40. The clerk is writing a report to be submitted along with the found property. What should he write as the total value of the found cash and property?
   a. $468
   b. $608
   c. $618
   d. $638
   e. $718

41. Out of 50 students, 16 are taking Spanish and 27 are taking French. If 9 students are in both classes, how many students are in neither class?
   a. 18
   b. 16
   c. 9
   d. 7
   e. 3

42. The student council at Jefferson Junior High School sponsored a competition between the seventh and eighth grade students to see which class could collect the most canned goods for a food drive. The results are recorded in the table below.

Cans Collected		
	Seventh Grade	Eight Grade
Week 1	46	71
Week 2	105	65
Week 3	89	83
Week 4	140	90
Subtotals	380	T
Total Cans Collected by Both Grades	689	

What value should take the place of T in the table?
   a. 309
   b. 380
   c. 520
   d. 599
   e. 1,069

43. The expression $(-12)(-10)(-3)$ simplifies to which of the following?
   a. −360
   b. −25
   c. −5
   d. 25
   e. 360

44. It takes a typing student 0.75 seconds to type one word. At this rate, how many words can the student type in 60 seconds?
   a. 4.5 words
   b. 8.0 words
   c. 45.0 words
   d. 75.0 words
   e. 80.0 words

45. If a physical education student burns 8.2 calories per minute while riding a bicycle, how many calories will the same student burn if she rides for 35 minutes?
   a. 246 calories
   b. 286 calories
   c. 287 calories
   d. 387 calories
   e. 980 calories

46. An orthodontist named Dr. Kelley charges $48 for an office visit, which is $\frac{2}{3}$ of what a dentist named Dr. John charges. How much does Dr. John charge for an office visit?
   a. $60
   b. $72
   c. $84
   d. $88.50
   e. $96

Use the following information to answer question 47.

A bicycle shop has a total of 55 bicycles in stock. Twelve are red, 5 are green, and 15 are blue. The bicycles are made by three different manufacturers: Regal, Duo, and XT.

47. Which of the following facts can be determined from the information given?
   a. the number of Regal bicycles
   b. the number of yellow bicycles
   c. the cost of a red Duo
   d. the ratio of road bicycles to mountain bicycles
   e. the ratio of red bicycles to green bicycles

48. Sage has a bag of marbles. The bag contains 16 black, 10 red, 10 blue, and 14 white marbles. What is the probability that Sage randomly takes a red marble from the bag and leaves the marble on a table and then takes a white marble from the bag?
   a. $\frac{1}{5}$
   b. $\frac{2}{7}$
   c. $\frac{12}{25}$
   d. $\frac{17}{35}$
   e. $\frac{18}{35}$

Use the following information to answer question 49.

Basic cable television service, which includes 16 channels, costs $15 a month. The initial labor fee to install the service is $25. A $65 deposit is required but will be refunded within two years if the customer's bills are paid in full. Other cable services may be added to the basic service: the movie channel service is $9.40 a month; the news channels are $7.50 a month; the arts channels are $5 a month; the sports channels are $4.80 a month.

49. A customer's first bill, including installation, totaled $112.50. This customer chose basic cable. Which additional service was chosen?
   a. the news channels
   b. the movie channels
   c. the arts channels
   d. the sports channels
   e. no additional services were chosen

50. Which of the following is the most appropriate unit for expressing the weight of a textbook?
   a. grams
   b. pounds
   c. quarts
   d. feet
   e. yards

Section 3: Essay Writing

Carefully read the two essay-writing topics that follow. On scratch paper, plan and write two essays, one on each topic. Be sure to address all points in the topic. Allow about 30 minutes for each essay.

Topic 1
Should public school students be required to wear uniforms? Supporters argue that, among other things, uniforms would improve discipline and build a strong sense of community and identity. On the other hand, opponents believe that uniforms limit students' freedom of expression and their development as individuals.

Write an essay in which you take a position on whether or not public school students should be required to wear uniforms to school. Be sure to support your position with logical arguments and specific examples.

Topic 2
Bob Maynard has said that "Problems are opportunities in disguise."

Write an essay describing a time in your life when a problem became an opportunity. How did you transform the situation? Explain what you did to turn the problem into an opportunity and how others can benefit from your experience.

45. If a physical education student burns 8.2 calories per minute while riding a bicycle, how many calories will the same student burn if she rides for 35 minutes?
   a. 246 calories
   b. 286 calories
   c. 287 calories
   d. 387 calories
   e. 980 calories

46. An orthodontist named Dr. Kelley charges $48 for an office visit, which is $\frac{2}{3}$ of what a dentist named Dr. John charges. How much does Dr. John charge for an office visit?
   a. $60
   b. $72
   c. $84
   d. $88.50
   e. $96

Use the following information to answer question 47.

A bicycle shop has a total of 55 bicycles in stock. Twelve are red, 5 are green, and 15 are blue. The bicycles are made by three different manufacturers: Regal, Duo, and XT.

47. Which of the following facts can be determined from the information given?
   a. the number of Regal bicycles
   b. the number of yellow bicycles
   c. the cost of a red Duo
   d. the ratio of road bicycles to mountain bicycles
   e. the ratio of red bicycles to green bicycles

48. Sage has a bag of marbles. The bag contains 16 black, 10 red, 10 blue, and 14 white marbles. What is the probability that Sage randomly takes a red marble from the bag and leaves the marble on a table and then takes a white marble from the bag?
   a. $\frac{1}{5}$
   b. $\frac{2}{7}$
   c. $\frac{12}{25}$
   d. $\frac{17}{35}$
   e. $\frac{18}{35}$

Use the following information to answer question 49.

Basic cable television service, which includes 16 channels, costs $15 a month. The initial labor fee to install the service is $25. A $65 deposit is required but will be refunded within two years if the customer's bills are paid in full. Other cable services may be added to the basic service: the movie channel service is $9.40 a month; the news channels are $7.50 a month; the arts channels are $5 a month; the sports channels are $4.80 a month.

49. A customer's first bill, including installation, totaled $112.50. This customer chose basic cable. Which additional service was chosen?
   a. the news channels
   b. the movie channels
   c. the arts channels
   d. the sports channels
   e. no additional services were chosen

50. Which of the following is the most appropriate unit for expressing the weight of a textbook?
   a. grams
   b. pounds
   c. quarts
   d. feet
   e. yards

Section 3: Essay Writing

Carefully read the two essay-writing topics that follow. On scratch paper, plan and write two essays, one on each topic. Be sure to address all points in the topic. Allow about 30 minutes for each essay.

Topic 1

Should public school students be required to wear uniforms? Supporters argue that, among other things, uniforms would improve discipline and build a strong sense of community and identity. On the other hand, opponents believe that uniforms limit students' freedom of expression and their development as individuals.

Write an essay in which you take a position on whether or not public school students should be required to wear uniforms to school. Be sure to support your position with logical arguments and specific examples.

Topic 2

Bob Maynard has said that "Problems are opportunities in disguise."

Write an essay describing a time in your life when a problem became an opportunity. How did you transform the situation? Explain what you did to turn the problem into an opportunity and how others can benefit from your experience.

Answers

Section 1: Reading Comprehension

1. **d.** See the second to last sentence of paragraph 4, which speaks of Mt. Desert Island as supporting *the flora and fauna of both zones, as well as beach, inland, and alpine plants.* The other choices are not mentioned in paragraph 4.

2. **a.** See the final sentence of paragraph 1 and the second sentence of paragraph 2. There is no support for the other choices.

3. **c.** Although all the choices are related to the glacial disturbance of the Maine shoreline, only marine fossils are spoken of as evidence that a mountain was once at shoreline level.

4. **d.** This is the choice that makes the most sense. Since the summer homes of the wealthy existed for years and apparently still existed at the time of the writing of the passage, it is illogical to say that they were either *remembered* (choice **a**) or *discouraged* from existing there (choice **b**), or that the town *endured* them (choice **e**). It is unreasonable to suppose that a town would pay for summer homes for wealthy people (choice **c**).

5. **c.** Paragraph 5 (see the second sentence) discusses the visitors to Acadia National Park, and what they can learn from their visits. Choices **a**, **b**, **d**, and **e** are not mentioned in the passage.

6. **a.** This answer is implied by the first three sentences of paragraph 1. Even though Maine was part of a mountain range, there is no evidence that it could now be described as *very mountainous* (choice **b**) because the original mountains sank into the sea. There is no support for choice **c**. Choices **d** and **e** are not mentioned in the passage.

7. **b.** Motion picture editing is the same as movie editing.

8. **a.** Architecture, civil spaces, electricity, and mechanics are all different areas of study.

9. **b.** The second paragraph describes places that a driver would enjoy seeing on Highway 1. Monterey Bay would be another place for a driver to enjoy.

10. **d.** The rest of the first sentence describes the first thoughts or impressions of taking a driving trip.

11. **c.** The first paragraph explains that driving has drawbacks, but that it may sometimes be the better travel choice. The second paragraph describes the things that a driver might see along California's Highway 1.

12. **e.** The phrase *farmers were happy* expresses an opinion

13. **a.** The paragraph describes how the city grew and declined, but the last sentence describes the government honoring the city.

14. **d.** Buses accounted for 13% of the traffic. The other segment of the circle graph that is 13% is motorcycles.

15. **c.** The paragraph describes the benefits of red light cameras, and this sentence offers another benefit.

16. **d.** This is the only sentence that follows that is logical in the given context. It makes sense that the play was in danger of closing. Choices **a** and **b** do not make syntactical sense, as the *however* in the next sentence contradicts them. The ideas mentioned in in choices **c** and **e** aren't mentioned anywhere in the passage.

17. **e.** The passage supports choice **e** by describing the success that the opening of *Menagerie*

enjoyed as well as stating that Williams brought poetry and imagination back to the theater that was offering, at the time, mostly realism to audiences. Choices **a** and **d** are never mentioned in the passage. Choice **b** is incorrect because, although the producers were thinking about closing the production, they are never described as narrow-minded. In fact, it makes sense that they would want to close down a potentially unsuccessful play. Choice **c** is incorrect because it is the opposite of the correct answer. The plot and characters were atypical of post–World War II plays, which is why *Menagerie* was so successful.

18. b. Choice **b** is the best synonym of *overweening*. Another clue is the word that follows, *meddlesome*.

19. c. This choice is supported by the same statement that provides the correct answer to question 17. It can be inferred that the success of *Menagerie* represented a change in post–World War II theater, since Williams is recognized as bringing poetry and imagination back to a stage that was in "the throes of post–World War II realism." Choice **a** is never mentioned or implied in the passage, and, although *Menagerie* was an important play, the passage doesn't state that it was the most important play of the twentieth century, making choice **b** incorrect. Choices **d** and **e** are entirely inaccurate; clearly the play was well received by the public.

20. e. Choices **a** and **c** are incorrect because the bus driver needs to see that each passenger has an exhibit ticket stub in order to grant half fare. Choice **b** is incorrect because the passage doesn't say that a person without an exhibit stub isn't allowed to ride the bus, but rather, that he or she must pay full fare. Choice **d** is a viable option, but the driver would still need to collect the full fare.

21. d. The third sentence in the passage is a clue to this correct answer. *As part of its ongoing effort to promote diversity awareness* implies that the University regularly does this. Choice **a** is incorrect because—although it may be true—it is never mentioned or implied in the passage. Choice **b** is incorrect because the passage doesn't mention the original price of the fare, nor does it imply that it is very expensive. Choice **c** is incorrect because although the University and the Cultural Center are joining forces on this venture, nowhere does it say that this is a regular occurrence. Choice **e** is incorrect because the reader is not given any information on how hard the bus drivers work during the other months of the year.

22. a. Although students in the other classes might find the passage's subject matter somewhat appropriate, the passage talks mainly about physiological changes to astronauts in space.

23. d. The passage says that in the face of light pollution *we lose our connection with something profoundly important to the human spirit, our sense of wonder.* The other choices are not mentioned in the passage.

24. e. Choices **a**, **b**, and **d** do not make sense in the context of the passage. Choice **c** opposes common sense—it *is* expected that there would be controversy between loggers and sawmill owners and environmentalists.

25. c. The clue is in the following sentence: "In 1990, the species was listed as threatened, mostly due to the loss of habitat as a result of logging." Because the species was losing its habitat because of logging, it can be inferred that the court wanted to put a stop to the possible extinction of the Northern Spotted Owl by prohibiting any more deforestation. Nothing in the passage implies that loggers should be looking for work elsewhere (choice **a**), or that people were interested in putting a stop to environmentalists heavily lobbying for the owl's protection (choice **b**). Nowhere does the passage mention that sawmills were in need of job applicants (choice **d**). And, although the passage mentions that owls hunt and kill rodents, nowhere does it say that it is a priority to maintain this behavior (choice **e**).

26. e. It is clear that the author of the passage disapproves of the loggers' behavior when the author uses the word *petulant*, which means "childish," in the last sentence to describe them.

27. b. In the previous sentence, the author says that the loggers reacted in a "vicious manner." Including quotes from the bumper stickers clearly serves to support this statement. Choice **a** is tricky, but technically, it is not as strong a choice as **b**. The author has no reason to show that loggers band together (choice **d**), and choice **e** does not make sense.

28. d. A wind speed of 173 miles per hour falls between 158 and 206, which is the range for an F3 tornado.

29. b. Applying words such as *mild, moderate, significant, severe, devastating, cataclysmic,* and *overwhelming* to the kinds of damage done by a tornado is a means of describing the damage. A word like *devastating*, for example, is not what we think of as *scientific* or *objective* (choices **a** and **c**), and most of the words have negative connotations and therefore are not *whimsical* (choice **e**). Neither the table nor the language is trying to *persuade* (choice **d**), except perhaps secondarily.

30. b. The connotations of words like *bonds* and *constraints* in the passage suggest a *confined space* of criticism where the mind must be allowed to find some movement or *play*. None of the other choices make sense in the context of the passage.

31. c. The word *awe* implies reverence, dread, and wonder, so the adjective *awesome* is the best choice to describe a place that is *dangerous and full of wonders* (second sentence of the second paragraph). Choices **a** and **b** both describe a part of the hero's journey but neither describes the whole of it. Choice **d** is incorrect because the hero's journey is described in the passage in very serious terms, not in *whimsical* (playful or fanciful) terms at all. The words *trials* and *adventures* do not suggest anything mundane.

32. e. The first sentence of the passage describes Campbell's hero as *archetypal*. An archetype is a personage or pattern that occurs in literature and human thought often enough to be considered universal. Also, in the second sentence, the author of the passage mentions *the collective unconscious of all humankind*. The *faces* in the title belong to the *hero*, not to *villagers*, *countries*, *languages*, or *adventures* (choices **a**, **b**, **c**, and **d**).

33. a. The passage states that the hero's tale will *enlighten* his fellows, but that it will also be *dangerous*. Such a story would surely be radically mind-altering. Choice **b** is directly contradicted in the passage. If the hero's tale would terrify people *to no good end*, it could not possibly be enlightening. There is nothing in the passage to imply that the tale is *a warning of catastrophe, a dangerous lie,* or *a parable* (choices **c**, **d**, and **e**).

34. b. The definition of the word *boon* is *blessing*. What the hero brings back may be a kind of *gift*, *charm*, or *prize* (choices **a**, **c**, and **d**), but those words do not necessarily connote blessing or enlightenment.

35. a. The paragraph describes only the similarity between the hero's journey and the poet's. The other choices are not reflected in the passage.

36. e. The last sentence in the passage says that *the kingdom of the unconscious mind* goes down into *unsuspected Aladdin caves*. The story of *Aladdin* is a fairy tale (choice **b**), but neither this nor the other choices are in the passage.

37. d. *Instead* makes the most sense in this context, as the sentence serves to explain an opposing idea in the previous sentence. The remaining choices do not make sense in the context of the passage.

38. c. The answer to this question can be found in the following sentence: "The word's translation into English is most likely the source of confusion regarding the disease's symptoms."

39. a. The passage explains schizophrenia; therefore, choice **a** makes the most sense. The passage doesn't go into any detail about actual people who have schizophrenia (choice **b**), nor does it discuss how to cope with it (choice **c**) or how to live with it (choice **e**).

40. d. Choice **d** is the only one that is directly stated in the passage. Nowhere does the passage say that schizophrenia is curable (choice **a**). The passage does not say that the onset of schizophrenia happens only in young adulthood (choice **b**); it says that the onset *usually* takes place then. Although one of the negative symptoms of schizophrenia includes a lack of motivation, nowhere does the passage state that *all* schizophrenics have this symptom (choice **c**). The passage states that schizophrenia is managed with antipsychotic medication but does not state that the symptoms disappear completely (choice **e**).

41. d. Choice **a** is incorrect because the passage clearly states that the HAV in the fourth vaccine is formalin-inactivated: *The fourth vaccine is made out of HAV that has been purified from infected human diploid cell cultures and <u>also inactivated with formalin</u>*. Choice **b** is incorrect—the passage never says that the three vaccines are more immunogenic than the fourth. In fact, it says that there are four highly immunogenic vaccines available. Choice **c** can be tricky if you don't read carefully. The phrase *the HAV in each is then formalin-inactivated and adsorbed to an aluminum hydroxide adjuvant* refers to the three vaccines, making the first part of choice **c** correct. But, the second part of choice **c** reads . . . *the fourth vaccine is purified*, when, in fact, the HAV that *makes up* the vaccine is purified, *not* the vaccine itself. Choice **e** is incorrect because the passage never mentions whether the three vaccines target influenza-primed antibody-presenting cells.

42. a. The answer can be found in the sentence *The fourth vaccine's virosomes, which have a protein or lipid from the envelope of the virus attached to their membranes, possess the antigenic, or antibody-stimulating properties of the virus, and in effect, transport the vaccine*. Choice **b** is incorrect: Virosomes *target* influenza-primed antibody-presenting cells and macrophages, not *transport* them. Choices **c** and **e** are incorrect because virosomes have a protein or a lipid from the envelope of the virus attached to their membranes—they are not made of them. Choice **d** is incorrect; nowhere in the passage is it mentioned that virosomes transport fibroblasts.

43. b. Students would look at the cost-savings of a community college if they could not afford university tuition.

44. c. The passage describes how students can take two years of classes at the community college, and then transfer the class credits to a four-year college.

45. b. The answer can be found in the sentence *. . . and destroys pancreatic beta cells—the ones that manufacture insulin.* Choice **a** is incorrect; insulin, not the pancreatic beta cells, is responsible for bringing glucose from the bloodstream into the cells. Choice **c** is incorrect because nowhere does the passage say that pancreatic beta cells stabilize the metabolism. If anything, that is one of the jobs of insulin. Choices **d** and **e** are incorrect, as pancreatic beta cells are never linked with the body's fuel production or making glucose.

46. d. Choice **a** is incorrect because the passage never says that people with Type II cannot manage their diabetes with regular insulin injections. Choice **b** is incorrect because the passage clearly states that both types of diabetes were previously known by other names (but are now known as *Type I* and *Type II*). Choice **c** is incorrect for two reasons. The first is that Type II can cause the body to produce excessive amounts of insulin. The second is that choice **c** mentions nothing about Type II. Choice **e** is incorrect because both types of diabetes are marked by high levels of blood glucose. The first sentence in the passage states this. Also, choice **e** reads that Type II *always* results in high levels of insulin, whereas the passage says that the pancreas *may* react by producing too much insulin.

47. c. This passage provides information to social workers about music therapy, as the title in choice **c** indicates. Choice **e** is incorrect because the first sentence speaks of mental and physical health professionals *referring* their clients and patients to music therapists; the second sentence indicates that *It* (meaning a *referral*) *seems a particularly good choice for the social worker.* Choice **d** is possible, but does not summarize the passage as well as choice **c**. Choices **a** and **b** refer to topics not covered in the passage.

48. e. Although the other choices may be correct, they require knowledge beyond the passage. Based on the information in the passage, choice **e** fits best.

49. a. Based particularly on the last sentence of the passage, choice **a** fits best. The other choices are beyond the scope of the passage.

50. c. Choice **c** provides the best outline of the passage. The other choices all contain points that are not covered by the passage.

Section 2: Mathematics

1. a. −0.15 is less than −0.02, the least number in the range.

2. c. January is approximately 38,000; February is approximately 41,000, and April is approximately 26,000. These added together give a total of 105,000.

3. c. The buses arrive 53 minutes after they leave. Therefore, the bus will arrive at 8:13.

4. b. $3 divided by $50 is .06. This is an increase of 0.06, or 6%.

5. c. Mr. Judah can supervise the bus zone for 30 minutes, from 2:10 to 2:40. If he then drives to the Central Administration Building for 35 minutes, he would arrive on time at 3:15 P.M.

DIAGNOSTIC CBEST EXAM

6. d. Stanine scores are represented by the whole numbers 1 through 9. Students who score a 4 or less have performed worse than 50% of students taking the test. Students who score over a 5 have performed better than 50% of students taking the test. The only whole number given that is greater than 5 is 6.

7. a. $-12 + -4 + -7 = -23$

8. e. According to the graph, of the choices given, the fewest acres burned in 2004.

9. c. The bar on the graph is over the 100,000 mark.

10. e. To answer this question, both *Acres Burned* and *Dollars Spent* must be considered. The ratio between the two is greater in 2005 than in the other years.

11. a. In April, the dotted line (representing the average) is closest to the solid line (representing 2005 rainfall).

12. d. Read the dotted line for September.

13. b. The graph shows that during January, February, and April, rainfall amounts were above average.

14. b. Since the price is given at a per-hour rate, the number of hours worked is needed to find the price of the fence.

15. c. $15.50 per hour × 7.5 hours per day × 5 days per week is $581.25. This can be estimated by multiplying 15 × 8 × 5, which equals $600. Choice **c** is the only answer that is close to this estimate.

16. b. The number of papers graded is arrived at by multiplying the rate for each grader by the time spent by each grader. Melissa grades 5 papers an hour for 3 hours, or 15 papers; Joe grades 4 papers an hour for 2 hours, or 8 papers, so together, they grade 23 papers. Because there are 50 papers, the percentage graded is $\frac{23}{50}$, which is equal to 46%.

17. e. A yardstick is 36 inches long; add that to the 28 inches of rope, and you will get 64 inches as the longest distance James can measure.

18. d. Each term in the pattern is the sum of sequential odd numbers 1, 1 + 3, 1 + 3 + 5, 1 + 3 + 5 + 7, and so on.

19. d. 3 inches every 2 hours = 1.5 inches per hour × 5 hours = 7.5 inches.

20. b. Convert each of the fractions to a decimal. $1\frac{3}{4}$ = 1.75 and $2\frac{1}{2}$ = 2.5. The only choice between 1.75 and 2.5 is 2.3.

21. d. The area of a rectangle is found by multiplying width times height. If the width is 3 cm, and the area is 24 square cm, then the height must be 8 cm. Therefore, the perimeter of the rectangle is found by adding the lengths of the sides: 3 + 8 + 3 + 8 = 22.

22. e. Three feet equals 36 inches; add 4 inches to get 40 inches total; 40 divided by 5 is 8.

23. d. 4.29 is greater than 4.209, and 4.209 is greater than 4.029.

24. d. Six buses will be full, and one bus will hold the remaining 58 students. This means the district needs seven buses all together.

25. d. The volume of concrete is 27 cubic feet. As noted in the previous answer explanation, the volume is length times width times depth or height, or $(L)(W)(D)$, so $(L)(W)(D)$ equals 27. We're told that the length L is 6 times the width W, so L equals $6W$. We're also told that the depth is 6 inches, or 0.5 feet. Substituting what we know about the length and depth into the original equation and solving for W, we get $(L)(W)(D) = (6W)(W)(0.5) = 27$. $3W^2$ equals 27. W^2 equals 9, so W equals 3. To get the length, we remember that L equals $6W$, so L equals $(6)(3)$, or 18 feet.

26. a. First, you find out how long the entire hike can be, based on the rate at which the hikers are using their supplies. $\frac{2/5}{3} = \frac{1}{x}$, where 1 is the total amount of supplies and x is the number of days for the whole hike. Cross multiplying, you get $\frac{2}{5}x = 3$, so $x = \frac{(3)(5)}{2}$, or $7\frac{1}{2}$ days for the length of the entire hike. This means that the hikers could go forward for 3.75 days together before they would have to turn around. They have already hiked for 3 days. 3.75 minus 3 equals 0.75 for the amount of time they can now go forward before having to turn around.

27. c. Three tons is 6,000 pounds. 6,000 pounds times 16 ounces per pound is 96,000 ounces. The total weight of each daily ration is 12 ounces plus 18 ounces plus 18 ounces, or 48 ounces. 96,000 divided by 48 equals 2,000 troops supplied. 2,000 divided by 10 days equals 200 troops supplied per day.

28. d. 26 forms times 8 hours is 208 forms per day per clerk. 5,600 divided by 208 is approximately 26.9. Since you can't hire 0.9 of a clerk, you have to hire 27 clerks for the day.

29. b. The women's combined rate of travel is 35 miles per hour plus 15 miles per hour, which is equal to 50 miles per hour. 2,100 miles divided by 50 miles per hour equals 42 hours.

30. d. The student's average would include the highest four exam scores of 96, 91, 87, and 82, so $\frac{96 + 91 + 87 + 82}{4} = 89$.

31. e. An equation can be used to solve this problem: $3x - 15 = 21$. The solution to this equation is $x = 12$.

32. e. This can be most quickly and easily solved by rounding the numbers to the nearest ten cents. Therefore, $2 \times \$3 + \$3.40 + 2 \times \$4 + \$2 = \$19.40$. The nearest and most reasonable answer would be **e** or $19.10.

33. b. Solve this problem with the following equation: $37\frac{1}{2}$ hours $- 26\frac{1}{4}$ hours $= 11\frac{1}{4}$ hours.

34. d. Solve this problem with the following equation: 4 candy bars × $0.40 + 3 soft drinks × $0.50 = $3.10.

35. e. To find this solution, add the distance to the track to the distance run at the track ($7 \times \frac{1}{4} = 3\frac{1}{4}$) to his distance home: $\frac{3}{4} + 1\frac{3}{4} + \frac{3}{4} = 3\frac{1}{4}$.

36. c. There are 5 spaces of 4 feet and 4 desks of 3 feet; this adds to 32 feet.

37. b. An algebraic equation should be used: $K - 20 = \frac{1}{2}(M - 20)$; $K = 40$. Therefore, $M = 60$.

38. a. The original number of cars is known, and the number sold is known, so the number remaining can be calculated.

39. c. The two rings valued at $150 have a total value of $300, but remember that there is another ring valued at only $70, so the correct answer is $610.

40. c. The value of the handbag ($150) must be included in the total of $618.

41. b. This problem can be solved with a Venn diagram.

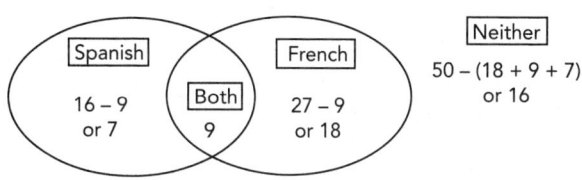

42. a. The letter T stands for the subtotal for grade 8. $71 + 65 + 83 + 90 = 309$

43. a. $12 \times 10 \times 3$ is 360. Since there are an odd number of negative factors, the product is negative.

44. e. This problem is solved by dividing 60 (the words) by 0.75 (the time), which gives 80 words.

45. c. Use multiplication to solve this problem. $8.2 \times 35 = 287$.

46. b. You know the ratio of Dr. Kelley's charge to Dr. John's charge is 2:3 or $\frac{2}{3}$. To find what Dr. John charges, you can use the equation $\frac{2}{3} = \frac{48}{x}$. Cross multiplying and dividing by 2, we find that $x = 72$.

47. e. Because the only categories quantified are colors of bikes, only the ratio of red bikes to green bikes can be found.

48. d. The probability of first drawing a red marble is $\frac{10}{50}$, or $\frac{1}{5}$. The probability of the next marble being white is $\frac{14}{49}$, or $\frac{2}{7}$. The sum of these two fractions is $\frac{17}{35}$.

49. a. The labor fee ($25) plus the deposit ($65) plus the basic service ($15) equals $105. The difference between the total bill, $112.50, and $105 is $7.50, the cost of the news channels.

50. b. Pounds are a unit of weight that is large enough to describe a heavy book.

Section 3: Essay Writing

Following are the criteria for scoring CBEST essays.

A "4" essay is a coherent writing sample that addresses the assigned topic and is aimed at a specific audience. Additionally, it has the following characteristics:

- a main idea and/or a central point of view that is focused; its reasoning is sound
- points of discussion that are clear and arranged logically
- assertions that are supported with specific, relevant detail
- word choice and usage that is accurate and precise
- sentences that have complexity and variety, with clear syntax; paragraphs that are coherent (minor mechanical flaws are acceptable)
- style and language that are appropriate to the assigned audience and purpose

A "3" essay is an adequate writing sample that generally addresses the assigned topic, but may neglect or only vaguely address one of the assigned tasks; it is aimed at a specific audience. Generally, it has the following additional characteristics:

- a main idea and/or a central point of view and adequate reasoning
- organization of ideas that is effective; the meaning of the ideas is clear
- generalizations that are adequately, though unevenly, supported
- word choice and language usage that are adequate; mistakes exist, but do not interfere with meaning
- some errors in sentence and paragraph structure, but not so many as to be confusing
- word choice and style is appropriate to a given audience

A "2" essay is an incompletely formed writing sample that attempts to address the topic and to communicate a message to the assigned audience but is generally incomplete or inappropriate. It has the following additional characteristics:

- a main point, but one which loses focus; reasoning that is simplistic
- ineffective organization that causes the response to lack clarity
- generalizations that are only partially supported; supporting details that are irrelevant or unclear
- imprecise language usage; word choice that distracts the reader
- mechanical errors; errors in syntax; errors in paragraphing
- style that is monotonous or choppy

A "1" essay is an inadequately formed writing sample that only marginally addresses the topic and fails to communicate its message to, or is inappropriate to, a specific audience. Additionally, it has the following characteristics:

- general incoherence and inadequate focus, lack of a main idea or consistent point of view; illogical reasoning
- ineffective organization and unclear meaning throughout
- unsupported generalizations and assertions; details that are irrelevant and presented in a confusing manner
- language use that is imprecise, with serious and distracting errors
- many serious errors in mechanics, sentence syntax, and paragraphing

Following are examples of scored essays for Topics 1 and 2.

Topic 1

Pass—Score = 4

Though it may seem to contradict the ideal of democracy upon which our public school system is based, requiring public school students to wear uniforms is a good idea. In fact, uniforms would help schools provide a better education to all students by evening out socio-economic differences and improving discipline among students.

Style is important, especially to children and teenagers who are busy trying to figure out who they are and what they believe in. But in many schools today, kids are so concerned about what they wear that clothing becomes a major distraction—even an obsession. Many students today are too busy to study because they're working after school so they can afford the latest fashions. If students were required to wear uniforms, they would have less pressure to be "best dressed" and more time to devote to their studies.

More importantly, the competition over who has the hottest clothes can be devastating to the self-esteem of students from lower income families.

Because uniforms would require everyone to wear the same outfits, students from poorer families would not have to attend school in beat-up hand-me-downs and wouldn't have to face the kind of teasing they often get from students who can afford designer jeans and $150 sneakers. True, students from wealthier families will be able to wear nicer shoes and accessories, but in general the uniforms will create an evening-out that will enable poorer students to develop a stronger sense of self.

Contrary to what opponents argue, uniforms will not create uniformity. Just because students are dressed the same does not mean they won't be able to develop as individuals. In fact, because uniforms enable students to stop worrying so much about their appearance, students can focus more on who they are on the inside and on what they're supposed to be learning in the classroom.

Furthermore, uniforms will improve discipline in the schools. Whenever a group of people dresses alike, they automatically have a sense of community, a sense of common purpose. Uniforms mean something. School uniforms will constantly remind students that they are indeed in school—and they're in school to learn. Getting dressed for school itself will be a form of discipline that students will carry into the classroom.

Though many students will complain, requiring public school students to wear uniforms makes sense. Students will learn more—both about themselves and about the world around them.

Marginal Pass—Score = 3

I don't think that requiring public school students to wear uniforms is a good idea. The way the student dresses makes a powerful statement about who he or she is, and the school years are an important time for them to explore their identities. Uniforms would undermine that. They would also have little, if any, positive affect on students with disipline problems.

Each student has their own personality, and one way he expresses who he is is through his clothing. Clothes are an important way for young people to show others how they feel about themselves and what is important to them. If public school students are forced to wear uniforms, this important form of self-expression will be taken away.

I remember back when I was in junior high school. My parents had given me complete freedom to buy my back to school wardrobe. They took me to the mall and let me choose everything, from sweaters and shirts to socks and shoes. I'll never forget how independent that made me feel. I could choose clothing that I liked. I did make a few bad choices, but at least those were my choices. Students today, I am sure, would feel the same way.

Besides, Americans value individuality. What happens to that value in an environment where everybody looks the same?

Though disipline in schools is a serious concern, uniforms are not the answer. Disipline problems usually come from a lack of disipline at home, and that's a problem that uniforms can't begin to address. A student who is rowdy in the classroom isn't going to change his behavior because he is wearing a white shirt and tie. In fact, disipline problems might increase if students are required to wear uniforms. Students often make trouble because they want attention. Well-behaved students who used to get attention from how they dressed might now become trouble-makers so they can continue to get attention.

Uniforms are not the answer to the problems public school students face. In fact, because they'll restrict individuality and may even increase disiplinary problems, they'll only add to the problem.

Marginal Fail—Score = 2

I don't think that requiring public school students to wear uniforms is a good idea. Each student has their own identity and express who he is through clothing. The school years are an important in finding one's personality. Uniforms would also have little, if any, positive affect on students with disipline problems.

In junior high school I let my children buy their back-to-school wardrobe, anything they wanted. I let them choose everything. I'll never forget how that made them feel. As they would say, awesome! They could choose clothing that they liked.

We are told to be yourself. But how can a young person be in a country where everybody is the same.

Disipline in schools is of a serious concern, uniforms are not the answer. It is the home life of many students that make bad behavior. If the parents use drugs or dont disipline children at home, thats a problem that the school and uniforms can't do anything about. A student who is causing trouble at school isn't going to change their behavior because they are wearing a white blouse or pleated skirt. In fact, disipline problems might even get worse if students are required to wear uniforms because of not getting enough attention about the way he or she is dressed.

Uniforms are not the answer to the problems public school students face. In fact, because they will keep them from being who they are they will make it worse.

Fail—Score = 1

Public school students should wear uniforms to. Not just private school students. I do not want to teach in a private school; but I like them wearing a uniform every day. The look neat and well-groom no matter if they are low income or high income. Social level doesnt matter.

Wearing uniforms is good because they build a sense of community. Everyone from the same school wear the same clothes. The students know if someone is from there school right away. It makes it easier for students, rich or poor, to make friends with people. They don't have to worry about what to wear in the morning because they always know.

Also they don't have to spend as much money on cloths.

Many students think it is unfair that public school students could wear whatever they wanted. Maybe private school students shouldn't wear uniforms either. Then everyone would be able to dress the way they want to and be individulistic.

Some people say uniforms would make bad students behave better. Because they wouldn't always be talking about who has a better sneakers or better jeans. They might have paid more attention in school like they should of, and then everyone could learn more.

Topic 2
Pass—Score = 4

Life is full of problems, but how we approach those problems often determines whether we're happy or miserable. Bob Maynard says that "Problems are opportunities in disguise." If we approach problems with Maynard's attitude, we can see that problems are really opportunities to learn about ourselves and others. They enable us to live happier and more fulfilling lives.

Maynard's quote applies to all kinds of problems. I faced a problem just last week when our kitchen sink developed a serious leak. There was water all over our kitchen floor and piles of dishes to be washed. But our landlord was out of town for the week. I have a big family—I have six children—so we couldn't afford to wait until he got back, and I couldn't afford a couple hundred dollars to pay for a plumber on my own. So I took the opportunity to learn how to fix it myself. I went to the library and found a great fix-it-yourself book. In just a few hours, I figured out what was causing the leak and how to stop it. If it weren't for that problem, I probably would have relied on plummers and landlords all my life. Now I know I can handle leaky pipes by myself.

I think it's important to remember that no matter how big a problem is, it's still an opportunity. Whatever kind of situation we face, problems give us the chance to learn and grow, both physically and mentally. For example, when I had a problem with my car and couldn't afford the repairs right away, my problem became an opportunity to get some exercise—something I'd been wanting to do anyway. I had to walk a mile each day to get to the bus stop and back. But in the meantime, I got the chance to start getting back in shape, and I saved a lot on gas.

I've come to realize that problems are really part of what makes life worth living. Problems challenge us and give us the opportunity to do things we've never done before, to learn things we never knew before. They teach us what we're capable of doing. They give us the chance to surprise ourselves.

Marginal Pass—Score = 3

Just the word "problem" can send some of us into a panic. But problems can be good things, too. Problems are situations that make us think and force us to be creative and resourceful. They can also teach us things we didn't know before.

For example, I had a problem in school a few years ago when I couldn't understand my math class. I started failing my quizzes and homework assignments. I wasn't sure what to do, so finally I went to the teacher and asked for help. She said she would arrange for me to be tutored by another student who was her best student. In return, though, I'd have to help that student around school. I wasn't sure what she meant by that until I met my tutor. She was differently abled and used a wheelchair to get around.

My job was to help her carry her books from class to class. I'd never even spoken to someone in a wheelchair before and I was a little scared. But she turned out to be the nicest person I've ever spent time with. She helped me understand everything I need to know for math class and she taught me a lot about what it's like to be disabled. I learned to appreciate everything that I have, and I also know that people with disabilities are special not because of what they can't do, but because of who they are.

So you see that wonderful things can come out of problems. You just have to remember to look for the positive things and not focus on the negative.

Marginal Fail—Score = 2

The word "problem" is a negative word but its just an opportunity as Mr. Bob Maynard has said. It can be teaching tool besides.

For example, I had a problem with my son last year when he wanted a bigger allowance. I said no and he had to earn it. He mowed the lawn and in the fall he raked leaves. In the winter he shovelled the walk. After that he apreciated it more. Its not the problem but the sollution that matters. My son learning the value of work and earning money. (It taught me the value of money to when I had to give him a bigger allowance!) After that he could get what he wanted at Toys Are Us and not have to beg. Which was better for me too. Sometimes we forget that both children and there parents can learn a lot from problems and we can teach our children the value of overcoming trouble. Which is as important as keeping them out of trouble. As well we can teach them the value of money. That is one aspect of a problem that we manytimes forget.

So problems are a good teaching tool as well as a good way to let you're children learn, to look at the silver lining behind every cloud.

Fail—Score = 1

I agree with the quote that problems are opportunities in disguise. Sometimes problems are opportunities, too.

I have a lot of problems like anyone else does. Sometimes there very difficult and I don't no how to handle them. When I have a really big problem, I sometimes ask my parents or freinds for advise. Sometimes they help, sometimes they don't, then I have to figure out how to handle it myself.

One time I had a big problem. Where someone stole my wallet and I had to get to a job interview. But I had no money and no ID. This happened in school. So I went to the principles office and reported it. He called the man I was supposed to interview with. Who rescheduled the interview for me. So I still had the opportunity to interview and I'm proud to say I got the job. In fact I'm still working there!

Problems can be opportunities if you just look at them that way. Instead of the other way around.

Scoring

Because it is necessary for you to do well on all three sections of the CBEST—Reading Comprehension, Mathematics, and Essay Writing—you must figure your score on each section separately. Reading Comprehension and Mathematics are scored the same way: First find the number of questions you got right in each section. Questions you skipped or got wrong don't count; just add up how many questions you got right out of the 50 questions in each section. If you get approximately 70% of the answers right on each section, you should pass the test. The following table will help you check your math by giving you percentage equivalents for some possible scores.

NUMBER OF QUESTIONS RIGHT	APPROXIMATE PERCENTAGE
50	100%
46	92%
43	86%
39	78%
35	70%
32	64%
28	56%
25	50%

You should get a score of at least 70% on both the Reading Comprehension section and the Mathematics section to be absolutely certain to pass those portions of the CBEST. (The actual number you receive on the real CBEST will *not* be "70," however, as the scores are converted from raw scores to scaled scores. But for the purpose of finding out if you passed the practice exams in this book, a percentage is just fine.)

In addition to achieving a score of 70% on the Reading Comprehension and Mathematics sections, you must receive a passing score on the Essay Writing section of the CBEST. On this portion, each essay you write will be scored by two readers who have been specially trained for this task. The criteria are outlined in detail on pages 60–61, but generally the essays are scored as follows:

4 = Pass (an excellent and well-formed essay)
3 = Marginal Pass (an average and adequately formed essay)
2 = Marginal Fail (a partially formed but substandard essay)
1 = Fail (an inadequately formed essay)

Your score will be a combination of the two readers' judgments, somewhere between a possible high of 8 and a low of 2. The best way to see how you did on your essays for this diagnostic exam is to give your essays and the scoring criteria to a teacher and ask him or her to score your essays for you.

What's much more important than your scores, for now, is how you did on each of the basic skills tested by the exam. You need to diagnose your strengths and weaknesses so that you can concentrate your efforts as you prepare for the exam.

Use your percentage scores in conjunction with the LearningExpress Test Preparation system in Chapter 2 of this book to help you devise a study plan. Then turn to the CBEST Mini-Course in Chapter 4, which covers each of the basic skills tested on the CBEST in 24 half-hour lessons. You should plan to spend more time on the lessons that correspond to the questions you found hardest and less time on the lessons that correspond to areas in which you did well.

CHAPTER 4 ▶ CBEST MINI-COURSE

CHAPTER SUMMARY
In just 24 lessons, the CBEST Mini-Course gives you the essentials you need to pass the CBEST. By spending just half an hour on each lesson—more on the areas that give you trouble, less on the areas you feel confident about—you can increase your CBEST score and earn your California or Oregon teaching credential.

Each of the 24 lessons in this chapter reviews one important CBEST skill. You can either move through the Mini-Course sequentially or choose the areas you need to study most and skip directly to them. If you find you need more help after completing the lessons in any one area, be sure to consult the More Help section at the end of this chapter.

Here's an outline of what you'll find in this Mini-Course:

Reading 1: General Strategies (page 70)
Reading 2: Organization Questions (page 73)
Reading 3: Unmasking the Main Idea (page 76)
Reading 4: About the Author (page 79)
Reading 5: Definite Details and Tables of Contents (page 82
Reading 6: Impressive Implications (page 86)
Reading 7: Wizard Words, Departed Parts, and Other Oddities (page 88)
Reading 8: Graphs (also applies to Math) (page 94)

Math 1:   Words, Words, Words (page 97)
Math 2:   Know the Score (page 101)
Math 3:   Rounding, Estimation, and Decimal Equivalents (page 106)
Math 4:   Fractions (page 110)
Math 5:   Measurement (page 113)
Math 6:   Ratios, Proportions, and Percents (page 118)
Math 7:   Algebra (page 123)
Math 8:   Probability and Combinations (page 128)
Math 9:   The Word Problem Game (page 130)
Math 10:   The CA SOLVE Approach to Word Problems (page 134)
Math 11:   Logic and Venn Diagrams (page 137)
Writing 1:   Outlining the Essay (page 140)
Writing 2:   Writing the Introduction (page 142)
Writing 3:   The Sandwich Paragraphs and the Last Slice (page 145)
Writing 4:   The Sentence Doctor (page 149)
Writing 5:   Finishing Touches (page 152)

More Help with Reading, Math, and Writing (page 156)

Most types of questions discussed in each lesson are accompanied by a gray box that gives steps for solving that type of question. Look for the gray box on each page and read it before you try the sample questions.

Reading 1: General Strategies

The reading comprehension section is composed of 50 multiple-choice questions on a variety of passages. The passages are created to simulate high school and college-level materials, student textbooks, teacher's guides and enrichment materials, and books on student behavior or psychology. This section explores some general strategies for all kinds of passages and questions. The sections that follow look in detail at each kind of question you might be asked.

Seven Approaches

How do you approach reading comprehension questions? Here are some suggestions from former CBEST takers.

- **The Concentrator:** "I read the passage thoroughly before I look at the questions. After concentrating on the passage, I can find the answers to the questions if I don't already know the answer from my careful reading."
- **The Skimmer:** "I skim the passage before looking at the questions. I can always go back and find the answers because I will know how the passage is arranged."
- **The Cautious Reader:** "I read each question and all the answer choices first. I want to know what the questions are about before I read the passage so I will know what to look for. Then I read the passage two or three times until I am sure I understand it completely."
- **The Game Player:** "I read the questions first and try to answer them from what I already know or can figure out. Then I read the passage to see whether I am right. After I have figured out the answers as best I can, the information in the passage lets me know if I am right or not."
- **The Educated Guesser:** "I read the questions first, but not the answers. When I find the answer in the passage, I look for it among the answer choices."
- **The Psychic:** "I think that the test designers write questions to match the same order as the passage. So I read the first question, then read the first part of the passage until I find the answer. Then I read

the second question and go to the next part of the passage. I do this until I have answered all the questions."

- **The Efficiency Expert:** "First, I look at the questions and do the questions that have line numbers that indicate where the answer is to be found. Then I skim the passage for the key words I read in the other questions. This way I sometimes do not even have to read the whole passage."

If you don't already have a preferred method, try some of these approaches as you work through the practice exercises in this book. See which method suits your strengths.

Hints for Reading the Passages

Try Shortcuts
Practice will help you determine whether you need to read the questions first, the answers first, or some combination of both. Try some of the shortcuts listed previously to find out which works for you.

Associate with the Passage
Every passage has something to do with real-life situations. Your mission is to discover the answers to questions such as:

- What is the author trying to express?
- Who might the author be?
- Does the author tell readers in the beginning what to expect later in the passage?
- How does the author structure the work to convey meaning?
- Does the author make any statements that might surprise or interest you?
- To what conclusions is the author leading readers? What conclusions are stated?

If the passage seems boring or discusses a topic that is foreign to you, try imagining that your best friend is talking to you on the same subject, and it really interests him or her. It might not be your thing, but it's your friend's, so listen to every detail and nuance of what your friend has to say and try to relate to it.

To Mark or Not to Mark
Some test takers find it helpful to underline text or make notes in the margins to designate the stated subject, supporting facts, conclusions, and so on. For others, marking a passage seems a waste of time. You are free to make as many marks as you want on the test booklet, so if marking helps, go for it. And if you are the type of person who prefers to mark up a test, don't sign up for the computer version! You won't have a way to mark passages. If you are not sure, now is the time to try out this method. If you decide to mark a passage, don't mark so much that the bulk of the passage is obscured. Marking a few key words and ideas is more helpful than underlining the majority of the passage.

Notice Transitions
Pay special attention to words that give you an insight into the author's purpose or that change the context of the passage, such as however, nevertheless, and so on. In at least one passage, these words will be left for you to fill in. This topic will be discussed in more detail in Reading Lesson 7.

Hints for Reading the Questions
Reading the questions carefully is just as important as reading the answers.

Read the Questions as Carefully as the Passage
It is crucial that you read the questions and answers as carefully as you read the passage. Should you read all the answer choices or stop when you have found one

that seems right? Test takers differ on this. Some who read all the answers become confused or worry about wasting time. Others feel more secure when they can eliminate every answer but the right one. It's up to you to find your best method.

Know Question Types

Being familiar with the types of questions that appear on the CBEST, and the kinds of wrong answers that each type is likely to include, can help you find the right answers with confidence. The lessons after this one will show you how to recognize the different question types and how to quickly choose the best answer.

Answer Only from the Passage

Everything you need to know has to be somewhere in the passage. While it is helpful to have some knowledge of the subject in order to better understand the author, don't rely on your experience to answer the question. The outside information you know may not be relevant to the passage, so make sure the answer you choose is supported by the passage.

Not or *Except*

Look for words in the question such as NOT or EXCEPT, especially if you cannot find a correct answer or there seems to be more than one answer. For example, a question might read: "Which of the following facts is NOT stated in the passage?"

Eliminate

Eliminate all the answers that are obviously off the subject or otherwise wrong. Many test takers find that questions often have two answers that seem more correct than the others. If this is the case, check the passage for key words or information that makes one answer more correct than the rest. Don't get frustrated if you find two answers that could be right. Instead, ask yourself, "Which answer is best, considering this particular passage?" If, after trying out all the strategies you learn in this book, you are still left with two answers, go ahead and guess, and get on with the test.

None Left?

If you eliminate all of the answers, go back over the eliminated answers to determine whether there might be another meaning for any of them. Try to find a reason that would make any of the answers correct. If there is no possible way an answer could be right—for example, it is completely off the subject—then eliminate that answer. Remember that you are looking for the answer that is best, considering the particular passage.

Marking the Unknown Question

Should you mark questions to come back to later? If you do, you will probably have to read the passage again, which can waste valuable time. If an answer jumps out at you after reading the passage once or twice, choose it. Many teachers and test takers recommend going with your first answer, your "gut" instinct. To save time and avoid reading passages more than once, answer all the questions about one passage before continuing on to the next passage.

Using the Steps

The lessons that follow discuss types of reading comprehension questions you may encounter. They offer sample question beginnings, as well as steps for solving each type of problem. There is no need to memorize all the steps. They are tips that clue you into what the test makers expect. If you are able to find the answer by your own methods without looking at the steps, so much the better. The steps are not there to bog you down, but if any of them can help you, use them.

Reading 2: Organization Questions

Passages on the CBEST are always organized logically. Learning to recognize that organization may also give you some ideas on organizing your essays in the Writing section. In this lesson, you'll learn about two types of organization questions: structure and misplaced sentences.

Structure Questions

Structure questions have stems (the question part) that start out like these:

- Which of the following best represents the arrangement of the passage?
- Which of the following best describes the organization of the passage?
- The sequence of the passage is best represented by which of the following?

Where to Find Structure Answers in the Passage

To answer structure questions, you will need to skim the passage carefully enough to understand the structure of each paragraph; that is, whether it gives a statistic, an example, a quote, an opinion, and so on.

Sample Passage and Questions

Try the six Success Steps on the structure questions that follow this passage.

Many extended-time programs use heterogeneous grouping of multi-age and/or multi-ability students. Mixed-ability grouping is based on the theory that lower-ability students benefit from working in small groups with their higher-achieving peers, and high-ability students reinforce their knowledge by sharing with their lower-achieving peers. Researchers also have found that multi-age grouping benefits students' mental health as well as academic achievement and contributes to positive attitudes toward school.

Because the voluntary nature of participation in an extended-time program results in a range of student ages and skills, heterogeneous groups may result naturally. Often, however, extended-time program planners arrange groups so that high- and low-ability students work together—with the expectation of cooperative rather than competitive learning. In Chicago's ASPIRA program, students are

Six Success Steps for Structure Passages

1. Skim the passage or read the topic sentences to understand the structure of each paragraph and the purpose of the passage.
2. Notice the logical sequence of ideas that the author uses.
3. The sentences in the answer should reflect the order of information in the passage. Does the first part of the answer match the purpose of the first part of the passage? Do they state a theory, introduce a topic, quote a famous person?
4. Read the answer choices. Eliminate any of the answers that do not have the same general purpose as the first portion of the passage.
5. Go back to steps 3 and 4; look at the next few sentences.
6. You should have eliminated one or two answers. Read the remaining answers to see how well they reflect the rest of the passage. Then choose the answer that best matches the structure of the entire passage.

Two Success Steps for Misplaced Sentences

1. Read the passage to determine the main idea.
2. Be suspicious of any sentence that has no connection to the main idea.

selected for participation with a goal of mixing high achievers and at-risk participants, and these groups work together closely in all activities.

1. Which of the following best describes the structure of the passage?
    a. The passage begins with a hypothesis, and then gives an explanation and support for this theory.
    b. The passage starts with a main idea, gives an example, and then draws a conclusion.
    c. The passage opens with an introduction to the topic, then gives a more detailed account of the topic.
    d. The passage begins with a statement, supports that statement with research, and gives real life examples.
    e. The passage begins with an event and then continues the narrative.

2. Which of the following would be the best outline for the passage?
    a. I. Statement
       II. Facts
       III. Quotations
    b. I. Theory
       II. Practices
    c. I. Research
       II. Discussion
       III. Example
    d. I. Question
       II. Answer
       III. Support
    e. I. Quote
       II. Thesis
       III. Examples

Answer

Here's how you could use the six Success Steps to answer question 1.

1. It seems as though the passage is about students of different ages and abilities learning together.
2. The first paragraph tells why and the second tells how students come to be in groups of mixed age and ability.
3. The first sentence states a fact. The other sentences in the paragraph seem to cite research. It doesn't say so at first, but later it says, "Researchers also found . . . ," which implies that research was involved in the theories before that sentence.
4. Choices **c** and **e** are out. The passage does not give much introduction to the topic, and does not start with an event.
5. The next sentences support the topic sentence with research. The answer must be choice **d**.
6. For this question, you don't need to use this step.

If you use the same method to answer question 2, you will quickly eliminate choices **d** and **e** on the basis of the first few sentences. You eliminate **a** because there are no quotations. You are left with choices **b** and **c**, which are very close. Choice **c** contains a vague word, *discussion*, which could describe almost any kind of paragraph. Choice **b** is more precise. The first paragraph in the passage gives the theory, and the second gives the application of the theory. The better answer is choice **b**.

Seven Success Steps for Simple Main Idea Questions

1. While reading or skimming the passage, notice the general topic.
2. Go through the answer choices. Cross out any that are completely off the topic.
3. Cross out any answer choices that are too broad for a short passage. ("The constellations" might be the subject of a book, but not the main idea for a paragraph or two.)
4. Eliminate any answer that is on the general topic, but not the specific topic of the passage.
5. Cross out any that only deal with one sentence of a paragraph, or one paragraph of a longer passage.
6. If you are still left with two answers that seem to fit most of the sentences in the passage, then choose the one that is most precise or specific.
7. If you have crossed them all out, check the choices again. Carefully try to decide whether there is another meaning to any of the answer choices. If you're still stumped, go back to the answer that was the most specific and seemed to cover more of the passage than the others.

Misplaced Sentences

You may be asked to find the sentence that does not flow logically, or that is not necessary to the purpose of the passage. Such questions often start out like this:

- Which sentence, if omitted from the passage, would be least likely to interrupt the sequence of ideas?
- Which of the following is least relevant to the main idea of the passage?

Where to Find Misplaced Sentences

You will usually be directed to a particular paragraph in a passage. If the first sentence states the main idea of the paragraph, it is unlikely to be the misplaced sentence, but you should read each sentence in the paragraph carefully, thinking about its relevance to the main idea.

Sample Passage and Question

(1) Long ago, humans used animals only for food. (2) Humans also ate plant products, such as fruits, vegetables, and leaves. (3) But eventually, humans saw that animals could provide work, protection, and transportation. (4) In nature, animals are suspicious of other animals and protect themselves. (5) Over time, humans have been able to change this behavior in some animals. (6) These animals look to humans for leadership. (7) This is called domestication. (8) Domesticated animal species become naturally used to living around and interacting with humans.

3. Which of the following numbered sentences is least relevant to the main idea of the paragraph?
   a. Sentence 2
   b. Sentence 3
   c. Sentence 6
   d. Sentence 7
   e. Sentence 8

Answer

The passage describes the history of animal domestication. Sentence 2 talks about other things that humans eat. This has nothing to do with domestication. All of the other sentence choices focus on how animals changed from wild to domesticated. The answer choice is **a**.

Preparing for Organization Questions

To further prepare for the test, as you read any book, magazine, or paper, you might want to take note of different ways paragraphs are structured and how sentences follow in a logical sequence.

Reading 3: Unmasking the Main Idea

Main idea questions can be put in three categories. The first asks for a simple sentence or title that includes the main topic of the passage. The second asks questions about the author's thoughts or intentions in writing the passage. Then there are those that ask for a paraphrase of all the main ideas in the passage.

Main Idea Questions

Main idea questions take a variety of forms:

- What is the main idea of the passage?
- The best title for this passage would be . . .
- What is the theme of the passage?
- The central thought of the passage is . . .

How to Find Main Idea Answers in the Passage

To answer main idea questions, you sometimes do not have to read the whole passage. The main idea is often stated at the beginning or end of the passage. Sometimes you can glean the main idea by looking for the topic sentences of each paragraph of the passage.

Sample Passage and Question

The goal is to discover the sequence of bases in the DNA. If this is a mitochondrial DNA fragment, the sequence will match the person's mother and maternal relatives. The DNA is divided down the center like a zipper. Heat is used to cause the division. Only one half of the DNA (one side of the zipper) is used. The sequence of bases will be discovered by re-creating the other half of the DNA.

The next goal is to use the half of the DNA that was saved to reconstruct the other half. This process will show the sequence of bases. Bases A and T always bind to each other, and bases C and G always bind to each other. The idea is to put one-half of a DNA strand in a test tube with some free bases and an enzyme that causes the free bases to attach to the half strand, rezipping the zipper. Modified bases are also added so that the location of that base on the "zipper" can be marked. In this way, the sequence of bases can be discovered. Each test tube contains thousands of copies of the saved half of the DNA strand, and a radioactive primer that will attach at the start location of every strand so that all operations start at the same place on every strand. Also included are DNA polymerase, which is an enzyme that acts as a "glue" to attach the free bases to the half DNA strand, and all four bases, which are free and unattached. There is also a modified base; each test tube has a different base that has been modified to act as a marker during reconstruction.

At the end of the process, thousands of reconstructed strands will be in each test tube. Some of these strands will be complete, but some of them will have been terminated by a modified base so they will be shorter. Each strand will have the same sequence of bases, but the strands will terminate at different positions where A is found. The reason that some of the strands do not terminate at base A is that a normal instead of a modified base A has attached at some of the base A locations. There is a test tube for each base. Therefore, there are reconstructed strands that terminate with C in the test tube with modified C bases, strands that terminate with G in the test tube with modified G bases, and strands that terminate with T in the test tube with modified T bases. The four test tubes are used in order to tell the difference between bases, since the strands and bases all look alike. However, the same test can be done in one test tube if fluorescent dyes are used to tag the modified bases.

1. Which of the following best describes the main topic of the passage?
   a. DNA can be linked to clues in a criminal investigation.
   b. Learning about the genetic code is important.
   c. The role of modified bases is part of the pieces of reading DNA.
   d. Dyes are used to tell the difference between bases.
   e. Reading base A strands is done at the end of the process.

Answer

Use the Success Steps to help you answer the question.

1. The general topic seems to have to do with the DNA strands in the test tube and some marked ends that help people read them.
2. It looks as though **a** is off the topic because the passage does not mention criminal investigations.
3. Choice **b** seems too broad.
4. There don't seem to be any answer choices that are on the general topic but not the specific topic.
5. Choices **d** and **e** have to do with only one part of the passage.

You don't have to use steps 6 and 7, because you have one answer left: Choice **c** is the best fit.

Sample Passage and Question

Try your hand at another passage and main idea question.

Successful programs make the extended-time curriculum challenging but not overwhelming. Research indicates that a challenging curriculum should accommodate individual student needs, coordinate with other instruction, and focus on more than remedial work. For example, the TAP Summer Youth Employment Program, which serves a large number of students living in housing projects, teaches basic skills that students need for communicating with employers and coworkers, and it also provides students with the challenge of putting these skills to use while working in their communities.

2. Which of the following would be the best title for the passage?
   a. An Appropriately Challenging Curriculum
   b. Some Successful Programs
   c. Implementing Individualized Learning
   d. Steps in Curriculum Innovation
   e. The TAP Summer Youth Employment Program

Answer

Again, apply the seven Success Steps.

1. The passage seems to be about the curriculum for a program outside of school.
2. It looks as if all the choices are on the general topic.
3. Choices **b** and **d** are too broad.
4. Choice **c** is on the general topic, but not on the subject of the paragraph.
5. Choice **e** has to do with only a part of the passage. The paragraph is mostly about the elements of a challenging curriculum. Therefore, choice **a** would make the best title. Once again, you did not have to use steps 6 and 7.

Perfect Paraphrases

There will probably be at least one question that asks you to paraphrase an entire passage. Paraphrase questions can be troublesome because the choices are so long. However, only one of the five answers is correct, and a careful, attentive approach will help you find it.

Seven Success Steps for Paraphrase Questions

1. Read or skim the passage, noting or underlining important ideas.
2. Look for phrases that restate the main ideas you underlined.
3. Eliminate answers that contain phrases that contradict ideas in the passage.
4. Eliminate answers that are off the topic or only address part of the passage.
5. Eliminate answers that include ideas that the author has not mentioned.
6. If you are left with two choices, choose the most complete one.
7. If you have eliminated every choice, take the paraphrase that contains the most main ideas without adding new ideas.

Paraphrase questions tend to start out like this:

- Which of the following best paraphrases the ideas in the passage?
- The best summary of the passage is . . .
- Which of the following is the best summation of the ideas in the passage?
- Which of the following best restates the main ideas of the passage?

How to Find Paraphrase Answers in the Passage

The main ideas of the passage can be found in each of the paragraphs, or in sections of the paragraphs. If you can follow the way the author has logically arranged the passage, you are more likely to find the correct answer to a paraphrase question.

Sample Passage and Question

Extended-time programs often feature innovative scheduling, as program staff work to maintain participation and respond to students' and parents' varied schedules and family or employment commitments. Offering students flexibility and some choice regarding when they participate in extended learning may be as simple as offering homework sessions when children need them most—after school and before dinner—as Kids Crew and the Omaha After-School Study Centers do. Or, it may mean keeping early and late hours to meet the childcare needs of parents who work more than one job or support extended families, as the Yuk Yau Child Development Center does. Another example of such flexibility is the Florida Summer Institute for At-Risk Migrant Students, which is a residential program so that students' participation does not disrupt their migrant families' travels.

3. Which of the following paraphrases best summarizes the passage?
   a. After-school programs should help children finish their homework after school.
   b. Kids Crew and other programs meet the needs of children.
   c. There are several ways to schedule programs outside of school time to meet the needs of students and families.
   d. Extended-time programs can be innovative, and Yuk Yau Child Development Center is an example of this.
   e. Extended hours may need to be late or early to accommodate families' needs.

Answer

Walk through the steps:

1. The flow goes like this: innovative scheduling—family needs—examples: after school, early and late care, residential.
2. Choices **a**, **c**, **d**, and **e** have words and ideas noted in Step 1.

Six Success Steps for Author Questions

1. For author questions, eliminate answers that do not match the general topic. If it is a scientific passage, the author is probably objectively trying to disseminate information, so you might eliminate answers that suggest the author is trying to change the reader's behavior in any way. If it is a persuasive paragraph, however, the author is not simply conveying information. For questions on the author's intended audience, eliminate audiences that are significantly less or more technical than the author's style.
2. Eliminate answers that say the opposite of what the author is trying to say.
3. Look for a climax in the passage, a sentence or two that describes the author's purpose or audience. Then look for an answer that says the same thing in different words. Also, be on the lookout for clue words that could hint at the audience.
4. Look for words that indicate a change or shift in the author's meaning. Sometimes the author's purpose will follow words such as *however*, or be found somewhere in sentences beginning with words like *although* or *instead of*.
5. If you are looking for an author's tone, put the answer choices in order from very negative to very positive. Look for adjectives that describe the way the author feels about a topic; then look for synonyms or the same tone in the answer choices.
6. If you are left with two choices, look at the topic of the passage and decide what might be an appropriate response to the topic. If the topic discusses a dangerous future situation, an appropriate response of the author might be a warning.

---

3. None of the choices is contrary to the passage. That tactic is usually used with persuasive passages.
4. The choices are all on the topic, but **a**, **b**, and **e** deal with only part of the paragraph.
5. All the ideas are in the passage.
6. You are left with choices **c** and **d**. Choice **d** only mentions only one example, and the passage gives three. Choice **c** does not mention any examples specifically, but encompasses all the examples as well as the idea of the paragraph. You can conclude that the answer is choice **c**, and you don't have to use step 7.

Preparing for Main Idea Questions

For extra practice, check out some test books from the library that have reading comprehension sections and practice answering main idea questions until you feel very confident.

Reading 4: About the Author

Test passages were not written to torture test takers. Authors write to communicate; that is, they *want* you to understand their ideas and arguments. To that end, they usually will try to write as clearly and logically as possible. To read these passages efficiently, therefore, you need to try to get in the mind of the author. Give this author your undivided attention and try to understand what the author took the time and trouble to write. As you read, ask yourself these questions:

- Who is this person?
- Can I detect anything about the author?
- From what perspective does the author write?
- How does the author think?
- What was the author trying to accomplish?
- For whom was the author writing?

Sample question stems for author questions might include the following:

- The author's primary purpose is to . . .
- The author is primarily concerned with . . .
- The main focus of the author is . . .
- In what publication might this passage be found?
- The author is writing primarily for what kind of audience?
- Which best describes the author's relationship with . . .
- Which best describes the feeling of the author toward his subject?
- The attitude of the author toward . . .

How to Find Author Answers in the Passage

You may discover the author's purpose, like the main idea, in the first or last sentence of the passage, or by looking at the topic sentences of the paragraphs. You can also skim the passage for descriptive words that reveal the bias of the author. The subject of the passage and the absence or presence of technical language are two of the main clues toward discovering the author's intended audience.

Sample Passage and Questions

Lincoln's 1863 Thanksgiving Proclamation

It is the duty of nations as well as of men to own their dependence upon the overruling power of God; to confess their sins and transgressions in humble sorrow, yet with assured hope that genuine repentance will lead to mercy and pardon; and to recognize the sublime truth, announced in the Holy Scriptures and proven by all history, that those nations are blessed whose God is the Lord.

We know that by His divine law, nations, like individuals, are subjected to punishments and chastisements in this world. May we not justly fear that the awful calamity of civil war which now desolates the land may be a punishment inflicted upon us for our presumptuous sins, to the needful end of our national reformation as a whole people?

We have been the recipients of the choicest bounties of heaven; we have been preserved these many years in peace and prosperity; we have grown in numbers, wealth and power as no other nation has ever grown.

But we have forgotten God. We have forgotten the gracious hand which preserved us in peace and multiplied and enriched and strengthened us, and we have vainly imagined, in the deceitfulness of our hearts, that all these blessings were produced by some superior wisdom and virtue of our own. Intoxicated with unbroken success, we have become too self-sufficient to feel the necessity of redeeming and preserving grace, too proud to pray to the God that made us.

It has seemed to me fit and proper that God should be solemnly, reverently and gratefully acknowledged, as with one heart and one voice, by the whole American people. I do therefore invite my fellow citizens in every part of the United States, and also those who are at sea and those who are sojourning in foreign lands, to set apart and observe the last Thursday of November as a day of Thanksgiving and praise to our beneficent Father who dwelleth in the heavens.

1. Lincoln's purpose in proclaiming a holiday was to
   a. make peace with Native Americans.
   b. celebrate cultural awareness.
   c. thank God for blessings and favor.
   d. bring complaints as well as thankfulness before God.
   e. promote separation of church and state.

Answer
Use the six Success Steps to answer the question.

1. Choices **a** and **b** do not match the general topic.
2. Choice **e** says the opposite of what Lincoln meant; he was proposing that all Americans thank God.
3. The last sentence seems to be a climax. Both choice **c** and choice **d** contain the idea of thankfulness.
4. The word *but* at the beginning of the fourth paragraph seems to indicate a shift, but that shift is really part of Lincoln's meaning; he is contrasting the blessings America has experienced with Americans' having forgotten God.
5. This isn't a tone question, so you don't need this step.
6. You're left with choices **c** and **d**. The holiday was about thanking God, not bringing complaints. Look again for a mention of complaints in the passage. There isn't one, so the closest answer is **c**.

Sample Passage and Questions
Now try the steps on the questions that follow this passage.

The most significant research results produced are as follows: In the area of micro-ecological adaptation and evolutionary process, our research has shown that regardless of the complexity of the selection force and the biological traits, the rate of evolutionary change of the plant populations has been rapid and the results are even better than we expected. Further study of the interactions between plants and their soil environments found that a successful colonization of plant species in soils with elevated toxic levels of soil chemical compounds such as selenium may be achieved in the presence of other chemical compounds (such as sulfate) that could alleviate the toxic effects and improve the conditions for colonization. The knowledge generated by these ecological studies has made it possible to apply the research with more confidence.

2. In what publication might this passage be published?
   a. a college *Introduction to Biology* textbook
   b. a general encyclopedia
   c. a bulletin to parents
   d. a science teacher's manual
   e. a book of dissertation abstracts

3. The author's primary purpose is to
   a. persuade.
   b. inform.
   c. entertain.
   d. explain.
   e. display.

Answer
Here's how you could use the steps on question 2.

1. This is a rather technical passage. Eliminate choices **a**, **c** and maybe even **b**.
2. Although no choice disagrees with the author, a science teacher's manual would have hints in it for teaching children. There are no clues that this is a teacher's manual; choice **d** is gone.
3. There is no climax.
4. There are clue words, though they're not easy to find. The author mentions *research* that is being done. Encyclopedias don't include current research, so choice **b** is eliminated. That leaves you with choice **e**. This makes sense because a dissertation is someone's research. (You don't need to use steps 5–6.)

Six Success Steps for Detail Questions

1. When reading the passage, notice the way it is arranged. For example, if the passage is on the intelligence of bees, the bees' sense of direction might be in the first paragraph. The bees' communication system might be discussed in the second paragraph.
2. Check the question for the detail you are looking for and search in the proper section of the paragraph. For example, if you were asked about the bees' inner compasses, you would look in the first paragraph of the two previously mentioned.
3. Skim for key words. Look through the passage for the words that are in the question. Once you find the words, find the answer in that sentence.
4. Eliminate answers that contain facts not found in the passage. If an answer choice is not in the passage, it is not the right answer, even if it is true. Also eliminate choices that are found in the passage, but that do not answer the question.
5. If the passage is complex and you are having trouble trying to find the answer, you may need to start several lines above the key word. For example, suppose the passage is comparing two kinds of fish, and the question asks for the head size of one kind. You find the word *head* in a context like this: "Although their tails are the same, the four-inch head size of the latter is about twice the head size of the former, which makes them easier to prey upon." You may need to go back a sentence or two to discover which fish has the bigger head and is easier to prey upon.
6. Do not let technical words stop you from answering the question. You are not being tested on technical language alone. There is always enough information in the passage to answer a detail question without previous knowledge of the topic.

For question 3, you have a purpose question.

1. This is a fairly scientific passage. That would not be entertaining, so eliminate **c**. Also, *display* is not a purpose for writing, so eliminate choice **e**. There is no sense that the author is trying to persuade the reader in this passage, so eliminate choice **a**.

2–5. You don't need these steps for this question.

6. We are left with *inform* and *explain*. To inform is to tell, whereas to explain is closer to teaching. The author does not teach here, but just tells. The best choice is **b**.

Reading 5: Definite Details and Parts of a Book

Most people find both detail questions and questions on parts of a book fairly easy to answer, because the answers are right there on the page. You have probably answered detail questions often in your education. In every subject, most of the questions at the end of the chapters in your textbook have been detail questions—and you used the parts of a book to find the chapter you wanted or key word quickly and easily. These questions mean (relatively) easy points for you. All you need are some strategies that can help enhance your speed and accuracy.

Detail questions ask about one specific fact in the passage. They are signaled by question words such as *what, when,* or *where.* You'll often find the phrase "according to the passage" in a detail question.

How to Find Detail Answers in the Passage

Detail answers are usually in the body of the paragraphs. They are usually not in the main idea sentences.

Sample Passage and Questions

Factors that can be used to calculate breast cancer risk include information about a woman's age, ethnicity, family history, number of pregnancies, age at the time of the first live birth, and others, which have been recognized more recently, such as the use hormonal replacement therapy. Some of the tools used for risk evaluation do not guarantee a 100% accurate analysis of a female's specific situation, because they exclude, for instance, clues that could clearly lead the diagnostician to suspect a genetic predisposition to breast cancer.

In general, women can be expected to have a cumulative lifetime risk of developing breast cancer of 1 in 7 or 8, which is modified by one or several of the specific risk factors previously mentioned. Because the risk is measured in terms of a "cumulative lifetime," the possibility of developing breast cancer for a 30-year-old is significantly lower than the same patient's risk when she reaches age 90. The term *cumulative lifetime risk*, which represents the possible occurrence, or development of the problem over a lifetime, must not be misinterpreted to express the prevalence of the disease. *Prevalence* simply refers to the existing cases of the problem in a group of women at a given moment in life.

It is important to understand that risk evaluation is but one piece of the puzzle, and breast cancer prevention should involve more than merely evaluating a woman's risk profile. Appropriate examinations, correctly utilized tests and consistent follow-ups are necessary components of a well-planned prevention initiative.

1. Which of the following risk factors is NOT mentioned in the paragraph?
   a. age
   b. age at the time of the first live birth
   c. age of a first-degree relative at the time of breast cancer diagnosis
   d. ethnicity
   e. family history

2. According to the passage, what does *cumulative lifetime risk* refer to?
   a. existing cases of the problem
   b. prevalence
   c. the possibility of developing the problem over a lifetime
   d. a genetic predisposition
   e. a risk factor

3. With which of the following statements would the author of the passage most likely agree?
   a. The use of hormonal replacement therapy cannot be used as a breast cancer risk factor.
   b. Women of from ages 30 through 90 have the same chance of developing breast cancer.
   c. *Prevalence* and *cumulative lifetime risk* can be used interchangeably.
   d. Evaluating a woman's risk profile is not enough to prevent breast cancer.
   e. Risk evaluation is 100% accurate.

Four Success Steps for Parts of a Book Questions

1. Read the question and answer choices first. Then skim the passage and mark the parts that might have the information you are seeking.
2. Look at the answer choices and eliminate any that are clearly wrong.
3. If you are left with multiple choices, choose the one that best answers the question.
4. If you are asked for the organization of the passage, look at the table of contents, section headings, and similar sections. Compare the organization of the information to the answers. Choose the answer that offers the best description.

Answers

For detail questions, you don't necessarily have to work through all of the steps. Here are some tips on how you might have answered the questions.

1. **c.** The answer can be found by referring to the first sentence in the passage. All of the choices, except for choice **c**, are listed there.
2. **c.** The beauty of detail questions is that the answers are always directly stated in the passage. There is no need to infer tone or meaning. This time, the answer can be found in the sentence that reads: "The term *cumulative lifetime risk*, which represents the possible occurrence, or development of the problem over a lifetime . . ."
3. **d.** Although this question may appear to be an inference question rather than a detail one, do not be fooled. All of the answer choices refer to details found in the passage. Choice **d** is the only one that is directly stated. The rest of the choices are the exact opposite of what is stated in the passage.

Parts of a Book Questions

Questions on parts of a book are some of the most straightforward questions in the Reading section. Parts of a book may include the table of contents, index, chapters, etc. You'll recognize these types of questions immediately by the appearance of the passage. Questions may ask something like the following:

- On which pages should one look to find information about . . . ?
- Which of the following best describes the organizational pattern . . . ?
- In which part of the book would one find information about . . . ?

How to Find Answers to Parts of a Book Questions

The answers to these questions have to be in the passage. There are usually fewer words in the table of contents, index, or section headings than in paragraphs. This makes it easier for you to skim, and the information is usually arranged in a logical manner.

Sample Table of Contents and Questions

Preparing Your Family for an Earthquake
The Plan 2
General Tips 4
Essentials 5
Sanitation 6
Safety 6
Cooking 7
Tools 9

4. On what page would you look to find a recommendation for stocking paper plates and cups?
   a. 2
   b. 4
   c. 6
   d. 7
   e. 9

5. In what way is this table of contents arranged?
   a. alphabetically
   b. by category
   c. chronologically
   d. by age
   e. by task

Answers

Here's how you would use the steps on question 4:

1. Looking down the table of contents, mark *Essentials*, *Sanitation*, and *Cooking*.
2. Eliminate **a**, **b**, and **e**.
3. The *Essentials* page is not listed in the answers, so that leaves you with *Sanitation* and *Cooking*. The choice that best fits the subject is *Cooking*, choice **d**.
4. This step doesn't apply.

Question 5 deals with organization, so go straight to step 4. Looking at the answer choices, you can see that the list is not alphabetical, so eliminate answer choice **a**. Choices **c** and **d** are not relevant to the subject. Choice **b** is better than **e** because the table is not talking necessarily about things to do, but categories of survival aids. Choice **b** is the correct answer.

Sample Index and Questions

Use the excerpt below from an index to answer the question that follows.

Chinatowns
　　arrival of immigrants in, 34
　　businesses in, 71–73
　　celebrations of births, 94–95
　　changing patterns in, 99–100
　　community organizations in, 60–63
　　development of, 53, 57–59
　　education in, 62–64
Chinese Americans
　　acceptance grows toward, 79–80
　　attacked by Native Americans, 26–27

6. On which page(s) should one look to find information about a group working to preserve the history of Chinatown?
   a. 62–64
   b. 60–63
   c. 34
   d. 26–27
   e. 79–80

Answers

Here's how you would use the steps on question 6:

1. Looking through the index entries, mark *arrival of immigrants in*, *businesses in*, *community organizations in*, *development of*, and *education in*, which are each possible answers
2. Eliminate **d** and **e**, as these choices do not correspond with any of the marked entries.
3. The pages for *businesses in* and *development of* are not given as choices. You are left with *immigrants in*, *community organizations in*, and *education in*. Of these choices, a group working to preserve the history of a community like Chinatown would best be described as a community organization. The best answer is **b**.
4. This step does not apply.

Nine Success Steps for Implication Questions

1. Skim the passage to discover how the passage is organized and find the sentences that relate to the question's topic.
2. Eliminate any answers that are off the topic.
3. Eliminate any answers that parrot sentences in the passage, using the same or similar words.
4. Look for an answer choice that draws a conclusion from information in the passage. For example, if the passage says that all unripe fruit is green, look for an answer choice that states that no unripe fruit is orange or red. If you find one like that, great! Most implication answers are not that easy to find.
5. Eliminate any answers that are unreasonable, that cannot be drawn from facts in the passage.
6. Eliminate any answers that can be concluded from the statements in the passage, but do not answer the question.
7. Ask yourself these questions:
   - If the author were to write another paragraph following this one, what might it be about?
   - If the author were to explain the ideas in the paragraph in more detail or more explicitly, what more would be written?
   - If the author could draw a conclusion from what has been written so far, what facts could be put together to form that conclusion and what would that conclusion be?
8. If you are still left with two answers, choose the answer that is only one step removed from the statements in the passage. Go with the choice that can be most clearly concluded from the statements in the passage.
9. If you have no answers left, look in another part of the passage for additional clue facts. Any choice using the same words as the passage is definitely not the correct answer. Check for answer choices that may mean something different from what you read, or that may contain answers to the questions you asked yourself in step 7.

Reading 6: Impressive Implications

Implication questions can be easily confused with detail questions. However, an implication question asks you to make an inference about the author's intent, rather than simply locating a detail in the passage. Knowing how implication questions are likely to be phrased will help you distinguish between the two question types. Implication question stems usually include words like these:

- The author **implies** that ...
- The author **suggests** that ...
- It can be **concluded** from this passage that ...
- The passage **implies** that ...
- The narrator **hints** that ...
- It can be **inferred** from the passage that ...
- Which of the following is **closest** to the author's **outlook** on ... ?

How to Find Implication Answers

Implications are not directly stated in the passage. If you find an answer choice in the passage, it is not the right answer. Look, however, for items, people, events, or ideas in the passage that might relate to other items, people, events, or ideas in the passage.

Sample Passage and Question

Many educational reformers have focused their efforts over the last decade on instructional practices such as cooperative learning that emphasize problem solving and decision making over solitary reliance on memorization of facts and theories. Furthermore, programs that emphasize problem solving and decision making directly address the national education goal of helping students prepare "for responsible citizenship, further learning, and productive employment in our modern economy." Several programs described here offer strategies for addressing problem solving and decision making, ranging from in-class discussions and the use of board games to designing and conducting community service activities. For example, tutors at Raising Academic Achievement focus on problem-solving skills and are trained to help students *think, explore, solve, and look back* when working on mathematics problems.

1. Which of the following can be inferred from the information in the passage?
   a. Tutors at Raising Academic Achievement help ensure that students will be productively employed when they become adults.
   b. Cooperative learning emphasizes problem-solving techniques.
   c. Playing board games increases problem-solving skills.
   d. Responsible citizenship should be taught in school.
   e. Tutors at Raising Academic Achievement help students solve math problems.

Answer

Walk through the steps.

1. The passage is short and the question offers no topic or location clues.
2. It looks as though choice **d** is off the topic since the paragraph is not about teaching responsible citizenship; it is only mentioned in passing.
3. Choice **b** is mentioned in the first sentence. Choices **c** and **e** are also mentioned. That gives us our answer already. Is choice **a** the answer? The passage does not explicitly state that the tutors will help future employment, but it does say that tutors help with problem-solving skills and that problem-solving skills will help with future employment. Choice **a** is one step removed from the facts of the passage, so it is the right answer.

You didn't need to use steps 4–9.

This short passage does not offer clues to where in the paragraph the answer might be.

Sample Passage and Questions

For some educators, the current emphasis in schools on science and technology are leading students away from a solid, well-rounded education. Focusing on science and technical skills may prepare students for college and technical careers, but at the cost of the ability to think and write logically and clearly. Proponents of returning to a classical education advocate the inclusion of humanities classes in the core curriculum, where learners can learn skills that could be applied to multiple courses. This would result in teachers reducing their focus on standardized tests, and it would give them back the freedom to design courses that instruct learners in the skills they need to become thriving adults rather than just successful students.

Six Success Steps for Word-in-Context Questions

1. Locate the word and read a few lines above the word to understand the context. Notice any context clues—words or phrases that explain the meaning of the word.
2. Eliminate any answers that have nothing to do with the passage or the context.
3. You may encounter an answer choice that is a different part of speech from the word or phrase in the question. Think for a minute to make sure this answer choice doesn't have an alternate meaning that is the same part of speech, and if it doesn't, eliminate it.
4. Place the remaining words in the blank and read to see which one fits best.
5. If you know the meaning of the word, make sure the passage uses the word in the same way. Many of the answers will be different possible meanings of the word in question.
6. Look for clues in root words, prefixes, and suffixes.

---

2. Which of the following assumptions most influenced the writer's argument in the passage?
   a. The number of students dropping out of school due to lack of science and technical skills is rising at an alarming rate.
   b. Classroom teachers stay up-to-date with trends in education and change their teaching styles accordingly.
   c. Most teachers focus too closely on the curriculum outlined in the textbooks rather than design lessons to the skills of the students in class. Most teachers focus too closely on the curriculum outlined in the textbooks rather than design lessons to the skills of the students in class.
   d. Students coming out of science- and technology-based programs do not become adults with well-rounded skills.
   e. Students prefer fine arts classes to science and technology classes.

Answer

Here's how you use the Success Steps to answer question 2:

1. There are no clues in the question.
2. All of the answers relate to teachers, students, or schools, so each is a possible answer.
3. Choices **c** and **d** mimic the language of the passage.
4. Choice **c** describes teachers depending too much on the lessons in textbooks. The passage does not talk about problems with textbooks, but the courses that students are offered. This may not be the best answer.
5. To ensure that choice **c** should be eliminated, look more closely at **d**. This choice indicates that science and technology classes do not offer enough skills to students. The passage indicates that more liberal arts classes should be offered rather than focusing on science and technology. Choice **d** is the best answer.

You don't need steps 6–9.

Reading 7: Wizard Words, Departed Parts, and Other Oddities

This section will review most of the rest of the kinds of reading questions you will be likely to encounter on the CBEST: words in context, fill-in-the-blanks, extra evidence, order, and opinion vs. fact. Most test takers do not find these questions to be among the most difficult on CBEST, so knowing what to expect will help you to work through them easily. This lesson

Three Success Steps for Fact vs. Opinion Questions

1. Read through the sentences looking for opinion words.
2. If a sentence sounds as though it could be a news item, found in a textbook, or otherwise verified, it is probably a fact. If it sounds like a judgment that can't be proven, then it is probably an opinion.
3. If you are left with two answers, choose the one that is most strongly a *value judgment*.

is a little longer than the rest, but you can easily accomplish it in half an hour by skimming over the passages, working on the sample questions, and then concentrating on any of the question types that give you trouble.

Words in Context

Questions on words in context have stems like these:

- What is the best synonym for _____ as it is used in the passage?
- Which of the following is the best meaning of _____ as it is used in the second sentence?

How to Find Word-in-Context Answers

Answers to word-in-context questions are found in the sentences immediately preceding, including, and following the word. Usually, there is some explanation nearby—some synonym for the word or paraphrase of its meaning.

Sample Passage and Question

There is no universally agreed upon definition of *intelligence*. However, a commonly used one is "the ability to reason, plan, solve problems, think abstractly, comprehend complex ideas, learn quickly, and learn from experience."

The most common method used to measure intelligence is the IQ (Intelligence Quotient) Test, which measures mental ability. The scientific community, however, is divided on whether or not the IQ Test can actually measure intelligence. This is because many researchers believe that there are several kinds of intelligence—such as logical, spatial, verbal, emotional, and kinesthetic—and that they cannot all be measured simply by taking an IQ Test.

Out of all of the types of intelligence that are thought to exist, it is emotional intelligence (EI) that is a relatively <u>nascent</u> concept. This is quite unlike IQ, which has almost 100 years of research to support it. Emotional intelligence refers to the ability to understand your emotions and those of people around you. This high level of self-awareness, then, allows a person to keep anxiety from hampering his or her ability to think clearly. It provides one with the ability to self-motivate and persevere in the face of setbacks. In short, a high EI helps one succeed in life, and this has been proven in various research studies.

IQ, in turn, has offered little explanation for the discrepancies between the destinies of people who have been afforded equal opportunities and schooling, for example. In fact, research has shown that people with high IQs or high test scores in college are not necessarily more successful in terms of salary, status in their fields, or productivity in middle age than their lower scoring counterparts are. Recent data shows that the ability to handle frustrations, control emotions, and get along with other people makes the most difference in the quality of one's life. In essence, people who score well on tests are good at achievement as measured by grades or scores, but this skill says nothing about how they will react to the ups and downs that life will surely bring.

Two Success Steps for Order Questions

1. Skim the passage for key words found in the question.
2. Read the section mentioned and then read the sentences immediately after or before the section depending on the question. If the question asks what happened last, look toward the end of the passage and look for key words such as *finally* or *in conclusion*.

Culturally, we are entirely focused on academic success, and do little in the way of emotional education, yet it is precisely this that accounts for an immense part of our future success and happiness. Continuing to expand research in the field of EI will surely benefit future generations.

1. The word *nascent*, as it is used in the passage, most nearly means
   a. old.
   b. proven.
   c. hypothetical.
   d. emerging.
   e. misinterpreted.

Answer

The overall content of the passage is about the recent and, up until now, largely ignored research in the field of EI. For a more detailed clue, the answer can be deciphered by reading the sentence that follows the one with the word nascent in it. It reads: "This is quite unlike IQ, which has almost one hundred years of research to support it." Then, if EI is unlike, or opposite, IQ in the sense that the latter has "almost one hundred years of research to support it," it can be inferred that EI does not have as many years of research to support it. Therefore, it must be a new or emerging concept.

Opinion versus Fact

A statement is considered a fact if it can be proven as true. An opinion is a statement that can reasonably be disputed by others. *The earth revolves around the sun* is a fact. Astronomers can prove that this is true. *This is an interesting movie* is an opinion. One person might not find the movie as interesting as another person. *Interesting* is a statement of opinion. Fact or opinion questions have stems like these:

- Which of the following is a statement of fact?
- Which of the numbered sentences constitutes an opinion, not a fact?

How to Find Opinion-vs.-Fact Answers

You don't have to read the passage to find the answer if the statements and opinions are listed in the answers. If you are referred to numbered sentences, look there.

Static electricity is found in many places. One example of static electricity is when your hair stands up after taking off a hat or wool sweater in winter. Another example of static electricity is lightning. Lightning occurs when an electrical charge builds up and then discharges from the clouds. Creating an experiment about static electricity is simple. We can perform an experiment to see how static electricity works.

Seven Success Steps for Fill-in-the-Blank Questions

1. Read the entire sentence, or pair of sentences, that contains the blanks.
2. The sentences should give you all the clues you need. Each sentence is likely to be made up of two statements that are compatible or contradictory. If they are compatible, words like *also* or *because* should be used. If they are contradictory, you will need words such as *while*, *even if*, or *although*.
3. Decide whether the first or last blank has the most clues and work with that one first.
4. If one sentence gives you all the clues you need, look at the answer choices to see which one contains a word in the right location that will fit. For example, if the first sentence contains two statements that contradict each other, cover the second set of words in each choice and look only at the first words. Eliminate any choices such as *because* or *since* that do not suggest there will be a contradiction or turn in the sentence. Eliminate the whole answer. Do not even consider the second part of the answer.
5. Next, turn to the other blank. If it is a structure blank, the word might indicate its placement in the sentence. For example, *finally* or *as a result* would probably be answers for an end of a passage, not a beginning. *However* cannot begin a passage.
6. Note the type of passage. A story might use the word *meanwhile*, directions would use *next* or *finally*, and *consequently* or *as a result* might be used in a persuasive or scientific passage.
7. Substitute the remaining words in the remaining blank and choose the one that fits the best.

---

2. Which of the following is NOT a statement of fact?
   a. One example of static electricity is when your hair stands up after taking off a hat or wool sweater in winter.
   b. Lightning occurs when an electrical charge builds up and then discharges from the clouds.
   c. Creating an experiment about static electricity is simple.
   d. We can perform an experiment to see how static electricity works.
   e. Static electricity is found in many places.

Answer
Choice **c** is the answer. All of the other choices can be proven true. Choice **c**, however, is not a statement of fact. A person might not find the experiment simple at all. Therefore, the sentence is considered an opinion.

Order

Order questions are easy to spot; they ask you what comes before or after some other incident or event. Question stems look like these:

- In the paragraph, what event immediately follows...?
- What incident precedes...?
- In what order should you...?
- According to the passage, what should you do after...?

How to Find Order Answers

Usually, a part of the passage is mentioned in order questions. The question will let you know whether to look after or before the section you found. The question could also point you directly to a specific part of the passage such as the beginning or the end.

Four Success Steps for Additional Information Questions

1. If there is a blank to fill, read the passage up to the blank line and then the sentence following it. Notice the relationship between the sentence before and after it. If there is no blank, skim the passage for a main idea or hypothesis.
2. Choose the sentence to fit in the blank that best continues the flow of the paragraph. If the sentence after the blank shows there was a turn in thought, choose the answer that turns the thought.
3. If there is no blank, choose the answer that might complete the thought of the author.
4. If the question calls for the least likely statement, use a sentence that breaks the flow or contradicts the author. The same is true for a question that calls for a statement that would weaken the stand of the author.

Sample Passage and Question

So, how can people who do not intrinsically have high EIs help themselves deal with frustration and setbacks? One of the increasingly popular ways is through cognitive behavioral therapy (CBT). Proponents of CBT believe that it is not the ups and downs of life that cause you anxiety, but rather, how you interpret them. Here's how it works: First, there is a precipitating event. Next—usually immediately—you interpret the event by thinking about it. After you analyze the situation with your thoughts, or cognitions, you develop your feelings about it. In other words, you cannot derive an emotion, positive or negative, without first having a thought. Therefore, increasing EI involves helping people recognize their thought patterns and modifying them when necessary.

3. According to the passage, proponents of CBT believe that which of the following events occurs last?
   a. frustration
   b. a precipitating event
   c. cognitions
   d. developing your feelings
   e. interpreting an event

Answer

The answer is choice **d**. The order in which events occur before feelings are derived is detailed in the fifth paragraph. Choices **b**, **c**, and e are all steps in the process, but none is the last step. Note, also, that choices c and e are essentially the same step. Choice **a** is incorrect because the passage states that feelings come last, not specifically the feeling of frustration.

Fill in the Blanks

Fill-in-the-blank questions come in two types. One type asks you to fill in a couple of words. The other type asks you to fill in a whole sentence. Turn to **Additional Information** (page 93) for the kind that deals with a whole sentence. Questions that ask you for a few words have stems like these:

- Which words, if inserted in order, would best complete the second paragraph?
- Which of the following phrases would best fit in the blank?

How to Find Fill-in-the-Blank Answers

There are two kinds of word blanks. One can be filled by reading the sentence. The other requires an understanding of the structure of the passage.

Sample Passage and Question

Typically, people think of genius, whether it manifests in Mozart's composing symphonies at age five or Einstein's discovery of relativity, as having a quality not just of the supernatural, but also of the eccentric. People see genius as a "good" abnormality; moreover, they think of genius as a completely unpredictable abnormality. Until recently, psychologists regarded the quirks of genius as too erratic to describe intelligibly; however, Anna Findley's groundbreaking study uncovers predictable patterns in the biographies of geniuses. These patterns do not dispel the common belief, however, that there is a kind of supernatural intervention in the lives of unusually talented men and women, even though they occur with regularity. —, Findley shows that all geniuses experience three intensely productive periods in their lives, one of which always occurs shortly before their deaths; this is true whether the genius lives to 19 or 90.

4. Which word or phrase, if inserted into the blank space, best defines the relationship of the last sentence in the passage to the one preceding it?
   a. For example
   b. Despite this
   c. However
   d. In other words

Answer

The correct answer is **a**. The final sentence is an instance of a regular pattern that still has an uncanny quality. Choices **b** and **c** would introduce a sentence with an idea contradicting the preceding. Choice **d** would indicate that the final sentence is a restatement of the preceding, which it is not.

Additional Information

Some questions may ask you to identify additional information that would fit in the passage, either in the form of a blank sentence that has been left in the passage or in the form of a question about what information would help or hurt the author's argument. The questions look like this:

- Which sentence, if inserted in the blank, would best complete the meaning of the paragraph?
- Which statement, if true, would most strengthen the author's argument?
- Which of the following facts would most weaken the author's argument?

How to Find Additional Information Answers

To find the answer to these questions, you need to skim the paragraph or passage for a main idea, purpose, or hypothesis.

Sample Question

Go back to the passage on page 92 to answer this question.

5. Which of the following statements, if true, would be LEAST likely to strengthen the paragraph about CBT for emotion regulation?
   a. It is important to recognize that thoughts or cognitions are not facts, but rather interpretations that may or may not be true.
   b. Being mindful about initial cognitive reactions to events is crucial to modifying your emotions.
   c. Another effective way to regulate emotions is through dialectical behavior therapy.
   d. Here's an example: Your boss calls you into his office (the precipitating event). You assume you're being let go, reprimanded, or something equally unpleasant (thoughts). Suddenly, you're nervous and fearful (feeling).

Three Success Steps for Working with Graphs

1. Read the graph carefully. Read all around the graph, including the title and the key.
2. Some questions may try to trick you by leaving out numbers. If all the numbers are not given, it is a very good idea to fill in all the missing numbers on the graph. To do this, you will need to know the value of each increment.
3. Sometimes, instead of reading bars or lines, you can compare differences by using a piece of paper to measure from one point to another or from the end of one bar to the end of another.

e. As you can see, your thoughts have a significant impact on your emotions.

Answer

The answer is choice **c**. This sentence does not strengthen the case about the effectiveness of cognitive behavior therapy in emotion regulation. On the contrary, this would only distract from the main point of this paragraph, as well as interrupt the flow. Choices **a** and **b** add additional information about how CBT works; choice **e** is a concluding statement. Choice **d** would be a relevant example to the "steps" involved in how feelings are generated.

Reading 8: Graphs

Graphs are found in both the reading and the math sections of the test. This section will give examples of the different types of graphs you may encounter on the CBEST. Try your hand at the sample graphs and questions in this section.

Histograms and Bar Graphs

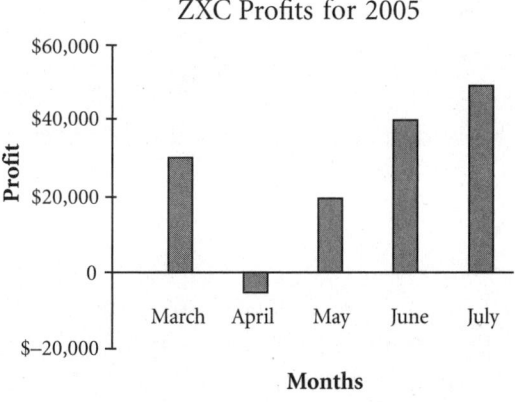

1. Between which two months was the change in profits for ZXC the greatest?
   a. February and March
   b. March and April
   c. April and May
   d. May and June
   e. June and July

2. Between which two months did the profits for ZXC increase the most?
   a. February and March
   b. March and April
   c. April and May
   d. May and June
   e. June and July

Answers

1. b. The change was the greatest between March and April. Choice **a** is irrelevant, as February is not mentioned on the graph.

2. c. April's bar ends on the downward side. Measuring with a piece of paper, you can see that it is farther from April's bottom to May's top than it is from May's top to June's top. You could also use the numbers for these months to determine when the greatest increase occurred.

Line Graphs

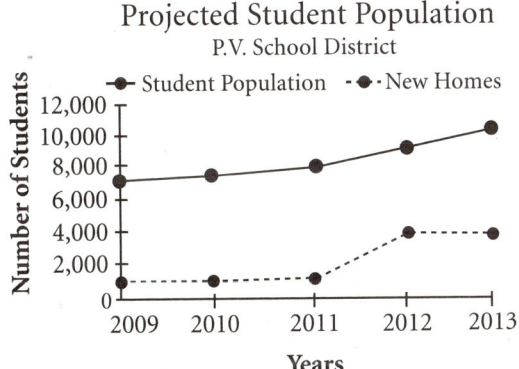

3. In what year is the increase in student population projected to be less than the increase in the number of new homes built?
   a. 2009
   b. 2010
   c. 2011
   d. 2012
   e. 2013

Answer

The answer is choice **c**. A look at the graph shows that for 2011 to 2012, there was a sharper increase in the number of new homes built than in student population. The line slopes up more steeply there for houses than it does for student population. Percent of increase is a different question and might yield a different answer. Check Ratios, Proportions, and Percents (page 114) for details on percents.

Picture Graphs

MEMBERSHIP OF THE MTAC

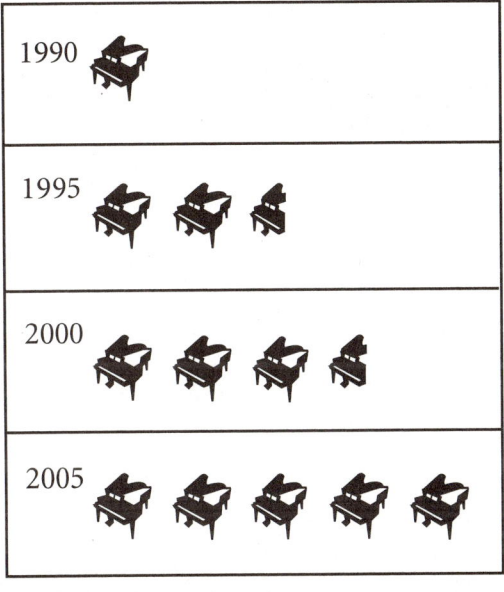

 Represents 500 members

4. How many MTAC members were there in 2000?
   a. $3\frac{1}{2}$
   b. 350
   c. 700
   d. 1,750
   e. 2,250

Answer

It is important to read the key at the bottom of the graph. Each piano represents 500 members. Half a piano represents 250 members. The year 2000 has $3\frac{1}{2}$ pianos. This represents 1,750 members. The answer is choice **d**.

Circle Graphs

Save the Caves Foundation Income

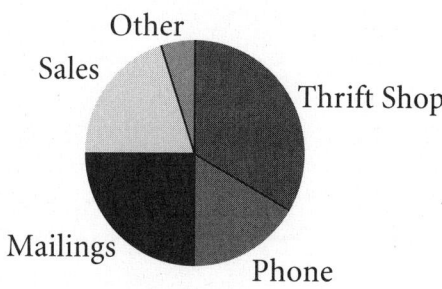

Use the graph below to answer the question that follows.

2010 Spending of College Senior

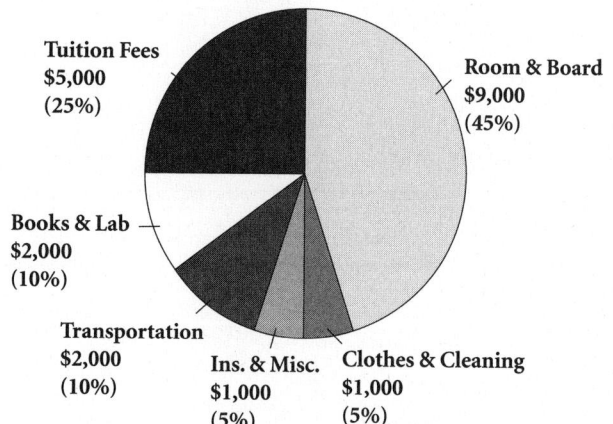

5. Which category represents approximately $\frac{1}{4}$ of the income for the Save the Caves Foundation?
   a. Mailings
   b. Sales
   c. Thrift Shop
   d. Phone
   e. Other

Answer

Look for the section that takes up approximately $\frac{1}{4}$ of the circle. The answer is choice **a**.

6. What percent of spending were direct college expenses?
   a. 25%
   b. 70%
   c. 80%
   d. 90%
   e. 100%

Answer

Room and board, tuition, and books and lab fees are all college expenses. By adding the percentages together, you get a total of 80%. Choice **c** is correct.

Oddballs

Some graphs are just plain odd.

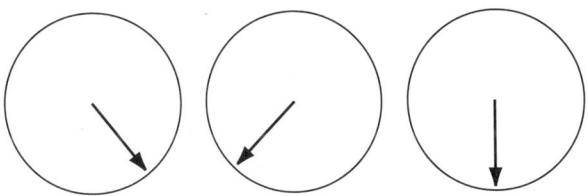

All right, here's a challenge.

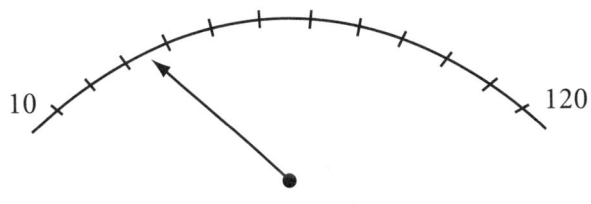

7. The circles above represent the dials on an electric meter. What reading do they represent?
   a. 476
   b. 465
   c. 466
   d. 486
   e. 487

8. Which number best represents the speed indicated on the speedometer above?
   a. $12\frac{1}{2}$
   b. $30\frac{1}{2}$
   c. 35
   d. $40\frac{1}{2}$
   e. 45

Answer

There are no clues whatsoever on the graphs. A look at the answer choices reveals that all are three digits and that all begin with the digit 4. It follows that each circle represents a digit. If so, the first dial has to represent 4. If the first dial represents 4, and the arrow is nearly halfway around (assuming the dials go clockwise), then half is probably 5. In that case, the last circle represents 5, which tells you your answer, choice **b**. It makes sense that the middle digit of 465 is 6, since the middle circle's arrow goes just a bit past the 5 mark. Questions similar to this one have appeared on the test, so it's important that you be prepared to think creatively.

Answer

It is very important to label the graph in order to answer this question. If there are 11 segments between 10 and 120, each segment must represent 10 mph. The arrow is pointing halfway between 30 and 40. Halfway between 30 and 40 is 35, so the answer is choice c.

Math 1: Know the Score

You will find many questions on the CBEST related to scoring students' exams. As you have probably learned in college, you can score students in a number of ways: stanine scores, percentiles, and averages. Each of these can appear on the CBEST, so it is important that you remember how to interpret or calculate each type of score.

Sample Stanine Question

You usually find stanine scores on norm-referenced standardized tests. In other words, stanines are used on tests where student performance is compared to that of other students on the same tests. *Stanine* is short for standard nine-point scale, and stanine scores range from 9 to 1. Using so few numbers means the scores can be interpreted quickly and easily. Stanine scores are usually grouped as above average (9, 8, 7), average (6, 5, 4), and below average (3, 2, 1).

1. Franklin is in the seventh grade and takes a standardized math test. Use his test scores below to answer the question that follows.

Raw Score	Stanine
65	7

   Franklin's test scores indicate that
   a. he scored as well as or better than 65 of the test takers.
   b. he answered 65% of the questions correctly.
   c. he performed better than 70% of the students who took the test.
   d. he is a bit above average compared to all of the other students who took the test.
   e. he missed two of the nine questions on the exam.

Answer

The raw score means how many questions were answered correctly. Without knowing the total number of questions, we can't convert that raw score to a percentile. And the raw score certainly doesn't tell how Franklin compares to anyone else, so we can eliminate choices a and b. Remember that the stanine is very general. It is not converted to a percentile, so eliminate choice c. The scale from 1 to 9 does not indicate the number of problems correct, so choice e can be eliminated. Choice d is correct and makes sense, as 7 is the lowest score that is considered above average.

Sample Percentile Question

Percentile scores are also used to report students' results on norm-referenced standardized tests. Percentiles are more specific than stanines, ranking students on a scale from 1 to 99. Here's an example: A student scored in the 68th percentile on a science test. This means that the student earned a score that is higher than 68% of all other students who took the test. In other words, if 100,000 students took the test, the student in the 68th percentile scored higher than 68,000 students.

> **HOT TIP**
> Don't confuse percentile scores with the percentage of questions answered correctly. Percentile scores are like stanines—they allow you to compare one student's scores with the other students who took the test.

2. Nita is in the fourth grade and takes a standardized reading test. Use her test scores below to answer the question that follows.

Raw Score	Percentile
42	84

   Nita's test scores indicate that
   a. she scored as good as or better than 84% of the test takers.
   b. she answered 84% of the questions correctly.
   c. she performed better than 42% of the students who took the test.
   d. she answered 42 questions correctly out of 84 questions.
   e. she only had time to answer 42 questions on the exam.

Four Success Steps for Average Problems

1. In order to use the formula $\frac{\text{Sum of the Numbers}}{\text{Number of Numbers}}$ = Average, draw a horizontal line.
2. Write in all the information you know. Put the number of numbers under the line and the average beside the line. Unless you know the whole sum, leave the top of the line blank.
3. Multiply the number of numbers by the average. This will give you the sum of the numbers.
4. Using this sum, solve the problem.

Answer

Choice **b** confuses percentile and percent of answers correct, so eliminate that option. Again, the raw score only means how many questions were answered correctly. The raw score is not turned into a percentile, doesn't tell how Nita compares to anyone else, and doesn't tell how many problems she answered, so we can eliminate choices **c** and **e**. Choice **d** combines the raw and percentile information, which is not how the scores are used. Choice **a** is correct and makes sense, as it shows the percentile score as how Nita did compared to others who took the test.

Averages

You probably remember how you solved average problems way back in elementary school. You added up the numbers, divided by the number of numbers, divided by the number of numbers, and the average popped out. Here's this process in algebraic form:

$$\frac{\text{Sum of the Numbers}}{\text{Number of Numbers}} = \text{Average}$$

What makes CBEST average problems more difficult is that not all of the numbers will be given for you to add. You'll have to find some of the numbers.

Sample Average Question

3. Sean loved to go out with his friends, but he knew he'd be grounded if he didn't get 80% for the semester in his English class. His test scores were as follows: 67%, 79%, 75%, 82%, and 78%. He had two more tests left to go. One was tomorrow, but his best friend Jason had invited him to his birthday party tonight. If he studied very hard and got 100% on his last test, what could he get by with tomorrow and achieve the 80%?
   a. 65%
   b. 72%
   c. 76.2%
   d. 79%
   e. 80.2%

Answer

Use the four Success Steps to solve the problem.

1. Draw the horizontal line: ———
2. Write in the information: $\frac{\quad}{7} = 80\%$
3. Multiply the *number of numbers* by the *average* to obtain the *sum of the numbers*: $7 \times 80 = 560$
4. The number 560 has to be the final *sum of the numbers*. So far, if you add up all the scores, Sean has a total of 381. With the 100 he plans to get on the last test, his total will be 481. Since he needs a sum of 560 for the average of the seven tests to be 80, he needs 79 more points. The answer is choice **d**.

Four Success Steps for Frequency Chart Questions

1. Read the question and look at the chart. Make sure you understand what the different columns represent.
2. If a question asks you to find the average, multiply the numbers in the frequency column by the numbers in the column of data values.
3. Add the figures you got by multiplying.
4. Divide the total sum by the sum of the left column. This will give you the average.

Sample Average Question

4. On an overseas trip, Jackie and her husband are allowed five suitcases that average 110 pounds each. They want to pack in all the peanut butter and mango nectar they can carry to their family in Italy. They weighed their first four suitcases and the weights were as follows: 135, 75, 90, and 120 pounds. How much weight are they allowed to carry in their fifth bag?

Answer

1. Draw the horizontal line: ———
2. Write in the information: $\frac{}{5} = 110$
3. Multiply the *number of numbers* by the *average* to obtain the *sum of the numbers*:
   $5 \times 110 = 550$.
4. The total weight they can carry is 550 lbs. and they already have 420 lbs. (135 + 75 + 90 + 120), so the fifth suitcase can weigh as much as 550 − 420, or 130 lbs.

Frequency Charts

Some average problems on the CBEST use frequency charts.

Sample Frequency Chart Question

5. The following list shows class scores for a Science 101 quiz. What is the average of the scores?

# of Students	Score
10	100
15	90
3	80
2	70

a. 28.5
b. 85
c. 91
d. 95
e. 100

Answer

Use the four Success Steps to solve the problem.

1. In this frequency chart, the test score is given on the right, and the number of students who received each grade is on the left: 10 students got a 100, 15 got a 90, etc.
2. Multiply the number of students by the score, because to find the average, each student's grade has to be added individually:

   $10 \times 100 = 1,000$
   $15 \times 90 = 1,350$
   $3 \times 80 = 240$
   $2 \times 70 = 140$

3. Then add the multiplied scores:

   $1{,}000 + 1{,}350 + 240 + 140 = 2{,}730$

4. Divide the total number of students, 30 (10 + 15 + 3 + 2), into 2,730 to get the average: $\frac{2{,}730}{30} = 91$.

Other Average Problems

There are other kinds of averages besides the *mean,* which is usually what is meant when the word *average* is used:

- *Median* is the middle number in a data set after the set is ordered.
- *Mode* is the number that occurs most frequently.
- *Range* is the difference between the highest and lowest number.

Sample Median Question

6. What is the median of 6, 8, 3, 9, 4, 3, and 12?
   a. 2
   b. 6
   c. 9
   d. 10
   e. 12

Answer

To get a *median,* put the numbers in order—3, 3, 4, 6, 8, 9, 12—and choose the middle number: 6. If there are an even number of numbers, average the middle two (you probably won't have to do that on the CBEST).

Mode

The *mode* is the number used most frequently in a series of numbers. In the sample median question, the mode is 3 because 3 appears twice and all other numbers are used only once. Look again at the frequency table from the frequency chart sample question. Can you find the mode? More students (15) earned a score of 90 than any other score. Therefore, the mode is 90.

Range

To obtain the *range,* subtract the smallest number from the largest number. The range in the median sample question is 12 − 3, or 9. The range in the frequency chart sample question is 100 − 70, or 30.

Math 2: Numbers Working Together

In the last lesson, you learned about typical scoring questions that appear on the CBEST, as well as average problems. This lesson will discuss ways in which numbers relate to each other and work together. You will need this information to solve simple algebra and perform certain arithmetic functions that will be part of some CBEST problems.

Adding and Subtracting Integers

The following sample questions are examples of the types of problems about adding and subtracting you may see on the CBEST. The answers are given later in this lesson.

Adding Positive Numbers

You probably already know that if a positive number, such as 5, is added to another positive number, such as 7, the answer will turn out to be a positive number: 12.

Adding Negative Numbers

Suppose you had two negative numbers to add together, such as −5 and −7. Here are two methods that make working with negative numbers easier:

- **Number line:** If you were to add −5 and −7 on a number line, you would start from 0. You would then proceed back five numbers to −5. From there, you would proceed back seven more (−7), which would leave you at the answer: −12.

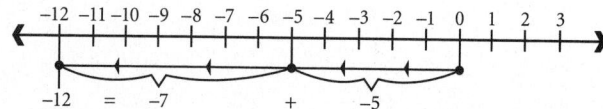

- **Bank account:** Negative numbers put you further in debt. If you started with a balance of zero and withdrew $5, you would have a balance of −5. If you withdrew $7 more, you would be in debt $12, or −12.

> **HOT TIP**
> When adding two negative numbers, just add the two values and place a negative in front of the answer. For instance, in the problem (−3) + (−6), first think 3 + 6 = 9, and then place a negative sign in front of the answer: −9.

Adding a Negative Number to a Positive Number

When adding a positive number and a negative number, such as 8 + (−15), you can use the number line or the bank account approach.

- **Number line:** Start from 0. Go 8 to the right and then move 15 spaces to the left. This will leave you at the correct answer: −7.

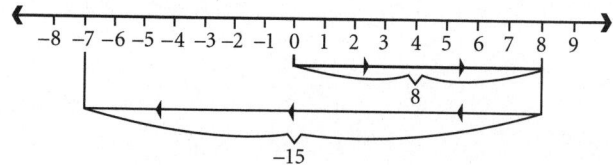

- **Bank account:** You put $8 in your bank account and take out $15. Oops, you've overdrawn, and you're left with a balance of −7.

Now try a problem with the negative number first: −6 + 7.

- **Number line:** Start from 0. Go 6 to the left since 6 is negative, then 7 to the right. You'll end up on the answer: 1.

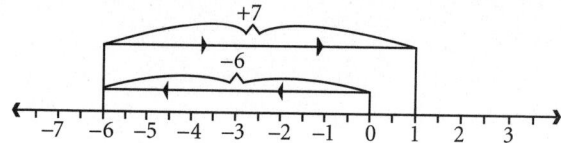

- **Bank account:** You take $6 out of your bank account and put in $7. You have one dollar more than you had before.

> **HOT TIP**
> When adding a positive and a negative number, simply subtract the smaller number from the larger number and give the answer the sign (− or +) of the larger number.

Subtracting Negative Numbers

Two minus signs next to each other may look strange, but they actually indicate one of the simplest operations; two negative signs together can be changed into one plus sign. For instance, the problem 9 − (− 7) will give you the same answer as 9 + 7.

- **Number line:** From 0, go 9 to the right. The first minus would send the 7 to the left, but another negative sign *negates* that operation, so 7 ends up going to the right as though there had been no negatives at all. The answer is 9 + 7, or 16.

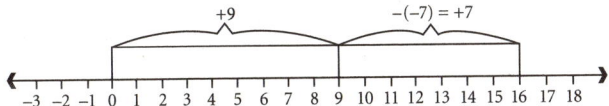

- **Bank account:** You deposit $9 in the bank. A negative would be a withdrawal, but there is another negative, so do a negative withdrawal; that is, deposit another $7. You have deposited a total of $16.

> **HOT TIP**
> When subtracting a negative number, change the two minus signs to addition signs.

Sample Integer Questions

1. Every month, Alice's paycheck of $1,500 goes directly into her bank account. Each month, Alice pays $800 on her mortgage payment and $500 for food and all other monthly expenses. She spends $1,650 per year on her car (insurance, gas, repairs, and maintenance), $500 per year for gifts, and $450 per year for property tax. What will be her bank balance at the end of a year?
   a. $500
   b. $300
   c. 0
   d. −$200
   e. −$400

2. A submarine is submerged 2,000 feet below the sea. An airplane directly over head is flying 32,000 feet above sea level. What is the difference in their altitudes?
   a. 30,000 feet
   b. 31,000 feet
   c. 32,000 feet
   d. 33,000 feet
   e. 34,000 feet

Answers to Sample Integer Questions

1. **d.** One way to find this answer is to first figure out Alice's monthly balance—what's left after she pays her monthly expenses: $1,500 − ($800 + $500), which equals $200. Then multiply this by 12 months to get $2,400, which is her yearly balance. Her yearly spending is $2,600 ($1,650 + $500 + $450). Her yearly balance minus her yearly spending will give you the answer: $2,400 − $2,600 = −$200.

2. **e.** The airplane's altitude is a positive 32,000 feet above sea level, and the submarine is a negative 2,000 below the water. Finding the difference between the two looks like this: 32,000 − (−2,000). Since you're subtracting a negative number, you need to add the two numbers, giving you a total distance of 34,000 feet.

Multiplying and Dividing Integers

Multiplying and dividing integers is not as complicated as adding and subtracting them.

Two Positives

When a positive number is multiplied or divided by a positive number, the result is positive: $4 \times 50 = 200$ and $50 \div 2 = 25$.

> **HOT TIP**
>
> Multiplication and division can be written three different ways.
> - **Multiplication:** You can write 3×4, $3(4)$, and $3 \cdot 4$. When working with a variable, such as z, $3 \times z$ may be written $3z$, without parentheses. Additionally, a negative sign directly outside a parentheses means to multiply anything inside the parentheses by negative 1. For example: $-(a) = -a$, and $-(xy) = -xy$.
> - **Division:** You can write $30 \div 4$, $4\overline{)30}$, or $\frac{30}{4}$. Variables in division can come in many forms. It's important to know these different forms when taking a multiple-choice exam. For example, $\frac{1}{2}y$ is the same as $\frac{y}{2}$, not $\frac{1}{2y}$.

Two Negatives

When two negative numbers are multiplied or divided, the result is positive: $-5 \times -5 = +25$ and $-36 \div -6 = +6$. Commit this rule to memory.

Negative and Positive

When a negative number is multiplied by a positive number, the result is negative. Multiplying -3 by 6 means that -3 is added together six times, so you will get a negative answer, -18. On the number line, you will go back three units six times. In your bank account, you will end up owing $18 after $3 is removed from your bank account six times.

Order of Operations

You may be given a problem with more than one operation, like this:

$$3 + 5 \times 2^2 + \frac{14}{(2+5)}$$

If you simply work from left to right, your answer will be 140, and it will be wrong. But, be assured, 140 will probably be one of the answer choices. The following phrase will help you remember the correct order of operations:

Please Excuse My Dear Aunt Sally

1. **P stands for *Parentheses*.** In the example, $2 + 5$ is in parentheses. That operation should be done first: $3 + 5 \times 2^2 + \frac{14}{7}$.
2. **E stands for *Exponents*.** Those are the numbers that are smaller in size and higher on the page than the others and indicate the number of times to multiply the number by itself. Thus, 5^3 means $5 \times 5 \times 5$. In the example problem, 2^2 means that 2 should be multiplied by itself twice: $2 \times 2 = 4$. So now the problem reads $3 + 5 \times 4 + \frac{14}{7}$.
3. **M and D stand for *Multiplication* and *Division*.** The next step is to do the multiplication and division from left to right: $3 + 20 + 2$.
4. **A and S stand for *Addition* and *Subtraction*.** The last step is to add and subtract from left to right: 25.

CBEST MINI-COURSE

Practice
Match the descriptions in the first column with an appropriate answer from the second column. The answers may be used more than once.

__ **3.** negative times or divided by a negative

__ **4.** negative times or divided by a positive

__ **5.** negative plus a negative

__ **6.** positive minus a negative

__ **7.** negative minus a negative

__ **8.** positive plus a negative

__ **9.** $8 + 3(40 - 10) - 9$

__ **10.** $2 + 5 + 6 \times \frac{4}{3} + 69$

__ **11.** $-97 - (-8)$

__ **12.** $100 + -11$

__ **13.** $-21(-4)$

__ **14.** $21(-4)$

__ **15.** $-21(4)$

__ **16.** $-14 - 70$

a. 89
b. 84
c. 56
d. −20
e. −84
f. −89
g. positive
h. negative
i. Change the double negative to a positive and follow rule **j**.
j. Subtract one from the other and select the sign of the largest number.

Answers

3. g.	**7.** i.	**11.** f.	**15.** e.
4. h.	**8.** j.	**12.** a.	**16.** e.
5. h.	**9.** a.	**13.** b.	
6. g.	**10.** b.	**14.** e.	

Seven Success Steps for Rounding Questions

1. Locate the place. If the question calls for rounding to the nearest ten, look at the tens place. Notice the place digit. Realize that the place digit will either stay the same or go up one.
2. Look at the digit to the right of the place digit—the **right-hand** neighbor.
3. If the right-hand neighbor is less than 5, the place digit stays the same.
4. If the right-hand neighbor is 5 or more, the place digit goes up one.
5. If the place digit is 9, and the right-hand neighbor is 5 or more, then turn the place digit to 0 and raise the **left-hand** neighbor up one.
6. If instead of a place, the question calls for rounding to a certain number of significant digits, count that number of digits starting from the left to reach the place digit. Now start with step 1.
7. If the specified place was to the left of the decimal point, change all the digits to the right of the place digit to 0.

Math 3: Rounding, Estimation, and Decimal Equivalents

The questions on the CBEST will include number rounding, estimation, and decimal equivalents. Most teachers studying for the CBEST need only a very basic brush up on these topics in order to master them. If you need a more thorough review, check out some of the books listed in the "More Help" section at the end of this chapter.

Rounding

Numbers are made up of digits that each represent a different value according to their position in the number. For instance, in the number 4,312.796, the 2 is in the ones place and equals 2 units. The 1 is in the tens place and equals 1 ten (10). The 3 is in the hundreds place and equals 3 hundreds (300). The 4 in the thousands place equals 4 thousands (4,000). To the right of the decimal, the 7 is in the tenths place and equals seven tenths (0.7, or $\frac{7}{10}$). The 9 is in the hundredths place and equals 9 hundredths (0.09, or $\frac{9}{100}$). The 6 is in the thousandths place and equals 6 thousandths (0.006, or $\frac{6}{1,000}$).

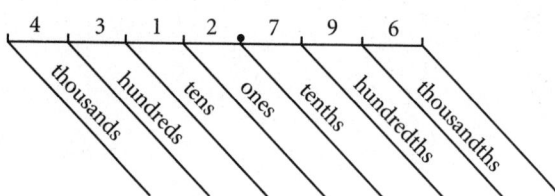

In a rounding question, you will be asked to round to the nearest tenths, hundreds, or other place.

Sample Rounding Question

1. Round 4,312.986 to the nearest tenth.
   a. 4,310.0
   b. 4,312.8
   c. 4,312.9
   d. 4,313.0
   e. 4,312.98

Three Success Steps for Estimation Problems

To do a problem like this, you might want to try some of the following strategies:

1. See whether you can round one number up and the other one down. This works best if one number is above its rounded value by about the same amount the second number is below its rounded value. Round the larger number up and the smaller number down for a fairly accurate estimate. For example, if the numbers were 71 and 89, you take one from 71 to get 70 and add one to 89 to get 90. 70 × 90 is very close to 71 × 89.
2. Eliminate answers that are further away from those you obtained in steps 1 and 2. For example, for 71 and 89, if answers given were 70 × 85 and 70 × 90, you can eliminate the former choice because 85 is further from 89 than 90 is.
3. After eliminating, you can always multiply (subtract, add, divide) out the remaining answers to make sure your answer is correct.

Answer

Find the answer by walking through the Success Steps.

1. The digit is 9, so it will either stay 9 or go to 0.
2. The digit 8 is to the right of 9.
3. This step does not apply; 8 is not less than 5.
4. The 9 goes up one because 8 is more than 5.
5. Change 9 to 0 and change 2 to 3. The answer is **d**, 4,313.0.

(Steps 6 and 7 don't apply.)

Practice

Now try a few more rounding questions.

2. Round 45.789 to the nearest hundredth.
3. Round 296.45 to the nearest ten.
4. Round 139.521 to the nearest whole number.

Answers

2. The digit you need to look at is 8; it will either stay 8 or go up to 9. The number 9 is to the right of 8; 9 is more than 5, so you change 8 to 9. The answer is 45.79.
3. The digit is 9; the 9 will either stay 9 or go to 0. The number 6 is to the right of 9; it is more than 5, so change 9 to 0 and apply step 5, raising the 2 to the left of 9 to 3. Now apply step 7, and change digits to the right of the tens place to 0. The answer is 300.
4. A whole number is the same as the ones place. Look at the number to the right of the ones place. Since it is a 5, the ones place should round up. But here, the ones place is already 9. So adding one more turns that to 10. So bump the tens place up by one ten, change the ones to zero, and drop the digits behind the decimal. The answer is 140.

Estimation

Estimation requires rounding numbers before adding, subtracting, multiplying, or dividing. If you are given numerical answers, you might just want to multiply the two numbers without estimation and pick the answer that is the closest. Most likely, however, the problem will be more complicated than that.

Sample Estimation Question

5. 42×57 is closest to
   a. 45×60
   b. 40×55
   c. 40×50
   d. 40×60
   e. 45×50

Answer

Here's how you could use the Success Steps to answer the sample question:

1. You can round 42 down and 57 up, resulting in choice **d**.
2. Rounding the numbers to one significant digit yields **d** also.
3. Check the remaining answers. The product of choice **b** is 2,200. The product of choice **d** is 2,400. The actual product is 2,394, which makes choice **d** the closest, and therefore the correct answer.

Decimal Equivalents

You may be asked to compare two numbers to tell which one is greater. In many cases, you will need to know some basic decimal and percentage equivalents.

Decimal-Fraction Questions

See how many of these you already know. For questions 6–11, state the decimal equivalent.

6. $\frac{1}{2}$

7. $\frac{3}{4}$

8. $\frac{4}{5}$

9. $\frac{1}{8}$

10. $\frac{1}{3}$

11. $1\frac{1}{6}$

For questions 12–14, determine which number is greater.

12. a. 0.93
    b. 0.9039

13. a. 0.339
    b. $\frac{1}{3}$

14. a. $1\frac{43}{91}$
    b. 1.52

Answers

6. 0.5
7. 0.75
8. 0.8
9. 0.125
10. $0.33\overline{3}$
11. $1.16\overline{6}$

12. **a.** To compare these numbers more easily, add zeros after the shorter number to make the numbers both the same length: 0.93 = 0.9300. Compare 0.9300 and 0.9039. Then take out the decimals. You can see that 9,300 is larger than 9,039.

13. **a.** Extending the number would yield $0.33\overline{3}$. (A line over a number means the number repeats indefinitely.) The number 333 is less than 339.

14. **b.** Instead of dividing the denominator (91) into the numerator (45), look to see whether the two choices are close to any common number. You might notice that both numbers almost equal $\frac{1}{2}$. 45 is less than half of 91, so $\frac{45}{91}$ is less than half. Half in decimals is 0.5 or 0.50; 0.52 is greater than 0.50, so it is greater than half. Thus, choice **b** is greater.

Decimal-Percentage Equivalents

You may already know that when you deposit money in an account that earns 5% interest, you multiply the money in the bank by 0.05 to find out your interest for the year. 5% in decimal form is 0.05.

> **HOT TIP**
> To change a percent to a decimal, move the decimal point two places to the left. To change a decimal to a percent, move the decimal point two places to the right. If there is no decimal indicated in the number, it is assumed that the decimal is after the ones place, or to the right of the number.

The percent always looks larger than its decimal equivalent. Here are some examples:

Number	Written as a Percent
0.05	5%
0.9	90%
0.002	0.2%
0.0004	0.04%
3	300%

Questions
Rewrite the following numbers as percents.

15. 0.07

16. 0.8

17. 0.45

18. 6.8

19. 1

20. 345

21. 0.125

Rewrite the following percents as decimals.

22. 5%

23. 0.7%

24. 0.09%

25. 49%

26. 764%

Answers
15. 7%
16. 80%
17. 45%
18. 680%
19. 100%
20. 34,500%
21. 12.5%
22. 0.05
23. 0.007
24. 0.0009
25. 0.49
26. 7.64

Common Equivalents

Here are some common decimal, percent, and fraction equivalents you should have at your fingertips. A line over a number indicates that the number is repeated indefinitely.

CONVERSION TABLE		
Decimal	%	Fraction
0.25	25%	$\frac{1}{4}$
0.50	50%	$\frac{1}{2}$
0.75	75%	$\frac{3}{4}$
0.10	10%	$\frac{1}{10}$
0.20	20%	$\frac{1}{5}$
0.40	40%	$\frac{2}{5}$
0.60	60%	$\frac{3}{5}$
0.80	80%	$\frac{4}{5}$
$0.33\overline{3}$	$33\frac{1}{3}$%	$\frac{1}{3}$
$0.66\overline{6}$	$66\frac{2}{3}$%	$\frac{2}{3}$

For more on fraction and decimal equivalents, see the next lesson.

Math 4: Fractions

Many test takers have had difficulty with fractions in the past, but if you are one of them, don't worry—now that you have had a few more years of education and are a little wiser, fractions may not be as intimidating as they once seemed.

Comparing Fractions

A CBEST question may ask you to compare two fractions, or a fraction to a decimal. To compare two fractions, use the laser beam method:

1. Two laser beams are racing toward each other.
2. They both hit numbers and bounce off up to the number in the opposite corner, multiplying the two numbers as they go.
3. Examine the numbers that result. The largest number is beside the largest fraction. Use the laser beam method to compare $\frac{5}{16}$ and $\frac{2}{5}$.

$$(25) \; \frac{5}{16} \; \times \; \frac{2}{5} \; (32)$$

$32 > 25$, so $\frac{2}{5} > \frac{5}{16}$.

HOT TIP

To change a fraction into a decimal, you simply divide the denominator of the fraction into the numerator, like this:

$$\frac{3}{8} = 8\overline{)3.000} \quad \begin{array}{r} 0.375 \\ \hline 24 \\ 60 \\ 56 \\ 40 \end{array}$$

Practice

Which number is greatest?

1. a. 0.25
   b. $\frac{11}{48}$

2. a. $\frac{4}{5}$
   b. 0.75

3. a. $2\frac{3}{7}$
   b. $1\frac{4}{9}$

Which number is less?

4. a. $\frac{3}{13}$
   b. $\frac{2}{11}$

5. a. 0.95

   b. $\frac{9}{10}$

6. a. $\frac{1}{3}$

   b. 0.3387

Answers

1. a. $11 \div 48 = 0.23 < 0.25$
2. a. $\frac{4}{5} = 0.8$ $80 > 75$
3. b. The whole number for choice **a** is greater than the whole number for choice **b**. Do not take the time to compare the fractions. The whole numbers give you your answer.
4. b. Use the laser beam method.
5. b. $\frac{9}{10} = 0.9$ $90 < 95$
6. a. $\frac{1}{3} = 0.\overline{33}$ $3{,}387 > 3{,}333$

Reducing and Expanding Fractions

Fractions can be reduced by dividing the same number into both the numerator and the denominator.

- $\frac{2}{4} = \frac{1}{2}$ because both the numerator and denominator can be divided by 2.
- $\frac{24}{36} = \frac{2}{3}$ because both the numerator and denominator can be divided by 12.

Fractions can be expanded by multiplying the numerator and the denominator by the same number.

- $\frac{1}{8} = \frac{2}{16} = \frac{5}{40}$ because the original numerator and the denominator are both multiplied by 2, and then by 5.

Adding and Subtracting Fractions

When adding fractions that have the same denominators, add the numerators, and then reduce if necessary:

$$\tfrac{1}{4} + \tfrac{5}{4} = \tfrac{6}{4} = 1\tfrac{2}{4} = 1\tfrac{1}{2}$$

When subtracting fractions that have the same denominators, subtract the numerators. Then reduce if necessary:

$$\tfrac{5}{7} - \tfrac{3}{7} = \tfrac{2}{7}$$

When adding or subtracting fractions with different denominators, find common denominators before performing the operations. For example, in the problem $\frac{3}{8} + \frac{1}{6}$, the lowest common denominator of 6 and 8 is 24.

Convert both fractions to 24ths: $\frac{3}{8} = \frac{9}{24}$
$\frac{1}{6} = \frac{4}{24}$

Add the new fractions: $\frac{9}{24} + \frac{4}{24} = \frac{13}{24}$

To subtract instead of add the fractions, after finding the common denominator, subtract the resulting numerators: $\frac{9}{24} - \frac{4}{24} = \frac{5}{24}$.

When adding mixed numbers, there is no need to rewrite the numbers as improper fractions. Simply add the fraction parts. Then add the integers. When finished, add the two parts together. Don't forget to "carry (regroup)" if the fractions add up to more than 1.

$$\begin{array}{r} 13\tfrac{5}{7} \\ + \, 6\tfrac{6}{7} \\ \hline 19\tfrac{11}{7} \end{array}$$

$\frac{11}{7} = 1\tfrac{4}{7}$
$1\tfrac{4}{7} + 19 = 20\tfrac{4}{7}$

Subtraction uses the same principle. Subtract the bottom fraction from the top fraction, and the bottom integer from the top integer. If the top fraction is less than the bottom one, then take the following steps:

1. Find the common denominator of the fractions.
2. Add that number to the numerator of the top fraction.
3. Subtract 1 from the top integer.
4. Subtract as usual.

Suppose the previous problem were a subtraction problem instead of addition:

$$13\frac{5}{7}$$
$$-6\frac{6}{7}$$

1. Find the common denominator of the fractions: 7
2. Add that number to the numerator of the top fraction: $5 + 7 = 12$
3. Subtract one from the top integer: $13 - 1 = 12$
4. Subtract as usual: $12\frac{12}{7}$
$$-6\frac{6}{7}$$
$$6\frac{6}{7}$$

HOT TIP
When adding or subtracting fractions, you can use the laser beam method.
1. First, cross multiply:

$$\frac{1}{6} + \frac{3}{7} = \overset{7}{\frac{1}{6}} \times \overset{18}{\frac{3}{7}}$$

2. Next, multiply the denominators: $6 \times 7 = 42$
3. Add or subtract the top numbers as appropriate and place them over the multiplied denominator to get your answer: $7 + 18 = 25$
$$\frac{25}{42}$$

Multiplying and Dividing Fractions

When multiplying fractions, simply multiply the numerators and then multiply the denominators:

$$\frac{5}{6} \times \frac{7}{8} = \frac{35}{48}$$

When dividing, turn the second fraction upside-down (finding its reciprocal), then multiply across:

$\frac{1}{2} \div \frac{2}{3}$ can be found by taking $\frac{1}{2} \times \frac{3}{2} = \frac{3}{4}$

When working with problems that involve mixed numbers such as $6\frac{1}{2} \times 5\frac{1}{3}$, change the numbers to improper fractions before multiplying. With $6\frac{1}{2}$, multiply the denominator, 2, by the whole number, 6, to get 12, then add the numerator, 1, for a total of 13. Place 13 over the original denominator, 2. The result is $\frac{13}{2}$.

HOT TIP
When you're working with two fractions and the numerator of one fraction can be divided by the same number as the denominator of the fraction or of the other fraction, you can reduce even before you multiply:

$$6\frac{1}{2} \times 5\frac{1}{3} = \frac{13}{2} \times \frac{16}{3}$$

Divide both the 2 and the 16 by 2:

$$\frac{13}{\cancel{2}\,1} \times \frac{\cancel{16}\,8}{3} = \frac{104}{3} = 34\frac{2}{3}$$

When multiplying or dividing a fraction and an integer, place the integer over 1 and proceed as if it were a fraction.

$$13 \times \frac{1}{2} = \frac{13}{1} \times \frac{1}{2} = \frac{13}{2} = 6\frac{1}{2}$$

CBEST MINI-COURSE

Choosing an Answer

When you come up with an answer in which the numerator is greater than the denominator, the answer may be given in that form, as an improper fraction. But if the answers are mixed numbers, divide the denominator into the numerator. Any remainder is placed over the original denominator. In the case of $\frac{208}{6}$, 208 divided by 6 is 34 with a remainder of 4, yielding $34\frac{4}{6}$. This answer probably will not be a choice, so reduce $\frac{4}{6}$ to $\frac{2}{3}$. If $\frac{208}{6}$ is not an answer choice, $34\frac{2}{3}$ probably will be. But don't worry about having to choose between these two answers. You will probably not encounter two forms of the same number, unless the question specifically asks for a fully reduced answer.

Practice

Have you improved your skills with fractions? Try these for practice:

1. $5\frac{1}{2} + 4\frac{2}{3} + 6\frac{1}{6} =$

2. $3\frac{6}{11} \times 1\frac{1}{39} =$

3. $5\frac{3}{4} - 2\frac{1}{2} =$

4. $8\frac{1}{8} - 2\frac{5}{8} =$

5. A recipe calls for $2\frac{3}{4}$ cups of flour. Jessica wanted to triple the recipe. How many cups of flour would she need?
   a. $7\frac{3}{4}$
   b. $7\frac{7}{8}$
   c. $8\frac{1}{4}$
   d. $8\frac{1}{2}$
   e. $8\frac{3}{4}$

Answers

1. $16\frac{1}{3}$. The least common denominator is 6.
2. $\frac{40}{11}$ or $3\frac{7}{11}$
3. $3\frac{1}{4}$
4. $5\frac{1}{2}$
5. Jessica needs to multiply $2\frac{3}{4}$ cups of flour by 3.
   $2\frac{3}{4} \times 3 = \frac{11}{4} \times \frac{3}{1} = \frac{33}{4} = 8\frac{1}{4}$

For more practice, look at some of the books in the "More Help" section.

> **HOT TIP**
> On the CBEST, there is usually one question that goes something like this:
> A school of 240 children want to go on a field trip. A bus can hold 50 children. How many buses are needed? Among the answers are 4, $\frac{4}{45}$, and 5. Four buses would not be enough. There is no such thing as $\frac{4}{5}$ of a bus. So 5 is the answer.

Math 5: Measurement

There are certain numbers, formulas, and measurements that you will be expected to know when working some CBEST problems. It's a good idea to put them on flash cards for memorization.

Common Measurements

You will be asked to figure problems using standard measurement of length, weight, and volume as well as speed, time, and temperature. Here are the common measurements you may be asked to use.

Weight Measurements

Weight measurements are usually measured on a scale.

1 pound = 16 ounces
1 ton = 2,000 pounds

Liquid and Dry Measurements

Liquid and dry measurements are usually made in a measuring spoon, cup, or larger container. Think of the dairy department of your grocery store. Units smaller than a cup probably will not be on the test.

1 cup = 8 ounces
1 pint = 2 cups = 16 ounces
1 quart = 2 pints
1 quart = 4 cups = 32 ounces
$\frac{1}{2}$ gallon = 2 quarts
$\frac{1}{2}$ gallon = 4 pints = 8 cups
$\frac{1}{2}$ gallon = 64 ounces
1 gallon = 2 half gallons
1 gallon = 16 cups = 4 quarts
1 gallon = 128 ounces

Distance

Distance can be measured by rulers or tape measures. In a car, miles are measured by an odometer.

1 foot = 12 inches
1 yard = 3 feet
1 yard = 36 inches
1 mile = 5,280 feet
1 mile = 1,760 yards

Temperature

Temperature is measured by a thermometer in degrees. The only tricky thing here is to be clear on the distinction between "above zero" and "below zero" numbers. If you can't visualize the distance between 40 below and 65 above 0, a rereading of Math Lesson 2 on negative numbers might help.

Speed

Speed is usually measured by speedometers in miles per hour. Time, distance, and rate problems are discussed in Math Lesson 7.

Time

Time can be measured by a clock or by a calendar. You can figure out the number of seconds in an hour (3,600) by multiplying 60 seconds by 60 minutes.

1 minute = 60 seconds
1 hour = 60 minutes = 3,600 seconds
1 day = 24 hours = 1,440 minutes
1 week = 7 days = 168 hours
1 year = 12 months = 52 weeks = 365 days

Sample Measurement Question

1. The diagram below shows an enclosed pasture. One section runs diagonally, and all other sections run north to south or east to west. The fence posts measure eight feet apart except for the diagonal section. Which statement best describes the perimeter of the pasture. P, in feet?

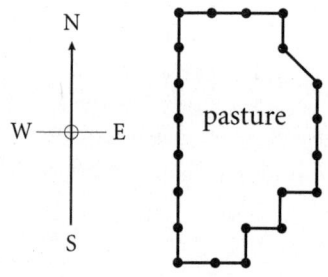

a. $P > 168$
b. $P = 168$
c. $P < 160$
d. $P > 220$
e. $P = 220$

Answer

In this problem, you are asked to find the statement that best describes the perimeter. Remember that the perimeter is the distance around the pasture. There are 20 posts that connect from north to south or east to west. Since these posts are 8 feet apart, this means that distance is 20 × 8 feet, or 160 feet. But what about that diagonal length of fence? This looks longer than the other sections of fence. In addition, you may remember from geometry that the hypotenuse of a right triangle is longer than the legs of the triangle. So this diagonal fence must be more than 8 feet long. The perimeter is 160 plus a bit more than 8. In other words, the fence is only a bit longer than 168 feet, so the best answer is **a**.

Practice

Try your hand at some additional measurement problems.

2. Casey bought 3 lbs. 5 oz. of boneless chicken at $1.60 per pound. How much did she pay?
   a. $0.50
   b. $4.80
   c. $5.30
   d. $8.80
   e. $12

3. Frank cut 2'8" off a 6'3" board. How much was left?
   a. 3'5"
   b. 4'5"
   c. 3'7"
   d. 4'7"
   e. cannot be determined

4. Eight scouts each need two 3' dowels for some banners they are making. Before being cut, the dowels are 10 feet long. How many dowels should the scoutmaster buy?
   a. 2
   b. 3
   c. 4
   d. 5
   e. 6

5. Three full containers each held one of the following amounts: one ounce, one cup, and one quart. If all three containers were dumped into a gallon jar, how much room would be left?
   a. $2\frac{9}{16}$ pints
   b. $5\frac{7}{16}$ pints
   c. $6\frac{5}{16}$ pints
   d. $9\frac{15}{16}$ pints
   e. $14\frac{15}{16}$ pints

Use the information below to answer the question that follows.

Monday	Tuesday	Wednesday	Thursday	Friday
38°F	43°F	44°F	–3°F	15°F

6. As part of a science unit on weather, students recorded the outdoor temperature at school at 7:30 A.M. for five consecutive mornings. What was the difference between the week's warmest and coldest temperatures?
   a. –44°F
   b. –3°F
   c. 41°F
   d. 47°F
   e. 87°F

7. Cooking a turkey takes 20 minutes for every pound in an oven heated to 350°. If a turkey weighing 20 pounds has to be ready by 2:00 P.M. at the latest, when should the turkey be put in the preheated oven?

a. 6:20 A.M.
b. 6:40 A.M.
c. 7:00 A.M.
d. 7:20 A.M.
e. 7:40 A.M.

Answers

2. This problem can be solved at least two ways. You can turn the ounces into $\frac{5}{16}$ of a pound and multiply $1.60 \times 3\frac{5}{16}$. Alternately, you can multiply 1.60 by 3, then multiply 1.60 by $\frac{5}{16}$ and add the two together. Choice **c** is the answer.

3. When subtracting 8 inches from 3 inches, borrow one foot from the 6 feet. Add 12 inches to the 3 inches to get 15"; 15 − 8 = 7 and 5 − 2 is 3. The answer is choice **c**.

4. The trick here is to realize that the 10' dowels are really only good for 9' since the scouts need 3' pieces. The scouts need a total of 48': 8 × 2 × 3 = 48. Five dowels would be good for only 45', but six dowels would provide more than enough (54'). The answer is choice **e**.

5. There are 128 ounces in a gallon. 128 − 1 oz. = 127 oz. 127 − 8 oz. (1 cup) = 119 oz. 119 − 32 oz. (1 qt.) = 87 oz. There are 16 ounces in 1 pint, so $\frac{87}{16} = 5\frac{7}{16}$ pt. The correct answer is choice **b**.

6. The warmest morning temperature is 44°F. The coldest morning temperature is −3°F. Asking for the difference indicates that this is a subtraction problem. 44−(−3) = 44 + 3 = 47. The correct answer is **d**.

7. Multiply 20 × 20 to get the total time. Convert the answer, 400, from minutes to hours by dividing by 60, to get $6\frac{2}{3}$, or 6 hours 40 minutes. From noon to 2 P.M. is 2 hours. Subtract the remaining 4 hours and 40 minutes from 12 noon; think of 12 noon as 11 plus 60 minutes. 11:60 − 4:40 = 7:20 A.M. The correct answer is choice **d**.

Perimeter Formulas

Following are important formulas you need to know.

Rectangle

2(length) + 2(width). To measure the distance around a rectangular object, you should find the measure of two lengths and two widths.

Square

4(side). To measure the distance around a square object, you should find the measure of one side and multiply it by 4.

Triangle

Side + side + side. Add the length of each of the three sides.

Circle

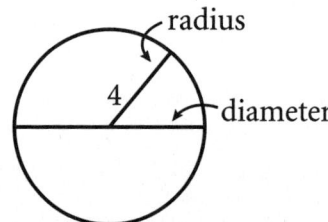

The **diameter** of a circle goes from one point on the circle through the center, and all the way to another point on the circle. The length of the radius (*r*) is half of the diameter. When working with π, consider the following: The symbol π is usually found in the answers so that you don't have to worry about converting it to a number. But if π is not found in the answers, and the question calls for an approximate answer, you can estimate by substituting 3 for π. The question may also tell you to use $\frac{22}{7}$ or 3.14.

Circumference: $2\pi r$. Circumference is to a circle what perimeter is to a rectangle. Multiply the radius by 2 and look for the answers. If π is not in the answer choices, multiply by 3. In the example above, the circumference is $2\pi 4$, or about 8π.

Other Perimeters

For any perimeter, just add the outside lengths all the way around.

Practice

8. The perimeter of a square room is 36 feet. How long is each side?
   a. 6 feet
   b. 9 feet
   c. 12 feet
   d. 18 feet
   e. 144 feet

9. What is the perimeter of a triangle with sides measuring 10 inches, 14 inches, and 15 inches?
   a. 24 inches
   b. 29 inches
   c. 34 inches
   d. 39 inches
   e. 44 feet

10. A rectangle has a perimeter of 28 inches. Which of the following could be the dimensions of the rectangle?
    a. 10 inches by 8 inches
    b. 4 inches by 7 inches
    c. 14 inches by 2 inches
    d. 6 inches by 8 inches
    e. 10 inches by 18 inches

11. What is the circumference of the circle below?

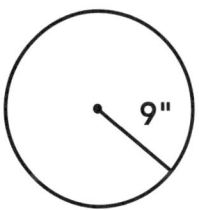

   a. 9π inches
   b. 18π inches
   c. 27π inches
   d. 81π inches
   e. 90π inches

Answers

8. Since the formula for the perimeter of a square is $4 \times$ side, we know that $4 \times$ side $= 36$. Since $4 \times 9 = 36$, each side must be 9 feet long. The correct answer is **b**.
9. The formula for the perimeter of a triangle is side + side + side. $10 + 14 + 15 = 39$. The correct answer is **d**.
10. Since the formula for the perimeter of a rectangle is 2(length) + 2(width), you can check each number pair to see which gives you an answer of 28. Since $2(6) + 2(8) = 12 + 16 = 28$, the correct answer is **d**.
11. The formula for circumference is $2(\pi)$(radius). Plug the radius into the formula and you get $2(\pi)(9)$, or 18π. The correct answer is **b**.

Math 6: Ratios, Proportions, and Percents

Ratios and proportions, along with their cousins, percents, are sure to appear on the CBEST. A good understanding of these topics can help you pick up valuable points on the math section of the test.

The Three-Step Ratio

The three-step ratio asks for the ratio of one quantity to another.

Sample Three-Step Ratio Question

Use the three steps to help you work out the following problem.

1. Which of the following expresses the ratio of 2 yards to 6 inches?
   a. 1:3
   b. 3:1
   c. 1:12
   d. 9:1
   e. 12:1

Answer

1. One yard is 36 inches, so 2 yards is 72 inches. Thus, the ratio becomes 72:6. (The quantities can also be put in yards.)
2. This ratio can be expressed as $\frac{72}{6}$ or 72:6. In this problem, 72:6 is the form that is used in the answers.
3. Since the answer is not there, reduce. 72 inches:6 inches = 12:1. The answer is choice **e**. Notice that choice **c**, 1:12, is backward, and therefore incorrect.

Practice

Try the three steps on the following problems.

2. Find the ratio of 3 cups to 16 ounces.
   a. 2:3
   b. 3:16
   c. 16:3
   d. 3:1
   e. 3:2

> **HOT TIP**
> - You can eliminate two of the choices for question 2 immediately. You know that 3:16 or 16:3 can't be right because the units haven't been converted yet.
> - In question 3, choices **b** and **c** are the same ratios. There can't be two right answers, so they can be eliminated. Six feet is two yards. Reducing 2:20 makes 1:10.

3. Find the ratio of 6 feet to 20 yards.
   a. 10:1
   b. 6:20
   c. 3:10
   d. 20:6
   e. 1:10

4. Find the ratio of 2 pounds to 4 ounces.
   a. 2:4
   b. 2:1
   c. 1:8
   d. 8:1
   e. 8:5

Three Success Steps for Ratios

1. Put the quantities in the same units of measurement (inches, yards, seconds, etc.).
2. Put the quantities in order and in the form given by the answer choices.
3. If the answer you come up with isn't a choice, reduce.

---

5. In a certain class, the ratio of children who preferred magenta to chartreuse was 3:4. What was the ratio of those who preferred magenta to the total students in the class? **Hint:** Add 3 and 4 to get the total.
   a. 7:3
   b. 3:4
   c. 4:3
   d. 3:7
   e. 4:7

6. In a certain factory, employees were either foremen or assembly workers. The ratio of foremen to assembly workers was 1 to 7. What is the ratio of the assembly workers to the total number of employees?
   a. 1:7
   b. 7:1
   c. 7:8
   d. 8:7
   e. 2:14

Answers
2. e.
3. e.
4. d.
5. d.
6. c.

Proportions

The four-step proportion solution is used when there are two ratios. One ratio will have both numbers given, and you will be asked to find one of the numbers from the other ratio.

Sample Proportion Question

7. The ratio of home games won to total games played was 13 to 20. If home teams won 78 games, how many games were played?

Answer

This problem can be solved in four steps.

1. Notice the two categories: home team wins and total games played. Place one category over the other in writing.

   $\frac{\text{Home wins}}{\text{Total games}}$ or $\frac{H}{T}$

   Note: This step is frequently omitted by test takers in order to save time, but the omission of this step causes most of the mistakes made on proportion problems.

Four Success Steps for Proportions

1. Label the categories or units of quantities in the problem to illustrate exactly what you're working with.
2. Set up the complete pair of numbers in ratio form.
3. Set up the second ratio, using a variable for the missing value.
4. Cross multiply to find the missing number.

2. In the previous problem, the width ratio with the smaller values is complete (13 to 20), and you're being asked to find the larger, real-life ratio. Work with the complete ratio first. Decide which numbers from the ratio go with each written category. Be careful; if you set up the ratio wrong, you will most probably get an answer that is one of the answer choices, but it will be the wrong answer.

   Notice which category is mentioned first: "The number of HOME games won to TOTAL games played..." Then check to see what number is first: "...was 13 to 20." Thirteen is first, so 13 goes with home games; 20 goes with the total games.

   $$\frac{H}{T} = \frac{13}{20}$$

3. Determine whether the remaining number in the problem best fits home wins or total games. "If home teams won 78 games" indicates that the 78 goes in the home-team row. The number of total games played isn't given, so that spot is filled with an x.

   $$\frac{H}{T} = \frac{13}{20} = \frac{78}{x}$$

4. Now cross multiply. Multiply the two numbers on opposite corners: 20×78. Then divide by the number that is left (13).

   $$\frac{20 \times 78}{13} = \frac{1{,}560}{13} = 120$$

HOT TIP
After you cross multiply and wind up with one fraction, you can divide one of the numbers in the numerator and the denominator by the same factor to avoid long computations. In the previous example, $13 \div 13 = 1$ and $78 \div 13 = 6$.

$$\frac{20 \times \cancel{78}^{6}}{\cancel{13}_{1}} = 120$$

The problem would then be much simpler: $20 \times 6 = 120$.

Practice
Try the four steps on the following problems.

8. On a blueprint, $\frac{1}{2}$ inch equals 2 feet. If a hall is supposed to be 56 feet wide, how many inches wide will the hall be on the blueprint?
   a. $1\frac{1}{6}$
   b. $4\frac{2}{3}$
   c. $9\frac{1}{3}$
   d. 14
   e. $18\frac{2}{3}$

9. In a certain recipe, 2 cups of flour are needed to serve 5 people. If 20 guests are coming, how much flour will be needed?
   a. 50
   b. 30
   c. 12
   d. 10
   e. 8

10. A certain district needs 2 buses for every 75 students who live out of town. If there are 225 students who live out of town, how many buses are needed?
    a. 4
    b. 6
    c. 8
    d. 10
    e. 11

Answers
8. d.
9. e.
10. b.

Percents

There are five basic types of percent problems on the CBEST. As is true with most other types of problems on the CBEST, percent problems most often appear in word-problem format. Percents can be done by using ratios or by algebra. Since ratios have just been covered, this section will explain the ratio method.

Percents can be fairly simple if you memorize these few relationships: $\frac{is}{of}$, $\frac{part}{whole}$, $\frac{percent}{100}$.

Sample Finding Part of a Whole Question

11. There are 500 flights out of Los Angeles every hour. Five percent are international flights. How many international flights leave Los Angeles every hour?

Answer
1. You are being asked to find a part of the 500 flights. The 500 flights is the whole. The percent is 5. You need to find the part. 5% is fairly small, and considering that 20% of 500 is 100, you know your answer will be less than 100.
2. The second sentence has an implied pronoun. The sentence can be rephrased "Five percent *of them* are international flights." *Them* refers to the number 500.
3. The question is *How many...* Use the other sentences to reconstruct the question so it includes all the necessary information. The problem is asking "5% of 500 (them) are how many (international flights)?" The question is now conveniently set up.
4. *Are* is the verb; 500 and 5% are on the left side of the verb and *how many* is on the right side. *How many* is all by itself, so it goes on top of the ratio in the form of a variable; 500 is next to the *of*, so it goes on the bottom. At this point, check to see that the part is over the whole.

$$\frac{x}{500} =$$

5. The 5 goes over 100.

$$\frac{x}{500} \qquad \frac{5}{100}$$

6. The two are equal to each other.

$$\frac{x}{500} = \frac{5}{100}$$

7. Solve.

$$\frac{500 \times 5}{100} = \frac{\cancel{500}^{5} \times 5}{\cancel{100}_{1}} = 25$$

8. Twenty-five international flights leave every hour.

Sample Finding Part of a Whole Question

12. In a certain laboratory, 60%, or 12, of the mice worked a maze in less than one minute. How many mice were there in the laboratory?

Answer
Once again, follow the eight Success Steps to solving this problem.

1. Twelve is part of the total number of mice in the laboratory. Sixty is the percent, which is more than half. Twelve must be more than half of the whole.
2. There are no pronouns.

Eight Success Steps for Solving Percent Problems

Feel free to skip steps whenever you don't need them.

1. Notice the numbers. Usually you are given two numbers and are asked to find a third. Are you given the whole, the part, or both ($\frac{part}{whole}$)? Is the percent given ($\frac{percent}{100}$)? Is the percent large or small? Is it more or less than half? Sometimes you can estimate the answer enough to eliminate some alien answers.
2. If there are pronouns in the problem, write the number to which they refer above the pronoun.
3. Find the question and underline the question word. Question words can include *how much is*, *what is*, *find*, etc. In longer word problems, you may have to translate the problem into a simple question you can use to find the answer.
4. Notice the verb in the question. The quantity that is by itself on one side of the verb is considered the *is*. Place this number over the number next to the *of* ($\frac{is}{of}$). If a question word is next to an *is* or *of*, put a variable in place of the number in that spot. If there is no *is* or no *of*, check to see whether one is implied. See whether you can rephrase the question, keeping the same meaning, but putting in the missing two-letter word. If all else fails, check to make sure the *part* is over the *whole*.
5. Place the percent over 100. If there is no percent, put a variable over 100 ($\frac{percent}{100}$).
6. Set the two fractions equal to each other.
7. Solve as you would a ratio.
8. Be sure to answer the question that was asked.

---

3. The problem is asking, "60% of what number (total mice) is 12?"
4. *Is* is the verb. The 12 is all by itself on the right of the verb. *What number* is next to the *of*. The 12 goes on top, the variable on the bottom.

    $\frac{12}{x}$

5. The 60 goes over 100.

    $\frac{60}{100}$

6. The two fractions are equal to each other.

    $\frac{12}{x} = \frac{60}{100}$

7. Solve.

    $\frac{12 \times 100}{60} = \frac{\cancel{12}^{4} \times \cancel{100}^{5}}{\cancel{60}_{1}^{3}} = 20$

8. There were 20 mice in the laboratory.

Sample Percent Question
13. Courtney sold a car for a friend for $6,000. Her friend gave her a $120 gift for helping with the sale. What percent of the sale was the gift?

Answer
1. The number 6,000 is the whole and 120 the part.
2. There are no pronouns, but there are words that stand for numbers. In the question at the end, the *sale* is 6,000 and the *gift* is 120.
3. The question is written out clearly: "What percent of 6,000 (sale) was 120 (gift)?"
4. *Was* is the verb. The number 120 is by itself on one side. It is the part, so it goes on top; 6,000 is near the *of* and is the whole, so it goes on the bottom.

    $\frac{120}{6,000}$

5. There is no percent, so x goes over 100.

$$\frac{x}{100}$$

6. The two equal each other.

$$\frac{120}{6{,}000} = \frac{x}{100}$$

7. Solve.

$$\frac{120 \times 100}{6{,}000} = \frac{\overset{2}{\cancel{120}} \times \overset{1}{\cancel{100}}}{\underset{1}{\cancel{6{,}000}}\ \cancel{100}} = 2$$

8. The gift was 2% of the sale.

Sample Percent Change Question

A change problem is a little bit different than a basic percent problem. To solve it, just remember that change goes over *old*: $\frac{change}{old}$

14. The Handy Brush company made $500 million in sales this year. Last year, the company made $400 million. What was the percent increase in sales this year?

Answer

First of all, what was the change in sales? Yes, 100 million. You got that by subtracting the two numbers. Which number is the oldest? Last year is older than this year, so 400 is the oldest. Therefore, 100 goes over 400.

$$\frac{100}{400}$$

The percent is the unknown figure, so a variable is placed over 100 and the two are made equal to each other. Cross multiply and solve for x.

$$\frac{100}{400} = \frac{x}{100} \quad \frac{100 \times \cancel{100}}{\cancel{400}} = \frac{100}{4} = 25$$

The answer is 25%. Note that if you had put 100 over 500, your answer would have come out differently.

Sample Interest Question

15. How much interest will Jill earn if she deposits $5,000 at 3% interest for six months?

Answer

Interest is a percent problem with time added. The formula for interest is $I = PRT$. I is the interest. P is the principal, R is the rate or percent, and T is the time in years. To find the interest, you simply multiply everything together. Be sure to put the time in years. You may change the percent to a decimal, or place it over 100.

$5{,}000$ (principal) $\times 0.03$ (percent) $\times \frac{1}{2}$ (year) $= \$75$.

Math 7: Algebra

Solving equations in algebra is like balancing a scale. The object is to keep both sides balanced while isolating the part you need on one side of the scale. For example, suppose you know that a novel weighs 8 ounces, and you want to find out how much your thick phone book weighs. You have five novels on one side of the scale, and your phone book and two novels on the other side. They balance perfectly. By taking two novels off each side, your phone book is alone and balances perfectly with the three novels on the other side. Then you know that your phone book weighs 3×8, or 24, ounces.

Plugging in Numbers

There are several types of algebra problems you may see on the CBEST. The first consists of a formula, perhaps one you have never seen, such as $Y = t + R - 3z$. You think, "I have never seen this..." and you are tempted to skip it. But wait, you read the question: What is Y if $t = 5$, $R = 12$, and $z = 1$? All you do is plug in the numbers and do simple arithmetic.

$$Y = t + R - 3z$$
$$Y = 5 + 12 - 3(1) = 14$$

Three Success Steps for Algebra Problems

In order to make a problem less confusing, try the WHO method:

1. **W**hat numbers are on the same side of the equation as the variable? There are two sides to the equal sign, the right side and the left side.
2. **H**ow are the numbers and the variable connected?
3. The **O**pposite is what? For example, the opposite of subtraction is addition.

Sample Question
1. Given the equation below, if $t = 5$ and $h = 7$, what is Q?

   $Q = t^2 - 3h$

Answer
You were right if you said 4.

$Q = t^2 - 3h$
$Q = 5^2 - 3(7)$
$Q = 25 - 21 = 4$

Solving an Equation

In the second type of question, you may actually be called upon to do algebra.

Sample Algebra Question
2. Given the equation below, if $Q = 15$ and $h = 1$, what is the value of t?

   $Q = t - 3h$

Answer
First, plug in the numbers you know and do as much arithmetic as you can:

$Q = t - 3h$
$15 = t - 3(1)$
$15 = t - 3$

1. What numbers are on the same side as the variable? 3
2. **H**ow are the numbers and the variable connected? With a minus sign.
3. The **O**pposite is what? Addition.

With that, add 3 to both sides to get your answer:

$15 = t - 3$
$\underline{+3 \quad +3}$
$18 = t$

Practice
Try these problems. You can probably do them in your head, but it's a good idea to practice the algebra because the problems get harder later.

3. $3x = 21$

4. $6 + x = 31$

5. $x - 7 = 24$

6. $\frac{x}{3} = 9$

7. $\frac{1}{3}x = 5$

Answers
3. 7
4. 25
5. 31
6. 27
7. 15

CBEST MINI-COURSE

Other Operations You Can Use

The following are some other ways you can use algebra on the CBEST.

Square Both Sides

When you're faced with a problem like $\sqrt{x} = 5$, you have to get x out from under the square root sign in order to solve it. The way to do this is to square both sides of the equation. Squaring is the opposite of taking a square root, and cancels it.

$$\sqrt{x} = 5$$
$$\sqrt{x}^2 = 5^2$$
$$x = 25$$

Take the Square Root of Both Sides

If the variable is squared, take the square root of both sides.

$$x^2 = 25$$
$$\sqrt{x^2} = \sqrt{25}$$
$$x = 5 \text{ or } x = -5, \text{ since } (-5)^2 \text{ also equals } 25$$

Flip Both Sides

If the answer calls for x and the x ends up as a denominator, the answer is unacceptable as is, because the question called for x, not $\frac{1}{x}$. If you have gotten this far in a problem, you can find the answer easily by flipping (taking the reciprocal of) both sides.

$$\frac{1}{x} = \frac{6}{7}$$
$$\frac{x}{1} = \frac{7}{6}$$
$$x = \frac{7}{6} \text{ or } 1\frac{1}{6}$$

Divide by a Fraction

To divide by a fraction, you take the reciprocal of the fraction and multiply.

$$\frac{3}{5}x = 15$$

Since the reciprocal of $\frac{3}{5}$ is $\frac{5}{3}$, multiply both sides by $\frac{5}{3}$:

$$\left(\frac{5}{3}\right)\frac{3}{5}x = 15\left(\frac{5}{3}\right)$$
$$x = \frac{15}{1}\left(\frac{5}{3}\right)$$

Reduce the fractions and multiply:

$$x = \frac{\overset{5}{\cancel{15}}}{1}\left(\frac{5}{\cancel{3}_1}\right) = 25$$

Practice

Solve for x:

8. $x^2 = 144$

9. $\sqrt{x} = 7$

10. $\frac{1}{x} = \frac{3}{4}$

11. $\frac{2}{3}x = 14$

Answers

8. 12 or −12
9. 49
10. $\frac{4}{3}$ or $1\frac{1}{3}$
11. 21

Multistep Problems

Now that you have mastered every algebraic trick you will need, let's juggle them around a little by doing multistep problems. Remember the order of operations: **Please Excuse My Dear Aunt Sally**—Parentheses, Exponents, Multiply and Divide, Add and Subtract? That order was necessary when putting numbers together. In algebra, numbers are pulled apart to isolate one variable. In general, then, it is easier to reverse the order of operations—add and subtract, then multiply and divide, then take square roots and exponents. Here is an example:

$$35 = 4x - 3$$

In this problem, you would add the 3 to both sides first. There is nothing wrong with dividing the 4 first, but remember, you must divide the whole side like this:

$$\frac{35}{4} = \frac{4x-3}{4} \text{ or } \frac{35}{4} = \frac{4x}{4} - \frac{3}{4}$$

As you can see, by adding first, you avoid working with fractions initally, making much less work for yourself:

$$35 = 4x - 3$$
$$+3 \quad\quad +3$$
$$38 = 4x$$

Then divide both sides by 4, resulting in the answer:

$$\frac{\cancel{38}^{19}}{\cancel{4}_{2}} = \frac{4x}{4}$$

$$x = \frac{19}{2} = 9\frac{1}{2}$$

Practice

Try these:

12. $5y - 7 = 28$

13. $x^2 + 6 = 31$

14. $\frac{4}{5}x - 5 = 15$

15. If $a - 2b = c$, what is a in terms of b and c?

Hint: When a question calls for a variable in terms of other variables, manipulate the equation until that variable is on a side by itself.

16. If $\frac{p}{3} + g = f$, what is p in terms of g and f?

Answers

12. $y = 7$
13. $x = 5, -5$
14. $x = 25$
15. $a = c + 2b$
16. $p = 3(f - g)$

Problems Involving Variables

Sometimes you'll find a problem on CBEST that has almost no numbers in it.

Sample Variable Question

17. John has 3 more than 10 times as many students in his choir class than Janet has in her special education class. If the number of students in John's class is v, and the number in Janet's class is s, which of the equations below does NOT express this information?

a. $v = 3 + 10s$
b. $v - 3 = 10s$
c. $\frac{v-3}{10} = s$
d. $10s - v = -3$
e. $v + 3 = 10s$

Three Success Steps for Distance, Rate, and Time Problems

1. First, write the formula. Don't skip this step! The formula for distance, rate, and time is $D = R \times T$. Remember this by putting all the letters in alphabetical order and putting in the equal sign as soon as possible. Or think of the word *DIRT*, where the *I* stands for *is*, which is always an equal sign.
2. Fill in the information.
3. Work out the problem.

Answer
After reading question 17, you're likely to come up with the equation in choice a. Since choice a is correct, it is not the right choice. Now manipulate the equation to see whether you can find an equivalent equation. If you subtract 3 from each side, choice b will result. From there, dividing both sides by 10, you come up with c. All those are equivalent equations. Choice d can be derived by using choice b and subtracting v from both sides. Choice e is not an equivalent and is therefore the correct answer.

Distance, Rate, and Time Problems
One type of problem made simpler by algebra is those involving distance, rate, and time. Your math review would not be complete unless you had at least one problem about trains leaving the station.

Sample Distance Problem
18. A train left the station near your home and went at a speed of 50 miles per hour for 3 hours. How far did it travel?
    a. 50 miles
    b. 100 miles
    c. 150 miles
    d. 200 miles
    e. 250 miles

Answer
Use the three Success Steps to work through the problem.

1. $D = R \times T$
2. $D = 50 \times 3$
3. $50 \times 3 = 150$

Practice
Try these:

19. How fast does a dirt bike go in one hour if it goes 60 miles every 3 hours?

20. How long does it take to go 180 miles at 60 miles per hour?

Answers
19. $R = 20$ miles per hour
20. $T = 3$ hours

HOT TIP

Another way to look at the distance formula is

$$\frac{D}{R|T}$$

When you're working out a problem, cross out the letter that represents the value you need to find. What remains will tell you the operation you need to perform to get the answer: the horizontal line means divide and the vertical line means multiply. For example, if you need to find R, cross it out. You're left with D and T. The line between them tells you to divide, so that's how you'll find R. This is a handy way to remember the formula, especially on tests, but use the method that makes the most sense to you.

Four Success Steps for Probability Questions

1. Make a fraction.
2. Place the total number of different possibilities on the bottom.
3. Place the number of possibilities that make an event true on the top.
4. If the answers are in a:b form, place the numerator of the fraction first, and the denominator second.

Math 8: Probability and Combinations

In this lesson, you'll have a chance to do problems on probability and on the number of possible combinations. These questions may be a little more advanced than those you did in school, but they will not be difficult for you if you master the information in this section.

Probability

Suppose you put one entry into a drawing that had 700 entrants. What would be your chances of winning? They would be 1 in 700 of course. Suppose you put in two entries. Your chances would then be 2 in 700, or reduced, 1 in 350. Probabilities are fairly simple if you remember the few tricks that are explained in this section.

Sample Probability Question

21. If a nickel were flipped thirteen times, what is the probability that heads would come up the thirteenth time?
    a. 1:3
    b. 1:2
    c. 1:9
    d. 1:27
    e. 1:8

Answer

Use the four Success Steps to solve the problem.

1. Form a fraction.
2. Each time a coin is flipped, there are two possibilities—heads or tails—so the number 2 goes on the bottom of the fraction. The thirteenth time, there are still going to be only two possibilities.
3. The number of possibilities that make the event (heads) true is 1. There is only one head on a coin. Therefore, the fraction is $\frac{1}{2}$. "Thirteen times" is extra information and does not have a bearing on this case.
4. The answer is choice **b**, 1:2. The numerator goes to the left of the colon and the denominator to the right.

Sample Probability Question

22. A spinner is divided into six equal parts. The parts are numbered 1–6. When a player spins the spinner, what are the chances the player will spin a number less than 3?

Answer

Once again, use the four Success Steps.

1. Form a fraction.
2. Total number of possibilities = 6. Therefore, 6 goes on the bottom.
3. Two goes on top, since there are two numbers that are less than 3: 1 and 2.
4. The answer is $\frac{2}{6}$, or reduced $\frac{1}{3}$, = 1:3.

CBEST MINI-COURSE

Combinations

Combination problems require you to make as many groups as possible given certain criteria. There are many different types of combination problems, so these questions need to be read carefully before attempting to solve them. One of the easiest ways to make combination problems into CBEST points is to make a chart called a tree diagram and list all the possibilities in a pattern. The following sample question is a typical CBEST combination problem.

Sample Combination Question

23. Shirley had three pairs of slacks and four blouses. How many different combinations of one pair of slacks and one blouse could she make?

a. 3
b. 4
c. 7
d. 12
e. 15

Answer

To see this problem more clearly, you may want to make a tree diagram:

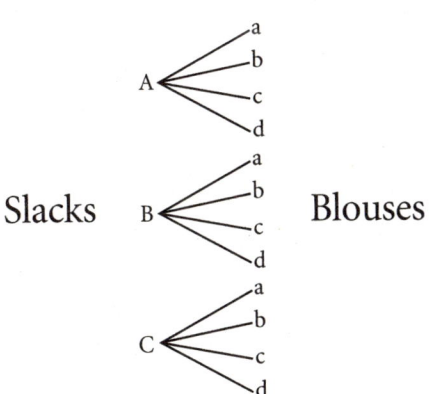

Each pair of slacks can be matched to four different blouses, making four different outfits for each pair of the three pairs of slacks, 3 × 4, for a total of 12 possible combinations.

Sample Combination Question

24. Five tennis players each played each other once. How many games were played?

a. 25
b. 20
c. 15
d. 10
e. 5

Answer

This combination problem is a little trickier in that there are not separate groups of items as there were for the slacks and blouses. This question involves the same players playing each other. But solving it is not difficult. First, take the total number of players and subtract one: 5 − 1 = 4. Add the numbers from 4 down: 1 + 2 + 3 + 4 = 10. To learn how this works, take a look at the following:

Letter the five players from *A* to *E*:

- *A* plays *B*, *C*, *D*, and *E* (4 games)
- *B* has already played *A*, so needs to play *C*, *D*, *E* (3 games)
- *C* has already played *A* and *B*, so needs to play *D*, *E* (2 games)
- *D* has already played *A*, *B*, and *C*, so needs to play *E* (1 game)
- *E* has played everyone

Adding up the number of games played (1 + 2 + 3 + 4) gives a total of 10, choice **d**.

This same question might be asked on the CBEST using the number of games five chess players played or the number of handshakes that occur when five people shake hands with each other once.

Other Combination Problems

Although the previous combination problems are the most common, other kinds of problems are possible. The best way to solve other combination problems is to make a list. When you notice a pattern, stop and multiply. For example, if you're asked to make all the possible combinations of three letters using the letters *A* through *D*, start with *A*:

AAA	ABA	ACA	ADA
AAB	ABB	ACB	ADB
AAC	ABC	ACC	ADC
AAD	ABD	ACD	ADD

There seem to be 16 possibilities that begin with *A*, so there are probably 16 that begin with *B* and 16 each that begin with *C* and *D*, so multiplying 16×4 will give you the total possible combinations: 64.

Math 9: The Word Problem Game

The directions for the word problem game are simple: While carefully observing a word problem, find all the math words and numbers in the problem. Eliminate the nonessential words and facts in order to find your answer.

Operations in Word Problems

To prepare for the game, make five columns on a sheet of paper. Write one of these words on the top of each column: **Add, Subtract, Multiply, Divide, Equals.** Now try to think of five words that tell you to add, five that tell you to subtract, and so on. If you can think of five for each column, you win the first round. If you can't think of five, you can cheat by looking at the following list.

How did you do?

0 = keep studying
1–3 for each = good
4–6 for each = great
7+ for each = excellent

- **Add:** *sum, plus, more than, larger than, greater than, and, increased by, added to, in all, altogether, total, combined with, together, lengthened by*
- **Subtract:** *difference, minus, decreased by, reduced by, diminished by, less, take away, subtract, lowered by, dropped by, shortened by, lightened by, less, less than, subtracted from, take from, deducted from.*
Note: The words in bold are *backwardswords*. (See the next section.)
- **Multiply:** *product, times, of, multiplied by, twice, thrice, squared, cubed, doubled, tripled, rows of, columns of*
- **Divide:** *quotient of, ratio of, halved, per, split, equal parts of, divided by, divided into, reciprocal*
Note: The words in bold are *backwardswords*. (See the following section.)
- **Equals:** *is, equal to, the same as, amounts to, equivalent to, gives us, represents*

Backwardswords

Backwardswords are words in a word problem that tend to throw off test takers; they indicate the opposite of the order in which the numbers appear in the problem. Only subtraction and division have *backwardswords*. Addition and multiplication come out the same no matter which number is written first: $2 + 6$ is the same as $6 + 2$, but $2 - 6$ is not the same as $6 - 2$. Using the numbers 10 and 7, notice the following translations:

Subtraction:

10 *minus* 7 is the same as $10 - 7$
10 *take away* 7 is $10 - 7$
10 *less* 7 is the same as $10 - 7$
But 10 *less than* 7 is the opposite, $7 - 10$
10 *subtracted from* 7 is also $7 - 10$

Four Success Steps for Converting Words to Algebra

In order to make an equation out of words, use these steps:

1. Find the verb. The verb is always the = sign.
2. Write in the numbers.
3. Write in the symbols for the other code words. Be careful of *backwardswords*.
4. If necessary, add parentheses.

Division:
10 *over* 7 is written $\frac{10}{7}$
The *quotient of* 10 and 7 is $\frac{10}{7}$
But 10 *divided into* 7 is written $\frac{7}{10}$
And the *reciprocal of* $\frac{10}{7}$ is $\frac{7}{10}$

HOT TIP
When setting up division problems in algebra, avoid using the division sign: ÷. Instead, use the division line: $\frac{3}{4}$.

Writing Word Problems in Algebraic Form
The following are exercises that will hep you translate words into equations.

Sample Word Conversion Questions
The following are simple problems to rewrite in algebraic form. Using N for a number, try writing out the problems below. Remember to add parentheses as needed to avoid order of operation problems.

1. Three added to a number gives us 6.
2. Six subtracted from a number is 50.

Answers
Use the four Success Steps to find the answer to question 1.

1. "Gives us" is the verb. Put in an equal sign: =
2. 3, 6, and N are the numbers: 3 N = 6
3. *Added* means +: $3 + N = 6$
4. No parentheses are needed.

Follow the Success Steps for question 2.

1. "Is" is the verb. Put in an equal sign: =
2. 6, N, and 50 are the numbers: 6 N = 50.
3. *Subtracted from* means –, but it is a *backwardsword*: $N - 6 = 50$.
4. No parentheses are needed.

Practice
Underline the *backwardswords*, then write the equations.

3. A number subtracted from 19 is 7.
4. Three less a number is 5.
5. Three less than a number is 5.
6. Nine less a number is –8.
7. A number taken from 6 is –10.
8. Thirty deducted from a number is 99.
9. The quotient of 4 and a number equals 2.
10. The reciprocal of 5 over a number is 10.
11. Six divided into a number is 3.

Change the following sentences into algebraic equations.

12. The sum of 60 and a number all multiplied by 2 amounts to 128.

13. Forty combined with twice a number is 46.

14. Nine dollars fewer than a number costs $29.

15. Seven feet lengthened by a number of feet all divided by 5 is equivalent to 4 feet.

16. Ninety subtracted from the sum of a number and one gives us 10.

17. Half a number plus 12 is the same as 36.

Answers
3. subtracted from, $19 - N = 7$
4. $3 - N = 5$
5. less than, $N - 3 = 5$
6. $9 - N = -8$
7. taken from, $6 - N = -10$
8. deducted from, $N - 30 = 99$
9. $\frac{4}{N} = 2$
10. reciprocal of, $\frac{N}{5} = 10$
11. divided into, $\frac{N}{6} = 3$
12. $(60 + N)2 = 128$ or $2(60 + N) = 128$
13. $40 + 2N = 46$
14. $N - \$9 = \$29$
15. $\frac{7+N}{5} = 4$
16. $(N + 1) - 90 = 10$
17. $\frac{N}{2} + 12 = 36$ or $\frac{1}{2}N + 12 = 36$

Words or Numbers?
Try these two problems and determine which is easier for you.

1. Three more than five times a number equals 23.

2. Jack had three more than five times the number of golf balls that Ralph had. If Jack had 23 golf balls, how many did Ralph have?

Answers
1. $23 = 3 + 5N$
2. $23 = 3 + 5N$

Did you notice that the two problems were the same, but the second one was more wordy? If question 1 was easier, you can work word problems more easily by eliminating nonessential words. If question 2 was easier, you can work out problems more easily by picturing actual situations. If they were both equally easy, then you have mastered this section. Go on to the section on two-variable problems, which is a little more difficult.

Practice
If you found wordy word problems difficult, here are some more to try:

18. Sally bought 6 less than twice the number of boxes of CDs that Raphael (R) bought. If Sally bought 4 boxes, how many did Raphael buy?

19. A 1-inch by 13-inch rectangle is cut off a piece of linoleum that was made up of three squares in a row; each had N inches on a side. This left 62 square inches in the original piece of linoleum. How long was each of the sides of the square?

20. Six was added to the number of sugar cubes in a jar. After that, the number was divided by 5. The result was 6. How many sugar cubes were in the jar?

Answers
18. Sally $= 2R - 6$. Substitute 4 for Sally: $4 = 2R - 6$
19. The first step is to find the dimensions of the original piece of linoleum by adding the area of the piece that was cut ($1 \times 13 = 13$ square inches) to

Three Success Steps for Problems with Two Variables

When turning "as many as" sentences into equations, consider the following steps.

1. Read the problem to decide which variable is least.
2. Combine the number given with the least variable.
3. Make the combined number equal to the larger amount.

---

the area of the remaining piece: 13 + 62 = 75 square inches. If we use S to represent the length of a side of one square, then the area of the square is S^2, and the area of all three squares is $3S^2$. The equation, then, will be $3S^2 = 75$. Dividing both sides by 3, we get $S^2 = 25$. Finally, take the square root of each side to get $S = 5$. The length of each side is 5 inches.

20. $\frac{6+N}{5} = 6$. Multiply both sides of the equation by 5, then subtract 6 from both sides of the equation: $5(\frac{6+N}{5}) = 6(5)$, $6 + N = 30$, $N = 24$. There are 24 sugar cubes in the jar.

Problems with Two Variables

In solving problems with two variables, you have to watch out for another backwards phrase: as many as.

Sample Two-Variable Questions

The following equations require the use of two variables. Choose the answers from the following:

a. $2x = y$
b. $2y = x$
c. $2 + x = y$
d. $2 + y = x$
e. none of the above

21. Twice the number of letters Joey has equals the number of letters Tina has. Joey = x, Tina = y.

22. Tuli corrected twice as many homework assignments as tests. Homework = x, tests = y.

Answers

21. **a.** *Equals* is the verb. Joey, or x, is on one side of the verb; Tina, or y, is on the other. A straight rendering will give you choice **a**, or $2x = y$, because Tina has twice as many letters as Joey has. To check, plug in 6 for y. If Tina has 6 letters, Joey will have $6 \div 2$, or 3 letters. The answer makes sense.

22. **b.** *Corrected* is the verb. Which did Tuli correct fewer of? Tests. You need to multiply 2 times the number of tests to reach the number of homework assignments. **Check:** If there are 6 tests, then there are 12 homework assignments: $2 \times 6 = 12$. This answer makes sense.

Practice

Now that you are clued in, try the following using these same answer choices.

a. $2x = y$
b. $2y = x$
c. $2 + x = y$
d. $2 + y = x$
e. none of the above

23. Sandra found two times as many conch shells as mussel shells. Conch = x, mussel = y.

24. Sharon walked two more miles today than she walked yesterday. Today = x, yesterday = y.

25. Martin won two more chess games than his brother won. His brother = x, Martin = y.

Answers

23. b.
24. d.
25. c.

Math 10: The CA SOLVE Approach to Word Problems

Of course, it helps to know the formula or method needed to solve a problem. But there are always those problems on the test that you don't recognize or can't remember how to do, and this may cause you a little anxiety. Even experienced math teachers experience that paralyzing feeling at times. But you shouldn't allow anxiety to conquer you. Nor should you jump into a problem and start figuring madly without a careful reading and analysis of the problem.

The CA SOLVE Approach

When approaching a word problem, you need the skills of a detective. Follow the CA SOLVE method to uncover the mystery behind a problem that is unfamiliar to you.

C Stands for Conquer

Conquer that queasy feeling—don't let it conquer you. To squelch it, try step A.

A Stands for Answer

Look at the answers and see if there are any similarities among them. Notice the form in which the answers are written. Are they all in cubic inches? Do they all contain pi? Are they all formulas?

S Stands for Subject Experience

Many problems are taken from real-life situations or are based on methods you already know. Ask: "Do I have any experience with this subject or with this type of problem? What might a problem about the subject be asking me? Can I remember anything that might relate to this problem?"

Eliminate experiences or methods of solving that don't seem to work. But be careful; sometimes sorting through your memory for experiences and methods takes a long time.

O Stands for Organize the Facts

Here are some ways to **organize** your data:

1. Look for clue words in the problem that tell you to add, subtract, multiply, or divide.
2. Try out each answer to see which one works. Look for answers to eliminate.
3. Think of formulas or methods that have worked for you in solving problems like this in the past. Write them down. There should be plenty of room on your test booklet for this.

> **HOT TIP**
> Don't try to keep a formula in your head as you solve the problem. Although writing does take time and effort, jotting down a formula is well worth it for three reasons: 1) A formula on paper will clear your head to work with the numbers; 2) You will have a visual image of the formula you can refer to and plug numbers into; 3) The formula will help you see exactly what operations you will need to perform to solve the problem.

L Stands for Live

Living the problem means pretending you're actually in the situation described in the word problem. To do this effectively, make up details concerning the events and the people in the problem as if you were part of the picture. This process can be done as you are reading the problem and should take only a few seconds.

V Stands for View

View the problem with different numbers to help you get a better sense of the steps you will need to take in order to solve it. This tactic is especially helpful when the sight of a large or complex number is so overwhelming that you just don't know where to start. For example, you might be intimidated by being asked to calculate how long it would take a rocket traveling 650 miles per hour to go 1,300,000 miles. To view the problem differently, you might think of how long it would take a car traveling 10 miles per hour to go 50 miles. Write down the steps you will take to solve the simpler problem, and then apply them to the more complex problem in just the same way.

E Stands for Eliminate

Eliminate answers you know are wrong. You may also spend a short time checking your answer if there is time.

Sample Question

Solve this problem using the CA SOLVE steps.

1. There are 651 children in a school. The ratio of boys to girls is 4:3. How many boys are there in the school?
   a. 40
   b. 325
   c. 372
   d. 400
   e. 468

Answer

1. **Subject Experience:** You know that 4 and 3 are only one apart and that 4 is greater. You can conclude from this that boys are a little over half the school population. Following up on that, you can cut 651 in half and eliminate any answers that are less than half. Furthermore, since there are three numbers in the problem and two are paired in a ratio, you can conclude that this is a ratio problem. Then you can think about what methods you used for ratio problems in the past.

2. **Organize:** The clue word *total* means *to add*. In the context in which it is used, it must mean girls plus boys equals 651. Also, since *boys* is written before *girls*, the ratio should be written *Boys:Girls*.

3. **Live:** Picture a group of three girls and four boys. Now picture more of these groups, so many more that the total would equal 651.

4. **View:** If there were only 4 boys and 3 girls in the school, there would still be a ratio of 4 to 3. Think of other numbers that have a ratio of 4:3, like 40 and 30. If there were 40 boys and 30 girls, there would be 70 students in total, so the answer has to be more than 40 boys. Move on to 400 boys and 300 girls—700 total students. Since the total in the problem is 651, 700 is too large, but it is close, so the answer has to be less than 400. This would narrow your choices to two.

5. **Eliminate:** Since you know from the previous step that the number of students has to be less than 400, you can eliminate choices **d** and **e**. Since you know that the number of boys is more than half the school population, you can eliminate choices **a** and **b**. You are left with choice **c**, the correct answer.

Quick Tips and Tricks

Below is a miscellaneous list of quick tips to help you solve word problems.

Work from the Answers

On some problems, you can plug in given answers to see which one works in a problem. Start with choice c. Then if you need a larger number, go down, and if you need a smaller answer, go up. That way, you don't have to try them all. Consider the following problem:

1. One-fifth of what number is 30?
   a. 6
   b. 20
   c. 50
   d. 120
   e. 150

Try **c**: $\frac{1}{5}$ of 50 is 10. A larger answer is needed.

Try **d**: $\frac{1}{5}$ of 120 is 24. Not yet, but getting closer.

Try **e**: $\frac{1}{5}$ of 150 is 30—Bingo!

Problems with Multiple Variables

If there are so many variables in a problem that your head is spinning, put in your own numbers. Make a chart of the numbers that go with each variable so there is less chance for you to get mixed up. Then write your answer next to the given answer choices. Work the answers using the numbers in your chart until one works out to match your original answer. In doing this, avoid the numbers 1 and 2 and using the same numbers twice. There may appear to be two or more right answers if you do.

Sample Multivariable Question

2. A man drove y miles every hour for z hours. If he gets w miles to the gallon of gas, how many gallons will he need?
   a. yzw
   b. $\frac{yz}{w}$
   c. $\frac{w}{yz}$
   d. $\frac{wy}{z}$
   e. $\frac{zw}{y}$

Answer

Picture yourself in the situation. If you drove 4 (y) miles every hour for 5 (z) hours, you would have driven 20 miles. If your car gets 10 (w) miles to the gallon, you would need 2 gallons. Since 2 is your answer, plug the numbers you came up with into the answer choices and see which one is correct. Choice **b** equals 2 and is therefore correct.

a. yzw $4 \times 5 \times 10 \neq 2$
b. $\frac{yz}{w}$ $\frac{4 \times 5}{10} = 2$
c. $\frac{w}{yz}$ $\frac{10}{4 \times 5} \neq 2$
d. $\frac{wy}{z}$ $\frac{10 \times 4}{5} \neq 2$
e. $\frac{zw}{y}$ $\frac{5 \times 10}{4} \neq 2$

Let the Answers Do the Math

When there is a lot of multiplication or division to do, you can use the answers to help you. Suppose you are asked to divide 9,765 by 31. The given answers are as follows:

   a. 324
   b. 316
   c. 315
   d. 314
   e. 312

You know then that the answer will be a three-digit number and that the hundreds place will be 3. The tens place will be either 1 or 2. Your division problem is practically worked out for you.

Problems with Too Much or Too Little

When you come across a problem that you think you know how to answer, but there seems to be a number left over that you just don't need in your equation, don't despair. It could very well be that the test writers threw in an extra number to throw you off. The key to not falling prey to this trick is to know your equations and check to make sure that the answer you came up with makes sense.

When you come across a problem that doesn't seem to give enough information to calculate an answer, don't skip it. Read carefully, because sometimes a question asks you to set up an equation using

One Success Step for *If* Problems

1. Pick some numbers and try it out!

variables, and doesn't ask you to solve the problem at all. If you are expected to actually solve a problem with what seems like too little information, experiment to discover how the information works together to lead to the answer. Try the CA SOLVE tips.

More Than One Way to Solve a Problem

Some questions ask you to find the only *wrong* way to solve a problem. In this type of question, do the computation yourself, and work from the answers. The choice that gives an answer different from the others has to be the wrong answer. Consider these choices:

    a. 5% of 60
    b. $\frac{5}{100} \times 60$
    c. 0.05×60
    d. $5 \times 60 \div 100$
    e. 5×60

All of the answers compute to 3 except choice **e**, which turns out to be 300. Therefore, choice **e** must be the correct answer.

Math 11: Logic and Venn Diagrams

You deserve a break after all your hard work on math problems. This lesson is shorter than the others; unless logic problems give you a lot of trouble, you can probably spend less than half an hour on this lesson.

If Problems

If problems are among the easiest problems on the test if you know how to work them. A genuine *if* problem begins with the word *if* and then gives some kind of rule. Generally, these problems mention no numbers. In order for the problem to be valid, the rule has to be true for *any* numbers you put in.

Sample *If* Question

The following is a typical *if* problem. Experiment with this problem to see how the answer is always the same no matter what measurements you choose to use.

1. Which statement can be deduced from "If Kim moves to Ohio, then she will get homesick"?
    a. Kim does not get homesick because she moved to Ohio.
    b. Kim will get homesick, but she does not move to Ohio.
    c. Kim moves to Ohio, and then she gets homesick.
    d. Kim does not move to Ohio, and she does not get homesick.
    e. Kim will get homesick, and she will move back from Ohio.

Answer

Answer **c** is the best decuction that can be made from the statement. The statement indicates that Kim will get homesick if she moves to Ohio. First she makes the move, and then she gets homesick.

Practice
Try another one:

2. If a coat was reduced 20% and then further reduced 20%, what is the total percent discount off the original price?
   a. 28%
   b. 36%
   c. 40%
   d. 44%
   e. 50%

> **HOT TIP**
> When choosing numbers for *if* problems, choose small numbers. When working with percents, start with 100.

Answer
Since this question concerns percents, make the coat's beginning price $100. A 20% discount will reduce the cost to $80. The second time 20% is taken off, it is taken off $80, not $100. Twenty percent of 80 is 16. That brings the cost down to $64 (80 − 16 = 64). The original price of the coat, 100, minus 64 is 36. One hundred down to 64 is a 36% reduction. So two successive discounts of 20% equal not a 40%, but a 36% total reduction.

Venn Diagrams
Venn diagrams provide a way to visualize groups in relationship to each other. Words such as some, all, and none commonly appear in these types of questions.

In Venn diagram problems, you are given two or more categories of objects. First, draw a circle representing one of the categories. Second, draw another circle representing the other category. Draw the second circle according to these rules:

1. If the question says that ALL of a category is the second category, place the second circle around the first.

   Example: All pigs (*p*) are animals (*a*).

   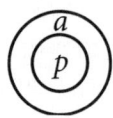

2. If the question says that SOME of a category is the second category, place the second circle so that it cuts through (overlaps) the first circle.

   Example: Some parrots (*p*) are talking birds (*t*).

   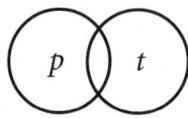

3. If the question says NO, meaning that none of the first category is in the second category, make the second circle completely separate from the first.

   Example: No cats (*c*) are fish (*f*).

   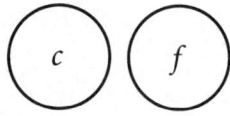

Sample Venn Diagram Question

3. All bipeds (*B*) are two headed (*TH*). Which diagram shows the relationship between bipeds and two-headed?

a.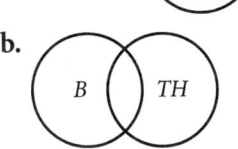

b.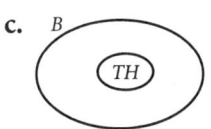

c.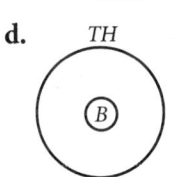

d.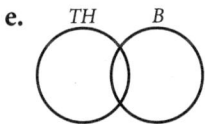

e.
TH *B*

Answer
The question says ALL, so the two-headed circle surrounds the circle denoting bipeds. The answer is choice **d**.

More Than Two Categories
Should there be more than two categories, proceed in the same way.

Example: Some candy bars (*c*) are sweet (*s*), but no bananas (*b*) are candy bars.

The sweet circle will cut through the candy bar circle. Since the problem did not specify where bananas and sweet intersect, bananas can have several positions. The banana circle can be outside both circles completely:

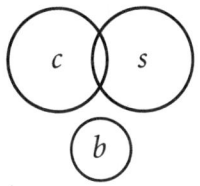

The banana circle can intersect the sweet circle:

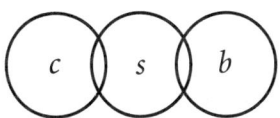

Or the banana circle can be completely inside the sweet circle but not touching the candy bar shape:

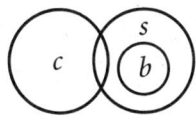

HOT TIP

Even when there are no pictures of Venn diagrams in the answers, you can often solve this type of problem by drawing the diagram one way and visualizing all the possible positions of the circles given the facts in the problem.

Writing 1: Outlining the Essay

You will be required to write two essays during your test time. One essay may be an expository essay, and the other a personal narrative. The expository essay will ask you to explain or describe something related to a current or well-known issue. The personal narrative essay question will relate to an experience you remember. You will need to convince the reader of your side of the issue. You will need to communicate your experience to the reader in such a way that the reader will be able to understand and appreciate your experience. The evaluators are not concerned about whether or not the facts are correct—they are solely judging your writing ability.

Unlike math, writing is flexible. There are many different ways to convey the same meaning. You can pass the test with any logical arrangement of paragraphs and ideas that are "clearly communicated." Most CBEST and English instructors recommend a five-paragraph essay, which is a standard formula. The five-paragraph essay assures that your ideas are logically and effectively arranged, and gives you a chance to develop three complete ideas. The more thorough the essay, the better rating is is likely to receive.

In writing both essays, there are five areas in which you need to show mastery.

1. **Clarity:** You must communicate your ideas clearly. Choose your words carefully so readers understand exactly what you mean.
2. **Focus:** Every sentence you write should relate to your topic. If a sentence is not reiterating your idea or providing an example, it probably isn't needed.
3. **Support:** Stating a thesis is not enough. You must give examples and reasons that support your thesis. The stronger the support, the better.
4. **Conventions:** Writing conventions include spelling, punctuation, capitalization, grammar, and paragraph structure. Your writing should show that you have a handle on all of these skills.
5. **Logic:** The logic you use in your writing should be extremely clear. This is not the time to dazzle the scorers with your creative approach to the topic. Follow the "sandwich" model, where you introduce your thesis statement, support your thesis statement, and then use the thesis again in your conclusion.

The first step in achieving such an essay is to come up with a plan or outline. You should spend the first four or five of the 30 minutes allowed in organizing your essay. This first writing lesson will show you how. The rest of the writing lessons will show you where to go from there.

Outlining the Expository Essay

Following are some tips on how to use your first four or five minutes in planning an expository essay, based on an essay topic similar to the one found in the diagnostic exam in Chapter 3.

Sample Expository Essay Question
1. What would you recommend as a dress code for your local public school?

Minute 1
During the first minute, read the questions carefully and decide what you want to say. You will not be graded on whether the scorers agree or disagree with your answer. Rather, they are interested in how well you communicate your answer to the question.

Minutes 2 and 3
Quickly think of and answer questions that apply to your topic. These questions can be adapted to the ideas

you will include in your paper. Jot down your ideas in a place on your test booklet that will be easily accessible as you write. Examples of how you might do this for the topic of school dress code are provided here.

- What do you know about the topic?
  Standardized dress code—students wear solid-color shirts and khaki pants.

- What are some reasons for the dress code you chose?
  Could eliminate problems with peer pressure and clothes, be less expensive, eliminate arguments between parents and students about what is appropriate clothing, reduce discipline issues related to clothing, and schools could organize clothing exchanges for gently used clothes that students have outgrown.

- What are the drawbacks to your suggestion? How could these problems be avoided?
  Families may have to buy new clothes not budgeted for; clothing exchanges can help with that.
  Students not expressing personality with standardized clothing; give opportunities for special clothing days throughout the school year.

- Whose opinion would support your thesis?
  Use quotes from parents, school administrators, even kids who don't want to keep up with expensive trends.

Minutes 4 and 5
When you have finished, organize your notes into three strong subtopics. You may use the three strongest reasons for the dress code you described, or you may organize the subtopics by the three groups that benefit from the plan. Under each subtopic, write examples and quotes that describe and support the subtopic.

Keep in mind that your essay doesn't have to have *only* three body paragraphs, though it shouldn't have *fewer* than three. Three is a good, solid number of main points to include, so plan on writing three body paragraphs right from the outset. You don't want to run out of time because you planned more paragraphs than you needed.

For an expository essay, you should progress from the weakest point to the strongest point. This means that you should choose the subtopic you have the least support for and write that paragraph first. The third subtopic paragraph should be the one you can write about best.

Outlining the Personal Narrative Essay
The process of outlining a personal narrative essay is similar to that of outlining an expository essay. You should still plan on taking the first four or five minutes for this process. The following steps will show you how to tackle a topic like the following:

Sample Personal Narrative Essay Question
2. Describe an event from your elementary school years that has affected the way you live your life today.

Minute 1
In order to answer a question like this, you need to search your memory and pick out an event or a person that had a significant impact in your life. Although you can use a made-up person or event, it may not be to your advantage. A familiar person or event is easier to write about. You will be able to visualize the details and communicate them to your reader.

You should also try to choose an event that has had a significant impact, will grab your reader's attention, and will make them feel or grow along with you. Writing about someone who inspired you to be a giving person or helped you overcome shyness is preferable to someone who taught you to avoid poison ivy or improve your penmanship. Something with a greater, more profound impact on your life is preferable to something trivial.

Minutes 2 and 3

Once you have chosen your topic, try to remember the events as they took place. Consider these questions:

1. What about you then was different than it is now?
2. Who were the principal actors?
3. How long did the situation last?
4. How did the event start, when did you first meet the person, or when were you first aware of what was happening?
5. How did you feel in the beginning?
6. How did the scene unfold?
7. What did you see, hear, taste, touch, and smell during the process?
8. What were the events that led up to the climax, and how did the climax take place?
9. How does the situation still affect you today?

Minutes 4 and 5

Place your thoughts in logical sequence on your paper. One logical sequence might be chronological order: Describe each of three parts of the event in detail and give your reactions, if necessary, as you go along. Alternately, if there are three people or groups of people involved, you could write a paragraph dedicated to each perspective of the event. Or you might want to write in the first paragraph about the event itself; in the second, talk about ways in which the situation affected you immediately, and in the third, explain how the situation affects you today. Any logical sequence will work. Jot the main ideas of your three subtopics down in your test booklet and refer to them as you write. Try to limit your time to just five minutes each.

Practice

Try outlining the following essay topics using the hints you've learned.

- What is the purpose of the Internet? Include different points of view, including those of consumers and Internet-related businesses.

- Many times in life there are choices to make. Sometimes people find themselves at a fork in life's road. Tell about such a time in your life and how you chose what road to take.

Writing 2: Writing the Introduction

You have your outline. You know exactly what points you are going to make. It is time to write your introduction. The introduction can be the most fun paragraph of your essay to write. You will have the opportunity to be creative and to show off your line of thinking or reasoning.)

The Outline

Let's say you decide to write about using school uniforms as a dress code policy. (Remember, it doesn't matter what dress code topic you chose. This is just an example.) Your outline on your scratch paper may look something like this:

Parents—Save money, can use hand-me-downs, save wear on good clothes, buying clothes easier, survey shows parents hate free dress days, less pressure from children and fewer fights over money for clothes.

Children—Low-income children feel as well-dressed as peers, feel more of a sense of belonging, easier and faster to dress in morning, don't have to worry about what others think, more disciplined and calmer at school.

School staff—Experts say fewer fights at school, less bullying and teasing, more school loyalty among children so builds school community, parents less stressed so fewer calls for advice, frees officials to do other things like academics.

Conclusion: In the end, children and families benefit.

Three Parts of an Introduction

A surefire formula for a good introduction has three parts: an attention-grabber, an orientation for the reader, and a thesis statement. The thesis statement is indispensable; you can play around with the other parts a bit.

Grab the Reader's Attention

This is your chance to be creative. The purpose of the first sentence or two of your introduction is to engage your reader.

You may start your introduction with a question or statement that engages the reader's imagination.

How would your life change if you could wear a practical, comfortable uniform to work? Imagine a school auditorium full of alert children, all dressed neatly in blue and white uniforms, reciting the Pledge of Allegiance. Imagine these same children happily running out to play in their blue shorts and white oxford shirts, playing tag and flying on swings.

Orient the Reader

Whether or not you choose to use a "starter" like what you just read, you will need one or more sentences to orient your reader. Write as if your reader is an alien from outer space who knows nothing about your subject. You will need to introduce the topic and give some background information. Here's an example:

Over 98% of our nation's schools have some kind of dress code for their students. Twenty percent of these codes designate a certain color and style of dress. Some of these uniform regulations even include specifics on shoes, socks, sweaters, and jackets. Over 1,000 schools each year are added to the ranks of those that have adopted stricter uniform policies for their students.

> **HOT TIP**
>
> It is perfectly fine to create facts, figures, and quotes. The test makers want to know if you can write. They are not testing your knowledge of the subject.
>
> But don't stew over a quote. It's important to get your ideas down on paper before you run out of time. If you can't think of something good right away, leave a line blank at the beginning of your essay so that you can put one in later if you have time.

For an expository essay, another kind of orientation states the other side of the argument briefly:

Whether or not to dress public school children alike has been the subject of much controversy in recent decades. Opponents suggest that requiring uniforms will stifle children's ability to choose, squash necessary individuality, and infringe on the rights of children and families. Although there is some justification for these arguments, the benefits of uniforms far outweigh the disadvantages.

State Your Thesis

The third piece of your introduction includes a sentence stating your three main points. The purpose of this sentence is to tell readers what you are going to tell them. The thesis sentence is taken from the three main points of your outline. Put these in order from the least important to the most important. Look at your arguments for each topic and put last the one for which you can make the best case.

Do you feel that you can write the best support for school administrators and the least support for parents? If that is the case, then you should write about benefits to parents first, then children, and finally school administrators.

Alternatively, you can use any number of words in phrases or even whole sentences that summarize the ideas you are going to write about. This is not the place to give much detail, however, or you will have nothing to develop in the next paragraphs.

Uniform policies provide relief for parents, enhance self-esteem in children, and facilitate learning at school.

Putting It All Together

Here's one possible introduction, built out of the three pieces put together.

How would your life change if you could wear a practical, comfortable uniform to work? In many schools, uniform policies have been adopted. Over 98% of our nation's schools have some kind of dress code for their students. 20% of these codes designate a certain color and style of dress. Some of these uniform regulations even include specifics on shoes, socks, sweaters, and jackets. Over 1,000 schools each year are added to the ranks of those that have adopted stricter uniform policies for their students. Putting uniform dress code policies in place provide relief for parents, enhance self-esteem in children, and facilitate learning at school.

The sentences in the introductory paragraphs need to fit together so that they flow. Notice that the sentence, In many schools, uniform policies have been adopted, has been added to make a transition from the first sentence to the third. The first talks about work. The third gives statistics about schools. A transition from work to school is needed to put these two parts together.

Here's another possible introduction. In this case, no transitions were needed.

Imagine a school auditorium full of alert children, all dressed neatly in blue and white uniforms, reciting the Pledge of Allegiance. Imagine these same children happily running out to play in their blue shorts and white oxford shirts, playing tag and flying on swings. Whether or not to dress public school children alike has been the subject of much controversy in recent decades. Opponents suggest that requiring uniforms will stifle children's ability to choose, squash necessary individuality, and infringe on the rights of children and families. Although there is some justification for these arguments, the benefits of uniforms far outweigh the disadvantages. Adopting a uniform policy will benefit parents, children, and school staff.

Outlining a Personal Narrative Essay

When writing the introduction to a personal narrative essay, use a sentence or two to engage the reader. Next, give a little orientation by stating a few facts from your life that might help the reader understand what is to follow, or by restating the question. Then state your thesis.

Your orientation can go at least two ways. If the question asked you to describe a significant fork in the road, you might write:

- A brief description of your general situation at the time
- A general reflection on how people do occasionally or often come to forks in the road, or how every day is full of forks and choices, but one significant one you remember is . . .

For your thesis statement, you may choose to write three phrases such as:

My road to the fork was rocky, and the fork was perplexing, but the road I took was paved with happiness.

In this case, your three paragraphs will be on:

1. The events preceding the fork
2. The decisions that were before you
3. The result of the path you chose

Note that if the question called for you to write about your reasons for choosing the fork, or to write in detail about each decision that faced you, you would need to adapt your outline to answer the question. If the question asked only for reasons, you would describe the fork briefly in the background sentences, and outline three reasons in your thesis statement. If it told you to describe the fork and give the reasons, then in your thesis sentence you might write two phrases on the fork and one on the reasons, or one on the fork and two on the reasons.

> **HOT TIP**
> There is no wrong way to organize your paragraphs and thesis statement, as long as your essay shows clear evidence of logical arrangement.

Introduction Practice

Try writing introductions for the following topics. You'll need to write a brief outline first.

- Describe a time when you felt you took a significant step toward maturity.

- Many shoppers make their purchases on the Internet, which can create hardship for brick-and-mortar store owners. Discuss the benefits to shopping at stores as opposed to shopping online. Include the perspectives of both business owners and shoppers.

Writing 3: The Sandwich Paragraphs and the Last Slice

Once you have written your outline and your introduction, you need not concentrate so much on ideas; you already have them written down. In the body and conclusion of the essay, show off your style. Each of the three paragraphs after the introduction should contain a topic sentence and at least four supporting sentences. Your conclusion should restate your thesis and offer a few closing words.

Lesson Exercise

The sample sentences and paragraphs in this lesson contain mistakes in grammar, punctuation, diction, and even organization. See whether you can find all the errors, and try to correct them. You may need to simply rewrite some of the paragraphs for clarity. Then compare your revisions to the ones you will find in Writing Sections 4 and 5. There are many ways to rewrite the paragraphs; maybe you'll find a better way than the ones given. If you can do that, you're sure to pass the writing portion of the CBEST.

Topic Sentence and Supporting Sentences

Each paragraph should have a topic sentence. The topic sentence often begins the paragraph, and states the main idea of the paragraph in general. For each of the three paragraphs that will make up the body of your essay, one of the points from your outline will be used. That is why you made the outline. The subpoints you wrote down will be the subject of the rest of the sentences in the paragraph.

After composing the topic sentence, clarify and explain your main idea with supporting sentences. These sentences should be as detailed and descriptive as possible.

Go back to the uniform example and write some topic sentences and supporting sentences. Remember, the outline looked like this:

> **Parents**—Save money, can use hand-me-downs, save wear on good clothes, buying clothes easier, survey shows parents hate free dress days, less pressure from children and fewer fights over money for clothes.
> **Children**—Low-income children feel as well dressed as peers, feel more of a sense of belonging, easier and faster to dress in morning, don't have to worry about what others think, more disciplined and calmer at school.
> **School staff**—Experts say fewer fights at school, less bullying and teasing, more school loyalty among children so builds school community, parents less stressed so fewer calls for advice, frees officials to do other things, like academics. Principals and teachers love the uniform policy.
> **Conclusion:** In the end, children and families benefit.

These were the thesis examples:

- Adopting a school uniform policy will benefit parents, children, and school staff.
- Uniform policies provide relief for parents, enhance self-esteem in children, and facilitate learning at school.

> **HOT TIP**
> When you write your CBEST essay, be sure to leave yourself plenty of room for revisions by double-spacing or leaving extra-wide margins.

Your first reason in favor of uniforms is that parents benefit. To make things easier, you can copy the first part of the thesis statement. This provides you with a transition (see the next section) as well as a topic sentence:

In my opinion, a uniform policy will benefit parents.

Next, add your detailed reasons. Here is one possible way to write the first body paragraph. (Remember, the paragraphs in this lesson have mistakes in them. Can you correct them?)

In my opinion, a uniform policy will benefit parents. Because they are all the same style and shape and usually very well made, children can use the hand-me-downs of older siblings or even used ones bought from another child. Parents they were also able to save money by buying fewer school clothes for their children. Children, who are often demanding, will have already agreed on what clothes their parents will need to buy so there will be fewer arguments over clothes for school their parents will need to buy. Children and teachers like it too. Parents are generally in favor of uniforms because you do not have to provide your children with a different matched set of clothes for each day. After buying uniforms the first year, more peace was reportedly experienced by

> 95% of the parents interviewed and many surveys reported that it saved them an average of $100–$200 in clothing costs.

Notice how this paragraph has used some statistics—completely made-up ones—to provide support for the topic sentence. When you are writing your personal narrative essay, you should usually organize the supporting sentences in chronological order, or in order of importance. Lots of descriptive detail and maybe even some conversation, when appropriate, will help support your main point and make your essay clear and compelling to your reader.

Now, how about a topic sentence for each of the other two body paragraphs?

> Children benefit from a school uniform policy. Uniforms cost no extra money for teachers and administrators, yet the benefits are great.

These sentences are OK for now, but your essay needs transitions from one paragraph to another. The first topic from your thesis statement gave your first body paragraph an automatic transition from the introduction. Now you need something that will link the first body paragraph to the second, and the second to the third.

Transition Sentences

A transition sentence joins two paragraphs together in some way. Usually, an idea taken from one paragraph links with an idea in a second paragraph. This is done in one sentence. Sometimes you can do this at the end of one paragraph to link it to the next, but often it's effective to build your transition right into your topic sentence, as you did with the first body paragraph.

For instance, take the topic sentence for your second body paragraph:

> Children benefit from a school uniform policy.

How can you link parents, the subject of your first body paragraph, to children? Try something like this:

> Not only are parents happy to see a uniform policy in place, but their children benefit as well.

Voilà, a transition that links together body paragraphs one and two.

You can also put your transition at the end of the previous paragraph, rather than at the beginning of the new one. For instance, you can put a sentence like this at the end of your paragraph on children to lead into the paragraph about teachers and administrators:

> Children are happy with the school uniform policy, but not as happy as their teachers and principals.

Now add the subpoints from your outline to your second and third body paragraphs. (Are you still looking for the mistakes in these paragraphs?)

> Not only are parents happy to see a uniform policy in place, but their children benefit as well. If you were poor wouldn't you feel bad if you were not dressed as well as your peers. Children who dress differently are alienated from cliques at school and left to feel like outsiders and are teased unmercifully and end up losing a lot of self-esteem and so maybe they will grow up bitter and make bad choices in life that could hurt themselves or someone else. Dressing in uniform eliminates that problem. Instead you feel a sense of belonging. You are less distractd by cumparing your clothes to others so you are more apd to be relaxed and quieter in school. This enables them to learn more. Children might be happy with the school uniform policy but not as happy as their teachers and principals

Uniforms cost no extra money for teachers and administrators yet the benefits are great. There is less competition in school so there is less fights. The reason is because there is less bullying and teasing and there is a lot less complaints. Instead, principals and teachers were able to use uniforms to build school pride and loyalty. Administrators and teachers will be able to concentrate on what they love to do most—teach—instead of dealing with problems from children and parents.

> **HOT TIP**
> Write neatly if you are taking the paper version of the test! The scorers do not want to take time to stop and decipher your words. If a word appears illegible or spelled wrong (an *i* looks like an *e*), erase the letter or word neatly and write it again. If your handwriting is illegible, print.

The Conclusion

The concluding paragraph is one of the most difficult to compose. A good format to follow is to first restate your thesis, and then try for a "clincher," something that will leave your readers with a sense of closure.

So in the first sentence or two, restate your thesis. Do not add any new ideas here.

Adopting a uniform policy will lighten the burden of parents. It will promote cheerfulness and scholarship in children. Lastly, it will free the time and talents of teachers and administrators.

The concluding paragraph in a personal narrative essay could sum up the story.

I can look back now on that day long ago. I was at the crossroads. I knew I loved children and that my parents would be proud. I signed up for teacher training.

The last sentence or two should contain the clincher. Its purpose is to end the paragraph gracefully and leave the reader with a sense of finality.

> **HOT TIP**
> Although you aren't required to write a title, it helps the judges to see that you are an organized and thoughtful writer. Leave a few lines blank at the beginning of your essay, since you might not come up with a title until you're nearly finished. Make sure your title captures the main idea of your essay. "Uniforms: Boon or Bane?" would not be appropriate for an essay that mostly deals with the positive reasons for uniforms because it suggests there are two sides to the story. "In Praise of Uniforms" would be better.

The last sentence of an expository essay may be a call to action, a question, a prediction, or a personal comment. You might add one of these clinchers to the thesis summary on school uniforms:

What are we waiting for? We need to talk to our teachers, principals, and school boards, and give our children ALL the tools we can that are essential for their growth and development.

Since school uniforms do so much good, would you want your school to miss out?

For a personal narrative essay, this last sentence could state your opinion, or talk about someone, even yourself, who will never be the same. You might add one of these sentences about your decision to go into teacher training:

I am glad I did.
My world will never be the same.
I often wonder how many children's lives will be changed because of one decision on that one April day.

It can be difficult to write this last sentence or two, but you need to supply your readers with something that makes your essay memorable.

Once you have your ideas down on paper, it's important to see that they are clearly and correctly expressed—unlike the paragraphs found in this lesson. Go on to Writing 4 and Writing 5 to see how to make your sentence structure and word choice work for you.

Writing 4: The Sentence Doctor

Even more important than a logical structure is the content of your essay. Generalizations need to be supported with exact and specific details, which you are free to make up. Your choice of words needs to be precise, your sentences varied, and your paragraphs unified. Your paragraphs should have connections between them so that your whole essay flows from one thought to another. Let us look at some of the sentence elements that make up good paragraphs.

Parallelism

Your thesis statement should use parallel form. Parallel writing serves to aid casual readers, impress test evaluators, and excite English teachers. The preceding sentence is an example of parallel writing—as were the sample thesis statements in the previous section. Parallel writing occurs when a series of phrases or sentences follow the same form. In the second sentence of this paragraph, there are three phrases that are parallel that are in the same form: verb, adjective, noun.

Verb	Adjective	Noun
aid	casual	readers
impress	test	evaluators
excite	English	teachers

Parallelism Practice

Test and strengthen your skill at parallelism. Change each sentence to correct faulty parallelism.

1. Ramona bought a necklace that had ruby charms, silver links, and it also had an adjustable clasp.
2. Sweet, playful, and being happy, dogs make the best pets.
3. Being healthy is more desirable than to be wealthy.
4. To be a good doctor requires patience, dedication, and having good ethics.
5. Exhausted, but with dedication, the tennis player kept chasing down balls.
6. To be considered for this job you need to have impeccable references, on-the-job experience, and to retain the services of a knowledgeable headhunter.

Answers

1. Ramona bought a necklace that had ruby charms, silver links, and an adjustable clasp.
2. Sweet, playful, and happy, dogs make the best pets.
3. To be a good doctor requires patience, dedication, and ethics.
4. To be a good doctor requires patience, dedication, and good ethics.
5. Exhausted, but dedicated, the tennis player kept chasing down balls.
6. To be considered for this job you need to have impeccable references, on-the-job experience, and a knowledgeable headhunter.

Varied Sentence Structure

Within your paragraph, your sentences should be varied. It makes your essay more interesting and shows the test evaluators that you have mastered different sentence structures.

There are two types of sentence variation: sentence length and sentence structure. Sentence length should not be a problem. Put in some long sentences and some short ones. For varying the structure of a sentence, you might need to brush up on parts of speech and different types of clauses and phrases. If this is the case, go to your local library and check out a book on grammar, or check out some of the books on writing listed at the end of this chapter. The idea is not to be able to name all the different types of clauses, but only to be able to add some variety to your writing. The following exercise provides a few examples of various sentence structures.

Practice with Varied Sentence Structures
Rewrite the sentences so that they begin with the part of speech indicated.
1. The cat scurried away quickly. (adverb)
2. The runner, muscular from weight-lifting, won the marathon. (adjective)
3. One must be limber to be a good gymnast. (infinitive)
4. I store my scrapbook under my bed. (prepositional phrase)
5. I hit an ice patch skiing down the slope. (participle)
6. The law will not be passed if enough people do not sign the petition. (adverb clause)

Answers
1. Quickly, the cat scurried away.
2. Muscular from weight-lifting, the runner won the marathon.
3. To be a good gymnast, one must be limber.
4. Under my bed I store my scrapbook.
5. Skiing down the slope, I hit an ice patch.
6. If enough people do not sign the petition, the law will not be passed.

For an additional exercise, try writing sentences that begin with these words:

After	Unless
Although	Where
As	Wherever
Because	While
Since	

Dangling Clauses
When beginning your sentences with a clause, try to avoid dangling clauses. A dangling modifier is a word, phrase, or clause that doesn't logically modify any other word in the sentence.

Walking home from school, the wind blew over a rose bush.

It sounds as if the *wind* was walking home from school! Instead you should write:

Walking home from school, I saw the wind blow over a rose bush.

Now the phrase *walking home from school* logically modifies the noun *I*.

If you start off with a clause, make sure that the *who* or *what* referred to in the clause begins the next part of the sentence.

Look for dangling clauses in the first body paragraph from the last lesson. You should find two.

In my opinion, a uniform policy will benefit parents. Because they are all the same style and shape and usually very well made, children can use the hand-me-downs of older siblings or other children. Parents they were also able to save money by buying fewer school clothes for their children. Children, who are often demanding, will have already agreed on what clothes their parents will need to buy so there will be fewer arguments over clothes for school their parents *will need to buy. Children and teachers like it too. Parents are generally in favor of uniforms because you do not have to provide your children with a different matched set of clothes for each day. After buying uniforms the first year, more peace was reportedly experienced by 95% of the parents interviewed and many surveys reported that it saved them an average of $100–$200 in clothing costs.*

Did you find them? Look at the second sentence.

Because they are all the same style and shape and usually very well made, children can use the hand-me-downs of older siblings or other children.

What is the same style and shape? The sentence says the children are. Here is a corrected version:

Because they are all the same style and shape and usually very well made, uniforms can be passed down from an older child to a younger one, or even sold.

Now look at the last sentence of the paragraph.

After buying uniforms the first year, more peace was reportedly experienced by 95% of the parents interviewed and many surveys reported that it saved them an average of $100–$200 in clothing costs.

Was it the peace that was buying the uniforms? Let's correct it:

On a recent survey, 95% of parents new to school uniforms attributed an increased feeling of peace to the adoption of the uniform policy. Parents also reportedly saved an average of $100–$200 on school clothes per child the first year.

Opinion Starters

There's a problem with the first sentence of that paragraph, too. Never start a sentence with "In my opinion" or "I think." If you didn't think it, you wouldn't be writing it. The first sentence of the first body paragraph should read simply:

A uniform policy will benefit parents.

Over and Over

Avoid redundancy. Try to keep your sentences as succinct as possible without losing meaning. Make every word and phrase count. Here's an example of a redundant sentence from the first body paragraph:

Children, who are often demanding, will have already agreed on what clothes their parents will need to buy so there will be fewer arguments over clothes for school their parents will need to buy.

The phrase *will need to buy* is in there twice. Get rid of it. *Children, who are often demanding* can be changed to *Demanding children*. The words *for school* can be left out, because that's a given. So now you have a shorter, more effective sentence:

Demanding children will have already agreed on what clothes their parents will need to buy, so there will be fewer arguments.

> **HOT TIP**
> Make sure you have a quality eraser—unless you are perfect! Find an eraser that will erase pencil marks from newsprint without leaving smudges or tearing. Avoid replacing a word with another by writing darker over the first word without erasing first. When you need to add a word, avoid "^" marks. Erase the words before and after the word you will put in, and put three words in place of two.

Sentence Stowaways and Sentence Order

Avoid writing sentences that are not on the same general topic as the rest of the paragraph. Did you notice the stowaway in the paragraph on parents? The sentence Children and teachers like it too does not belong in that paragraph.

The order of the sentences in your paragraph is just as important as the order of the paragraphs in your essay. If you are writing about money parents will save, put all the sentences on money together. Provide transitions for your sentences, just as you did with your paragraphs. You can join sentences with words such as *besides, second, lastly,* and so on, or you can add subtopic sentences.

Try rearranging the paragraph on parents in a logical order. You have two subtopics: money and peace in the family. So add a subtopic sentence to announce the first subidea:

First, uniforms would save parents money.

The fake survey you added at the end of the paragraph reports statistics on both money and peace, so that's a great way to tie the two topics together. The rest of the sentences should all fit under one of the two subtopics. If you have something that doesn't fit, just leave it out. Here's one way to provide a more logical organization:

A uniform policy will benefit parents. First, uniforms will save parents money. Parents will not have to provide their children with a different matched set of clothes for each day, so they will need to buy fewer school clothes for their children. Because uniforms are all the same style and shape and usually very well made, they can be passed down from an older child to a younger one, or even sold. On a recent survey, parents new to school uniforms reportedly saved a whopping $100-$200 on school clothes per child the first year. The survey also reported that 95% of parents attributed an increased feeling of peace to the adoption of the uniform policy. Children will have already agreed on what clothes their parents will need to buy, so there will be fewer arguments.

Writing 5: Finishing Touches

The scorers who read your essay will be on the lookout for precise wording and careful, accurate usage. This lesson will review some common errors.

Punctuation Deficit

A question mark goes at the end of a question. Use few, if any, exclamation points in your essay and always end your sentences with a period. There are many rules for using commas. Here are the most common places for a comma:

- at the end of long clauses
- to separate three or more words in a series
- between the clauses of a compound sentence
- around nonessential words and clauses
- wherever the meaning of the sentence would not be clear without one

If these rules aren't familiar, you can find more information in the same books listed at the end of this chapter.

As you proofread, check to see whether your essay flows well. If additional punctuation is necessary to get your point across, use it—but don't go overboard by throwing in commas where they are not necessary. Can you find the punctuation errors in the following paragraph?

Not only are parents happy to see a uniform policy in place, but their children benefit as well. If you were from a low-income home wouldn't you feel bad if you were not dressed as well as your peers. Children who dress differently are usually alienated from cliques at school and left to feel like outsiders. Often they are teased unmercifully. Dressing in uniform eliminates that problem. Instead you feel a sense of belonging. You are less distractd by cumparing your clothes to others so you are more apd to be relaxed and queiter in school. This enables them to learn more. Children might be happy with the school uniform policy but not as happy as their teachers and principals

> **HOT TIP**
>
> Spend the last few minutes of exam time proofreading to see whether you included everything you had to say, used the same verb tense and person throughout, and whether your words are clear. There is no time for big revisions, but check for such details as periods after sentences and spelling.

The second sentence is a question; it should have a question mark. Because the question doesn't start until after a phrase, the phrase should be set off by a comma.

If you were from a low-income home, wouldn't you feel bad if you were not dressed as well as your peers?

There could be a comma after *Instead* at the beginning of the fifth sentence. This comma may not be necessary in some circumstances, but you are changing the flow of thought here, and you want the readers to know it.

Instead, you feel a sense of belonging.

The sixth sentence contains a compound sentence that should be set off with a comma. The last sentence could also use a comma to separate a long clause from the main sentence, particularly since you are once again switching gears. Lastly, don't let the fact that you're almost done make you forget to put a period at the end of the last sentence.

You are less distractd by cumparing your clothes to others, so you are more apd to be relaxed and queiter in school. This enables them to learn more. Children might be happy with the school uniform policy, but not as happy as their teachers and principals.

Identity Disorder

Keep the same person throughout the essay: *I* and *me* or *you*, or *they* and *them*. It is all right to address the reader as *you* to ask a question, but the facts and statements should match each other. In the following paragraph, the subject of the first and third sentences is "children." You need to continue to talk about children in the third person throughout the paragraph.

Not only are parents happy to see a uniform policy in place, but their children benefit as well. If you were from a low-income household, wouldn't you feel bad if you were not dressed as well as your peers? Children who dress differently are usually alienated from cliques at school and left to feel like outsiders. Often, they are teased unmercifully. Dressing in uniform eliminates that problem. Instead, they feel a sense of belonging. They are less distractd by cumparing their clothes to others, so they are more apd to be relaxed and queiter in school.

The second sentence is not talking about children, but is addressing the reader, so it's OK to use *you* and *your*. The last two sentences talk about children, not about the reader, so those sentences should use *they* and *their*, not *you* and *your*.

Spelling Abnormality Disorder

You have to write quickly during the exam, but you should save a couple of minutes at the end to check your work for spelling errors. Often, our minds go faster than our pencils, and left alone, our pencils make a lot of mistakes. Did you find the misspelled words in the second body paragraph on school uniforms?

> They are less distractd by cumparing their clothes to others so they are more apd to be relaxed and queiter in school.

Let's fix it:

> They are less distracted by comparing their clothes to others so they are more apt to be relaxed and quieter in school.

Forked Tongue Disease

Be on the lookout for words or even sentences that might have two different meanings. Now that we've fixed the spelling errors in the previous sentence, look again to see how it might be confusing. Does the sentence mean that comparing their clothes is less distracting? And what are they comparing their clothes to? To other people? There are too many meanings for this sentence. It needs to be revised.

> Children do not need to compare their clothing with that of others, so they have fewer distractions.

Less Than Insufficient Mistreatment

Remember to use problem words correctly. Try to avoid double negatives, but if you must use them, make sure you are saying what you really mean. If you have time, you can brush up on other problem words such as *lay* and *lie*, *all together* and *altogether*, and so on. Discussions on these topics can be found in the grammar books listed at the end of this chapter. Check the problem words in the following sentences from the third body paragraph.

> There is less competition in school so there is less fights. The reason is because there is less bullying and teasing and there is a lot less complaints.

The word *fewer* refers to a quantity that can be counted.

> There are fewer boys in the class.
> There are fewer mistakes in this paragraph than in the last one.

Less refers to a quantity that cannot be counted, but might be able to be measured.

> There is less water in that cup now that you drank from it.

In this sentence, competition cannot be counted, so *less* is the right word. But the number of fights can be counted, so *fewer* should replace *less*. In the second sentence, the bullying and teasing in general are hard to count, so *less* is the right word. If the sentence was worded to read "incidences of teasing," then *fewer* would be used because incidences can be counted. Complaints can be counted, so *fewer* should be used. *Fewer* takes the verb *are* and *less* takes the verb *is*.

You can also get rid of the redundant *The reason is because*. Maybe you can show off some parallelism here. And why not name the actors in this sentence?

> Because there is less competition in school, teachers and administrators report that there are fewer fights, less bullying, and fewer complaints from the students.

Tense All Over

Unless there is a very good reason for doing otherwise, the same tense should be used throughout your essay.

The tense of the sentence should change only if you are writing about actions or events that take place at different times. See whether you can find the tense mistakes in the following paragraph.

> *Uniforms cost no extra money for teachers and administrators yet the benefits are great. Because there is less competition in school, teachers and administrators report that there are fewer fights, less bullying, and fewer complaints from the students. Instead, principals and teachers were able to use uniforms to build school pride and loyalty. Administrators and teachers will be able to concentrate on what they love to do most, teach, instead of dealing with problems from children and parents.*

The first part of the paragraph is in present tense. The past tense verb *were able* in the third sentence should be changed to the present *are able*. In the last sentence, the future tense *will be able* should be also be changed to the present *are able*.

> *Instead, principals and teachers are able to use uniforms to build school pride and loyalty. Administrators and teachers are able to concentrate on what they love to do most, teach, instead of dealing with problems from children and parents.*

Sewing It Up

Notice how the few remaining problems with transitions have been cleaned up in this final version of the essay on school uniforms. The body paragraph on teachers and administrators ended with too strong a statement—no one will believe that school personnel will have *no* problems from children just because of uniforms—so that statement has been softened. This final version also has a title.

In Praise of School Uniforms

Imagine a school auditorium full of alert children, all dressed neatly in blue and white uniforms, reciting the Pledge of Allegiance. Imagine these same children happily running out to play in their blue shorts and white oxford shirts, playing tag and flying on swings. Whether or not to dress public school children alike has been the subject of much controversy in recent decades. Opponents suggest that requiring uniforms will stifle children's ability to choose, squash necessary individuality, and infringe on the rights of children and families. Although there is some justification for these arguments, the benefits of uniforms far outweigh the disadvantages. Adopting a uniform policy will benefit parents, children, and the school staff.

A uniform policy will benefit parents. Uniforms save parents money. Parents will not have to provide their children with a different matched set of clothes for each day, so fewer school clothes will be needed. Because uniforms are all the same style and shape and usually very well made, they can be passed down from an older child to a younger one, or even sold. On a recent survey, parents new to school uniforms estimated they saved up to $1,000 on school clothes per child the first year alone. The survey also reported that 95% of parents attributed an increased feeling of peace to the adoption of the uniform policy. Children will have already agreed on what clothes their parents will need to buy, so there will be fewer arguments on this often touchy subject.

Not only are parents happy to see a uniform policy in place, but their children benefit as well. If you were from a low-income home, wouldn't you feel badly if you were not dressed as well as your peers? Children who dress differently are usually alienated from cliques at school and left to feel like outsiders. Often they are teased unmercifully. Dressing in uniform eliminates that problem. Instead, uniformed children feel an increased sense of belonging that enables them to be more relaxed and quieter in school. Children do not need to compare their clothing with that of others, so they have fewer distractions during their learning time. Children like the policy because there is less nagging at home and dressing for school is much easier.

Parents and children are not the only ones who are better off with school uniforms. Teachers and administrators love them too. Uniforms cost the school no extra money, yet the benefits are great. Because there is less competition in school, teachers and administrators report that less time is spent mediating because there are fewer fights, less bullying, and fewer complaints from students. Administrators and teachers can use the time they save to do what they are paid to do—build school loyalty, form young minds, and teach basic skills. Teachers report a more peaceful classroom, and administrators report a more cooperative student body.

Adopting a uniform policy will lighten the burden of parents. It will promote cheerfulness and scholarship in children. Lastly, it will free the time and talents of teachers and administrators. What are we waiting for? We need to talk to our teachers, principals, and school boards, and give our children all the tools we can that will enhance their growth and development.

More Help with Reading, Math, and Writing

If any or all of the three subjects covered in the mini-course are especially tough for you, you may want to consider doing some further reading. Following is a list of particularly useful books for preparing for the skills tested on the CBEST.

Reading
- *501 Reading Comprehension Questions*, 4th edition (LearningExpress)
    Fast, focused practice to help you improve your skills.
- *Reading Comprehension Success in 20 Minutes a Day*, 4th edition (LearningExpress)
    A 20-step book that covers all the basics of reading well; especially useful for those preparing for exams like the CBEST.

Book List
The best way to improve your reading skills is to read as often as you can. Here is a list of well-known books that may interest you:

Running with Scissors by Augusten Burroughs (Autobiography)

A Long Way Gone: Memoirs of a Boy Soldier by Ishmael Beah (Autobiography)

To Kill a Mockingbird by Harper Lee (Coming of Age)

The Perks of Being a Wallflower by Stephen Chbosky (Coming of Age)

The Stand by Stephen King (Horror)

Rosemary's Baby by Ira Levin (Horror)

Fahrenheit 451 by Ray Bradbury (Science Fiction)

The Giver by Lois Lowry (Science Fiction)

Band of Brothers: E Company, 506th Regiment, 101st Airborne from Normandy to Hitler's Eagle's Nest by Stephen E. Ambrose (War)

The Art of War by Sun Tzu (War)

Harry Potter and the Deathly Hallows by J.K. Rowling (Fantasy)

Eragon by Christopher Paolini (Fantasy)

The Good Earth by Pearl S. Buck (Historical Fiction)

The Book Thief by Markus Zusak (Historical Fiction)

Along Came a Spider by James Patterson (Thriller)

The Bourne Identity by Robert Ludlum (Thriller)

A Brief History of Time by Stephen W. Hawking (Science)

A Short History of Nearly Everything by Bill Bryson (Science)

Math

- *Algebra Success in 20 Minutes a Day, 4th edition* (LearningExpress)

  Equations, inequalities, powers, and roots—master algebra now!

- *Geometry Success in 20 Minutes a Day, 3rd edition* (LearningExpress)

  Focused practice to help refine your geometry skills.

- *Math Essentials, 3rd edition* (LearningExpress)

  If you have trouble with fractions, decimals, or percents, this book offers an easy, step-by-step review.

- *1001 Math Problems, 3rd edition* (LearningExpress)

  Fast, focused practice to help you improve your math skills!

- *Practical Math Success in 20 Minutes a Day, 4th edition* (LearningExpress)

  Provides review of basic math skills and easy-to-follow examples with opportunities for practice.

- *Seeing Numbers* (LearningExpress)

  Specifically designed for the visual learner, this book explores shapes from many different perspectives.

- *501 Algebra Questions, 2nd edition* (LearningExpress)

  Covers basic to advanced algebra skills.

Writing

- *Grammar Essentials, 3rd edition* (LearningExpress)

  Gives a thorough review of all the rules of basic grammar; lots of exercises and examples make for a painless, and even fun, learning experience.

- *Grammar Success in 20 Minutes a Day, 2nd edition* (LearningExpress) A thorough and concise guide to grammar essentials with hundreds of practice questions.

- *501 Grammar and Writing Questions, 4th edition* (LearningExpress)

  Learn how to spot common grammar mistakes; compose correct sentences; organize clear, concise paragraphs; and much more!

- *Write Better Essays in Just 20 Minutes a Day, 2nd edition* (LearningExpress)

  Your guide to top test scores, this book teaches the mechanics of good essay writing. It's like having a personal tutor!

- *Writing Skills Success in 20 Minutes a Day, 4th edition* (LearningExpress)

  Covers all the basics of writing through step-by-step instruction and exercises; especially useful for those preparing for exams such as the CBEST.

CHAPTER

CBEST PRACTICE EXAM 1

CHAPTER SUMMARY
Here is another sample test based on the California Basic Educational Skills Test (CBEST). After working through the CBEST Mini-Course in Chapter 4, take this test to see how much your score has improved.

Like the actual CBEST, the exam that follows consists of three sections: 50 questions on Reading, 50 questions on Mathematics, and two essay topics in the Writing section. For this exam, you should simulate the actual test-taking experience as closely as you can. Find a quiet place to work where you won't be disturbed. Tear out the answer sheet on the next page and use a number 2 pencil to fill in the circles. Write your essays on a separate piece of paper. Allow yourself four hours for the exam: one and a half hours each for the reading and math sections and a half-hour each for the two essays. Set a timer or stopwatch, but do not worry too much if you go over the allotted time on this practice exam. You can work more on timing when you take the second practice exam in Chapter 6.

After the exam, use the answer key that follows it to see how you did and to find out why the correct answers are correct. As was the case for the diagnostic test, the answer key is followed by a section on how to score your exam.

LEARNINGEXPRESS ANSWER SHEET

Section 1: Reading Comprehension

Section 2: Mathematics

Section 1: Reading Comprehension

Answer questions 1–8 on the basis of the following passage.

(1) Produced in 1959, Lorraine Hansberry's play *A Raisin in the Sun* was a quietly revolutionary work that depicted African-American life in a fresh, new, and realistic way. The play made her the youngest American, the first African American, and the fifth woman to win the New York Drama Critics' Circle Award for Best Play of the Year. In 1961, it was produced as a film starring Sydney Poitier, and the play has since become a classic, providing inspiration for an entire generation of African-American writers.

(2) Hansberry was not only an artist but also a political activist and the daughter of activists. Born in Chicago in 1930, she was a member of a prominent family devoted to civil rights. Her father was a successful real estate broker who won an anti-segregation case before the Illinois Supreme Court in the mid-1930s, and her uncle was a Harvard professor. In her home, Hansberry was privileged to meet many influential cultural and intellectual leaders. Among them were artists and activists such as Paul Robeson, W.E.B. DuBois, and Langston Hughes.

(3) The success of *A Raisin in the Sun* helped gain an audience for her passionate views on social justice. It mirrors one of Hansberry's central artistic efforts, to free many people from the smothering effects of stereotyping by depicting the <u>wide array</u> of personality types and aspirations that exist within one Southside Chicago family. *A Raisin in the Sun* was followed by another play, produced in 1964, *The Sign in Sidney Brustein's Window*. This play is about an intellectual in Greenwich Village, New York City, a man who is open-minded and generous of spirit who, as Hansberry wrote, "cares about it all. It takes too much energy not to care."

(4) Lorraine Hansberry died on the final day of the latter play's run on Broadway. Her early death, at the age of 34, was unfortunate, as it cut short a brilliant and promising career, one that, even in its short span, changed the face of American theater. After her death, however, her influence continued to be felt. A dramatic adaptation of her autobiography, *To Be Young, Gifted, and Black*, consisted of vignettes based on Hansberry's plays, poems, and other writings. It was produced off Broadway in 1969 and appeared in book form the following year. Her play, *Les Blancs*, a drama set in Africa, was produced in 1970; and *A Raisin in the Sun* was adapted as a musical, *Raisin*, which won a Tony award in 1973.

(5) Even after her death, Hansberry's dramatic works have helped gain an audience for her essays and speeches on wide-ranging topics, from world peace to the evils of the mistreatment of minorities, no matter what their race, and especially for her works on the civil rights struggle and on the effort by Africans to be free of colonial rule. She was a woman, much like the characters in her best-known play, who was determined to be free of racial, cultural, or gender-based constraints.

1. The writer of the passage suggests that Hansberry's political beliefs had their origins in her experience as
   a. the daughter of politically active parents.
   b. a successful playwright in New York.
   c. a resident of Southside Chicago.
   d. an intellectual in Greenwich Village.
   e. a civil rights activist.

2. The main purpose of the passage is to
   a. praise Lorraine Hansberry's writings and illustrate their artistic and political influence.
   b. summarize Lorraine Hansberry's best-known works.
   c. demonstrate that if one is raised in a well-educated family, such as Lorraine Hansberry's, one is likely to succeed.
   d. show Lorraine Hansberry's difficult struggle and ultimate success as a young female writer.
   e. persuade students to read *A Raisin In The Sun*.

3. Hansberry's father earned his living as
   a. a civil rights worker.
   b. a banker.
   c. a real estate broker.
   d. an artist and activist.
   e. an attorney.

4. Paragraph 3 suggests that Hansberry's main purpose in writing *A Raisin in the Sun* was to
   a. win her father's approval.
   b. break down stereotypes.
   c. show people how interesting her own family was.
   d. earn the right to produce her own plays.
   e. win a Best Play award.

5. By including paragraphs 4 and 5, the author most likely intended to show that
   a. the civil rights struggle continued even after Hansberry died.
   b. Hansberry actually wrote more poems and essays than she did plays.
   c. *Raisin in the Sun* was more successful after Hansberry's death than it was before she died.
   d. Hansberry's work continued to influence people even after her death.
   e. Hansberry died unusually young.

6. According to the passage, how many women had won the New York Drama Critics' Circle Award for Best Play of the Year *before* Lorraine Hansberry did?
   a. none
   b. one
   c. four
   d. five
   e. six

7. As it is used in paragraph 3, the underlined phrase *wide array* most nearly means
   a. variety.
   b. gathering.
   c. arrangement.
   d. decoration.
   e. features.

8. According to the passage, which of the following dramatic works was based most directly on Hansberry's life?
   a. *A Raisin in the Sun*
   b. *Les Blancs*
   c. *The Sign in Sidney Brustein's Window*
   d. *To Be Young, Gifted, and Black*
   e. *Raisin*

Use the excerpt below from an index to answer question 9.

> Fainting
>   dealing with, 269–270
>   prevention, 269
> Falling and related injuries
>   broken bones, 268–269
>   prevention, 267
> Financial concerns, 21, 22, 23, 82–93
>   assessment of resources, 62
>   conservatorships, 83
>   financial advisors, 90-91
>   paying for equipment and supplies, 129
>   personal representatives, 89
>   power of attorney, 31, 65, 83, 99
>   private insurance, 65–71
>   questions about medical billing, 43
>   trusts, 82–83
>   veterans benefits, 68
>   wills, 82
> First aid, kids, 275
> Food, see Meals and feeding, Nutrition and diet
> Foot care, 170–171
> Foster care homes, 14, 18, 19–20, 66

9. On which page would one look to find information about how to designate a person to help with money decisions?
   a. 14
   b. 62
   c. 68
   d. 89
   e. 267

Answer questions 10–13 on the basis of the following passage.

Hypoglycemia, a condition marked by an extremely low level of blood sugar (glucose), affects one out of 1,000 people in the United States. The causes of hypoglycemia can include alcohol consumption; certain medications and cancers; kidney, liver, or heart disease; hormonal deficiencies; or hyperinsulinemia, a condition in which the pancreas releases too much insulin into the bloodstream.

Although insulin is the hormone primarily responsible for maintaining normal blood sugar levels, these levels can also become too low if the body's glucose production is interrupted. The liver and the kidneys are the organs responsible for glucose production, using a process called *gluconeogenesis*. Therefore, diseases of the liver and kidneys that impair gluconeogenesis can result in hypoglycemia.

Some symptoms of hypoglycemia are confusion, double or blurred vision, heart palpitations, anxiety, sweating, hunger, and seizures. To treat hypoglycemia, its underlying cause must first be determined. Urgent initial treatment, though, involves raising blood sugar levels by eating food or by taking glucose tablets.

10. The immediate concern of a person suffering from hypoglycemia is to
   a. get salt into the body.
   b. raise the body temperature.
   c. decrease blood sugar levels.
   d. increase blood sugar levels.
   e. determine its underlying cause.

11. According to the passage, if gluconeogenesis doesn't occur, then
   a. blood glucose levels can get too high.
   b. the body can't store glucose.
   c. hypoglycemia will always result.
   d. insulin production will be halted.
   e. blood glucose levels can get too low.

12. The main purpose of the passage is to
   a. warn people about the dangers of hypoglycemia.
   b. outline the causes of hypoglycemia.
   c. give an overview of hypoglycemia.
   d. offer treatment options for hypoglycemia.
   e. explain how the liver and kidneys can cause hypoglycemia.

13. This passage is most likely taken from
   a. a nutrition textbook.
   b. a scientific journal.
   c. a newspaper column.
   d. an essay about insulin deficiencies.
   e. a series on different blood sugar diseases.

Answer questions 14 and 15 on the basis of the following passage.

Poet William Blake believed that true religion is revealed through art, not through nature. For Blake, it is through art also that eternity is revealed. One does not have to die to reach eternity; eternity is the moment of vision. It is only through the reordering of sense impressions by the creative imagination that we are able, as Blake says in his "Auguries of Innocence," "To see the World in a Grain of Sand /. . . And Eternity in an hour."

14. Which of the following would best describe what Blake meant by the words *To see the World in a Grain of Sand / . . . And Eternity in an hour*?
   a. a moment of mystical enlightenment
   b. a religious conversion
   c. a moment of artistic inspiration
   d. an hallucinatory experience
   e. a return to a state of being without sin

15. Which of the following defines Blake's view of *nature* as described in the passage?
   a. the raw stuff of which the world is made but which does not represent ultimate reality
   b. the work of God in a state of innocence before it is corrupted by human beings
   c. the world made up of base and corrupt material before it is changed by the perception of the artist at the "moment of vision"
   d. the temporal world that will perish, as opposed to the world of artistic vision that will last forever
   e. the real world as it is perceived by ordinary people, as opposed to the fantasy world of the artist

Answer questions 16–18 on the basis of the following passage.

The word *autobahn* brings to mind speed demons driving high-performance sports cars at speeds near 200 miles per hour (321.9 kilometers per hour). But this speedway is mostly a pipe dream because the autobahn is just another word for the German highway system.

There are three autobahns, and only limited areas of these federal highways are without speed limits. On that small portion of roadway that doesn't have a speed limit, drivers can still break the law if they drive too fast through construction zones or cities. Police also expect drivers to travel at a speed appropriate for the weather. So racing down rain-slicked streets can earn a driver a ticket, too.

Germans are particularly strict in their traffic laws. _____ If the police stop a driver who is eating behind the wheel, they can give the driver a fine because this is driving in a distracted state. There is absolutely no passing on the right, and the left lane can only be used for passing. Drivers must leave at least two seconds of reaction time between cars on the road. Following too close is reason to suspend a driver's license for as long as three months.

16. Which sentence, if inserted into the blank line in the third paragraph, would be most consistent with the writer's purpose and intended audience?
   a. Some of the laws are even stricter than traffic laws in the United States.
   b. So many traffic laws have led to a surge in law offices specializing in traffic offenses.
   c. Tourists are a favorite target of German police, as they are not likely to know all of the traffic laws.
   d. The German traffic laws are the strictest in the world.
   e. Speed is the one area of German traffic law that is relaxed.

17. Which of the following is the best meaning of the phrase *a pipe dream* as it is used in the first paragraph of the passage?
   a. a part of a car
   b. a fantasy that won't come true
   c. something to hope for
   d. something that is smoky or foggy
   e. an illegal activity

18. Which of the following best organizes the main topics addressed in this passage?
   a. I. Definition of *autobahn*
       II. Speed and the autobahn
       III. Other rules of the road
   b. I. Location of the autobahn
       II. Cars on the autobahn
       III. Traffic laws
   c. I. High-performance cars
       II. Speed records on the autobahn
       III. Driving rules in Germany
   d. I. Speeds on European highways
       II. How fast to drive
       III. Speed-related laws
   e. I. Comparing U.S. and German cars
       II. Driving at high speeds
       III. Other traffic laws

Answer questions 19 and 20 on the basis of the following passage.

The fictional setting of Toni Morrison's novel *Sula*—the African-American section of Medallion, Ohio, a community called "the Bottom"—is a place where people, and even natural things, are apt to go awry, to break from their prescribed boundaries, a place where bizarre and unnatural happenings and strange reversals of the ordinary are commonplace. The very naming of the setting of *Sula* is a turning-upside-down of the expected; the Bottom is located high up in the hills. The novel is furthermore filled with images of mutilation, both psychological and physical. A great part of the lives of the characters, therefore, is taken up with making sense of the world, setting boundaries and devising methods to control what is essentially uncontrollable. One of the major devices used by the people of the Bottom is the seemingly universal one of creating a _____—in this case, the title character Sula—upon which to project both the evil they perceive outside themselves and the evil in their own hearts.

19. Based on the description of the setting of the novel *Sula*, which of the following adjectives would most likely describe the behavior of many of its residents?
   a. cowardly
   b. artistic
   c. unkempt
   d. arrogant
   e. eccentric

20. Which of the following words would BEST fit into the blank in the final sentence of the passage?
   a. victim
   b. hero
   c. leader
   d. scapegoat
   e. martyr

Answer questions 21–23 on the basis of the following passage.

For centuries, human beings have been trying to find an answer to the nature versus nurture debate. The nature theory proposes that human behavior is determined by DNA, the nurture theory that behavior is determined by environment and conditioning. Not many would argue that eye color and hair color are genetically predetermined, but when it comes to more abstract traits such as a shy or thrill-seeking personality, or athletic talent, the debate steamrolls on. Although proponents of the nature theory attribute these _____ traits to genetic encoding, those who believe in the nurture theory point to the many studies on infant and child conditioning that provide evidence that personality, skills, and tendencies can be influenced by environment.

21. Which of the following words would best fit into the blank in the fourth sentence of the passage?
   a. tactile
   b. intangible
   c. ephemeral
   d. mysterious
   e. straightforward

22. The main point of the passage is that
   a. human beings have long pondered nature versus nurture.
   b. everyone agrees that traits like hair color are controlled by DNA.
   c. there are two long-debated, contradictory views on the shaping of abstract human traits.
   d. studies on infants and children provide evidence that the nurture theory is true.
   e. human beings will never come up with an answer to the nature versus nurture debate.

23. The tone of the author can best be described as
   a. indifferent.
   b. persuasive.
   c. passionate.
   d. informational.
   e. biased.

Answer questions 24–26 on the basis of the following passage.

(1) A human embryo is smaller than the period at the end of this sentence, but that tiny embryo contains dozens of stem cells. (2) Stem cells start out as blank slates. (3) They have not developed into any particular type of cell. (4) Stem cells provide doctors and researchers with amazing opportunities. (5) They can develop into every kind of cell found in the

human body. (6) Researchers and doctors in all fields of medicine are looking into therapies involving stem cells. (7) Politicians and the public debate the ethics of using stem cells. (8) In order for stem-cell therapy to become practical, doctors and researchers must learn how to develop the stem cells into the desired tissues or organs.

24. Which of the following numbered sentence of the passage best expresses an opinion rather than a fact?
   a. Sentence 1
   b. Sentence 2
   c. Sentence 3
   d. Sentence 4
   e. Sentence 5

25. Which of the following numbered sentence is least relevant to the main idea of the paragraph?
   a. Sentence 9
   b. Sentence 8
   c. Sentence 7
   d. Sentence 6
   e. Sentence 5

26. Which title best conveys the main idea of the passage?
   a. Why We Study Stem Cells
   b. Stem Cells: Worth the Risk?
   c. Alzheimer's and Stem Cells
   d. The Future of Stem Cells
   e. Miracles of Medicine

Answer questions 27 and 28 on the basis of the following index from a forest management textbook.

INDEX

fire protection, 51–55, 108, 115

forest conflicts: European, 8, 91–93, 116–117, 133–134, 186–188

forest destruction and ecological decline, 143; and fire, 31–35; and industrialization, 156–173; and railways 27–29; and scientific forestry, 60–61; and villagers, 107, 115–116; and World Wars, 42–43, 46–47

forest fires, 72, 87, 100–105, 124; and pasture, 48, 51–53, 115–118; arson, 51, 122, 126–130; *see also* fire protection

forest law: breaches of, 34–41, 49–52, 55, 70, 115–116, 121–123; *see also* forest conflicts

forest management: and agrarian economy, 104–105, 121, 186–189; and imperial needs, 28, 35; and slash-and-burn farming, 12–18, 48; and commercial orientation of forests, peasant resistance to, 75–76, 89, 99–106

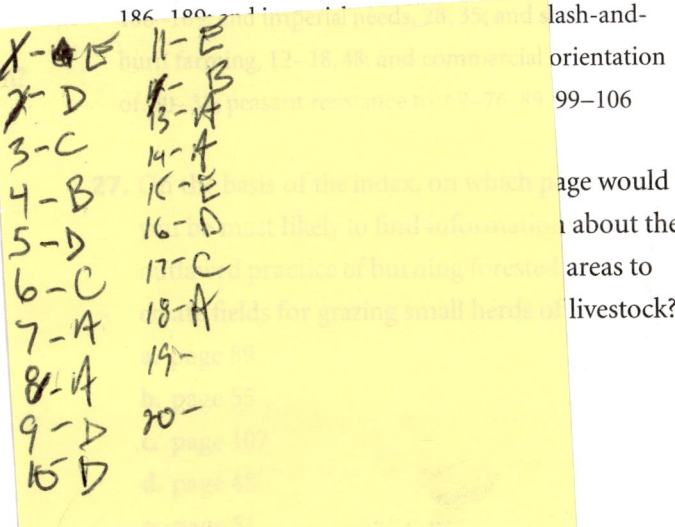

27. On the basis of the index, on which page would you be most likely to find information about the historical practice of burning forested areas to create fields for grazing small herds of livestock?
   a. page 89
   b. page 55
   c. page 107
   d. page 48
   e. page 51

28. On what cause of *forest destruction* does the author of the textbook focus most, from the evidence of the index?
   a. industrialization
   b. fire damage
   c. railroads
   d. ecological decline
   e. scientific forestry

Answer questions 29–31 on the basis of the following passage.

(1) To some, Benjamin Franklin is most well known as one of the Founding Fathers of the United States. (2) But Franklin did more than sign the Declaration of Independence. (3) He was also a scholar, author, printer, scientist, and inventor. (4) As a scientist, he researched electricity and was the first to put forward the model of electrical current we use in modern times by conducting a hazardous experiment. (5) Unbelievably, he proved that lightning was actually electricity by flying a kite during a thunderstorm. (6) The kite was struck by lightning, and Franklin used this newfound knowledge as the basis for his invention of the lightning rod. (7) Other of Franklin's inventions include bifocals and a stove.

(8) Clearly, Franklin was a man of many talents. (9) If he had not been involved in so many different ventures at once, he would have certainly produced more inventions.

29. Which of the following would be the most appropriate title for this passage?
   a. Benjamin Franklin
   b. Benjamin Franklin: A Founding Father
   c. Benjamin Franklin and Electricity
   d. Benjamin Franklin: A Man of Many Talents
   e. Benjamin Franklin: The Early Days

30. Which of the following numbered sentences represents an opinion rather than a fact?
   a. 2
   b. 3
   c. 5
   d. 8
   e. 9

31. Why is the word *Unbelievably* used in sentence 5?
   a. because there was no way to predict whether or not there would be a storm
   b. because that was a dangerous and uncontrollable way to conduct an experiment
   c. because no one had thought of conducting this type of experiment before
   d. because the experiment proved to be successful
   e. because there was no guarantee Franklin could prove his theory correct

Answer questions 32–35 on the basis of the following passage.

Jellyfish are creatures as fascinating as they are intimidating. Not fish at all, "jellies" as they are sometimes called, are actually invertebrates related to sea anemones and corals. Members of the phylum *Cnidaria*, jellyfish possess a structurally simple body plan. The dominant type of jelly has a medusoid—saucer or bell-shaped—form that displays radial symmetry, its body parts radiating from a central axis point. Jellyfish have no head, no heart, no bones, and no brain. Instead, they have a nerve net, which consists of receptors that can detect light, odor and other stimuli. _____.

Not all jellyfish sting, but the ones that do can cause a range of reactions in humans, varying from mild skin irritation to death. The stinging mechanism, or cnidoblast, is located on a jellyfish's tentacles or oral arms. Inside the cnidoblast is a nematocyst, which is a capsule that contains a trigger and the stinging structure. Although the stinging structure varies between the different species of jellyfish, it is usually made up of a hollow coiled thread lined with barbs. When nematocysts make contact with another object, they launch their threads into the jellyfish's victims, injecting toxins upon contact. Just one tentacle can have hundreds or even thousands of nematocysts, and their sting usually paralyzes or kills small prey.

32. Which if the following sentences, if inserted into the blank line, would best end the first paragraph and lead into the second?
    a. Some species of jellyfish are considered a delicacy by humans.
    b. Jellyfish cannot control their movements efficiently, and thus depend mostly on the changing tides for locomotion.
    c. Jellyfish are meat-eaters, and primarily feed on zooplankton and even other jellyfish.
    d. The best way to treat a jellyfish sting is to douse the affected area with vinegar after removing, with gloves, any tentacles left on the skin.
    e. To feed and defend themselves, jellyfish are equipped with a stinging apparatus.

33. Which of the following information is correct, according to the passage?
    a. Jellyfish are a type of sea anemone.
    b. Most jellyfish do not sting humans.
    c. Cnidoblasts are capsules inside nematocysts, which contain the jellyfish's stinging structure.
    d. Most jellyfish are shaped like a bell or saucer.
    e. Jellyfish and coral have no skeletons.

34. Which of the following choices outlines the main topics addressed in the passage?
    a. I. Explanation of why jellyfish are fascinating
       II. Locomotion methods of jellyfish
    b. I. Description of a jellyfish's body plan
       II. An explanation of the different ways that jellyfish respond to stimuli
    c. I. Biological classification of jellyfish
       II. Description of how jellyfish respond to being threatened by predators
    d. I. Comparison of jellyfish with other cnidarians
       II. Usefulness of the jellyfish's ability to sting
    e. I. General classification and characteristics of jellyfish
       II. Description of the form and function of a jellyfish's stinging apparatus

35. Which of the following best describes the purpose of the passage?
    a. to prove how fascinating and intimidating jellyfish are
    b. to explain the communication methods of jellyfish
    c. to provide a lively description of these mysterious creatures
    d. to describe jellyfish in an informative way
    e. to persuade people to observe jellyfish carefully

Answer question 36 on the basis of the following passage.

A book proposal has three major functions. First, it should sell a publisher on the commercial potential of the as-yet-to-be-written book. Second, the writing in the proposal itself should convince the publisher that the author has the ability to write the book. Finally, the proposal should show that the author has the background necessary to write the book.

36. Which of the following is the best meaning of the word *background* as it is used in the passage?
   a. something behind the main event
   b. something in a subordinated position
   c. one's ability to do something
   d. events leading up to something
   e. facts to help explain something

Answer questions 37–40 on the basis of the following passage.

Typically, the process of recycling paper begins by adding water and chemicals to it in a machine called a "pulper," which chops the paper into tiny pieces. The mixture is heated and eventually turns into a mushy pulp. This phase of the process is known as re-pulping. The pulp then goes through a screening process, where it is forced through a filter that eliminates small contaminants such as plastic or glue. Next, the pulp is cleaned and, if necessary, de-inked.

There are two different ways to de-ink pulp—one of them simply involves washing the pulp with water. Larger particles of ink, however, are removed through a process called flotation. During flotation, the pulp is poured into a large vat where a class of soaplike chemicals called surfactants and compressed air are added. The surfactants cause the pulp to separate from the ink, which then attaches to the air bubbles and rises to the top. These bubbles turn into foam, which is skimmed off and discarded. The use of surfactants, although effective, is costly, and chemicals that can replace them are being researched.

The final stage in the process is for the remaining pulp to be turned into paper. This involves adding chemicals and enough water to make the mixture 99.5% water. This mixture is sprayed onto wire screens in sheets, allowing water to drain from the pulp. As the sheets starts to resemble paper, they are heated, dried, and wound into giant rolls.

Through recycling, Americans recover approximately 50% of all the paper they use. Not all paper can be recycled, however. In fact, some recovered paper contains materials that are not paper fibers, such as those found in shiny magazine pages. Wood fibers, too, have a recycling limit—they can be recycled only five to seven times before they become too weak to be made into paper again.

37. One disadvantage of flotation is
   a. only large particles of ink can be removed.
   b. it is costly.
   c. it is time consuming.
   d. it uses chemicals harmful to the environment.
   e. it is not very effective.

38. The process that removes small contaminants from the pulp is
   a. de-inking.
   b. skimming.
   c. screening.
   d. recycling.
   e. re-pulping.

39. What is the purpose of this passage?
   a. to persuade more people to recycle
   b. to prove that paper recycling is cost-effective
   c. to inform the public about the recycling process
   d. to show that recycling is necessary for preserving the environment
   e. to clarify misconceptions about paper recycling

40. According to the passage, air is sometimes added in the de-inking phase so that
   a. ink separates from the pulp.
   b. the ink floats to the top.
   c. the surfactants are more effective.
   d. fewer surfactants are needed.
   e. the pulp doesn't weaken.

Use the graph below to answer question 41.

Acme Paper Products: Distribution of Products Sold Profits in 2001

Total Profit: $275 million

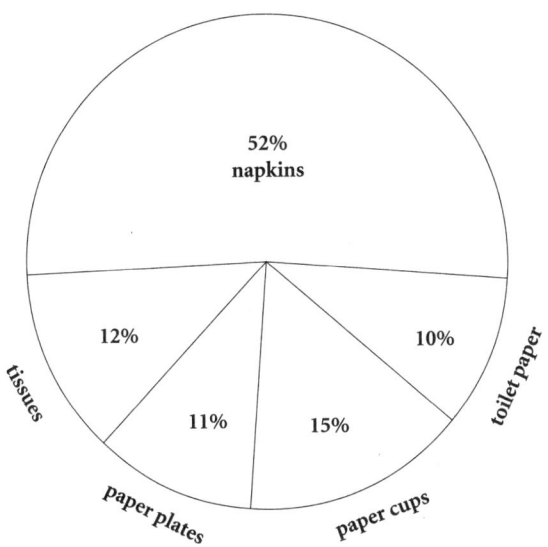

41. What percentage of Acme's products sold are NOT intended for use with food?
- a. 10%
- b. 12%
- c. 15%
- d. 22%
- e. 37%

Answer question 42 on the basis of the following passage.

The Internet has been in widespread use for well over a decade. The Internet allows for the dissemination of a large amount of information at high speeds and low cost. It also allows for anyone to easily conduct research on almost any topic. But information found on the Internet may come from unsubstantiated sources. Information gathered from the Internet should be carefully crosschecked with offline sources. When official documents need to be produced, consulting books, encyclopedias, and journals might still be best.

42. The paragraph best supports the statement that the Internet
- a. has changed considerably since it came into existence over a decade ago.
- b. is most effective when information it offers is double-checked.
- c. is inexpensive.
- d. allows for the dissemination of a lot of information.
- e. should be used for researching only unofficial information.

Answer question 43 on the basis of the following passage.

More and more office workers telecommute from offices in their own homes. The upside of telecommuting is both greater productivity and greater flexibility. Telecommuters produce, on average, 20% more than if they were to work in an office, and their flexible schedule allows them to balance both their family and work responsibilities.

43. The paragraph best supports the statement that telecommuters
- a. have more family responsibilities than workers who travel to the office.
- b. get more work done in a given time period than workers who travel to the office.
- c. produce a better quality work product than workers who travel to the office.
- d. are more flexible in their personal lives than workers who travel to the office.
- e. would do 20% more work if they were to work in an office.

Answer question 44 on the basis of the following passage.

Dermatologists classify sensitive skin four ways: acne, rosacea, skin that stings in contact with certain products, and allergic skin. These four types of sensitive skin are very different from each other. Skin with acne tends to contain oil and bacteria. Using oily products can make acne worse. People with rosacea experience flushing skin or broken blood vessels. People with stinging reactions must determine what chemicals or ingredients cause the stinging reactions and avoid them. Dermatologists can sometimes provide relief for the stinging reaction. People with allergic skin reactions can visit a dermatologist for testing and medications to relieve the allergic reactions.

44. Which of the following statements does NOT fit into the pattern of logic developed in the passage?
    a. It's not surprising that no single skin care product can solve the needs of every person with sensitive skin.
    b. Age and ethnicity make finding an effective skin care routine more complicated.
    c. Unfortunately, no two types of skin are alike.
    d. An appropriate skin care regimen will include cleansing to rid the skin of irritants and protection from future damage.
    e. All people with sensitive skin problems will benefit from using olive-oil-based skin products.

Answer question 45 on the basis of the following passage.

Keeping busy at important tasks is much more motivating than having too little to do. Today's employees are not afraid of responsibility. Most people are willing to take on extra responsibility in order to have more variety on their jobs. Along with more responsibility should come the authority to carry out some important tasks independently.

45. The paragraph best supports the statement that
    a. variety on the job helps increase employee motivation.
    b. employees like responsibility more than authority.
    c. to avoid boredom, many people do more work than their jobs require of them.
    d. today's employees are demanding more independence than ever before.
    e. office jobs in the past have carried little responsibility.

Answer questions 46–50 on the basis of the following passage.

When people discuss genetic cloning, they are generally referring to what is known more formally as "reproductive cloning." There are, however, two other types of cloning: DNA cloning and therapeutic cloning.

DNA cloning involves transferring a DNA fragment from a cell in one organism to a genetic element in another that is capable of self-replication. As this self-replicating element multiplies, the original DNA fragment is reproduced, allowing scientists to use it for research.

Reproductive cloning—like that used to clone the now-infamous sheep Dolly—uses a process called somatic cell nuclear transfer (SCNT) in which scientists transfer the genetic information of an adult cell to a female's egg cell whose nucleus, or center, has been removed. This newly "configured" egg divides, and once it becomes an embryo, it is transferred to the uterus of a female host where it is expected to grow to full term.

Therapeutic cloning involves producing human embryos in a process similar to the first stages of reproductive cloning. From these human embryos, scientist collect stem cells (doing so leaves the embryos inactive), which are valuable for research purposes because they can differentiate into any type of cell in the human body.

46. According to the passage, therapeutic cloning
   a. is similar to the process of reproductive cloning.
   b. has been banned by the federal government.
   c. is used to collect stem cells for research.
   d. has been frowned upon by scientists.
   e. is harmful to the female host.

47. This passage was most likely taken from
   a. a website explaining cloning and issues surrounding it.
   b. a scientific journal for geneticists.
   c. a daily newspaper.
   d. a history textbook.
   e. a government-funded website.

48. The main difference between reproductive cloning and therapeutic cloning is that
   a. reproductive cloning is used to study a specific DNA fragment, and therapeutic cloning is used to cure disease.
   b. in reproductive cloning the embryos are nurtured to grow to full term, and in therapeutic cloning the embryos are destroyed.
   c. reproductive cloning is controversial and therapeutic is not.
   d. an executive order was issued to ban therapeutic cloning but not to ban reproductive cloning.
   e. reproductive cloning is more useful than therapeutic cloning.

49. The best title for the passage would be
   a. Cloning and Its Implications.
   b. Cloning and Federal Intervention.
   c. Cloning: A Summary.
   d. Cloning and Private Funding.
   e. Pros and Cons of Cloning.

50. Toward cloning, it can be inferred that the author feels
   a. passionate.
   b. disapproving.
   c. respectful.
   d. weary.
   e. neutral.

Section 2: Mathematics

Use the following information to answer question 1.

If Linda purchases an item that costs $30 or less, she will pay with cash.
If Linda purchases an item that costs between $30 and $70, she will pay with a check.
If Linda purchases an item that costs $70 or more, she will use a credit card.

1. If Linda recently paid for a certain item using a check, which of the following statements could be true?
   a. The item costs $20.
   b. The item costs $80.
   c. If the item had cost $20 more, she would have paid with cash.
   d. The item costs at least $70.
   e. The item costs more than $25.

2. An elevator went from the bottom to the top of a building at an average speed of four feet/second, remained at the top of the building for 90 seconds, and then returned to the bottom at five feet/second. If the total elapsed time was four and a half minutes, how high is the tower?
   a. 20 feet
   b. 270 feet
   c. 360 feet
   d. 400 feet
   e. 3,600 feet

3. Miriam took a standardized test to measure her performance in reading. She earned a percentile score that showed she performed better than 70% of students who also took the test. Which stanine score could Miriam have received?
   a. 3
   b. 4
   c. 5
   d. 6
   e. 9

4. The price of a new car increases at a rate of about 4% annually. If the current cost of a certain car is $14,000, what will be the approximate cost next year?
   a. $14,040
   b. $14,400
   c. $14,560
   d. $14,800
   e. $15,100

Use the following graph to answer questions 5 and 6.

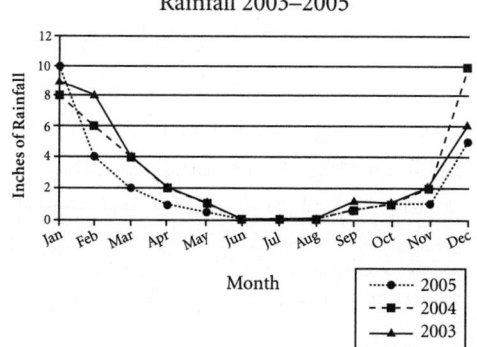

Rainfall 2003–2005

5. What month in 2004 had the most rainfall?
   a. January
   b. February
   c. March
   d. November
   e. December

6. What was the average (mean) rainfall in February for the three years?
   a. 4 inches
   b. 5 inches
   c. 6 inches
   d. 7 inches
   e. 8 inches

7. The Chen family traveled 75 miles to visit relatives. If they traveled $43\frac{1}{3}$ miles before they stopped at a gas station, how far was the gas station from their relatives' house?
   a. $31\frac{2}{3}$ miles
   b. $32\frac{2}{3}$ miles
   c. 35 miles
   d. $38\frac{1}{3}$ miles
   e. $43\frac{1}{3}$ miles

8. Roger has a bowl filled with strawberry and lemon candies. If 3 out of every 8 candies are strawberry, and there are 96 candies in the bowl, how many of the candies are lemon?
   a. 30
   b. 36
   c. 48
   d. 56
   e. 60

Use the table and the information below to answer question 9.

A recent survey polled 2,500 people about their reading habits. The results are as follows:

SURVEY REGARDING READING HABITS	
Books per month	Percentage
0	13
1–3	27
4–6	32
> 6	28

9. How many people surveyed had read books in the last month?
   a. 325
   b. 700
   c. 1,800
   d. 1,825
   e. 2,175

10. A certain university has 36,042 total students. Of these students, 16,534 are male. Approximately how many more women attend the university than men?
   a. 1,500
   b. 2,000
   c. 3,000
   d. 4,000
   e. 4,500

11. The highest elevation is Mount Everest, at 29,028 feet above sea level. The Dead Sea is the lowest elevation, at 1,312 feet below sea level. What is the difference between the two locations?
   a. −29,340 feet
   b. −27,716 feet
   c. 26,404 feet
   d. 27,716 feet
   e. 30,340 feet

12. Statistics show that 6% of the cars at a particular traffic light will run a red light on any given day. If 350 cars went through the intersection today, how many people could be expected to run the red light?
   a. 6
   b. 12
   c. 21
   d. 124
   e. 210

13. A certain congressional district has about 490,000 people living in it. The largest city in the area has 98,000 citizens. Which most accurately portrays the portion of the population made up by that city in the district?
   a. $\frac{1}{5}$
   b. $\frac{1}{4}$
   c. $\frac{2}{9}$
   d. $\frac{3}{4}$
   e. $\frac{4}{5}$

14. A recipe calls for $1\frac{1}{4}$ cups of flour. If Larry wants to make $2\frac{1}{2}$ times the recipe, how much flour does he need?
   a. $2\frac{3}{4}$
   b. $3\frac{1}{8}$
   c. $3\frac{1}{4}$
   d. $3\frac{5}{8}$
   e. $4\frac{1}{4}$

15. Thirty percent of the high school is involved in athletics. If 15% of the athletes play football, what percentage of the whole school plays football?
   a. 4.5%
   b. 9.0%
   c. 15%
   d. 30%
   e. 45%

16. Twenty percent of the people at a restaurant selected the dinner special. If 40 people did not select the special, how many people are eating at the restaurant?
   a. 10
   b. 20
   c. 40
   d. 50
   e. 60

17. John's Market sells milk for $2.24 per gallon. Food Supply sells the same milk for $2.08 per gallon. If Mitzi buys 2 gallons of milk at Food Supply instead of John's, how much will she save?
   a. $0.12
   b. $0.14
   c. $0.32
   d. $0.38
   e. $0.42

18. Kara uses 112 beads to make eight necklaces. If Kara uses the same number of beads on each necklace, how many beads are on each necklace?
   a. 8
   b. 10
   c. 12
   d. 14
   e. 16

Use the following information to answer question 19.

Textbooks are to be ordered in the following quantities:
   History: 24 books at $20 each
   Math: 20 books at $30 each
   Science: 15 books at $25 each

19. What is the total cost of the textbooks?
   a. $1,455
   b. $1,495
   c. $1,500
   d. $1,510
   e. $1,550

20. A small-town emergency room admits a patient on August 3 at 10:42 P.M. and another patient at 1:19 A.M. on August 4. How much time has elapsed between admissions?
   a. 1 hour 19 minutes
   b. 1 hour 37 minutes
   c. 2 hours 23 minutes
   d. 2 hours 37 minutes
   e. 3 hours 23 minutes

21. Nationwide, in one year, there were about 21,500 residential fires associated with furniture. Of these, 11,350 were caused by smoking materials. About what percent of the residential fires were smoking related?
   a. 47%
   b. 49%
   c. 50%
   d. 51%
   e. 53%

22. Jerry was $\frac{1}{3}$ as young as his grandfather 15 years ago. If the sum of their ages is 110, how old is Jerry's grandfather?
   a. 80
   b. 75
   c. 65
   d. 60
   e. 50

23. If $0.875x + 39 = -10$, what is the value of x?
   a. −56
   b. −49
   c. −10
   d. 49
   e. 56

24. An auto parts store delivery van traveled these distances during one week: 109.4 miles, 127.8 miles, 97.3 miles, 128.7 miles, and 225.4 miles. What other information is needed in order to find out how many gallons of gas were used by the delivery van during the week?
   a. the average speed traveled in miles per hour
   b. the cost of gasoline per gallon
   c. the number of drivers
   d. the mileage in miles per gallon for the van
   e. the number of deliveries the van made

The table below shows the relationship between the height of a tree and how long ago it was planted.

Number of Years after Planting	3	4	5
Height of Tree (in feet)	17	21	25

25. Which is the best prediction of the height of the tree seven years after it was planted?
   a. 28 feet
   b. 29 feet
   c. 32 feet
   d. 33 feet
   e. 36 feet

26. Jeremy cooked $2\frac{1}{3}$ dozen muffins for the school bake sale. Nona baked $2\frac{1}{2}$ dozen muffins for the sale. Jaime baked more muffins than Jeremy but less than Nona. Which could be an amount that Jaime baked?
   a. 2.0 dozen
   b. 2.3 dozen
   c. 2.4 dozen
   d. 2.5 dozen
   e. 2.6 dozen

Use the following table to answer question 27.

DISTANCE TRAVELED FROM CHICAGO WITH RESPECT TO TIME	
Time (hours)	Distance from Chicago (miles)
1	60
2	120
3	180
4	240

27. A train moving at a constant speed leaves Chicago for Los Angeles at time $t = 0$. If Los Angeles is 2,000 miles from Chicago, which of the following equations describes the distance from Los Angeles at any time t?
   a. $D(t) = 60t - 2{,}000$
   b. $D(t) = 60t$
   c. $D(t) = 2{,}000 - 60t$
   d. $D(t) = \frac{2{,}000}{60t}$
   e. $D(t) = 2{,}000 + 60t$

Use the following table and the information to answer question 28.

Felipe is planning to get cable Internet service. Two service providers, A and B, offer different rates as shown below.

CABLE INTERNET SERVICE RATES			
Provider	Free Hours	Base Charge	Hourly Charge
A	17.5	$20.00	$1.00
B	20	$20.00	$1.50

28. If Felipe plans on using 25 hours of cable Internet service per month, which of the following statements is true?
    a. Provider A will be cheaper.
    b. Provider B will be cheaper.
    c. The answer cannot be determined from the information given.
    d. The answer cannot be determined but could be if no hours were free.
    e. The providers will cost the same per month.

29. Rico found gasoline selling for $3.49 per gallon on Wednesday. On Thursday, he saw it selling for $3.399 per gallon. On Friday, he saw gas selling for $3.409 per gallon. Which sentence correctly shows the relationship between the numbers?
    a. 3.49 > 3.399 > 3.409
    b. 3.399 > 3.49 > 3.409
    c. 3.49 > 3.409 > 3.399
    d. 3.399 > 3.409 > 3.49
    e. 3.409 > 3.399 > 3.49

Use the following information to answer question 30.

Roger, Lucy, Mike, and Samantha are cousins. They all practice unique sports: One enjoys skiing, one enjoys fishing, one enjoys tennis, and one enjoys volleyball. Use the statements below to answer the question that follows.
   I. The cousin who fishes is female.
   II. Roger and Lucy hate sports with balls.
   III. Samantha is older than the cousin who fishes.

30. Who likes to fish?
    a. Roger
    b. Mike
    c. Samantha
    d. Lucy
    e. The answer cannot be determined from the information given.

31. Triangles *RST* and *MNO* are similar. What is the length of line segment *MO*?

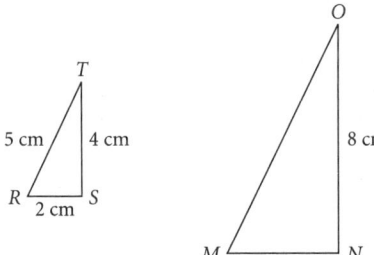

    a. 5 cm
    b. 10 cm
    c. 20 cm
    d. 32 cm
    e. 40 cm

32. Which number sentence is true?
   a. 0.27 < 0.027
   b. 2.7 < 0.0027
   c. 0.027 > 0.27
   d. 0.0027 < 0.027
   e. 0.27 > 2.7

33. Which of the following equations represents the phrase "8 times the sum of 5 and a number is equal to 28 times the number"?
   a. $8(5 + n) = 28n$
   b. $(8 \times 5) + n = 28n$
   c. $8n + 5 = 28n$
   d. $8(5 + n) = 28 + n$
   e. $\frac{5 + n}{8} = 28 + n$

34. The PTA at the local elementary school made gift baskets for teachers to celebrate the first day of school. They purchased 125 dry-erase markers to put into the gift baskets. Since the school has 21 teachers, how many dry-erase markers will be put in each gift basket if each teacher gets the same number of markers?
   a. 5
   b. 5.95
   c. 5 R 20
   d. 6
   e. 6 R 20

35. What is the value of the expression $6y - 4x$ when $y = 4$ and $x = -2$?
   a. −28
   b. −12
   c. 16
   d. 18
   e. 32

36. Keisha surveyed 60 people to find out their reading preferences. Of the people surveyed, 53 like to read fiction, 22 like to read nonfiction, and 15 like both. How many like to read fiction but not nonfiction?
   a. 53
   b. 38
   c. 35
   d. 31
   e. 7

Use the following diagram to answer item 37.

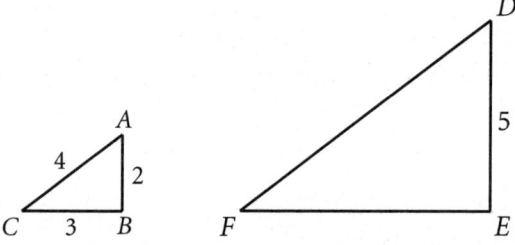

37. If the two triangles in the diagram are similar, with angle A equal to angle D, what is the perimeter of triangle DEF?
   a. 12
   b. 21
   c. 22.5
   d. 24.75
   e. 25.0

38. Helen has a jar with six blue, seven black, and five yellow marbles. If Helen picks a marble from the jar without looking, what is the probability that the marble is NOT yellow?
   a. $\frac{5}{18}$
   b. $\frac{1}{3}$
   c. $\frac{5}{13}$
   d. $\frac{13}{18}$
   e. $\frac{13}{5}$

39. The expression $(-11)(8)(-2)$ simplifies to which of the following?
   a. –176
   b. –88
   c. 88
   d. 90
   e. 176

40. Fourth grade student Larry Bond goes to the school nurse's office, where his temperature is found to be 102° Fahrenheit. What is his aproximate temperature in degrees Celsius? $C = \frac{5}{9}(F - 32)$
   a. 21.9
   b. 33.3
   c. 38.9
   d. 41.3
   e. 50.0

41. Three high schools can serve a town of 105,000 people. How many people could be served by four high schools?
   a. 130,000
   b. 135,000
   c. 140,000
   d. 145,000
   e. 150,000

42. A recipe serves four people and calls for $1\frac{1}{2}$ cups of broth. If you want to serve six people, how much broth do you need?
   a. 2 cups
   b. $2\frac{1}{4}$ cups
   c. $2\frac{1}{3}$ cups
   d. $2\frac{1}{2}$ cups
   e. $2\frac{3}{4}$ cups

43. Plattville is 80 miles west and 60 miles north of Quincy. How long is a direct route from Plattville to Quincy?
   a. 100 miles
   b. 110 miles
   c. 120 miles
   d. 140 miles
   e. 160 miles

44. Which of the following brands has the lowest unit cost?

Brand	W	X	Y	Z
Price	0.21	0.48	0.56	0.96
Weight in ounces	6	15	20	32

   a. W
   b. X
   c. Y
   d. Z
   e. They are equal in price.

45. A salesperson drives 2,142 miles in 6 days, stopping in 3 towns each day. How many miles does he average between stops?
   a. 714
   b. 357
   c. 238
   d. 119
   e. 87

46. A school cafeteria manager spends $540 on silverware. If a place setting includes 1 knife, 1 fork, and 2 spoons, how many place settings did the manager buy?
   a. 90
   b. 108
   c. 135
   d. 180
   e. There is not enough information to solve this problem.

47. An office uses 2 dozen pencils and $3\frac{1}{2}$ reams of paper each week. If pencils cost 5 cents each and a ream of paper costs $7.50, how much does it cost to supply the office for a week?
   a. $7.55
   b. $12.20
   c. $26.25
   d. $27.45
   e. $38.25

48. Which of the following is the most appropriate unit for expressing the capacity of a bathtub?
   a. pounds
   b. tons
   c. quarts
   d. ounces
   e. gallons

Use the following information to answer question 49.

Mr. James Rossen is just beginning a computer consulting firm and has purchased the following equipment:

- 3 telephones, each costing $125
- 2 computers, each costing $1,300
- 2 computer monitors, each costing $950
- 1 printer costing $600
- 1 fax machine costing $50

49. Mr. Rossen is reviewing his finances. What should he write as the total value of the equipment he has purchased so far?
   a. $3,025
   b. $3,275
   c. $5,400
   d. $5,525
   e. $6,525

50. Body mass index (BMI) is equal to weight in kilograms/(height in meters)^2. A man who weighs 64.8 kilograms has a BMI of 20. How tall is he?
   a. 1.8 meters
   b. 0.9 meters
   c. 2.16 meters
   d. 3.24 meters
   e. 1.62 meters

Section 3: Essay Writing

Carefully read the two essay-writing topics that follow. Plan and write two essays, one on each topic. Be sure to address all points in the topic. Allow about 30 minutes for each essay.

Topic 1

In his play, The Admirable Crighton, J.M. Barrie wrote, "Courage is the thing. All goes if courage goes."

Write an essay about a time in your life when you had the courage to do something or face something difficult, or when you feel you fell short. What did you learn from the experience?

Topic 2

Recently, American students are said to have fallen behind in the sciences, and some educators believe it is because American teachers are conducting science classes ineffectively.

Write an essay in which you suggest ways science classes could be conducted so as to more effectively challenge high school and college students.

Answers

Section 1: Reading Comprehension

1. **a.** The first paragraph speaks of Hansberry's being raised as the daughter of political activists. Choices **b**, **d**, and **e** are related to her beliefs but are not depicted as the origin of those beliefs. The passage does not say that Hansberry herself ever lived in Southside Chicago (choice **c**).

2. **a.** The passage begins and ends with praise of Hansberry's works and influence. Hansberry's works are summarized (choice **b**), but this is not the main purpose of the passage. Choice **c** is not necessarily true and is not in the passage. Lorraine Hansberry may have had a *difficult struggle* (choice **d**), but the struggle is not shown in the passage. The author tells about Hansberry's plays, but does not try to persuade students to read them (choice **e**).

3. **c.** See the third sentence of paragraph 2. Her father definitely worked in the cause of civil rights (choice **a**), but he did not earn his living that way (choice **e**). There was no mention of her father's being either a banker (choice **b**) or an artist (choice **d**).

4. **b.** This correct answer is clearly stated in the second sentence of paragraph 3. There is no support for the other choices.

5. **d.** Both paragraphs focus on how much Hansberry's work continued to be an influence even after she died. In paragraph 4, *Her influence continued to be felt*, and in paragraph 5, *Even after her death, her dramatic works have helped gain an audience for...* Choices **a** and **e** may be true, but this is not the main purpose of the paragraphs. There is no support for choice **b** or **c**.

6. **c.** See the second sentence of the first paragraph. She was the *fifth* woman to win the award, which means there were *four* women before her.

7. **a.** Choice **a** is the most logical choice, given the context of the sentence. It is illogical to describe personality types and aspirations as a *gathering, arrangement, decoration,* or *feature* (choices **b**, **c**, **d**, and **e**).

8. **d.** See paragraph 4, which describes *To Be Young, Gifted, and Black* as a dramatic adaptation of an autobiography. Choices **a** and **e** are wrong because there is no support for the idea that *Raisin* is based on Hansberry's family. *Les Blancs* is set in Africa, which rules out choice **b**. *The Sign in Sidney Brustein's Window* is about a man, which rules out choice **c**.

9. **d.** A person who helps with financial decisions could have a power of attorney or could be a personal representative. In the answer choices, only personal representative has a page number listed, which is page 89.

10. **d.** This is stated in the last paragraph: *Urgent initial treatment, though, involves raising blood sugar levels...* Choices **a** and **b** are never mentioned in the passage, and choice **c** is the opposite of the correct answer. Choice **e** is a treatment method for hypoglycemia, but it is used to treat it in the long run, not immediately.

11. **e.** The passage defines *gluconeogenesis* as the process by which the liver and kidneys produce glucose. The second paragraph states that blood sugar levels can become too low if glucose production is interrupted. Therefore, if gluconeogenesis doesn't occur, then blood sugar levels can become too low. Choices **a**, **b**, and **d** are never mentioned in the passage.

Although, according to the passage, hypoglycemia can result if the liver and kidneys are diseased, the passage doesn't say that hypoglycemia will *always* result if this is the case, making choice **c** incorrect.

12. c. The passage gives an overview of hypoglycemia by outlining its causes, symptoms, and treatment options. Choice **a** is incorrect because the passage does not warn the reader of the dangers of hypoglycemia—it is not written with a cautionary tone. Choice **b** is partly correct, but it is only one of the details outlined in the passage. Choices **d** and **e** are incorrect for the same reasons as choice **b**.

13. a. The passage contains objective information about hypoglycemia that one might find in a textbook. The information in the passage is written at an introductory level and is too general to be found in something as technical as a scientific journal (choice **b**). There is nothing new or noteworthy to make choice **c** an option. The passage is not about insulin deficiencies, making choice **d** incorrect. Choice **e** could be correct, but there is no clue that this passage is part of a series, so choice **a** is better.

14. a. According to the passage, Blake believed that through art (that is, *through the reordering of sense impressions by the creative imagination*), true religion is revealed. Artistic inspiration (choice **c**) might be involved, but the words *religion* and *moment of vision* point toward a mystical experience, rather than a primarily artistic one. There is no mention in the passage of *conversion* or *sin* (choices **b** and **e**) and no hint that the author views Blake's *moment of vision* as a false perception (*hallucinatory experience*, choice **d**).

15. a. The passage's tone and word choice (*true religion* and *eternity . . . revealed* through art) indicate that the world at *the moment of vision* is reality. There is no hint in the passage that nature represents a state of innocence for Blake (choice **b**)—the contrary is implied. The idea that nature is made up of *base and corrupt material* or that it will *perish* (choices **c** and **d**) are not in the passage. There is no evidence that Blake thought of the world of the artist as *fantasy* (choice **e**).

16. a. The paragraph details traffic laws that are generally stricter than those in the United States. It does not describe lawyers or tourism. We don't have enough information to know that the laws are the strictest in the world. The passage also already describes traffic laws related to speed. The best answer is choice **a**.

17. b. The passage describes how the idea that you can drive as fast as possible anywhere on the autobahn is not true, though some people wish it were. This sounds most like choice **b**.

18. a. The first paragraph explains what the autobahn is. The second paragraph talks about how and when speed is regulated on the autobahn. The third paragraph describes other German traffic laws.

19. e. The passage says of the people who live in "the Bottom" that they are *apt to go awry*, to *break from their natural boundaries*. A person who is *eccentric* is quirky or odd. Nowhere in the passage is it implied that the people are *cowardly, artistic, unkempt,* or *arrogant* (choices **a**, **b**, **c**, and **d**).

20. d. A *scapegoat* is one who is forced to bear the blame for others or upon whom the sins of a community are heaped. Choices **b** and **c** are incorrect because nowhere in the passage is it implied that Sula is a hero or leader, or even that "the Bottom" has such a personage. Sula may be a *victim* (choice **a**), but a community does not necessarily *project evil* onto a victim the way they do onto a scapegoat. Choice **e** does not make sense in the context of the passage. People do not project evil onto martyrs.

21. b. The sentence before the one in question describes the traits as abstract. Since the following sentence is discussing these same traits, choice **b**—the answer that is a synonym for abstract—is the best choice. Choice **a** most nearly means the opposite of abstract and intangible, so it is not correct. Choice **c** means short-lived, and thus doesn't make sense in the given context. Choice **d** almost works, but the connotation of mysterious is not right for this passage. Choice **e**, like choice **a**, is almost opposite of abstract.

22. c. Choice **a** is incorrect because although the passage implies people have long pondered nature versus nurture, it clearly presents this issue as a debate with a long history of two opposing viewpoints. Choices **b** and **d** are incorrect because they are only details mentioned in the passage, and neither is the main idea. Choice **e** is never mentioned or implied in the passage.

23. d. Choice **a** doesn't make sense; if the author were indifferent, he or she wouldn't have written the passage. Choice **b** is clearly not the case—the author is not trying to convince the reader of anything. Choice **c** is incorrect because the author remains neutral and takes no sides. Choice **e** is incorrect for the same reason as choice **c**. The author is not biased to either side.

24. d. Sentence 4 says, *Stem cells provide doctors and researchers with amazing opportunities*. Some people would find the research opportunities amazing. Those who oppose stem-cell research would not. The phrase *amazing opportunities* is an opinion.

25. c. Sentence 7 says, *Politicians and the public debate the ethics of using stem cells*. The rest of the paragraph describes what stem cells are and how they are driving research. The topic of ethics does not follow the main idea of the paragraph.

26. a. The paragraph describes how stem cells could be useful, as well as why doctors and researchers still need to study them. It does not discuss Alzheimer's disease or how stem cells could specifically be used in the future. There are no miracles described either. Although the ethical debate is mentioned, actual risks are not. The best answer is choice **a**.

27. e. Page 89 (choice **a**) deals with *peasant resistance*; page 55 (choice **b**) with *fire protection*; page 107 (choice **c**) with *villagers*; page 48 (choice **d**) with *slash-and-burn farming*. All might pertain somewhat to the question, but the index lists page 51 (choice **e**) under the topics of both *pasture* and *arson* (which is illegal burning), so it is the best choice.

28. a. Although there are more entries in the index having to do with fire, arson, and fire protection, the greatest number of pages listed under the topic of forest destruction is *industrialization*—18 pages.

29. d. The main thrust of the passage is that Franklin was multitalented; therefore, choice **d** is the best answer. Choice **a** is too vague, and choice **b** is too specific; furthermore, very little of the passage is devoted to Franklin's role as a Founding Father. The title in choice **c** is misleading—the passage does not focus solely on Franklin and his role in the discovery of electricity. Finally, choice **e** is incorrect because nowhere in the passage are the early days of Franklin mentioned.

30. e. All of the other choices are facts. Choice **e** is the only sentence that represents the author's opinion.

31. b. One doesn't need to know much about electricity to know that flying a kite during a thunderstorm is dangerous, but to obtain evidence from the passage that choice **b** is indeed correct, look to the last part of sentence 4, *. . . by conducting a hazardous experiment*. Choices **a**, **c**, **d**, and **e** are all viable options, but they are not nearly as strong as choice **b**.

32. e. The first paragraph describes a variety of jellyfish characteristics and functionality. Choice **e** describes yet another characteristic and introduces the topic that is discussed in the second paragraph. Choice **a** doesn't fit into the topic of the first paragraph. Choice **b** does describe another characteristic of jellyfish—how they move—but doesn't serve as a segue into the second paragraph like choice **e** does. Choice **c**, too, describes another characteristic of jellyfish—what they eat—but like choice **b**, doesn't serve as a segue into the second paragraph. Choice **d** doesn't fit into the first paragraph at all; the passage would have to first tell the reader that jellyfish sting before explaining how to treat a victim of a sting. Also, choice **d** is not a characteristic of jellyfish.

33. d. The correct answer can be found in the sentence: *The dominant type of jelly has a medusoid—saucer or bell-shaped—form. . .* Choice **a** is incorrect, as a sentence in the first paragraph states that jellyfish are related to sea anemones, not that they are a type of sea anemone. Choice **b** is never mentioned or implied in the passage. Choice **c** has part of the facts reversed—nematocysts are capsules inside cnidoblasts, not the other way around. Choice **e** is only partly true. The passage states that jellyfish have no skeleton, but it never says the same of corals.

34. e. Choice **a** is incorrect because, although the passage does state that jellyfish are fascinating, its purpose is not to explain why this is the case. Also, the passage never addresses the locomotion methods of jellyfish. Choice **b** is incorrect because a description of the jellyfish's body plan is only one of the details described in the passage, not its main idea. Also, the passage never explains the different ways that jellyfish respond to stimuli. The first part of choice **c** is correct, but the passage never describes how jellyfish respond to predators. Choice **d** is incorrect because the passage never really compares jellyfish to other cnidarians; it simply names some of its relatives.

35. d. Choice **a** is incorrect because the passage is not written in a persuasive way; therefore, it is not trying to prove anything. Choice **b** is incorrect, as the communication methods of jellyfish are never discussed in the passage. Choice **c** is not on target either; the passage is not written in a lively or entertaining tone, but rather in an informational one. Choice **e** is never mentioned or implied in the passage.

36. c. Any of the choices may be a definition of *background*; however, the context of the passage indicates that the word refers to the education and training of the proposed author—that is, the author's ability to write the book.

37. b. This is a detail question, and the answer can be found directly in the passage—in the last line of the second paragraph. The remaining choices are never mentioned in the passage.

38. c. This is another detail question, and the answer can be found in the first paragraph in the sentence that begins, *The pulp then goes through a screening process, . . .*

39. c. The passage presents no evidence or persuasive statements; therefore, choice **a** is incorrect. Nowhere in the passage are statements made supporting the idea that paper recycling is cost-effective, so choice **b** is incorrect. Choice **d** is incorrect because there is never anything mentioned in the passage about preserving the environment. Finally, choice **e** is incorrect because nowhere does the author mention a misconception that needs clarification.

40. b. This is a detail question, and the answer can be found in the following sentence part: *. . . which then attaches to the air bubbles and rises to the top.*

41. d. The items that are not made to be used with food are toilet paper and tissues. Add the percentages for these two categories together: 10% + 12% = 22%.

42. b. Although this passage is only one paragraph, its message is clear: Information found on the Internet is not always accurate and should be cross-checked with other sources. Choice **a** is incorrect because nowhere is it indicated that the Internet has changed considerably since it came into existence. Choices **c** and **d** are indeed found in the paragraph, but not expanded upon. Choice **e** is not indicated anywhere in the paragraph.

43. b. This choice is correct because the third sentence states that telecommuters produce 20% more than their on-location counterparts. Choice **a** is not mentioned in the paragraph. Choice **c** is incorrect because more productivity does not necessarily mean better quality. Choice **d** is not mentioned, and choice **e** is refuted in the final sentence.

44. e. The passage indicates that sensitive skin comes from different sources. It is unlikely that these different sources would all respond well to the same product. In addition, the passage states that skin with acne can be aggravated by products that contain oil.

45. a. The answer is stated in the first sentence. Choices **b**, **d**, and **e** are not mentioned in the paragraph. Choice **c** is attractive, but it is incorrect because the paragraph is talking about more responsibility and independence, not necessarily more work.

46. c. Choice **a** is misleading, but if you read the passage carefully, you'll know that it says therapeutic cloning is similar to the *first stages* of reproductive cloning—not to the entire process. Choice **b** is incorrect—according to the passage, using federal funds to research human cloning was banned, not researching therapeutic cloning. Choices **d** and **e** are never mentioned in the passage.

47. a. This passage is too casual to have been taken from a scientific journal for geneticists (choice **b**). Choice **c** is incorrect because the passage is not written like a newspaper article—there is no new information of note. The passage goes into too much detail about the process of cloning for choice **d** to be correct; furthermore, nothing in the passage is placed in a historical context. Choice **e** is incorrect because government involvement in cloning is given very little attention in the passage.

48. b. This is a detail question, and the answer can be found by referring back to paragraphs three and four.

49. c. Implications of cloning are never mentioned, so choice **a** is incorrect. Choice **b** is incorrect because the main focus of the article is not on federal intervention. The topics in choices **d** and **e** are never mentioned in the passage.

50. e. The passage is written to explain cloning—no opinions on it or feelings towards it are mentioned.

Section 2: Mathematics

1. e. Because Linda pays with a check only if an item costs more than $30, the item must have cost more than $25.

2. d. The elevator went at 4 f/s at a distance of x. The elevator returned at 5 f/s at the same distance, x. Change the total time to seconds because the units are in feet per second.
$(4 \times 2 + 1) \div 2 = 4.5 \times 60 = 270$ seconds.
Subtract the 90 seconds that the elevator was paused at the top of the building.
$270 - 90 = 180$
$\frac{x}{4} + \frac{x}{5} = 180$
Rewrite the fractions with common denominators:
$20\frac{x}{4} + 20\frac{x}{5} = 20 \times 180$
Simplify the expression:
$5x + 4x = 3,600$
$9x = 3,600$
$x = 400$
The tower is 400 feet tall.

3. d. A 70% percentile score is a bit better than average, as Miriam scored the same or better than 70% of the people that took the exam. The stanine scores of 3 and 4 are worse than average. A stanine score of 5 is average, and a stanine score of 9 is far above average. A stanine score of 6 is just a bit above average, so **d** is the best choice.

4. c. Four percent is equal to 0.04, so multiply 14,000 times 0.04 and then add the result to 14,000, for a total cost of $14,560.

5. e. From the line chart, 2004 is represented by the line with squares at each month. In December 2004, there were 10 inches of rainfall, the most that year.

6. c. The mean is the sum of the values divided by the number of values. Add $8 + 6 + 4 = 18$ inches, and then divide by 3 to get 6 inches.

7. a. If the gas station is $43\frac{1}{3}$ miles from their house, and their relatives live 75 miles away, the numbers are subtracted: $75 - 43\frac{1}{3} = 31\frac{2}{3}$.

8. e. If 3 of 8 are strawberry, then 5 of 8 are lemon: $96(\frac{5}{8}) = 60$ candies.

9. e. 13% had not read books; therefore, 87% had. 87% is equal to 0.87. $0.87 \times 2,500 = 2,175$ people.

10. c. To estimate quickly, the numbers can be rounded to 36,000 and 16,500. 36,000 students minus 16,500 male students is equal to 19,500 female students; 19,500 women minus 16,500 men is equal to 3,000 more women than men.

11. e. Asking for the difference between two values means to subtract the two values. The elevation of the Dead Sea should be written as a negative value because it is below sea level. The subtraction problem is $29,028 - (-1,312) = 29,028 + 1,312 = 30,340$.

12. c. 6% is equal to .06, so $0.06 \times 350 = 21$.

13. a. Rounding to close numbers helps. This is approximately 100,000 divided by 500,000, which is 0.20 or $\frac{1}{5}$.

14. b. $2\frac{1}{2} = 2.5$. $1\frac{1}{4} = 1.25$. $2.5 \times 1.25 = 3.125$ or $3\frac{1}{8}$.

15. a. Multiply the percentages by one another (30% = 0.30; 15% = 0.15). $0.30 \times 0.15 = 0.045$ or 4.5%.

16. d. If 20% are not eating the special, 80% are; 80% = 40 people. 40 divided by 0.80 = 50 people total.

17. c. To find the answer, work this equation: ($2.24 − $2.08) × 2 = $0.32.

18. d. Divide the number of beads by the number of necklaces: 112 ÷ 8 = 14 beads.

19. a. 24 history books at $20 each are $480. 20 math books at $30 each are $600. 15 science books at $25 each are $375. $480 + $600 + 375 = $1,455.

20. d. Between 10:42 and 12:42, two hours have elapsed. From 12:42 to 1:00, another 18 minutes have elapsed (60 − 42 = 18). Then from 1:00 to 1:19, there is another 19 minutes. Two hours + 18 minutes + 19 minutes = 2 hours, 37 minutes.

21. e. Division is used to arrive at a decimal, which can then be rounded to the nearest hundredth and converted to a percentage: 11,350 divided by 21,500 is approximately equal to 0.5279. 0.5279 rounded to the nearest hundredth is 0.53, or 53%.

22. b. This problem uses two algebraic equations to solve for the age. Jerry (J) and his grandfather (G) have a sum of ages of 110 years. Therefore, $J + G = 110$. Jerry was one-third as young as his grandfather 15 years ago. Therefore, $J - 15 = \frac{1}{3}(G - 15)$. Solve the first equation for J: $J = 110 - G$. Now substitute this value of J into the second equation: $110 - G - 15 = \frac{1}{3}(G - 15)$. Solve for G: $95 - G = \frac{1}{3}G - 5$; $100 = \frac{4}{3}G$; $G = 75$.

23. a. Subtract 39 from both sides of the equation: $0.875x = -49$. Since $0.875 = \frac{7}{8}$, multiply both sides of the equation by $\frac{8}{7}$: $x = (-49)(\frac{8}{7}) = -56$.

24. d. Look at this equation:
gallons $(\frac{miles}{gallon})$ = miles

To find the gallons of gas used, you could divide both sides of the equation by miles per gallon.

gallons = $\frac{miles}{(\frac{miles}{gallon})}$

So to solve this problem, you would need the mileage of the truck in miles per gallon.

25. d. If you look for a pattern in the table, you can see that as each year increases by one, the height of the tree increases by four. To get to year seven in the table, we would need to add two more years. If each year represents four feet, then two more years would represent eight more feet. 25 + 8 = 33. The best answer is choice **d**.

26. c. Change each fraction in the problem to a decimal.
$2\frac{1}{3} = 2.333 \qquad 2\frac{1}{2} = 2.5$
The only answer choice that is between 2.333 and 2.5 is choice **c**, 2.4.

27. c. The speed of the train is 60 miles per hour, obtained from the table. Therefore, the distance from Chicago would be equal to $60t$. However, as the train moves on, the distance decreases from Los Angeles, so there must be a function of $-60t$ in the equation. At time $t = 0$, the distance is 2,000 miles, so the function is $2,000 - 60t$.

28. e. The cost for 25 hours for both providers must be found. For provider A, the base charge is $20, plus 7.5 hours at $1 per hour. This is $27.50. For provider B, the base charge is $20, plus 5 hours at $1.50. This is also $27.50. Therefore, they will cost the same.

29. c. The largest value of the three given is $3.49, so this number should be listed first. This eliminates choices **b**, **d**, and **e**. The value 3.409 is greater than 3.399 because four-tenths is greater than three-tenths. This eliminates choice **a**.

30. d. This problem can be solved using only statements I and III. Since the cousin who fishes is female, either Lucy or Samantha likes to fish. Statement III eliminates Samantha, which leaves Lucy.

31. b. The dimensions of triangle MNO are double those of triangle RST. Line segment RT is 5 cm; therefore line segment MO is 10 cm.

32. b. The ones and tenths digits of 0.0027 and 0.027 are the same, but the hundredths digit of 0.027 (2) is greater than the hundredths digit of 0.0027 (0), so 0.027 > 0.0027.

33. a. The sum of 5 and a number is $5 + n$. 8 times that sum is $8(5 + n)$, and 28 times the number is equal to $28n$. Therefore, $8(5 + n) = 28n$.

34. a. This is a division problem. $125 \div 21 = 5$, remainder 20. However, the question asks how many markers would be placed in each gift basket. You would not place R 20 in each basket. This means that there are 20 leftover markers and that each basket would only get 5 markers.

35. e. Substitute 4 for y and -2 for x: $6(4) - (4)(-2) = 24 - (-8) = 24 + 8 = 32$.

36. b. Draw a Venn diagram to solve the problem.

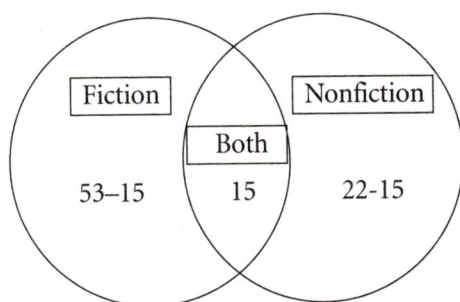

The problem does not say that 53 people like *only* fiction. It is possible that the people who enjoy fiction also enjoy nonfiction. By subtracting the number of people who enjoy both from the number that like fiction, you can find the number of people who only like fiction.

37. c. $\overline{DE}$ is 2.5 times greater than $\overline{AB}$; therefore, $\overline{EF}$ is 7.5 and $\overline{DF}$ is 10. Add the lengths of the three sides of DEF together to arrive at the perimeter.

38. d. The total number of marbles is 18. The marbles that are not yellow are blue and black. There are 6 blue marbles and 7 black marbles. $\frac{6}{18} + \frac{7}{18} = \frac{13}{18}$

39. e. First, multiply the three values together without regard to whether they are positive or negative.
$(11)(8)(2) = 176$
Two of the original numbers are negative. The product of two negative numbers is a positive number, so the final answer is positive.

40. c. Use the formula beginning with the operation in parentheses: 102 minus 32 equals 70. Then, multiply 70 by $\frac{5}{9}$ (first, multiply 70 by 5, then divide by 9) to get an answer of 38.888888, which rounds up to 38.9°.

41. c. The ratio of 105,000 : 3 is equal to the ratio of $x : 4$, or $\frac{105,000}{3} = \frac{x}{4}$, where x is the population served by four schools. Solve for x by multiplying 4 times 105,000 and then dividing by 3 to get 140,000.

42. b. $1\frac{1}{2}$ cups equals $\frac{3}{2}$ cups. The ratio is 6 people to 4 people, which is equal to the ratio of x to $\frac{3}{2}$. By cross multiplying, we get $6(\frac{3}{2})$ equals $4x$, or 9 equals $4x$. Dividing both sides by 9, we get $\frac{9}{4}$, or $2\frac{1}{4}$ cups.

43. a. The distance between Plattville and Quincy is the hypotenuse of a right triangle with sides of length 80 and 60. The length of the hypotenuse equals the square root of $(80^2 + 60^2)$, which equals the square root of $(6{,}400 + 3{,}600)$, which equals the square root of 10,000, which equals 100 miles.

44. c. You can find the price per ounce of each brand, as follows:

Brand	W	X	Y	Z
Price in cents per ounce:	$\frac{21}{6} = 3.5$	$\frac{48}{15} = 3.2$	$\frac{56}{20} = 2.8$	$\frac{96}{32} = 3.0$

It is then easy to see that Brand Y, at 2.8 cents per ounce, is the least expensive.

45. d. 2,142 divided by 6 days equals 357 miles per day. Then, 357 miles is divided by 3 stops, equaling an average of 119 miles between each stop.

46. e. There is not enough information to solve this problem. The price of one piece of silverware is needed to find the solution.

47. d. First find the total price of the pencils: (24 pencils)($0.05) equals $1.20. Then find the total price of the paper: (3.5 reams)($7.50 per ream) equals $26.25. Next, add the two totals together: $1.20 and $26.25 equals $27.45.

48. e. Only choices **c**, **d**, and **e** are units of capacity. Since a bathtub can hold any one of these units, you should choose the largest of the given capacities. The best answer is **e**.

49. d. It is important to remember to include all three telephones ($375 total), both computers ($2,600 total), and both monitors ($1,900 total) in the total value for the correct answer of $5,525.

50. a. Substituting known quantities into the formula yields $20 = \frac{64.8}{x^2}$. Next, you must multiply through by x^2 to get $20x^2 = 64.8$ and then divide through by 20 to get $x^2 = 3.24$. Now take the square root of both sides to get $x = 1.8$.

Section 3: Essay Writing

Following are the criteria for scoring CBEST essays.

A "4" essay is a coherent writing sample that addresses the assigned topic and is aimed at a specific audience. Additionally, it has the following characteristics:

- a main idea and/or a central point of view that is focused; its reasoning is sound
- points of discussion that are clear and arranged logically
- assertions that are supported with specific, relevant detail
- word choice and usage that is accurate and precise
- sentences that have complexity and variety, with clear syntax; paragraphs that are coherent (minor mechanical flaws are acceptable)
- style and language that are appropriate to the assigned audience and purpose

A "3" essay is an adequate writing sample that generally addresses the assigned topic, but may neglect or only vaguely address one of the assigned tasks; it is aimed at a specific audience. Generally, it has the following additional characteristics:

- a main idea and/or a central point of view and adequate reasoning
- organization of ideas that is effective; the meaning of the ideas is clear
- generalizations that are adequately, though unevenly, supported
- word choice and language usage that are adequate; mistakes exist but do not interfere with meaning
- some errors in sentence and paragraph structure, but not so many as to be confusing
- word choice and style that are appropriate to a given audience

A "2" essay is an incompletely formed writing sample that attempts to address the topic and to communicate a message to the assigned audience but is generally incomplete or inappropriate. It has the following additional characteristics:

- a main point, but one that loses focus; reasoning that is simplistic
- ineffective organization that causes the response to lack clarity
- generalizations that are only partially supported; supporting details that are irrelevant or unclear
- imprecise language usage; word choice that distracts the reader
- mechanical errors; errors in syntax; errors in paragraphing
- style that is monotonous or choppy

A "1" essay is an inadequately formed writing sample that only marginally addresses the topic and fails to communicate its message to, or is inappropriate to, a specific audience. Additionally, it has the following characteristics:

- general incoherence and inadequate focus, lack of a main idea or consistent point of view; illogical reasoning
- ineffective organization and unclear meaning throughout
- unsupported generalizations and assertions; details that are irrelevant and presented in a confusing manner
- language use that is imprecise, with serious and distracting errors
- many serious errors in mechanics, sentence syntax, and paragraphing

Following are examples of scored essays for Topics 1 and 2. (There are some deliberate errors in all the essays, so that you can tell how much latitude you have.)

Topic 1

Pass—Score = 4

Courage and cowardice seem like absolutes. We are often quick to label other people, or ourselves, either "brave" or "timid," "courageous" or "cowardly." However, one bright afternoon on a river deep in the wilds of the Ozark mountains, I learned that these qualities are as changable as mercury.

During a cross-country drive, my friend Nina and I decided to stop at a campsite in Missouri and spend the afternoon on a float trip down Big Piney River, 14 miles through the wilderness. We rented a canoe and paddled happily off.

Things went fine—for the first seven or eight miles. We gazed at the overhanging bluffs, commented on the wonderful variety of trees (it was spring, and the dogwood was in bloom), and marveled at the clarity of the water. Then, in approaching a bend in the river (which we later learned was called "Devil's Elbow") the current suddenly swept us in toward the bank, underneath the low-hanging branches of a weeping willow. The canoe tipped over and I was pulled under, my foot caught for just a few seconds on the submerged roots of the willow. Just as I surfaced, taking my first frantic gulp of air, I saw the canoe sweeping out, upright again, but empty, and Nina frantically swimming after it.

I knew I should help but I was petrified and hung my head in shame as I let my friend brave the treacherous rapids and haul the canoe back onto the gravel bar, while I stood by cravenly.

Then came the scream. Startled, I glanced up to see Nina, both hands over her eyes, dash off the gravel bar and back into the water. I gazed down into the canoe to see, coiled in the bottom of it, the unmistakeable, black-and-brown, checkerboard-patterned form of a copperhead snake. It had evidently been sunning itself peacefully on the weeping willow branch when we passed by underneath.

I don't know exactly why, but the supposedly inborn terror of snakes is something that has passed me by completely. I actually find them rather charming in a scaly sort of way.

Nina was still screaming, "Kill it!" But I was calm in a way that must have seemed smug. "We're in its home, it's not in ours," I informed her. And gently I prodded it with the oar until it reared up, slithered over the side of the canoe, and raced away—terrified, itself—into the underbrush.

Later that night, in our cozy, safe motel room, we agreed that we each had cold chills thinking about what might have happened. Still, I learned something important from the ordeal. I know that, had we encountered only the rapids, I might have come away ashamed, labeling myself a coward, and had we encountered only the snake, Nina might have done the same. And I also know that neither of us will ever again be quite so apt to brand another person as lacking courage. Because we will always know that, just around the corner, may be the snake or the bend in the river or the figure in the shadows or something else as yet unanticipated, that will cause our own blood to freeze.

Marginal Pass—Score = 3

Courage can be shown in many ways and by many kinds of people. One does not have to be rich, or educated, or even an adult to show true courage.

For example, a very heartbreaking thing happened in our family. It turned out all right but at the time it almost made us lose our faith. However, it also taught us a lesson regarding courage. In spite of his father's and my repeated warnings, my son Matt went ice fishing with some friends and fell through the ice into the fridgid water beneath. He is prone to do things that are dangerous no matter how many times he's told. Fortunately there were grown-ups near and they were able to throw him a life line and pull him to safety. However, when they got him onto shore they discovered he was unconsious. There were vital signs but they were weak, the paramedics pronounced him in grave danger.

He is his little sisters (Nan's) hero. He is 16 and she is 13, just at the age where she admires everything he does. When they took him to the hospital she insisted on going that night to see him, and she insisted on staying with me there. My husband thought we should insist she go home, but it was Christmas vacation for her so there was no real reason. So we talked it over and she stayed. She stayed every night for the whole week just to be by Matt's side. And when he woke up she was there. Her smiling face the was first thing he saw.

In spite of the fact she was just a child and it was frightning for her to be there beside her brother she loves so much, and had to wonder, every day if he would die, she stayed. So courage has many faces.

Marginal Fail—Score = 2

Courage is not something we are born with. It is something that we have to learn.

For example when your children are growing up you should teach them courage. Teach them to face lifes challanges and not to show there fear. For instance my father. Some people would say he was harsh, but back then I didnt think of it that way. One time he took me camping and I had a tent of my own. I wanted to crawl in with him but he said there was nothing to be afraid of. And I went to sleep sooner than I would have expect. He taught me not to be afriad.

There are many reasons for courage. In a war a solder has to be couragous and a mother has to be no less couragous if she is rasing a child alone and has to make a living. So, in me it is totally alright to be afriad as long as you face your fear. I have been greatful to him ever since that night.

Sometimes parents know what is best for there kids even if at the time it seems like a harsh thing. I learned not to show my fear that night, which is an important point to courage. In everyday life it is important to learn how to be strong. If we dont learn from our parents, like I did from my father, then we have to learn it after we grow up. But it is better to learn it, as a child. I have never been as afriad as I was that night, and I learned a valuble lesson from it.

Fail—Score = 1

Courage is important in a battle and also ordinary life. In a war if your buddy depends on you and you let him down he might die. Courage is also important in daly life. If you have sicknes in the family or if you enconter a mugger on the street you will need all the courage you can get. There are many dangers in life that only courage will see you through.

Once, my apartment was burglerised and they stole a TV and micro-wave. I didnt have very much. They took some money to. I felt afraid when I walked in and saw things moved or gone. But I call the police and waited for them inside my apartment which was brave and also some might say stupid! But the police came and took my statement and also later caught the guy. Another time my girlfreind and I were in my apartment and we looked out the window and there was somebody suspisious out in front. It turned out to be a false alarm but she was scard and she said because I was calm it made her feel better. So courage was important to me, in my relationship with my girlfreind.

So courage is importand not only in war but also in life.

Topic 2
Pass—Score = 4

The best way for teachers to boost their students' science test scores is to stop worrying quite so much about the scores and start being concerned about making the students excited by science.

Before ever asking students to memorize facts, the teacher should demonstrate a scientific process or, better, teach the students how to experiment for themselves, allowing them to apprehend the process with their senses before trying to fix it in their intellect. For example, the teacher might pass around an ant farm in the class room and let the students observe the little critters skittering behind the glass, going about their complex, individual tasks, before asking the student to read that ants have a rigid social structure, just as people do. If possible, it would be even better to take them on a field trip to observe a real ant-hill or to see how other kinds of real animals behave, say on a farm or in a zoo. The teacher might allow the students to create a chemical reaction in a beaker—taking care of course that they don't blow themselves up—before asking them to memorize the formula.

When I was small, I had first-hand experience with this kind of teaching. My father built a telescope (a painstaking project that should only be taken on out of love because it is a very difficult, intricate task—I recall that even he swore a lot during that period!). The telescope had a clock at its base that kept it fixed on the moon or stars rather than turning as the earth turns. When my father switched off the clock, I remember watching through the eyepiece, fascinated at how quickly the stars drifted out of my field of vision—it took only seconds—and even more fascinated to realize that what I was seeing was us floating so swiftly through space. He told me the magical names of the geological formations on the moon, such as the crater called "The Sea of Tranquility." When I looked through the lens, the pock-marked silvery disc of the moon seemed as close as the hills behind our suburban house.

After that, I became interested in the statistics such as the rate of the rotation of the earth, the geophysical facts behind the making of the craters that form the moon's laughing face, in a way I never would have if the facts had been the starting point of a lecture.

This approach should be begun, not in high school or college, but in grade school or even in kindergarten. The facts are important, of course—without them, we can have no real understanding. But curiosity is as vital to learning as the ability to memorize—perhaps more so. Because curiosity will keep students learning long after they've passed their final test in school.

Marginal Pass—Score = 3

Science is important for many reasons, but especially because today's world is based on technology. If other countries get ahead of us in science the consequences may be dire. So it is extremely important for our students to excell.

The first and best way to teach science is to make the student see the practical application of it. For example, if the teacher is teaching botony, she might explain the medical uses of plants. Or if teaching physics, she might show a diagram of a rocket ship. Field trips are a good idea, as well, perhaps to a factory that makes dolls. The point is to make it practical and interesting to boys and girls alike.

When I was in high school I had a teacher named Mr. Wiley who let us mix things in jars and watch the results. Sometimes they were unexpected! Such as a kind of mushroom we planted that was poisonous and reminded us of the horror movies we all loved in those days. Mr. Wiley made it interesting in a personal way, so that it wasn't just dry facts. And he told us the practical uses, such as this particular kind of mushroom is used in the making of certain insect poison.

In this day and age it is important for all of us to know something about science because it affects all aspects of our lives, but for young people it is vital. Their livelihoods—and even their lives—may depend on that knowledge.

Marginal Fail—Score = 2

Science is a necesary skill because it can effect each one of us, such as the making of the hydrogen bomb or finding a cure for AIDS. It is responsable for TV, cars, and a host of other items we take for granted. So we all depend on it and need to learn it.

The best way to teach science is to have a good textbook and also good equiptment in the classroom. If the equiptment is poor there is no way they are going to learn it, which is why the poorer schools are behind the richer ones and also behind other countries. Its the most important factor in the classroom today.

Another way to teach science is through field trips and vidio-tapes. There are many tapes in the library and every school should have a good vidio system. Also a good library is important. And there are many places to take the class that they would find intresting.

When I was in school I thought science was boring. I wish I had learned more about it because I think it would make me a better teacher someday as well as better understand the world of technology. If we don't understand technology we are at it's mercy, and it is something we rely on to get us through our lives. Without science we would have no technilogical advances. If other countries are ahead of us it is our own fault for not putting science as a priority.

Fail—Score = 1

Science is importnt and we should teach it to our students in the right way. A scientist coming in to talk would be one way. Also experimints that the students can do. The reason it is important, is other countrys are ahead of us and we may have a war. Then if their tecnoligy is better they will take us over. So it is dangerous not to have students that know alot about science.

If we teach our children to relay too much on science and technoligy what will happen if it fails. If the computers fail we are in serious trouble. There is still no cure for cancer and our products cause polution. So science is important and our students should learn but it isnt everything and they should learn that they should study other things to, like how to make a good living for there family. And religion also knows things science can never know.

If we teach science in the right way our country will be better off as well as our children when they are caught up to the new melinnium.

Scoring

Once again, in order to evaluate how you did on this practice exam, start by scoring the three sections of the CBEST—Reading Comprehension, Mathematics, and Essay Writing—separately. You will recall that Reading Comprehension and Mathematics are scored the same way: First find the number of questions you got right out of the 50 questions in each section, then use the table below to check your math and find percentage equivalents for several possible scores.

Number of questions right	Approximate percentage
50	100%
46	92%
43	86%
39	78%
35	70%
32	64%
28	56%
25	50%

As previously stated, you will need a score of at least 70% on both the Reading Comprehension section and the Mathematics section to be certain to pass those portions of the CBEST. (Remember that the scores are converted from raw scores to scaled scores, so the actual number you receive on the real CBEST will *not* be "70"; however, for the purpose of finding out if you passed these practice exams, a percentage will work fine.) Besides achieving a score of 70% on the Reading Comprehension and Mathematics sections, you must receive a passing score on the Essay Writing section of the CBEST, which will be evaluated by trained readers. The criteria are outlined in detail in the Answers section, but generally the essays are scored as follows:

4 = Pass (an excellent and well-formed essay)

3 = Marginal Pass (an average and adequately formed essay)

2 = Marginal Fail (a partially formed but substandard essay)

1= Fail (an inadequately formed essay)

The best way to see how you did on your essays for this second practice exam is to give your essays and the scoring criteria to a teacher and ask him or her to score your essays for you.

You have probably seen improvement between your first practice exam score and this one; but if you didn't improve as much as you'd like, following are some options:

- **If you scored below 60%,** you may want to consider whether you're ready for the CBEST at this time. A good idea would be to take some brush-up courses, either at a university or community college nearby or online, in the areas you feel less sure of. If you don't have time for a course, you might try private tutoring.
- **If your score is in the 60% to 70% range,** you need to work as hard as you can to improve your skills. The LearningExpress books *Reading Comprehension Success in 20 Minutes a Day* and *Practical Math Success in 20 Minutes a Day* or other books from your public library will undoubtedly help. Also, reread and pay close attention to all the advice in Chapters 2 and 4 of this book in order to improve your score. It might also be helpful to ask friends and family to make up mock test questions and quiz you on them.
- **If your score is between 70% and 90%,** you could still benefit from additional work by going back to Chapter 4 and by brushing up your reading comprehension and general math skills before the exam.
- **If you scored above 90%,** that's great! This kind of score should make you a good candidate for a teaching job. Don't lose your edge, though; keep studying right up to the day before the exam.

Keep in mind that what's much more important than your scores, for now, is how you did on each of the basic skills tested by the exam. Using the advice in this section, diagnose your strengths and weaknesses so that you can concentrate your efforts as you prepare for the exam. Your percentage scores in conjunction with the LearningExpress Test Preparation System in Chapter 2 of this book will help you revise your study plan if need be. After your study plan is revised, turn again to the CBEST Mini-Course in Chapter 4, which covers each of the basic skills tested on the CBEST.

If you didn't score as well as you would like, ask yourself the following: Did I run out of time before I could answer all the questions? Did I go back and change my answers from right to wrong? Did I get flustered and sit staring at a difficult question for what seemed like hours? If you had any of these problems, once again, be sure to go over the LearningExpress Test Preparation System in Chapter 2 again to learn how to avoid them.

After working on your reading, writing, and math skills, take the second practice exam in Chapter 6 to see how much you've improved.

CHAPTER 6

CBEST PRACTICE EXAM 2

CHAPTER SUMMARY
This is the third of the four practice tests in this book based on the California Basic Educational Skills Test (CBEST). Use this test to see how much you've improved.

Like the previous CBEST exams in this book, this one is divided into three sections of the same types as the actual exam—the Reading Comprehension section, consisting of 50 multiple-choice questions; the Mathematics section, consisting of 50 multiple-choice questions; and the Essay Writing section, consisting of two topics on which you are to write essays.

For this exam, you should simulate the actual test-taking experience as closely as you can. Work in a quiet place away from interruptions. Tear out the answer sheet on the next page, and use a number 2 pencil to fill in the circles. (As you did for the other two exams, write your essays on a separate piece of paper.) Use a timer or stopwatch and allow yourself four hours for the exam: one and a half hours each for the reading and math sections and a half hour each for the two essays.

After the exam, use the answer key that follows it to see your progress on each section and to find out why the correct answers are correct and the incorrect ones incorrect. Then use the scoring section at the end of the exam to see how you did overall.

LEARNINGEXPRESS ANSWER SHEET

Section 1: Reading Comprehension

1. ⓐ ⓑ ⓒ ⓓ ⓔ	21. ⓐ ⓑ ⓒ ⓓ ⓔ	41. ⓐ ⓑ ⓒ ⓓ ⓔ
2. ⓐ ⓑ ⓒ ⓓ ⓔ	22. ⓐ ⓑ ⓒ ⓓ ⓔ	42. ⓐ ⓑ ⓒ ⓓ ⓔ
3. ⓐ ⓑ ⓒ ⓓ ⓔ	23. ⓐ ⓑ ⓒ ⓓ ⓔ	43. ⓐ ⓑ ⓒ ⓓ ⓔ
4. ⓐ ⓑ ⓒ ⓓ ⓔ	24. ⓐ ⓑ ⓒ ⓓ ⓔ	44. ⓐ ⓑ ⓒ ⓓ ⓔ
5. ⓐ ⓑ ⓒ ⓓ ⓔ	25. ⓐ ⓑ ⓒ ⓓ ⓔ	45. ⓐ ⓑ ⓒ ⓓ ⓔ
6. ⓐ ⓑ ⓒ ⓓ ⓔ	26. ⓐ ⓑ ⓒ ⓓ ⓔ	46. ⓐ ⓑ ⓒ ⓓ ⓔ
7. ⓐ ⓑ ⓒ ⓓ ⓔ	27. ⓐ ⓑ ⓒ ⓓ ⓔ	47. ⓐ ⓑ ⓒ ⓓ ⓔ
8. ⓐ ⓑ ⓒ ⓓ ⓔ	28. ⓐ ⓑ ⓒ ⓓ ⓔ	48. ⓐ ⓑ ⓒ ⓓ ⓔ
9. ⓐ ⓑ ⓒ ⓓ ⓔ	29. ⓐ ⓑ ⓒ ⓓ ⓔ	49. ⓐ ⓑ ⓒ ⓓ ⓔ
10. ⓐ ⓑ ⓒ ⓓ ⓔ	30. ⓐ ⓑ ⓒ ⓓ ⓔ	50. ⓐ ⓑ ⓒ ⓓ ⓔ
11. ⓐ ⓑ ⓒ ⓓ ⓔ	31. ⓐ ⓑ ⓒ ⓓ ⓔ	
12. ⓐ ⓑ ⓒ ⓓ ⓔ	32. ⓐ ⓑ ⓒ ⓓ ⓔ	
13. ⓐ ⓑ ⓒ ⓓ ⓔ	33. ⓐ ⓑ ⓒ ⓓ ⓔ	
14. ⓐ ⓑ ⓒ ⓓ ⓔ	34. ⓐ ⓑ ⓒ ⓓ ⓔ	
15. ⓐ ⓑ ⓒ ⓓ ⓔ	35. ⓐ ⓑ ⓒ ⓓ ⓔ	
16. ⓐ ⓑ ⓒ ⓓ ⓔ	36. ⓐ ⓑ ⓒ ⓓ ⓔ	
17. ⓐ ⓑ ⓒ ⓓ ⓔ	37. ⓐ ⓑ ⓒ ⓓ ⓔ	
18. ⓐ ⓑ ⓒ ⓓ ⓔ	38. ⓐ ⓑ ⓒ ⓓ ⓔ	
19. ⓐ ⓑ ⓒ ⓓ ⓔ	39. ⓐ ⓑ ⓒ ⓓ ⓔ	
20. ⓐ ⓑ ⓒ ⓓ ⓔ	40. ⓐ ⓑ ⓒ ⓓ ⓔ	

Section 2: Mathematics

1. ⓐ ⓑ ⓒ ⓓ ⓔ	21. ⓐ ⓑ ⓒ ⓓ ⓔ	41. ⓐ ⓑ ⓒ ⓓ ⓔ
2. ⓐ ⓑ ⓒ ⓓ ⓔ	22. ⓐ ⓑ ⓒ ⓓ ⓔ	42. ⓐ ⓑ ⓒ ⓓ ⓔ
3. ⓐ ⓑ ⓒ ⓓ ⓔ	23. ⓐ ⓑ ⓒ ⓓ ⓔ	43. ⓐ ⓑ ⓒ ⓓ ⓔ
4. ⓐ ⓑ ⓒ ⓓ ⓔ	24. ⓐ ⓑ ⓒ ⓓ ⓔ	44. ⓐ ⓑ ⓒ ⓓ ⓔ
5. ⓐ ⓑ ⓒ ⓓ ⓔ	25. ⓐ ⓑ ⓒ ⓓ ⓔ	45. ⓐ ⓑ ⓒ ⓓ ⓔ
6. ⓐ ⓑ ⓒ ⓓ ⓔ	26. ⓐ ⓑ ⓒ ⓓ ⓔ	46. ⓐ ⓑ ⓒ ⓓ ⓔ
7. ⓐ ⓑ ⓒ ⓓ ⓔ	27. ⓐ ⓑ ⓒ ⓓ ⓔ	47. ⓐ ⓑ ⓒ ⓓ ⓔ
8. ⓐ ⓑ ⓒ ⓓ ⓔ	28. ⓐ ⓑ ⓒ ⓓ ⓔ	48. ⓐ ⓑ ⓒ ⓓ ⓔ
9. ⓐ ⓑ ⓒ ⓓ ⓔ	29. ⓐ ⓑ ⓒ ⓓ ⓔ	49. ⓐ ⓑ ⓒ ⓓ ⓔ
10. ⓐ ⓑ ⓒ ⓓ ⓔ	30. ⓐ ⓑ ⓒ ⓓ ⓔ	50. ⓐ ⓑ ⓒ ⓓ ⓔ
11. ⓐ ⓑ ⓒ ⓓ ⓔ	31. ⓐ ⓑ ⓒ ⓓ ⓔ	
12. ⓐ ⓑ ⓒ ⓓ ⓔ	32. ⓐ ⓑ ⓒ ⓓ ⓔ	
13. ⓐ ⓑ ⓒ ⓓ ⓔ	33. ⓐ ⓑ ⓒ ⓓ ⓔ	
14. ⓐ ⓑ ⓒ ⓓ ⓔ	34. ⓐ ⓑ ⓒ ⓓ ⓔ	
15. ⓐ ⓑ ⓒ ⓓ ⓔ	35. ⓐ ⓑ ⓒ ⓓ ⓔ	
16. ⓐ ⓑ ⓒ ⓓ ⓔ	36. ⓐ ⓑ ⓒ ⓓ ⓔ	
17. ⓐ ⓑ ⓒ ⓓ ⓔ	37. ⓐ ⓑ ⓒ ⓓ ⓔ	
18. ⓐ ⓑ ⓒ ⓓ ⓔ	38. ⓐ ⓑ ⓒ ⓓ ⓔ	
19. ⓐ ⓑ ⓒ ⓓ ⓔ	39. ⓐ ⓑ ⓒ ⓓ ⓔ	
20. ⓐ ⓑ ⓒ ⓓ ⓔ	40. ⓐ ⓑ ⓒ ⓓ ⓔ	

Section 1: Reading Comprehension

Answer questions 1–8 on the basis of the following passage.

(1) Milton Hershey was born near the small village of Derry Church, Pennsylvania, in 1857. It was a modest beginning that did not foretell his later success. Milton only attended school through the fourth grade; at that point, he was apprenticed to a printer in a nearby town. Fortunately for all chocolate lovers, Milton did not excel as a printer. After a while, he left the printing business and was apprenticed to a Lancaster, Pennsylvania candy maker. It was apparent he had <u>found his calling in life</u> and, at the age of 18, he opened his own candy store in Philadelphia. In spite of his talents as a candy maker, the shop failed after six years.

(2) Milton Hershey's fans today may be surprised to learn that his first candy success came with the manufacture of caramel. After the failure of his Philadelphia store, Milton headed for Denver, where he learned the art of caramel making. There he took a job with a local manufacturer who insisted on using fresh milk in making his caramels; Milton saw that this made the caramels especially tasty. After a time in Denver, he once again attempted to open his own candy-making businesses in Chicago, New Orleans, and New York City. Finally, in 1886, he went to Lancaster, Pennsylvania, where he raised the money necessary to try again. This company—the Lancaster Caramel Company—made Milton's reputation as a master candy maker.

(3) In 1893, Milton attended the Chicago International Exposition, where he saw a display of German chocolate-making implements. Captivated by the equipment, he purchased it for his Lancaster candy factory and began producing chocolate, which he used for coating his caramels. By the next year, production had grown to include cocoa, sweet chocolate, and baking chocolate. The Hershey Chocolate company was born in 1894 as a <u>subsidiary</u> of the Lancaster Caramel Company. Six years later, Milton sold the caramel company, but retained the rights, and the equipment, to make chocolate. He believed that a large market of chocolate consumers was waiting for someone to produce reasonably priced candy. He was right.

(4) Milton Hershey returned to the village where he had been born, in the heart of dairy country, and opened his chocolate-manufacturing plant. With access to all the fresh milk he needed, he began producing the finest milk chocolate. The plant that opened in a small Pennsylvania village in 1905 is today the largest chocolate factory in the world. The confections created at this facility are favorites in the U.S. and internationally.

(5) The area where the factory is located is now known as Hershey, Pennsylvania. Within the first decades of its existence, the town thrived, as did the chocolate business. A bank, a school, churches, a department store, even a park and a trolley system all appeared in short order. Soon, the town even had a zoo. Today, a visit to the area reveals the Hershey Medical Center, Milton Hershey School, and Hershey's Chocolate World, a theme park where visitors are greeted by a giant Reese's Peanut Butter Cup. All of these things—and a huge number of happy chocolate lovers—were made possible because a caramel maker visited the Chicago Exposition of 1893!

1. The writer's main purpose in this passage is to
   a. recount the founding of the Hershey Chocolate Company.
   b. describe the process of manufacturing chocolate.
   c. compare the popularity of chocolate to that of other candies.
   d. explain how apprenticeships work.
   e. persuade readers to visit Hershey, Pennsylvania.

2. As it is used in paragraph 1, the underlined phrase *found his calling in life* most nearly means
   a. became educated.
   b. discovered a vocation.
   c. was a talented person.
   d. called on other people to help him.
   e. had good luck.

3. Which of the following statements is supported by information in the passage?
   a. Chocolate is popular in every country in the world.
   b. The Hershey Chocolate Company's factory is near Derry Church, Pennsylvania.
   c. Chocolate had never been manufactured in the United States before Milton Hershey did it.
   d. The Hershey Chocolate Company is run by Milton Hershey's children.
   e. The Hershey Chocolate Company has branches in Chicago, New Orleans, and New York City.

4. Which of the following words best describes Milton Hershey's character, as he is presented in the passage?
   a. defective
   b. determined
   c. carefree
   d. cautious
   e. greedy

5. According to the passage, Milton Hershey first began to produce chocolate in order to
   a. make cocoa and baking chocolate.
   b. save his caramel company from bankruptcy.
   c. make chocolate-covered caramels.
   d. attend the Chicago International Exposition.
   e. found a new town.

6. Which of the following best defines the underlined word *subsidiary* as used in paragraph 3?
   a. a company that is in financial trouble
   b. a company founded to compete with another company
   c. a company that is not incorporated
   d. a company controlled by another company
   e. a company owned by one person

7. The passage implies that Hershey opened his first chocolate company in
   a. Chicago.
   b. Denver.
   c. Philadelphia.
   d. Lancaster.
   e. Derry Church.

8. The author most likely included the information in paragraph 5 in order to show that
   a. Hershey's chocolate factory was so successful that a whole town was built around it.
   b. people all over the world have become tourists in Hershey, Pennsylvania.
   c. Hershey's chocolate factory has now become a successful theme park.
   d. Hershey moved back to the town where he was born.
   e. the Hershey Chocolate Company manufactures both chocolate and caramel.

Answer questions 9–12 on the basis of the following passage.

Students with allergic food reactions can display a wide range of symptoms. The most severe and potentially life threatening reaction is anaphylaxis. Anaphylaxis is a serious, whole-body allergic reaction that can lead to airway tightening or closure. Many students with diagnosed food allergies may have an anaphylactic reaction, even when the possibility has not been diagnosed. If a student should experience an anaphylactic reaction, epinephrine should be administered immediately.

Clear Creek Elementary School has epinephrine in the nurse's office. The epinephrine will be used for students with unknown allergies who experience an anaphylactic reaction. In addition, the epinephrine can be used for students with known allergies when their personal emergency medication does not function properly.

Symptoms of anaphylaxis affect many systems in the body, the most dangerous of which are breathing difficulties and a drop in blood pressure. Foods that most commonly cause anaphylaxis are peanuts, tree nuts, shellfish, milk, wheat, soy, fish, and eggs. These severe allergic reactions can occur within minutes of contact with the allergen, or a reaction can be delayed for up to two hours. There is presently no cure for food allergies. The key to preventing anaphylaxis is for the allergic student to avoid all contact with the allergen.

School employees should limit the contact between students with food allergies and the allergens. Discourage students from sharing food in the lunchroom. After one class of students eats lunch, the lunchroom tables should be wiped down to remove any food residue before other students sit down. If teachers choose to use food in classroom activities, they should use prepackaged food only and read labels to ensure no potential allergens are in the food.

9. How would you expect the author to feel about allowing homemade foods to be brought into classrooms?
   a. As long as the foods are not shared, they should be fine.
   b. Homemade foods are a treat that students should enjoy on special occasions.
   c. The teacher should remove the allergic student from the classroom when food is present.
   d. No homemade foods should be brought to class to minimize exposure to allergens.
   e. Homemade foods are healthier than store-bought, prepackaged foods.

10. Who would NOT be part of the intended audience for this passage?
    a. teachers
    b. school nurses
    c. school administrators
    d. parents
    e. students

11. What is the main idea of the passage?
    a. Students may have food allergies, so lunchrooms should be cleaned between each group of students.
    b. School nurses should be prepared to deal with students with undiagnosed food allergies.
    c. All school employees should try to prevent allergic reactions to food and know how to treat them.
    d. All students who have food allergies should have access to epinephrine in the nurse's office.
    e. Food allergies may be undiagnosed, so teachers must be prepared to recognize them.

12. The use of the word *presently* in the third paragraph serves to
   a. show that the school is using the epinephrine.
   b. hint that a cure is close to being available.
   c. request a gift of more epinephrine from the PTA.
   d. explain that the school does not keep the cure handy.
   e. indicate that a cure could be found in the future.

Answer questions 13–16 on the basis of the following passage.

In Ralph Waldo Emerson's view, although individual consciousness will eventually be lost, every living thing is part of the blessed Unity, part of the transcendent "over-soul" that is the universe. And so, in the main body of his philosophy, Emerson accepts the indifference of Nature to the individual life, and does not struggle against it. His acceptance of Nature as tending toward overall unity and good in spite of her indifference to the individual is curiously and ironically akin to the Puritan acceptance of the doctrine of Divine Election.

    In his "Personal Narrative," Jonathan Edwards writes that he finally has "a delightful conviction" of the doctrine of God's sovereignty, of God's choosing according to His divine and arbitrary will, "whom he would to eternal life, and rejecting whom he pleased …" He writes that the doctrine had formerly seemed _____ to him; however, it had finally come to seem "exceedingly pleasant, bright, and sweet." In "Fate," Emerson writes that "Nature will not mind drowning a man or a woman, but swallows your ship like a grain of dust," but that "the central intention of Nature [is] harmony and joy. Let us build altars to the Beautiful Necessity.…"

13. Which of the following statements would LEAST effectively support the view of both Emerson and Edwards toward the nature of the universe?
   a. God notices the fall of a sparrow.
   b. God is all-powerful and all-wise.
   c. The universe is a harmonious place.
   d. Nature is beautiful and good.
   e. One should accept the universal plan.

14. Which of the following best describes the main idea of the passage?
   a. As philosophers reflecting on the nature of the universe, Ralph Waldo Emerson and Jonathan Edwards are ironically akin to one another.
   b. Ralph Waldo Emerson believes that nature is indifferent to individuals; on the other hand, Jonathan Edwards believes God makes decisions about individuals, but based on His desires.
   c. Ralph Waldo Emerson believes in a world ruled by the transcendent oversoul of Nature, whereas Jonathan Edwards believes in a world ruled by a sovereign God.
   d. Ralph Waldo Emerson believes that individual consciousness will be lost after death, whereas Jonathan Edwards believes that the soul will go to heaven or hell.
   e. Ralph Waldo Emerson's acceptance of Nature's indifference to the individual is ironically similar to Jonathan Edwards' acceptance of the doctrine of Divine Election.

15. Which of the following terms best defines the doctrine of Divine Election as discussed in the passage?
   a. God's power
   b. the soul's redemption
   c. eternal damnation
   d. predestined salvation
   e. a state of grace

16. In the context of the passage, which of the following words would best fit in the blank?
   a. loving
   b. just
   c. horrible
   d. imperious
   e. satisfying

Answer question 17 on the basis of the following passage.

> Authentic Dhurrie rugs are hand-woven in India. Today, they are usually made of wool, but they are descendants of cotton floor- and bed-coverings. In fact, the name Dhurrie comes from the Indian word *dari*, which means "threads of cotton." The rugs are noted for their soft colors and their varieties of design and make a stunning focal point for any living room or dining room.

17. Which of the following is most likely the intended audience for the passage?
   a. people who are planning a trip to India
   b. people studying traditional Indian culture
   c. people who are studying Indian domestic customs
   d. people learning to operate a rug loom
   e. people who enjoy interior decorating

Answer questions 18 and 19 on the basis of the following passage.

> A healthy diet with proper nutrition is essential for maintaining good overall health. Since vitamins were discovered in the twentieth century, people have routinely been taking vitamin supplements for this purpose. The Recommended Dietary Allowance (RDA) is a frequently used nutritional standard for maintaining optimal health. The RDA specifies the recommended amount of a number of nutrients for people of both sexes and in many different age groups. The National Research Council's Committee on Diet and Health has proposed a definition of the RDA to be that amount of a nutrient which meets the needs of 98% of the population.
>
> The RDA approach _____. First, it is based on the assumption that it is possible to accurately define nutritional requirements for a given group. However, individual nutritional requirements can vary widely within each group. The efficiency with which a person converts food intake into nutrients can also vary widely. Certain foods when eaten in combination actually prevent the absorption of nutrients. For example, spinach combined with milk reduces the amount of calcium available to the body from the milk. Also, the RDA approach specifies a different dietary requirement for each age and sex; however, it is clearly unrealistic to expect families to prepare a different menu for each family member. Still, although we cannot rely solely upon RDA to ensure our overall long-term health, it can be a useful guide so long as its limitations are recognized.

18. Which of the following would best fit in the blank in the first sentence of paragraph 2?
   a. is based on studies by respected nutritionists
   b. has a number of shortcomings
   c. has been debunked in the last few years
   d. is full of holes
   e. is constantly being refined

19. With which of the following would the author most likely agree?
   a. The RDA approach should be replaced by a more realistic nutritional guide.
   b. The RDA approach should be supplemented with more specific nutritional guides.
   c. In spite of its flaws, the RDA approach is definitely the best guide to good nutrition.
   d. The RDA approach is most suitable for a large family.
   e. The RDA approach is too complicated for most consumers.

Answer questions 20–22 on the basis of the following passage.

Interactive whiteboards are phenomenal tools. They will do for chalk and felt erasers what cell phones have done to pay phones. They can present anything which can be displayed on a computer, including software, websites, and more. Interactive whiteboards also let teachers record the screens they display so they can be used again at a later time. This makes it very easy to review material or provide missed instruction to a student who was absent.

Educational publishers and software companies produce material designed for interactive whiteboards. Some of this is specific to a certain brand of whiteboard, but the ideas can be incorporated on most of them. Teachers do not, however, need to spend money on predesigned lessons to make great use of interactive whiteboards.

For example, teachers can use built-in maps to teach geography or map scale. Storytelling can take on digital and graphic elements. Then students can illustrate and write a book as a class. Recording features allow students to narrate the text. Teachers can save special lessons to share with parents during conferences and open houses. The whiteboard can become an electronic word wall. The possibilities are endless.

20. Which of the following publications would most likely contain this passage?
   a. a brochure for a specific brand of electronic whiteboard
   b. advertising from a company that creates interactive whiteboard activities
   c. an online tutorial that shows teachers how to use interactive whiteboards
   d. a memo from a school district announcing the purchase of interactive whiteboards
   e. a magazine aimed at giving teachers insights into educational technology

21. Which of the following is the best meaning of the phrase *what cell phones have done to pay phones* as it is used in the first paragraph of the passage?
   a. cost about a quarter
   b. easy to find
   c. needed in public places
   d. private versus public
   e. make obsolete

22. Which of the following best organizes the main topics addressed in this passage?
- **a.** I. Description of interactive whiteboards
  II. Where to get content for interactive whiteboards
  III. Ways to use interactive whiteboards
- **b.** I. Comparing interactive whiteboard brands
  II. Types of interactive whiteboard content
  III. Lesson ideas
- **c.** I. The invention of interactive whiteboards
  II. How companies are selling interactive whiteboards
  III. Incorporating interactive whiteboards in the classroom
- **d.** I. Benefits of interactive whiteboards
  II. Interactive whiteboards in schools
  III. Built-in features
- **e.** I. Comparing interactive whiteboards and chalkboards
  II. Publishing interactive whiteboard lessons
  III. Expected uses of interactive whiteboards

Answer questions 23–26 on the basis of the following passage.

Avenida 9 de Julio in Buenos Aires, Argentina, is the widest street in the world, measuring 400 feet in width and 8,500 feet in length. The idea for the avenue was born in 1895, when city officials wanted to create an avenue that joined the north of the city with the south. It was initially decided that the avenue would be 108 feet wide, and so the city began to buy the buildings and land within the 33-block radius that would be needed to begin construction. Since then, many more blocks have been demolished to lengthen and widen the avenue to its current measurements. Avenida 9 de Julio, which means "July 9th Avenue" in English, was so named to commemorate Argentinean Independence Day.

_____.

The obelisk, standing 219 feet tall with four sides, was built in 1936 under the direction of Argentinean architect Alberto Prebisch. One side of the monument represents the anniversary of the first founding of the city by Pedro Mendoza in 1536. Another side represents the site where the flag of Argentina was raised for the first time. A third side commemorates the first time Buenos Aires was proclaimed as the capital of Argentina, and the fourth commemorates the founding of the city by Juan de Garay for a second time in 1580.

23. Which of the following is the best title for this passage?
- **a.** Buenos Aires's Famous Monuments
- **b.** The Argentineans Take Pride in Their Capital City
- **c.** The Widest Street in the World
- **d.** The Obelisk and the History of Buenos Aires's Avenida 9 de Julio
- **e.** Famous Facts about Buenos Aires

24. Which sentence, if inserted in the blank space at the end of the first paragraph, would make the most sense and best lead into the second paragraph?
- **a.** The avenue commemorates important historical facts of the city in other ways, too.
- **b.** In the middle of the avenue, the commemorative tradition continues with an obelisk that was built to honor important historical dates.
- **c.** Many come to visit the avenue and the obelisk that stands at its center.
- **d.** Argentineans don't go to work on July 9.

25. The main purpose of the passage is to
   a. entice people to visit Buenos Aires.
   b. compare Avenida 9 de Julio with other avenues in the world.
   c. give a history of Buenos Aires's most famous sites.
   d. explain what the obelisk symbolizes.
   e. describe the evolution of Avenida 9 de Julio and the obelisk.

26. Which of the following information, if added to the passage, would strengthen it the most?
   a. an explanation of why the city was founded a second time
   b. how long the obelisk took to build
   c. the measurements of the second widest street in the world
   d. how Alberto Prebisch was chosen as the architect of the obelisk
   e. the date the avenue was completed

Answer questions 27–29 on the basis of the following passage.

Queen Elizabeth I of England, also known as the "Virgin Queen" because she never married, reigned from 1558 until 1603. Because of her decisive leadership skills, she inaugurated an era of prosperity in Tudor England. The period of her reign, therefore, is referred to as the Elizabethan Era, or the Golden Age of Elizabeth, as England flourished under her leadership.

_____, William Shakespeare's and Christopher Marlowe's writing thrived, Francis Drake became the first person to sail across the globe, Francis Bacon published his influential political works, and North America was explored and colonized.

_____ a successful English ruler, Queen Elizabeth had her share of political turmoil to contend with. In July 1588, for instance, King Philip of Spain dispatched a fleet of 130 ships—the Spanish Armada—to invade and conquer England. In retaliation, Elizabeth sent forth troops to defend her country. Instead of staying safely hidden inside her castle, Elizabeth joined her troops on the front. Once there, she gave a speech known today as the "Speech to the Troops at Tilbury," in which she famously said, "I know I have the body but of a weak and feeble woman; but I have the heart and stomach of a King, and of a King of England too!" The battle that followed resulted in a resounding victory for England. This increased the Queen's popularity with her subjects, and elevated the status of the country. England was no longer a second-rate sea power, but a powerful force that had crushed the mighty Spanish Empire.

27. Which words or phrases, if inserted in order into the blanks in the passage, would help the reader understand the sequence of the author's ideas?
   a. Therefore; Now
   b. However; Still
   c. In addition; Yet
   d. For example; Although
   e. For instance; On the other hand

28. According to the passage, Elizabeth's reign resulted in
   a. turmoil between England and Spain.
   b. victory over Spain in a decisive battle.
   c. England thriving in many areas.
   d. the publication of great works.
   e. the exploration and settling of new colonies.

29. Which of the following is the best meaning of the word *inaugurated* as it is used in the passage?
   a. initiated
   b. dedicated
   c. invested
   d. adjourn
   e. offer

Answer questions 30–32 on the basis of the following passage.

Alexander III of Macedon, more famously known as Alexander the Great, inherited his father's kingdom in 336 B.C. at the age of 20. Believing that he was the son of Greek gods, Alexander was not satisfied with receiving the throne as a gift. Soon after his <u>ascension</u>, he led his armies to conquer—against overwhelming odds—the Persian territories of Asia Minor, Syria, and Egypt without one defeat. With his victories, the young leader of the Greeks, ruler of Asia Minor, and Pharaoh of Egypt also became the Great King of Persia at age 25. Over the next eight years, Alexander conquered and founded more than 70 cities, building an empire that spanned over three continents and two million square miles. Being a hero was always Alexander's ambition, and he is even quoted as saying, "I would rather live a short life of glory than a long one of obscurity." After Alexander died in Babylon at the age of 33—still the ruler of his conquered lands—he got what he wanted: More than 2,300 years after his death, he is still remembered as a legendary figure.

30. According to the information in the passage, for how many years did Alexander reign?
   a. 20
   b. 8
   c. 13
   d. 5
   e. 15

31. Which of the following is the best meaning of the word *ascension* as it is used in the passage?
   a. advancement
   b. climb
   c. expansion
   d. jump
   e. increase

32. Which of the following, if added to the passage, would strengthen it the most?
   a. a description of where Alexander grew up and what he studied in school
   b. information on how his father ruled, to give the reader more insight into how Alexander came to be the military genius that he was
   c. a quote about Alexander's character by someone who knew him well
   d. how Alexander was able to conquer the land that he did against the overwhelming odds that he faced
   e. how Alexander ended up in Babylon and how he died there at such a young age

Answer questions 33 and 34 on the basis of the following index.

Freedom of Expression, 217–290
    Text of the First Amendment, 217
    Suppression of Message Content, 217–272
        Cohen v. California, 219–220
        Marketplace of Ideas, 221–225
            Abrams v. United States, 223
        Unprotected Categories, 225–259
            Chaplin v. New Hampshire, 226
            Obscenity, 232–239
                Miller v. California, 233–235
            Advocating (Imminent) Illegal Behavior, 239–242
                Schenck v. Ohio, 240
            Defamation, 242–246
                New York Times v. Sullivan, 243–245
            Fighting Words, 247–252
                Feiner v. New York, 249
        Mere rationality analysis, 252–260
            Brandenburg v. Ohio, 256–259
        Outside the Unprotected Categories, 260–272
            Regulations Presumed Unconstitutional, 260–263
                Metromedia, Inc. v. San Diego, 261–263
            Government's Interest, 264–272
                Chicago Police Department v. Mosley, 266–267
                Significance, 267
                      Widmar v. Vincent, 268–269
                Narrowly Drawn, 270–272
                      Boos v. Barry, 270–271
    Incidental Interference with Expression, 273–290
        Time, Place, and Manner, 274–277
            Clark v. Community for Creative Non-Violence, 275–276
        Forum, 278–283
            Hague v. CIO, 281–283
            Public, 279
            Not Public, 280
        Government's Interest, 283–290
            Schneider v. State, 284–286
            Significance, 286–287
            Narrowly Drawn, 287–289
            Available Alternatives, 289–290

33. On which pages should one look to find information about the categories of unprotected speech?
    a. 217–220
    b. 221–225
    c. 225–259
    d. 260–272
    e. 273–290

34. Which of the following best describes the organizational pattern used in the section of the book dealing with suppression of message content?
    a. by the types of publications involved
    b. by the courts that heard the cases
    c. by the dates of the court decisions
    d. by the forum in which the speech took place
    e. by the category of the content of the speech

Answer question 35 on the basis of the following passage.

(1) Scientists understand that Italy's Mount Vesuvius will erupt again, and many geologists and volcanologists believe that the volcano is overdue. (2) So the Vesuvius Observatory monitors volcanic indicators 24 hours a day. (3) Around 25,000 years old, Mount Vesuvius destroyed Pompeii and Herculaneum. (4) Today, about 600,000 people live at the base of the volcano, and they are all at risk in the event of an eruption. (5) The last time Vesuvius erupted was in 1944. (6) The eruption was minor, so it caused very little damage and only killed 26 people. (7) Researchers think that the next eruption won't be as small.

35. Which of the following numbered sentence from the passage best expresses an opinion rather than a fact?
    a. Sentence 2
    b. Sentence 3
    c. Sentence 4
    d. Sentence 5
    e. Sentence 6

Answer questions 36 and 37 on the basis of the following passage.

When the current measure used to calculate poverty levels was introduced in 1963, the poverty line for a family of two adults and two children was about $3,100. In 2004, there were 36.9 million people, or 14.5% of the U.S. population, with incomes below the poverty line. A proposed new way of measuring poverty levels would include for the first time the effects of work-related expenses such as transportation costs and child care costs on families' available income.

The largest effect of the new measure would be a decrease in the percentage of people in families receiving cash welfare who fall under the poverty line, and an increase in the percentage of people in working families who fall under it. People in families receiving cash welfare would make up 30% of the poor under the new measure, compared with 40% under the current measure. In contrast, people in working families would make up 59% of the poor under the new measure, compared with 51% under the current measure.

36. According to the 1963 standards, the current number of poor working families is approximately what proportion of the population?
a. 30%
b. 60%
c. 40%
d. 59%
e. 51%

37. One difference between the current measure and the proposed measure is the fact that
a. the proposed measure identifies fewer working poor.
b. the current measure identifies fewer working poor.
c. the proposed measure disregards expenses for basic needs.
d. the current measure includes more people with health insurance.
e. the current measure ignores the completely destitute.

Answer questions 38–41 on the basis of the following passage.

Solar power is a form of renewable energy, as unlike coal or other fossil fuels, it is an infinite resource. It also does not produce pollution or environmental damage like its nonrenewable counterparts do. When harnessed, solar power can be used to heat water and buildings and to generate electricity. Both of these processes are accomplished by collecting the solar radiation, or radiant energy, emitted by the sun. Radiant energy—which is the energy produced from electromagnetic waves—contains self-propagating power and movement.

Solar power is converted into electricity through a photovoltaic (PV) cell, which is a non-mechanical device usually made from silicon alloys. PVs consist of two layers. When particles of the sun's energy, or photons, strike the surface of a PV, they cause electrons to move from one layer to another. This imbalance of charge creates a voltage potential similar to the one created by the positive and negative terminals of a battery, resulting in electric current.

38. What would be the best title for this passage?
   a. Solar Power
   b. Solar Power: A Renewable Resource
   c. Harnessing Solar Power
   d. Converting Solar Power into Electricity
   e. Solar Power and the Environment

39. According to the passage, solar radiation is
   a. energy from electromagnetic waves.
   b. electricity.
   c. heat.
   d. similar to fossil fuels.
   e. an electron.

40. According to the passage, renewable energy
   a. is more cost-effective than nonrenewable energy.
   b. is difficult to harness.
   c. does not run out.
   d. can be used only to heat water and buildings and generate electricity.
   e. is growing in popularity.

41. According to the passage, photons are
   a. electrons.
   b. non-mechanical devices.
   c. silicone alloys.
   d. particles of the sun's energy.
   e. particles of electricity.

Answer questions 42–45 on the basis of the following passage.

By using tiny probes as neural prostheses, scientists may be able to restore nerve function in quadriplegics and make the blind see or the deaf hear. Thanks to advanced techniques, a single, small, implanted probe can stimulate individual neurons electrically or chemically and then record responses. Preliminary results suggest that the microprobe telemetry systems can be permanently implanted and replace damaged or missing nerves.

The tissue-compatible microprobes represent an advance over the typical aluminum wire electrodes used in studies of the cortex and other brain structures. Researchers accumulate much data using traditional electrodes, but there is a question of how much damage they cause to the nervous system. Microprobes, which are about as thin as a human hair, cause minimal damage and disruption of neurons when inserted into the brain.

In addition to recording nervous system impulses, the microprobes have minuscule channels that open the way for delivery of drugs, cellular growth factors, neurotransmitters, and other neuroactive compounds to a single neuron or to groups of neurons. Also, patients who lack certain biochemicals could receive doses via prostheses. The probes can have up to four channels, each with its own recording/stimulating electrode.

42. One similar feature of microprobes and wire electrodes is
   a. a minimal disturbance of neurons.
   b. the density of the material.
   c. the capacity for multiple leads.
   d. the substance from which they are made.
   e. their ability to generate information.

43. Which of the following best expresses the main idea of the passage?
   a. Microprobes require further technological advances before they can be used in humans.
   b. Wire electrodes are antiquated as a means for delivering neuroactive compounds to the brain.
   c. Microprobes have great potential to help counteract neural damage.
   d. Technology now exists that may enable repair of the nervous system.
   e. Use of wire electrodes is being replaced by use of wire electrodes.

44. All of the following are mentioned in the passage as potential uses for prostheses EXCEPT
   a. transportation of medication.
   b. induction of physical movement.
   c. compensation for damaged nerves.
   d. transportation of growth factor.
   e. removal of biochemicals from the cortex.

45. The initial function of microprobe channels is to
   a. create pathways.
   b. disrupt neurons.
   c. replace ribbon cables.
   d. study the brain.
   e. induce sight and hearing in the blind and deaf.

Answer questions 46 and 47 on the basis of the following passage.

Pit bulls are one of the most misunderstood breeds. Technically, the term *pit bull* refers to a group of dogs that share similar characteristics, not to a specific breed. When people talk about pit bulls, however, they are generally referring to the American Pit Bull Terrier (APBT).

Contrary to popular myth, pit bulls love people and make excellent companions. However, pit bulls are strong, energetic, and agile; therefore, they may not make the best pets for people who have never owned a dog before. They are energetic and need a lot of exercise and can be rambunctious without the proper training and socialization.

The APBT was originally bred to fight other dogs, and much of the negative attention the dogs receive is based on this genetic trait. Their breeding, however, does not mean that pit bulls should be put in a ring to fight other dogs—on the contrary—this is a cruel sport. Pits can remain loving and loyal companions if treated properly. Like any other dog, they become aggressive if abused and mistreated.

46. Based on the tone of the passage, the author's main purpose is to
 a. teach people how to train pit bulls.
 b. show how the pit bull's nature makes it a good pet.
 c. clarify misconceptions surrounding the pit bull.
 d. encourage people to adopt a pit bull.
 e. argue against pit-fighting as a sport.

47. According to the passage, adopting a pit bull is a good idea for people who
 a. are getting their first dog.
 b. have the time, experience, and patience to properly train them.
 c. are elderly or retired.
 d. live in an apartment.
 e. live in a large home.

Use the graph below to answer question 48.

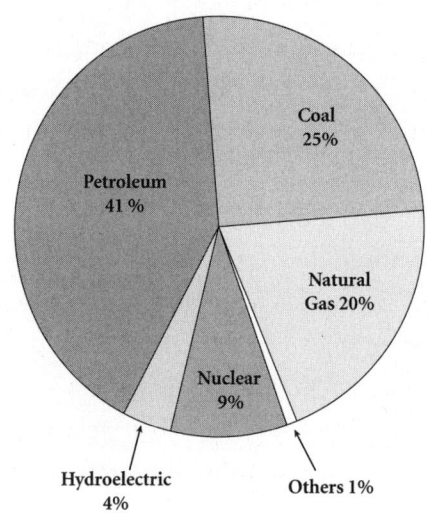

Energy Sources for Kane County Residents

48. What percentage of energy is NOT derived from fossil fuels?
 a. 4%
 b. 9%
 c. 10%
 d. 14%
 e. 34%

Answer questions 49 and 50 on the basis of the following table.

DISTRIBUTION OF OCCUPATIONS OF 200 ADULT MALES IN THE BAIDYA CASTE MADARIPUR VILLAGE, BENGAL, 1914

Occupation	Number
Farmers	02
Government service, clerks	44
Landowners	08
Lawyers	06
Newspapers and presses	05
No occupation	25
Not recorded	08
Students	68
Teachers	11
Trade and commerce	23

49. The largest number of men in the Baidya caste of Madaripur were involved in which field?
   a. education
   b. agriculture
   c. government
   d. publishing
   e. trade

50. How many men listed a field related to education as an occupation?
   a. 11
   b. 23
   c. 68
   d. 79
   e. 91

Section 2: Mathematics

1. Roger earned $24,355 this year, and $23,000 the year before. To the nearest $100, what did Roger earn in the past two years?
   a. $47,300
   b. $47,350
   c. $47,355
   d. $47,360
   e. $47,400

Use the information below to answer question 2.

A cafeteria has three different price options for lunch.
   For $2, a customer can get either a sandwich or two pieces of fruit.
   For $3, a customer can get a sandwich and one piece of fruit.
   For $4, a customer can get either two sandwiches, or a sandwich and two pieces of fruit.

2. If Jan has $6 to pay for lunch for her and her husband, which of the following is NOT a possible combination?
   a. three sandwiches and one piece of fruit
   b. two sandwiches and two pieces of fruit
   c. one sandwich and four pieces of fruit
   d. three sandwiches and no fruit
   e. one sandwich and three pieces of fruit

Use the following table to answer question 3.

PRODUCTION OF FARM-IT TRACTORS FOR THE MONTH OF APRIL	
FACTORY	APRIL OUTPUT
Dallas	450
Houston	425
Lubbock	
Amarillo	345
TOTAL	1,780

3. What was Lubbock's production in the month of April?
   a. 345
   b. 415
   c. 540
   d. 550
   e. 560

Use the pie chart to answer question 4.

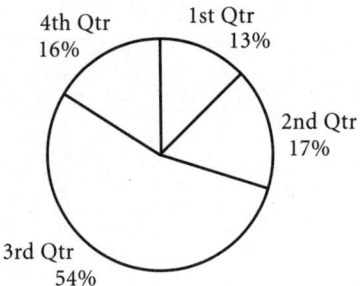

Sales for 2005

4. The chart shows quarterly sales for Cool-Air's air-conditioning units. Which of the following combinations contributed 70% to the total?
   a. 1st and 2nd quarters
   b. 1st and 3rd quarters
   c. 2nd and 3rd quarters
   d. 2nd and 4th quarters
   e. 3rd and 4th quarters

5. A car drove 294 miles in 4 hours and 54 minutes. What was the average speed of the car in miles per hour?
   a. 29 miles per hour
   b. 36 miles per hour
   c. 54 miles per hour
   d. 60 miles per hour
   e. 64 miles per hour

6. An average of 90% is needed on five tests to receive an A in a class. If a student received scores of 95, 85, 88, and 84 on the first four tests, what score will the student need to achieve on the fifth test to get an A?
   a. 90
   b. 92
   c. 94
   d. 96
   e. 98

7. A deck of cards contains 6 clubs, 10 spades, 2 hearts, and 14 diamonds. If one card is drawn from the deck, what is the probability that it will be either a spade or a diamond?
   a. $\frac{5}{6}$
   b. $\frac{3}{8}$
   c. $\frac{7}{16}$
   d. $\frac{2}{3}$
   e. $\frac{3}{4}$

8. Marco took a standardized test to measure his performance in history. He earned a stanine score that showed he performed a little below average compared to students who also took the test. Which stanine score could Marco have received?

   a. 1
   b. 2
   c. 4
   d. 5
   e. 6

9. What is the product of 200 and 2.104?

   a. 42.08
   b. 42.8
   c. 402.8
   d. 420.8
   e. 428

10. If a school buys three computers at a, b, and c dollars each, and the school gets a discount of 90%, which expression would determine the average price paid by the school?

   a. $\frac{0.9(a+b+c)}{3}$
   b. $\frac{(a+b+c)}{0.9}$
   c. $(a+b+c) \times 0.9$
   d. $\frac{(a+b+c)}{3}$
   e. $\frac{3(a+b+c)}{0.9}$

11. Roger wants to know if he has enough money to purchase several items. He needs three heads of lettuce, which cost $.99 each, and two boxes of cereal, which cost $3.49 each. He uses the expression $(3 \times \$.99) + (2 \times \$3.49)$ to calculate how much the items will cost. Which of the following expressions could also be used?

   a. $3 \times (\$3.49 + \$.99) - \$3.49$
   b. $3 \times (\$3.49 + \$.99)$
   c. $(2 + 3) \times (\$3.49 + \$.99)$
   d. $(2 \times 3) + (\$3.49 \times \$.99)$
   e. $3 \times (\$3.49 + \$.99) + \$3.49$

12. Rosa finds the average of her three most recent golf scores by using the following expression, where a, b, and c are the three scores: $\frac{a+b+c}{3} \times 100$. Which of the following would also determine the average of her scores?

   a. $(\frac{a}{3} + \frac{b}{3} + \frac{c}{3}) \times 100$
   b. $\frac{\frac{a+b+c}{3}}{100}$
   c. $(a+b+c) \times \frac{3}{100}$
   d. $\frac{a \times b \times c}{3 + 100}$
   e. $\frac{a+b+c}{3+100}$

13. Jim uses $\frac{3}{4}$ of a can of paint to cover $2\frac{1}{2}$ canvases. How much paint is needed to cover one canvas?

   a. $\frac{1}{4}$ cans
   b. $\frac{3}{10}$ cans
   c. $\frac{3}{8}$ cans
   d. $1\frac{7}{8}$ cans
   e. $3\frac{1}{3}$ cans

14. A 20 cc dosage of medication must be increased by 40%. What is the new dosage?
   a. 4 cc
   b. 8 cc
   c. 24 cc
   d. 28 cc
   e. 60 cc

15. The sticker price on a car is $18,500, but the dealer is offering an 8.8% discount. How much does the car cost?
   a. $16,280
   b. $16,872
   c. $17,020
   d. $17,082
   e. $20,128

16. In the Pinebrook school district last year, 220 students were vaccinated for measles, mumps, and rubella. Of those, 60% reported that they had the flu at some time in their lives. How many students had not had the flu previously?
   a. 36
   b. 55
   c. 88
   d. 126
   e. 132

17. A survey found that 341 out of 1,755 households were tuned into a particular football game on television. Approximately what percentage of the households was watching the football game on television?
   a. 5.2%
   b. 15%
   c. 19.4%
   d. 22.3%
   e. 27.1%

Answer questions 18–19 by referring to the following chart, which gives the causes of major home fires.

MAJOR CAUSES OF HOME FIRES IN THE PREVIOUS 4-YEAR PERIOD

Cause	Fires (% of Total)	Civilian Deaths (% of Total)
Heating equipment	161,500 (27.5%)	770 (16.8%)
Cooking equipment	104,800 (17.8%)	350 (7.7%)
Incendiary, suspicious	65,400 (11.1%)	620 (13.6%)
Electrical equipment	45,700 (7.8%)	440 (9.6%)
Other equipment	43,000 (7.3%)	240 (5.3%)
Smoking materials	39,300 (6.7%)	1,320 (28.9%)
Appliances, air conditioning	36,200 (6.2%)	120 (2.7%)
Exposure and other heat	28,600 (4.8%)	191 (4.2%)
Open flame	27,200 (4.6%)	130 (2.9%)
Child play	26,900 (4.6%)	370 (8.1%)
Natural causes	9,200 (1.6%)	10 (0.2%)

18. What is the percentage of the total fires caused by electrical equipment and other equipment combined?
   a. 7.8%
   b. 14.9%
   c. 15.1%
   d. 29.9%
   e. 30.0%

19. Of the following causes, which one has the highest ratio of total fires to percentage of deaths?
   a. heating equipment
   b. smoking materials
   c. exposure and other heat
   d. child play
   e. natural causes

20. The snack machine in the teachers' lounge accepts only quarters. Candy bars cost 25¢, packages of peanuts cost 75¢, and cans of cola cost 50¢. How many quarters are needed to buy two candy bars, one package of peanuts, and one can of cola?
   a. 8
   b. 7
   c. 6
   d. 5
   e. 4

21. Carlotta's credit card statement showed that she owed $450. She made a payment of $175, then she charged $27 for gas. She returned a lamp she had charged earlier for a refund of $49. Then she charged $25 at the bookstore. What is her new balance?
   a. $174
   b. $278
   c. $376
   d. $622
   e. $726

22. A child has a temperature of 40° C. What is the child's temperature in degrees Fahrenheit? $F = \frac{9}{5}C + 32$.
   a. 100° F
   b. 101° F
   c. 102° F
   d. 103° F
   e. 104° F

Answer question 23 on the basis of the following information.

Mr. Richard Tupper is purchasing gifts for his family. He stops to consider what else he has to buy. A quick mental inventory of his shopping bag so far reveals the following:

- 1 cashmere sweater valued at $260
- 3 diamond bracelets, each valued at $365
- 1 computer game valued at $78
- 1 cameo brooch valued at $130

Later, having coffee in the Food Court, he suddenly remembers that he has purchased only 2 diamond bracelets, not 3, and that the cashmere sweater was on sale for $245.

23. What is the total value of the gifts Mr. Tupper has purchased so far?
    a. $833
    b. $975
    c. $1,183
    d. $1,198
    e. $1,563

Answer questions 24-25 on the basis of the following list.

Here is a list of the ingredients needed to make 16 brownies.

Deluxe Brownies
$\frac{2}{3}$ cup butter
5 squares (1 ounce each) unsweetened chocolate
$1\frac{1}{2}$ cups sugar
2 teaspoons vanilla
2 eggs
1 cup flour

24. How much sugar is needed to make 8 brownies?
    a. $\frac{3}{4}$ cup
    b. 3 cups
    c. $\frac{2}{3}$ cup
    d. $\frac{5}{8}$ cup
    e. 1 cup

25. What is the greatest number of brownies that can be made if the baker has only 1 cup of butter?
    a. 12
    b. 16
    c. 24
    d. 28
    e. 32

26. One lap on a particular track at a local city park measures a third of a mile around. To run a total of four and two-thirds miles, how many complete laps must a person complete?
    a. 4
    b. 6
    c. 10
    d. 12
    e. 14

27. Wallace has 15 pounds of dough. If he uses $5\frac{7}{8}$ pounds of dough making pizza and $6\frac{1}{2}$ pounds of dough making bread, how much dough does he have left?
    a. $2\frac{1}{8}$ pounds
    b. $2\frac{3}{8}$ pounds
    c. $2\frac{5}{8}$ pounds
    d. $3\frac{3}{8}$ pounds
    e. $3\frac{5}{8}$ pounds

28. A floor plan is drawn to scale so that a quarter of an inch represents 2 feet. If a hall on the plan is 4 inches long, how long will the actual hall be when it is built?
   a. 2 feet
   b. 8 feet
   c. 16 feet
   d. 24 feet
   e. 32 feet

29. Student track team members have to buy running shoes at the full price of $84.50, but those who were also team members last term get a 15% discount. Those who have been team members for at least three terms get an additional 10% off the discounted price. How much does a student who has been a track team member at least three terms have to pay for shoes?
   a. $63.38
   b. $64.65
   c. $65.78
   d. $71.83
   e. $72.05

30. Of the 150 sixth grade students at Jamestown Middle School, 45 students play football, 30 students play basketball, and 42 students play soccer. What percentage of students does not play any sport?
   a. 15%
   b. 18%
   c. 20%
   d. 22%
   e. 28%

31. The basal metabolic rate (BMR) is the rate at which our bodies use calories. The BMR for a man in his twenties is about 1,700 calories per day. If 204 of those calories should come from protein, about what percent of this man's diet should be protein?
   a. 1.2%
   b. 8.3%
   c. 12%
   d. 16%
   e. 18%

32. The condition known as Down syndrome occurs in about 1 in 1,500 children whose mothers are in their twenties. About what percent of all children born to mothers in their twenties are likely to have Down syndrome?
   a. 0.0067%
   b. 0.67%
   c. 6.7%
   d. 0.067%
   e. 0.00067%

33. If a population of yeast cells grows from 10 to 320 in a period of 5 hours, what is the rate of growth?
   a. It doubles its numbers every half hour.
   b. It doubles its numbers every hour.
   c. It triples its numbers every hour.
   d. It doubles its numbers every two hours.
   e. It triples its numbers every two hours.

34. A certain water pollutant is unsafe at a level above 20 ppm (parts per million). A city's water supply now contains 50 ppm of this pollutant. What percentage of improvement will make the water safe?
   a. 30%
   b. 40%
   c. 50%
   d. 60%
   e. 70%

35. An insurance policy pays 80% of the first $20,000 of a certain patient's medical expenses, 60% of the next $40,000, and 40% of the $40,000 after that. If the patient's total medical bill is $92,000, how much will the policy pay?
   a. $36,800
   b. $49,600
   c. $52,800
   d. $73,600
   e. $80,000

36. Emilio bought oranges, apples, and grapes for a school party. The oranges and grapes cost the same amount, and the apples cost $3.99. What information would allow you to find the amount Emilio spent on the oranges?
   a. the cost per pound of oranges
   b. the cost per pound of grapes
   c. the total amount Emilio spent on fruit
   d. the number of oranges Emilio purchased
   e. the cost per pound of apples

37. Water is coming into a tank three times as fast as it is going out. After one hour, the tank contains 11,400 gallons of water. How fast is the water coming in?
   a. 2,850 gallons/hour
   b. 3,800 gallons/hour
   c. 5,700 gallons/hour
   d. 11,400 gallons/hour
   e. 17,100 gallons/hour

38. Neela must transport 5,120 pounds of sand using 8 trucks. If she dumps the same quantity of sand in each truck, how much sand will each truck transport?
   a. 605 pounds
   b. 640 pounds
   c. 650 pounds
   d. 675 pounds
   e. 765 pounds

39. A stocker at the grocery store builds a four-sided pyramid using cantaloupes. (Don't count the bottom as a side.) How many cantaloupes will there be in a pyramid that has six layers?
   a. 16
   b. 25
   c. 28
   d. 36
   e. 49

40. Michelle burns a CD for her mother that has $3\frac{1}{4}$ hours of music. She then burns a CD for her father that has $3\frac{1}{3}$ hours of music. Michelle then burns a CD for herself that is longer than her mother's and shorter than her father's. How long could her CD be?
   a. 3 hours 14 minutes
   b. 3 hours 15 minutes
   c. 3 hours 17 minutes
   d. 3 hours 20 minutes
   e. 3 hours 25 minutes

41. Ron is half as old as Sam, who is three times as old as Ted. The sum of their ages is 55. How old is Ron?
   a. 5
   b. 8
   c. 10
   d. 15
   e. 30

42. Abby has 42 math problems to complete for homework. If she has completed $\frac{5}{6}$ of them, how many does she have left to do?
   a. 7 problems
   b. 10 problems
   c. 12 problems
   d. 14 problems
   e. 35 problems

43. A gardener on a large estate determines that the length of garden hose needed to reach from the water spigot to a particular patch of prize-winning dragonsnaps is 175 feet. If the available garden hoses are 45 feet long, how many sections of hose, when connected together, will it take to reach the dragonsnaps?
   a. 2
   b. 3
   c. 4
   d. 5
   e. 6

44. To lower a fever of 105°, ice packs are applied for 1 minute and then removed for 5 minutes before being applied again. Each application lowers the fever by half a degree. How long will it take to lower the fever to 99°?
   a. 36 minutes
   b. 1 hour
   c. 1 hour and 7 minutes
   d. 1 hour and 15 minutes
   e. 1 hour and 30 minutes

45. Each sprinkler head in a sprinkler system sprays water at an average of 16 gallons per minute. If 5 sprinkler heads are flowing at the same time, how many gallons of water will be released in 10 minutes?
   a. 80
   b. 160
   c. 320
   d. 800
   e. 1650

46. Ron needs moving boxes to pack the books he has in his office. Each box can hold 16 books, and Ron needs to pack up 420 books. How many boxes does Ron need?
   a. 25
   b. 26
   c. 26.25
   d. 27
   e. 27.25

47. A deck of cards contains 52 cards, 13 from each suit. If a card is flipped over, what is the probability that it is a face card (J, Q, or K)?
   a. $\frac{13}{4}$
   b. $\frac{3}{13}$
   c. $\frac{3}{26}$
   d. $\frac{1}{26}$
   e. $\frac{3}{52}$

48. The length of a rectangle is three times its width. If the perimeter of the rectangle is 72 inches, what is the length of the rectangle?
   a. 9 inches
   b. 15 inches
   c. 18 inches
   d. 24 inches
   e. 27 inches

49. About how many liters of water will a 5-gallon container hold? (1 liter = 1.06 quarts)
   a. 5
   b. 11
   c. 19
   d. 20
   e. 21

50. A community contains 8,450 households. The fire department found that 7,120 of the households had a smoke detector in the house. About what percentage of the community's households had a smoke detector?
   a. 15%
   b. 30%
   c. 43%
   d. 72%
   e. 84%

Section 3: Essay Writing

Carefully read the two essay-writing topics that follow. Plan and write two essays, one on each topic. Be sure to address all points in the topic. Allow about 30 minutes for each essay.

Topic 1

In a review of Don DeLillo's novel White Noise, Jayne Anne Phillips writes that the characters are people "sleepwalking through a world where 'Coke is It!' and the TV is always on." On the other hand, television is said to have brought the world to people who would not have seen much of it otherwise, that it has made possible a "global village." Write an essay in which you express your opinion of the effect of television on individuals or on nations. Include specific detail from personal experience to back up your assertions.

Topic 2

Many studies indicate that students leaving high school do not have the business skills that employers desire. Describe how schools can prepare students for the demands of a job while also giving them the preparation to attend college. Be sure to back up your thesis statement with concrete examples and specific details.

Answers

Section 1: Reading Comprehension

1. **a.** Choice **a** is the best because it is the most complete statement of the material. Choices **c** and **d** focus on small details of the passage; choice **b** is not discussed in the passage. The passage is informative, not persuasive, so choice **e** is incorrect.

2. **b.** In the context of the paragraph, this is the only possible choice. Choice **a** can be ruled out because there is no evidence that Hershey *became educated*. It is true that Hershey *was a talented person* (choice **b**), but *was talented* is not the same as having *found* something. Choice **d** is incorrect because there is no evidence in paragraph 1 that Hershey called on anyone to help him. The passage talks about Hershey's hard work, but does not say he was lucky (choice **e**).

3. **b.** Because the passage states that Hershey *returned to the village where he had been born* to open his plant, and the passage also states that he was born near Derry Church, this statement must be accurate. The other choices cannot be supported. Although the writer mentions the popularity of chocolate internationally, you cannot assume that it is popular in every country (choice **a**), nor is there any indication that Milton Hershey was the first person to manufacture chocolate in the United States (choice **c**). Choice **d** is not discussed in the passage at all. The passage states that Hershey did not succeed in his candy-making ventures in other cities (choice **e**).

4. **b.** This is the best choice because the passage clearly shows Hershey's determination to be successful in the candy business. Although Hershey had some failures, he could not be described as *defective* (choice **a**). There is nothing to indicate that he was *carefree* (choice **c**), *cautious* (choice **d**), or *greedy* (choice **e**).

5. **c.** The third paragraph states that Hershey first used chocolate for *coating his caramels*. Choice **a** can be ruled out because he didn't make cocoa or baking chocolate until a year after he began producing chocolate. Choice **b** is not in the passage. Choice **d** is incorrect because he purchased the chocolate-making equipment at the Exposition. Choice **e** is incorrect because Hershey did not try to start a town.

6. **d.** This question tests your ability to use context clues to determine the intended meaning of a word. In paragraph 3, the passage says that *The Hershey Chocolate company was born in 1894 as a subsidiary of the Lancaster Caramel Company.* This indicates that a subsidiary company is one controlled by another company, choice **d**. Choices **a**, **b**, and **e** are illogical. Since the passage contains no discussion of whether any of Hershey's companies were incorporated, choice **c** can be ruled out.

7. **d.** This is an inference taken from paragraphs 3 and 4. Paragraph 3 indicates that Hershey's caramel company was in Lancaster and the chocolate company was a subsidiary. Paragraph 4 states that Hershey moved his plant in 1905, 11 years after he first got into the chocolate business. From these two facts, it is reasonable to conclude that the first chocolate business was in Lancaster.

8. **a.** This is the only choice that can be supported by the paragraph. Although tourists and caramel are mentioned in the passage (choices **b** and **e**), this is not the main purpose of the paragraph. There is a theme park in Hershey (choice **c**), but the chocolate factory still exists. Choice **d** can be ruled out because this information was given in paragraph 4.

9. d. The author implies that food residue could be a problem for students, so a student who spreads crumbs of an allergen food, even without sharing the food, could cause an allergic reaction. This eliminates choices **a** and **e**. Homemade foods could inadvertently contain an allergen, which would be dangerous to a child with food allergies. This eliminates choice **b**. Nothing in the passage indicates the need to remove students from an area due to the risk of allergies, so eliminate choice **c**. The best answer is choice **d**, and this mimics the language of the passage.

10. e. The passage describes how teachers and school administrators should manage students with food allergies. Nurses who are assigned to work in this school should be aware that they have epinephrine in the office. Parents with children who have food allergies would want to know how the school handles these food allergies. However, this is a passage about an elementary school. This passage is not written with language geared toward elementary-age children. The best choice is **e**.

11. c. Cleaning lunchroom tables is mentioned in only one paragraph, so eliminate choice **a**. School nurses are discussed, but so are teachers and administrators. Eliminate choice **b**. The passage does not dictate that students should have medicine in the nurse's office, so eliminate choice **d**. Choice **e** only describes part of the passage. The best choice is **c**, as the majority of the passage discusses how to prevent food allergies and how they are treated.

12. e. The base word, *present*, has multiple definitions, meaning right now, a gift, and in attendance. The passage only mentions a treatment if a child has an allergic reaction. It makes the most sense that there is not a cure right now but that one could be found in the future.

13. a. The final sentence states that *Nature will not mind drowning a man or a woman*, and sentence 4 speaks of Edwards' approval of God's *arbitrary* will; neither Nature nor God, as described in the passage, would notice *the fall of a sparrow*. Choice **b** is incorrect because Edwards has a *delightful conviction* in *God's sovereignty* (authority or power), which indicates that he believes God's judgment, no matter how arbitrary, is wise. Choices **c** and **d** are incorrect because Emerson speaks of Nature's intention as *harmony and joy*. Choice **e** is incorrect; both Emerson and Edwards believe God makes decisions about individuals based on the need of nature as a whole.

14. e. This choice says *how* the reflections of Emerson and Edwards are alike (that is, their acceptance of the arbitrary nature of Nature and God) and also speaks of the irony of the similarity between Emerson and Edwards, which is mentioned in the passage. Choice **a** is true, but is too general, since it does not say exactly how the two philosophers are alike. Choices **b**, **c**, and **d** are incorrect because they emphasize differences between the two world views, whereas the passage emphasizes similarities.

15. d. To be elected means to be chosen, and the passage speaks of *God's choosing according to his divine and arbitrary will, whom he would to eternal life* (i.e., to salvation). Being rejected is the opposite of being chosen or elected, so someone rejected would be damned (choice **c**). The other choices do not reflect an element of choice.

16. c. The word *horrible* most definitely contrasts to the words *exceedingly pleasant, bright, and sweet*, and the words *formerly* and *however* indicate that the sentence is describing a contrast. The other choices do not necessarily point to a contrast.

17. e. Although the people in the other choices might read this passage, it is not directed toward travelers, scholars, or readers (choices **a**, **b**, and **c**), nor is there anything in it about operating a loom (choice **d**). The last sentence indicates that the passage is directed toward interior decorators.

18. b. The blank is followed by a discussion of the shortcomings of the RDA approach. Choice **a** is incorrect because it does not lead into the discussion that follows regarding the RDA approach's shortcomings. Choice **c** is incorrect because it is contradicted by the final sentence of the passage, which states that the RDA approach remains a *useful guide*. Choice **d** is incorrect because its informal style is inconsistent with the style used in the rest of the passage. Choice **e** is incorrect because it does not lead into the discussion that follows, and there is nothing in the passage to indicate the RDA is changing.

19. b. Choice **b** is indicated by the final sentence, which indicates that the RDA approach is useful but has limitations, implying that a supplemental guide would be a good thing. Choice **a** is contradicted by the final sentence of the passage. Choice **c** is incorrect because the passage says the RDA approach is a *useful guide*, but does NOT say it is the best guide to good nutrition. Choice **d** is contradicted by the next-to-last sentence of the passage. The passage states that the RDA approach is frequently used, which indicates it is not too complicated, as stated in choice **e**.

20. e. If this were a brochure of one brand of interactive whiteboard, the passage would name only that brand. No brand name is given, so eliminate choice **a**. A company who made activities for the whiteboard would not suggest that a teacher could make activities for free, so eliminate choice **b**. The passage does not describe how to use the whiteboard, so eliminate choice **c**. A memo from a school district would tell who is receiving the whiteboards, the cost of the purchase, or more specific information relevant to schools. A magazine describing the interactive whiteboard would be the best answer.

21. e. Think about what cell phones have done to pay phones. Nearly every adult has a cell phone. This eliminates the need to use a pay phone, so businesses do not install pay phones anymore. In other words, pay phones are not needed, or obsolete.

22. a. The first paragraph describes what interactive whiteboards are and does not discuss features of different brands. Eliminate choice **b**. The second paragraph mentions that publishers and software companies make interactive whiteboard lessons, but so can teachers. This eliminates choices **c** and **d**. The third paragraph gives ideas for how the whiteboard could be used in lessons, so the best choice is **a**.

23. d. The passage talks about only one of Buenos Aires's famous monuments, so choice **a** is incorrect. There is never any mention of the Argentinean people taking pride in Buenos Aires, so choice **b** is incorrect. Choice **c** is

tricky because the passage is indeed about the "widest street in the world," but choice **d** is still the better choice of the two because it is more specific and descriptive. Choice **e** is much too vague.

24. b. Choice **a** doesn't mention the obelisk at all, and since the second paragraph starts with *The obelisk*, it's not the correct choice. Choice **c** doesn't flow smoothly from the sentence before it, nor does it introduce the obelisk—it is written as if the reader already knows about it. Choice **e** is completely irrelevant to the information in the passage.

25. e. Nothing in the passage suggests that people should visit Buenos Aires, making choice **a** incorrect. Choice **b** is incorrect; although the passage does say that Avenida 9 de Julio is wider than any other street in the world, that is not the main point of the passage. Choice **c** is incorrect because the passage gives the history of only one of the city's famous sites. The passage does explain what the obelisk symbolizes (choice **d**), but that is only a detail of the passage, not its main idea.

26. c. Choice **a** would add only a small detail (and one that is irrelevant to the history of the avenue and the obelisk) that wouldn't contribute much to the passage, so it is not the correct choice. Choices **b**, **d**, and **e** wouldn't hurt the passage, but since the passage is about the widest street in the world, giving the measurements of the second widest street in the world would strengthen it the most.

27. d. To determine what word goes into the sentence with the first blank, look to the sentence that precedes it—it states that England flourished under Elizabeth's leadership. The sentence with the blank lists examples that support that statement. Although the first term in choice **e** is *For instance*, the second word in the choice doesn't make sense within the context of the passage; therefore, choice **d** is the only option.

28. c. All of the other choices are, in fact, results of Elizabeth's reign, but each one reflects only *one* result. Choice **c** is the only one that addresses all of the results of her reign according to the passage.

29. a. Choices **b** and **c** are alternate definitions of *inaugurated*, but do not fit the context of the passage. Choice **d** has the opposite meaning to the word inaugurated, and choice **e** does not define the word at all.

30. c. If Alexander took the throne at 20 and died at 33, that means he reigned for 13 years.

31. a. The verb form of *ascension*, *ascend*, has more than one meaning. It can mean to *go up*, to *climb*, or to *rise*. It can also mean to *advance from a lower level or station*, such as one does when ascending the throne, which is the meaning of the word in the context of this passage. Choice **b** is incorrect for two reasons: It is the wrong definition of the word in this context, and it is a synonym for the verb form, *ascend*, not the noun form, *ascension*. Choices **c**, **d**, and **e** are not synonyms of *ascension*.

32. d. Since the reason Alexander is legendary is that he conquered so many lands at such a young age, information on how he was able to do this would strengthen the passage most. All of the other choices would add only minor details that would not add much to the passage.

33. c. Unprotected categories of expression are discussed on pages 225–259.

34. e. Although this information is about expression, it is not organized by the types of publications involved, choice **a**; and although the index contains court cases, it does not indicate which courts heard the cases—choice **b**—or the dates of the decisions, choice **c**. Choice **d**, the forum in which the speech took place, is an entry in the index, but does not impact its organization.

35. e. Sentence 6 says, *The eruption was minor, so it caused very little damage and only killed 26 people.* The people who had damage or lost a loved one may not consider the eruption a minor one. This is a statement of opinion.

36. e. See the last sentence of the passage for the correct answer, 51%.

37. b. The second paragraph states that the current measure identifies fewer working poor, so choice **a** is incorrect. The proposed measure does not disregard expenses for basic needs (choice **c**); it includes the value of non-cash benefits. The current measure identifies fewer people with health insurance (choice **d**). There is no indication in the passage that either measure ignores the destitute (choice **e**).

38. d. Choice **a** is too broad, and choice **b** refers to only one of the details in the passage, and one that is not expanded upon. Choice **c** is a close second to choice **d**, but the passage covers harnessing solar power only for electricity, not heat. Choice **e** is not covered in the passage.

39. a. This is a detail question. The answer can be found here: *... by collecting the solar radiation, or radiant energy, emitted by the sun. Radiant energy—which is the energy produced from electromagnetic waves ...*

40. c. Choices **a**, **b**, and **e** are never mentioned in the passage. Choice **d** would be right except for the word *only*, which makes the statement an absolute that is not found in the passage.

41. d. This is a detail question. The answer can be found in the following sentence in the second paragraph: *When particles of the sun's energy, or photons, strike the surface of a PV ...*

42. e. The second sentence of the first paragraph states that probes record responses. The second paragraph says that electrodes *accumulate much data*.

43. c. The tone throughout the passage suggests the potential for microprobes. They can be permanently implanted, they have advantages over electrodes, they are promising candidates for neural prostheses, they will have great accuracy, and they are flexible.

44. e. According to the third paragraph, people who *lack* biochemicals could receive doses via prostheses. However, there is no suggestion that removing biochemicals would be viable.

45. a. The first sentence of the third paragraph says that microprobes have channels that *open the way for delivery of drugs*. Studying the brain (choice **d**) is not the initial function of channels, though it is one of the uses of the probes themselves.

46. c. Although some parts (or all) of choices **a**, **b**, and **e** are mentioned in the passage, they are not the main point. Choice **d** is incorrect because it is not mentioned in the passage.

47. b. Because the passage mentions that pit bulls need a lot of exercise and proper training and socialization, it can be inferred that the author feels a pit bull owner should have time and experience to raise one. The opposite of choice **a** is mentioned in the passage, therefore it is incorrect. Although the passage never mentions the elderly or retired, it can be inferred that they might not make the best pit bull owners, as the author clearly states pit bulls require a lot of exercise. Even if this choice is slightly in the running, choice **b** is still the best answer. Choices **d** is an unlikely answer due to the reasons previously mentioned, and although choice **e** is a possibility, it is never mentioned in the passage, and choice **b** remains the best answer.

48. d. Coal, petroleum, and natural gas are all fossil fuels, so those numbers should be ignored. By adding the other percentages together, you get an answer of 14%.

49. a. The question asks for in which field the most men are *involved* instead of *employed*. The answer would include students, who are not necessarily salaried workers. Therefore, combining the number of students and teachers gives the largest number involved in education.

50. d. Both students and teachers have occupations related to education. The sum of these values is 79.

Section 2: Mathematics

1. e. $24,355 + $23,000 = $47,355. When this is rounded to the nearest $100, the answer is $47,400.

2. a. It would cost $7 to get three sandwiches and a piece of fruit.

3. e. The production for Lubbock is equal to the total minus the other productions: 1,780 − 450 − 425 − 345 = 560.

4. e. The 3rd and 4th quarters are 54% and 16%, respectively. This adds to 70%.

5. d. Mileage is calculated by dividing miles by the number of hours traveled, so change hours and minutes to hours.
$\frac{54}{60} = 0.9$
So the car drove 4.9 hours. Now divide 294 by 4.9, for an answer of 60.

6. e. An average of 90% is needed of a total of 500 points: 500 × 0.90 = 450, so 450 points are needed. Add all the other test scores together: 95 + 85 + 88 + 84 = 352. Now subtract that total from the total needed, in order to see what score the student must make to reach 90%: 450 − 352 = 98.

7. e. There are 6 + 10 + 2 + 14 = 32 total cards and 10 + 14 = 24 that are either spades or diamonds. The probability of drawing a card that is either a spade or a diamond is $\frac{24}{32} = \frac{3}{4}$.

8. c. A stanine score ranges from 1 to 9, with 1 being the lowest score and 9 being the highest, compared to other people taking the test. Since 5 is exactly in the middle of these numbers, that would be average, with just as many people performing better as those performing worse than the test taker. If 5 is average, 4 would be a little less than that, or a little below average.

9. d. (200)(2) = 400, (200)(0.1) = 20, (200)(.004) = 0.8; 400 + 20 + 0.8 = 420.8.

10. a. The 90% discount is over all three items; therefore the total price is $(a + b + c) \times 0.9$. The average is the total price divided by the number of computers: $\frac{0.9 \times (a + b + c)}{3}$.

11. a. Because there are three items at $0.99 and two items at $3.49, the sum of the two numbers minus $3.49 will give the cost.

12. a. This gives the same result as the equation provided; each score is divided by three.

13. **b.** Divide the number of cans of paint by the number of canvases: $2\frac{1}{2} = \frac{5}{2}, \frac{3}{4} \div \frac{5}{2} = \frac{3}{4} \times \frac{2}{5} = \frac{6}{20} = \frac{3}{10}$.

14. **d.** 40% of 20 cc equals (0.40)(20), which is 8. Adding 8 to 20 gives 28 cc.

15. **b.** 8.8% = 0.088. Multiply the discount by the sticker price, and then subtract that amount from the sticker price: ($18,500)(0.088) = $1,628; $18,500 – $1,628 = $16,872.

16. **c.** If 60% of the students had the flu previously, 40% had not had the disease. 40% of 220 is 88.

17. **c.** Divide 341 people watching the football game by the total of 1,755 households to arrive at about 19.4%.

18. **c.** Adding 7.8% (electrical equipment) and 7.3% (other equipment) is the way to arrive at the correct response of 15.1%.

19. **b.** Smoking materials account for only 6.7% of the fires but for 28.9% of the deaths.

20. **b.** Two candy bars require 2 quarters; one package of peanuts requires 3 quarters; one can of cola requires 2 quarters—for a total of 7 quarters.

21. **b.** Start with the credit card balance. Subtract refunds and payments from the balance, and add any charges to the balance. $450 – 175 + 27 – 49 + 25 = $278

22. **e.** Use the formula provided: $\frac{9}{5}(40) + 32 = 72 + 32 = 104$.

23. **c.** Add the corrected value of the sweater ($245) to the value of the two, not three, bracelets ($730), plus the other two items ($78 and $130), for a total of $1,183.

24. **a.** The recipe is for 16 brownies. Half of that, 8, would reduce the ingredients by half. Half of $1\frac{1}{2}$ cups of sugar is $\frac{3}{4}$ cup.

25. **c.** The recipe for 16 brownies calls for $\frac{2}{3}$ cup butter. An additional $\frac{1}{3}$ cup would make 8 more brownies, for a total of 24 brownies.

26. **e.** To solve this problem, think of each mile as requiring three laps (since each lap is one-third of a mile). So, to run four miles would take $4 \times 3 = 12$ laps, and the last two-thirds of a mile would require two more laps. A total of 14 laps would be needed.

27. **c.** First, find how much dough was used. Convert halves to eighths: $5\frac{7}{8} + 6\frac{4}{8} = 11\frac{11}{8} = 12\frac{3}{8}$. Then, subtract the total dough used from the original quantity of dough: $15 – 12\frac{3}{8} = 14\frac{8}{8} – 12\frac{3}{8} = 2\frac{5}{8}$ pounds.

28. **e.** Four inches is equal to 16 quarter inches, which is equal to (16)(2 feet) = 32 feet.

29. **b.** You can't just take 25% off the original price, because the 10% discount after three years of service is taken off the price that has already been reduced by 15%. Figure the problem in two steps: After the 15% discount, the price is $71.83. 90% of that—subtracting 10%—is $64.65.

30. **d.** There are $45 + 30 + 42 = 117$ students who play sports, which means that there are $150 – 117 = 33$ students who do not: $\frac{33}{150} = 0.22 = 22\%$.

31. **c.** The problem is solved by dividing 204 by 1,700. The answer, 0.12, is then converted to a percentage, 12%.

32. **d.** The simplest way to solve this problem is to divide 1 by 1,500, which is 0.0006667, and then count off two decimal places to arrive at the percentage, which is 0.06667%. Since the question asks *about what percentage*, the nearest value is 0.067%.

33. **b.** You can use trial and error to arrive at a solution to this problem. After the first hour, the number would be 20; after the second hour,

40; after the third hour, 80; after the fourth hour, 160; and after the fifth hour, 320; The other answer choices do not have the same outcome.

34. d. 30 ppm of the pollutant would have to be removed to bring the 50 ppm down to 20 ppm. 30 ppm represents 60% of 50 ppm.

35. c. You must break the 92,000 into the amounts mentioned in the policy: 92,000 = 20,000 + 40,000 + 32,000. The amount the policy will pay is (0.8)(20,000) + (0.6)(40,000) + (0.4)(32,000) = 16,000 + 24,000 + 12,800 = 52,800.

36. c. The problem says that the oranges and grapes cost the same. If the price of grapes is called g, then the total spent could be written like this:

$g + g + \$3.99$

or

$2g + \$3.99$

If you knew the total amount that Emilio spent, then you could write an equation:

$2g + \$3.99 = \text{Total}$

This would allow you to solve for g, so the best answer is **c**.

37. e. $3W$ equals water coming in, and W equals water going out. $3W - W = 11,400$, which implies that W is equal to 5,700 and $3W$ is equal to 17,100.

38. b. Divide 5,120 by 8: $5,120 \div 8 = 640$ pounds.

39. d. This problem can be solved by looking for a pattern.

Layer	Balls Added	Balls in This Layer
1 (top layer)	1	1
2	3	4 (1+3 = 4)
3	5	9 (4 + 5 = 9)
4	7	16 (9 + 7 = 16)
5	9	25 (16 + 9 = 25)
6	11	36 (25 + 11 = 36)

We know the second layer has to have four balls, as this is what forms the four sides of the pyramid. The next layer would place a ball between each of the balls in the layer above it, as well as one in the center. This sets up the pattern. Completing the table shows that **d** is the best choice.

40. c. Change each fraction into hours and minutes to better compare the times.

$3\frac{1}{4} = 3$ hours 15 minutes

$3\frac{1}{3} = 3$ hours 20 minutes

The only answer choice that is between 3 hours 15 minutes and 3 hours 20 minutes is **c**, 3 hours 17 minutes.

41. d. Let T equal Ted's age; S equal Sam's age, which is $3T$; and R equal Ron's age, which is $\frac{S}{2}$, or $\frac{3T}{2}$. The sum of the ages is 55: $\frac{3T}{2} + 3T + T = 55$. Convert the left side of the equation into fractions so you can add them: $\frac{3T}{2} + \frac{6T}{2} + \frac{2T}{2} = \frac{11T}{2}$. Now you have $\frac{11T}{2} = 55$. Multiply both sides by 2: $11T = 110$. Divide through by 11 to get $T = 10$. That is Ted's age. Sam is three times Ted's age, or 30. Ron is half Sam's age, or 15 years old.

42. a. If she has completed $\frac{5}{6}$ of them, then $\frac{1}{6}$ remain for her to do: $(42)(\frac{1}{6}) = 7$ problems.

43. c. The answer is arrived at by first dividing 175 by 45. Since the answer is approximately 3.89, not a whole number, the gardener needs 4 sections of hose. Three sections of hose would be too short.

44. c. The difference between 105 and 99 is 6 degrees. Application of the ice pack plus a "resting" period of 5 minutes before reapplication means that the temperature is lowered by half a degree every six minutes, or 1 degree every 12 minutes. Six degrees times 12 minutes per degree equals 72 minutes; however, the temperature becomes 99 degrees after the final application, prior to any "resting" period.

Subtract 5 from 72: 72 − 5 = 67 minutes, or 1 hour and 7 minutes.

45. d. Multiply 16 times 5 to find out how many gallons all five sprinklers will release in one minute. Then multiply the result (80 gallons per minute) by the number of minutes (10) to get 800 gallons.

46. d. Divide the number of books by the number of books that can fit in each box. 420 ÷ 16 = 26.25. However, Ron cannot buy 0.25 of a box. Instead, Ron would need to buy another box for the remaining books. This means he needs 27 boxes.

47. b. There are 3 face cards from all four suits, making 12 face cars in all. The chance of drawing a face card is 12 out of 52. Write this as a fraction and reduce it to lowest terms. $\frac{12}{52} \div \frac{4}{4} = \frac{3}{13}$

48. e. If the width of the rectangle is w, then the length is $3w$. The perimeter of a rectangle is equal to twice the length plus twice the width: $72 = 2(3w) + 2(w)$, $72 = 6w + 2w$, $72 = 8w$, $w = 9$ inches. If the width is 9 inches, then the length is $(9)(3) = 27$ inches.

49. c. There are four quarts to a gallon. There are therefore 20 quarts in a 5-gallon container. Divide 20 by 1.06 quarts per liter to get approximately 18.86 liters and then round off to 19.

50. e. Division is used to arrive at a decimal, which can then be rounded to the nearest hundredth and converted to a percentage: 7,120 ÷ 8,450 is equal to approximately 0.8426, rounded to the nearest hundredth is 0.84, or 84%.

Section 3: Essay Writing

Following are the criteria for scoring CBEST essays.

A "4" essay is a coherent writing sample that addresses the assigned topic and is aimed at a specific audience. Additionally, it has the following characteristics:

- a main idea and/or a central point of view that is focused; its reasoning is sound
- points of discussion that are clear and arranged logically
- assertions that are supported with specific, relevant detail
- word choice and usage that is accurate and precise
- sentences that have complexity and variety, with clear syntax; paragraphs that are coherent (minor mechanical flaws are acceptable)
- style and language appropriate to the assigned audience and purpose

A "3" essay is an adequate writing sample that generally addresses the assigned topic, but may neglect or only vaguely address one of the assigned tasks; it is aimed at a specific audience. Generally, it has the following additional characteristics:

- a main idea and/or a central point of view and adequate reasoning
- organization of ideas that is effective; the meaning of the ideas is clear
- organization of ideas that is effective; rhe meaning of the ideas is clear
- generalizations that are adequately, though unevenly, supported
- word choice and language usage that are adequate; mistakes exist but these do not interfere with meaning
- some errors in sentence and paragraph structure, but not so many as to be confusing

- word choice and style appropriate to a given audience

A "2" essay is an incompletely formed writing sample that attempts to address the topic and to communicate a message to the assigned audience but is generally incomplete or inappropriate. It has the following additional characteristics:

- a main point, but one that loses focus; reasoning that is simplistic
- ineffective organization that causes the response to lack clarity
- generalizations that are only partially supported; supporting details that are irrelevant or unclear
- imprecise language usage; word choice that distracts the reader
- mechanical errors; errors in syntax; errors in paragraphing
- style that is monotonous or choppy

A "1" essay is an inadequately formed writing sample that only marginally addresses the topic and fails to communicate its message to, or is inappropriate to, a specific audience. Additionally, it has the following characteristics:

- general incoherence and inadequate focus, lack of a main idea or consistent point of view; illogical reasoning
- ineffective organization and unclear meaning throughout
- unsupported generalizations and assertions; details that are irrelevant and presented in a confusing manner
- language use that is imprecise, with serious and distracting errors
- many serious errors in mechanics, sentence syntax, and paragraphing

Following are examples of scored essays for Topics 1 and 2. (There are some deliberate errors in all the essays, so that you can tell how much latitude you have.)

Topic 1
Pass—Score = 4

I like TV. It's relaxing after a hard day, and the quotation above is correct—TV has enabled us to see places we've never gotten to go, and it has made possible a global village. But it has its dark side, too.

Take for example the case of Darrell, who, in 1989, married Sherry, a good friend of mine. Their wedding was lovely, held outdoors to the music of guitars and tamborines, on a sunlit spring day, all their friends present. I'd flown in from a thousand miles away just for the wedding, so it was a couple of years before I made it back to visit them again. By that time they'd bought a small two-bedroom house and had acquired a cat, an orange-striped, 15-pound scrapper named Chester.

But I had been in their home only hours before I realized something was wrong. During supper Darrell was cordial and seemed glad to have me there. We had pasta and wine and talked about old times. After supper, he excused himself and went into the family room and turned on the TV. Over coffee, Sherry told me he was addicted. "If there's nothing else on, he'll watch the weather channel for hours." She told me that the addiction had come on gradually. "We used to take nature walks and go to museums but not anymore."

And sure enough, the whole weekend I was visiting, Darrell spent most of the time in front of the TV. He watched good shows and bad, sitcoms and specials and old movies. The old movies kept him up til 2:00 A.M. on both Friday and Saturday nights. "They're having a Fred Astaire marathon," he explained over breakfast on Sunday. "That Fred Astaire is something else,"

A couple of years later, Sherry called me in tears to tell me she couldn't stand it anymore. "I've filed for divorce," she said. "I can't compete with Barbara Walters and that guy on the Travel Channel. I can't even compete with the dog food commercials."

I had some vacation coming from my job, so I flew back to cheer her up. By the time I got there, she and Darrell had already moved out of their house, and she just had a few things to pick up from Darrell's apartment that he had packed but decided he didn't want. He'd given Sherry a key to his apartment, because their divorce really was friendly, so we let ourselves in. The main light was a soft blue from the TV. He waved at us cheerfully, then burst into laughter. He was watching "Funniest Home Videos."

"This guys a hoot," was all he said to me after not having seen me for two years "Do you ever watch this show?"

I don't think TV is Darrell's only problem, but I do suspect its constant chatter keeps him from facing his demons. It's a passive medium—even the Explorer channel, which makes you feel you've made a trip to someplace like Sri Lanka, although you never saw how brilliant the sunlight could be in that part of the world, or feel the warm sand under your feet.

Darrell did say one last thing to Sherry as we were preparing to leave, after we'd gathered up a bag of her leftover stuff plus Chester. She leaned down to kiss him and bumped the remote. A flickering took place on the TV screen, yellow lines and text, something about an adjustment being needed.

"Oh, watch out, honey," Darrell said, grabbing the remote and punching some buttons. "You'll mess up the colors."

Marginal Pass—Score = 3

Many people say they don't watch television, and I say good for them! There is very little on TV today that is worth watching. And yet, for all that, it has an important place in society. I believe, for example, that it is an excellent teaching tool for kids who have had less than a sterling formal education in the lower grades. It's something they can relate to and something they will have in common with the other people in their class. It's something they have in common with the teacher, for that matter. And that is all-important.

Television opens a window on the world that is unique. It helps students to see more of the world than any generation before them has been able to see. With a simple flick of the switch they can look in and watch the goings-on in congress; or travel down the Ganges river or see the Scotish highlands. They can learn about other cultures, learn how to cook or build a house. They can witness events half a world away as soon as they take place.

Here is one advantage of television, as it can be used as a teaching tool. In classrooms today, especially in community colleges, for example, there are students from every strata of society, from many different social classes. Television is one thing they have in common and can bring about lively discussions and a meeting of the minds. Rich and poor alike, privileged or under privileged, all have looked through that tiny window and see wonders and horrors, current events and events long-past. And all can be used as fodder for lively class discussion, for making the subjects we're teaching come alive.

We might take pride in saying we never watch television, but we shouldn't be so quick to put it down—especially as it pertains to teaching. Television is one thing students have in common, and I think it was Winston Churchhill who said, "The only thing worse than democracy is any other form of government." I think the same can be said for television: "The only thing worse than television is no television." Sure, theres a lot on that's not worth watching, but theres also a lot that is. And to ignore it's influence is to ignore an excellent, if flawed, teaching tool.

Marginal Fail—Score = 2

I sometimes wish TV had never been invented. Especially for the younger generation, who get much of their information about the world in a distorted fashion from "the box." Of course it is entertaining after a hard day, but at the end what have you gained?

And the news gets distorted. We get our news from "a reliabel source" but who is that? Some gossip columnist in Washington or New York that has nothing to do with our real life. We get to see how rotten our politicions are and maybe thats a good thing because earlier in history they could cover it up. We get to watch them on TV and judge for ourself instead of taking someone else's word for it. So television can be a good thing if watched in moderation.

Another way TV corrupts society is through advertizing. It tells us to buy, buy, buy. It gives us super models and sport's figures to tell you what to buy and where. It gives you movie stars advertizing even in a TV movie away from comercials, by holding a can of Coke or other product. All of which subliminaly tells you to buy Coke. They say they even have messages flashed on the screen so on the commercial you will get up and go to the kitchen. I find myself bringing home products I never even use. The worse thing is the shows in which dificult life situatsions get solved in a half hour. You could never do it in real life but on TV it is easy. It gives us a erronous view of the world.

I think we should try to do away with it in our homes even if it is hard. After all, its your baby-sitter and advise-giver, and even your friend if you are lonely. But give it a week to be away from it and then watch intermitently. You're life will be better for it.

Fail—Score = 1

TV can be good or bad depending on how you look at it. It can be all you do if you are not careful. It can take you away from your kids if you use it as a baby sitter or when you come home from work that is all you do. Also you will never get the real story. You will never know if they are telling the truth or trying a snow job to sell you something.

I grew up with television like most peopel. It is a good thing if you try to learn from it. It probably will help in a class room discussion if the children all watch the same show. In grade school where I went we had current events and television had it's place.

One example is the news. We know if we are going to war the minute the president makes his decission. We can watch it all happening. We can know if there is a scandel in Washington. And the latest medical facts are on TV. So TV can be good in that aspect.

It can be bad to. For example the shows for teen agers. When I was a teen ager I liked them, all the music and the dancing. But now it is diferent. Drugs are spread through MTV because of the musicions who you can tell do them. And they are models for our kids.

But in some aspects TV is good and in some it is bad. I think spending time away from it will make you feel better. all the news is bad news. But you can get an education too if you just watch public TV. It is good in some aspects and bad in some.

Topic 2
Pass—Score = 4

Not every high school graduate will go on to higher education. In addition, many students who choose to go to college or trade school will have to work in order to pay for tuition, books, and other school-related expenses. This means that most students coming out of high school need to have skills that employers are looking for. While the focus of high school classes may be in academic content areas, teachers can incorporate job skills into their classes to ensure that students can succeed as employees as well as students.

Employers are looking for workers with problem-solving skills. Teachers will not necessarily teach the problem situations that students would experience in any given business. However, the more opportunities students have to think through solutions to problems, the more flexible the students' thinking will become. But if students are told how to solve problems rather than thinking of solutions on their own, the problem-solving skills that employers need will never be learned. Math and science classes provide many opportunities for students to attack problems with different techniques. This type of teaching takes more time, as students may fail at some attempts and need time to think of other approaches. These problem-solving opportunities should be incorporated into the classroom as often as possible.

In addition to problem solving, employers expect their workers to multitask. Being able to manage more than one assignment at a time requires good time-management skills. Often, teachers make decisions for students as to how to prioritize assignments. Some schools even avoid time-management problems by dictating which days students can get assignments in each subject. It would better serve students to take class time to explicitly teach how to keep a schedule, how to use time-management tools like software or planners, and how to prioritize. Homeroom time would be ideal for this instruction, as a short five- to ten-minute lesson every few days would not be burdensome to the teacher. Students would be better prepared for college as well as future employment.

Finally, students need to learn effective communication skills. In a typical high school, students would expect to write in English and History classes. Essays and creative writing would be common. However, these are rarely the types of communication skills students would need on the job. Instead, students may need to write instructions, memos, or explanations for decisions that they made. Again, math and science classes can help fill in this gap. Instead of writing equations and symbolic solutions, students can instead write words to describe steps in a process or a solution to a problem. If students are given problem-solving opportunities, they can then follow the lesson with a description of how they chose the problem-solving method and what the results were. Not only will this help students when they are on the job, but teachers will be able to use the writing to judge how well the students understand the concept.

Many schools offer classes and programs that prepare students to enter the workforce. junior achievement, business courses, and even community in schools programs bring business concepts into the schools. However, in many instances, only students who choose to participate in these programs experience them. Often, college-track students are too busy with college-prep courses and extracurricular activities to complete a college resume. Making time to teach skills that all employees need would benefit the students in the future when they get a job. These skills would also benefit them as they complete their high school education, as they can improve their problem solving, time management, and communication skills in class.

Marginal Pass—Score = 3

Not every student will go to college. Some college students need jobs to pay for tuition, books, and other school-related expenses. This means that most students coming out of high school need to have job skills. While the focus in high school may be on high school classes, teachers can teach job skills in their classes to help students on the job.

Employers are looking for workers who can solve problems. Teachers don't normally teach business situations in a science class, but they can teach problem solving. Then students can use the problem-solving skills on the job. Math and science classes give students the chance to solve problems. Teachers need to give students enough time to try the problem solving, especially if they don't succeed in solving the problem. Teachers can use problem solving often.

Employers will look for people who can multitask, too. This means the employees can take on more than one assignment and manage this time well. Often, teachers tell kids what assignments should be done first or are most important. Instead, teachers should give students planners and show them how to use them. This would make better students and better employees.

Also, students need to write. In school, students write essays, poems, and stories. These don't help much on the job. Workers write other things, like receipts or e-mails. English teachers can teach this type of writing, too. It will give teachers a different type of assignment to grade, and students would probably be glad to write something short and fun like a receipt. I had to do that on my first job, and I didn't understand words like subtotal and total. I would have been glad to have a teacher help with something like that.

Students can choose to take business classes in school, which certainly helps when they go get a job. But at some point, nearly every high school student needs to get a job. So schools should take the time to teach skills that employers look for, like problem solving, multitasking, and time management. Then students will be better employees, whether they get a job in high school, in college, or after they graduate.

Marginal Fail—Score = 2

At some point, every student will need a job. I know I do! Why don't you teach them what they need to know on the job? We can have teachers cover that material along with the other subjects they teach.

Teachers are busy already, I know. Maybe we can invite speakers into the classroom to teach some of the job skills. Another idea would be to have parents come in and do like a show and tell. They can show how they do math, science, history, or English on the job. Teachers would probably like the break, and the kids would see what people do when they work.

We need to teach kids how to solve problems. Learning how to solve an algebra problem or dissect a frog isn't all that useful. So teachers should think of things that apply more to the real world. Then they can do math and science about those problems instead. This will be a lot of help when the kids go to work, right?

Writing is important, too. Lots of times kids get a job and someone asks them to write a report. Then they're like, what? So the writing that students do in school should be more like the kind of writing they would have to do at work, like reports and e-mails and memos.

I also think that students should learn how to be more organized. My father uses his computer to keep track of his appointments and meetings. He gets a reminder a few minutes before he is supposed to be somewhere, so he's never late. Learning a software like that would be a really great idea. That would mean that all of the students would have to have a computer, so that might be expensive. Maybe businesses would help pay for them if they knew kids would know how to use the software when they came to work.

Since everyone is going to eventually get a job, the sooner students know how to be a good worker, the better. So schools should teach things like solving problems, keeping a schedule, and how to write. Then kids getting jobs out of school would have better skills and might even make more money.

Fail—Score = 1

I haven't had a real job yet, just babysitting and dog-sitting, so I don't know a hole lot about stuff to do in an office. Plus I want to be a teacher, so the things I'll do are really different than office stuff. But it never hurts to learn something new. I really hate it when I go somewhere and the person working doesn't have a clue. Like how to make change or let you know that your appointment is running late. Those people shuold have got more training.

If I were going to teach someone what to do on the job, I would make sure they knew math. How dumb is it that they can't give you change without the cash register telling them how much they should give back. So math teachers could teach making change. Then they could teach how to understand a pay check. That hole gross and nets thing is really confusing. Once I get my teaching job I will probly figure that out. Oh, and taxes, too.

Workers should also be polite. I can not stand it when people don't look at you when they talk to you. Like they are too busy to stop and do what they are payed for. So speech classes could practice polite conversation, do role playing like at the doctor's office, and stuff like that.

I know some kids that took jobs right out of high school. I don't know where they learned to do the job unless someone there teached them all of it. But those jobs must not be that hard. Most people learn to do the work stuff at college. That's where I'm going to learn about how to teach kids and give grades and stuff. It's harder work, so that's why I have to go to college.

Scoring

Again, evaluate how you did on this practice exam by scoring the three sections—Reading Comprehension, Mathematics, and Essay Writing—separately. For both Reading Comprehension and Mathematics, use the same scoring method: First, find the number of questions you got right out of the 50 questions in each section, then use the following table to check your math and find percentage equivalents for several possible scores.

Number of questions right	Approximate percentage
50	100%
46	92%
43	86%
39	78%
35	70%
32	64%
28	56%
25	50%

If you achieve a score of at least 70% on both the Reading Comprehension section and the Mathematics section, you will most likely pass those portions of the CBEST. (Remember that the scores are converted from raw scores to scaled scores, so the actual number you receive on the real CBEST will *not* be "70"; however, a percentage will work for the purpose of finding out if you passed the practice exams.) In addition, as mentioned in previous chapters, you must receive a passing score on the Essay Writing section of the CBEST, which will be evaluated by trained readers. The criteria are outlined in detail in the Answers section, but generally the essays are scored as follows.

4 = Pass (an excellent and well-formed essay)
3 = Marginal Pass (an average and adequately formed essay)
2 = Marginal Fail (a partially formed but substandard essay)
1 = Fail (an inadequately formed essay)

To see how you did on your essays for this third and final practice exam, be sure to give them and the scoring criteria to a teacher and ask him or her to score your essays for you.

You have probably seen improvement between your first practice exam score and this one, but if you didn't improve as much as you'd like, following are some options for you to consider:

- **If you scored below 60%,** you may want to reconsider whether you're ready for the CBEST at this time. A good idea would be to take some brush-up courses, either at a university or community college nearby or online, in the areas you feel less sure of. If you don't have time for a course, you might try private tutoring.
- **If your score is in the 60% to 70% range,** you will want to work as hard as you can to improve your skills. The LearningExpress books *Reading Comprehension Success in 20 Minutes a Day* and *Practical Math Success in 20 Minutes a Day* or other books from your public library will undoubtedly help. Also, reread and pay close attention to all the advice in Chapters 2 and 4 of this book in order to improve your score. It might also be helpful to ask friends and family to make up mock test questions and quiz you on them.
- **If your score is between 70% and 80%,** you could still benefit from additional work by going back to Chapter 4 and by brushing up your reading, math, and writing skills before the exam.

- **If you scored above 80%,** that's great! This kind of score should make it easy for you to pass the official CBEST. Don't lose your edge, though; keep studying right up to the day before the exam.

There's an old joke that goes like this: In New York City, a man stops a second man on the street and asks, "How do I get to Carnegie Hall?" The second man answers, "Practice."

The key to success in almost any pursuit is to prepare for all you're worth. By taking the practice exams in this book, you've made yourself better prepared than other people who may be taking the exam with you. You've diagnosed where your strengths and weaknesses lie and learned how to deal with the various kinds of questions that will appear on the test. So go into the exam with confidence, knowing that you're ready and equipped to do your best.

CHAPTER 7

CBEST PRACTICE EXAM 3

CHAPTER SUMMARY
This is the final practice test based on the California Basic Educational Skills Test. Use this test to determine what concepts you may want to review before test day.

Like the other three practice exams in this book, this exam is divided into three sections just like the official CBEST—the Reading Comprehension section, consisting of 50 multiple-choice questions; the Mathematics section, consisting of 50 multiple-choice questions; and the Essay Writing section, consisting of two topics on which you are to write essays.

In order to simulate the official CBEST, tear out the answer sheet on the next page and use a number 2 pencil to fill in the circles. (As you did for exams 1 and 2, write your essays on a separate piece of paper.) Use a timer or stopwatch and allow yourself four hours for the exam: one and a half hours each for the Reading and Math sections and a half hour each for the two essays.

After the exam, use the answer key that follows to see your progress on each section and to find out why the correct answers are correct and the incorrect ones are incorrect. Then, use the scoring section at the end of the exam to see how well you did overall.

LEARNINGEXPRESS ANSWER SHEET

Section 1: Reading Comprehension

1. ⓐ ⓑ ⓒ ⓓ ⓔ	21. ⓐ ⓑ ⓒ ⓓ ⓔ	41. ⓐ ⓑ ⓒ ⓓ ⓔ
2. ⓐ ⓑ ⓒ ⓓ ⓔ	22. ⓐ ⓑ ⓒ ⓓ ⓔ	42. ⓐ ⓑ ⓒ ⓓ ⓔ
3. ⓐ ⓑ ⓒ ⓓ ⓔ	23. ⓐ ⓑ ⓒ ⓓ ⓔ	43. ⓐ ⓑ ⓒ ⓓ ⓔ
4. ⓐ ⓑ ⓒ ⓓ ⓔ	24. ⓐ ⓑ ⓒ ⓓ ⓔ	44. ⓐ ⓑ ⓒ ⓓ ⓔ
5. ⓐ ⓑ ⓒ ⓓ ⓔ	25. ⓐ ⓑ ⓒ ⓓ ⓔ	45. ⓐ ⓑ ⓒ ⓓ ⓔ
6. ⓐ ⓑ ⓒ ⓓ ⓔ	26. ⓐ ⓑ ⓒ ⓓ ⓔ	46. ⓐ ⓑ ⓒ ⓓ ⓔ
7. ⓐ ⓑ ⓒ ⓓ ⓔ	27. ⓐ ⓑ ⓒ ⓓ ⓔ	47. ⓐ ⓑ ⓒ ⓓ ⓔ
8. ⓐ ⓑ ⓒ ⓓ ⓔ	28. ⓐ ⓑ ⓒ ⓓ ⓔ	48. ⓐ ⓑ ⓒ ⓓ ⓔ
9. ⓐ ⓑ ⓒ ⓓ ⓔ	29. ⓐ ⓑ ⓒ ⓓ ⓔ	49. ⓐ ⓑ ⓒ ⓓ ⓔ
10. ⓐ ⓑ ⓒ ⓓ ⓔ	30. ⓐ ⓑ ⓒ ⓓ ⓔ	50. ⓐ ⓑ ⓒ ⓓ ⓔ
11. ⓐ ⓑ ⓒ ⓓ ⓔ	31. ⓐ ⓑ ⓒ ⓓ ⓔ	
12. ⓐ ⓑ ⓒ ⓓ ⓔ	32. ⓐ ⓑ ⓒ ⓓ ⓔ	
13. ⓐ ⓑ ⓒ ⓓ ⓔ	33. ⓐ ⓑ ⓒ ⓓ ⓔ	
14. ⓐ ⓑ ⓒ ⓓ ⓔ	34. ⓐ ⓑ ⓒ ⓓ ⓔ	
15. ⓐ ⓑ ⓒ ⓓ ⓔ	35. ⓐ ⓑ ⓒ ⓓ ⓔ	
16. ⓐ ⓑ ⓒ ⓓ ⓔ	36. ⓐ ⓑ ⓒ ⓓ ⓔ	
17. ⓐ ⓑ ⓒ ⓓ ⓔ	37. ⓐ ⓑ ⓒ ⓓ ⓔ	
18. ⓐ ⓑ ⓒ ⓓ ⓔ	38. ⓐ ⓑ ⓒ ⓓ ⓔ	
19. ⓐ ⓑ ⓒ ⓓ ⓔ	39. ⓐ ⓑ ⓒ ⓓ ⓔ	
20. ⓐ ⓑ ⓒ ⓓ ⓔ	40. ⓐ ⓑ ⓒ ⓓ ⓔ	

Section 2: Mathematics

1. ⓐ ⓑ ⓒ ⓓ ⓔ	21. ⓐ ⓑ ⓒ ⓓ ⓔ	41. ⓐ ⓑ ⓒ ⓓ ⓔ
2. ⓐ ⓑ ⓒ ⓓ ⓔ	22. ⓐ ⓑ ⓒ ⓓ ⓔ	42. ⓐ ⓑ ⓒ ⓓ ⓔ
3. ⓐ ⓑ ⓒ ⓓ ⓔ	23. ⓐ ⓑ ⓒ ⓓ ⓔ	43. ⓐ ⓑ ⓒ ⓓ ⓔ
4. ⓐ ⓑ ⓒ ⓓ ⓔ	24. ⓐ ⓑ ⓒ ⓓ ⓔ	44. ⓐ ⓑ ⓒ ⓓ ⓔ
5. ⓐ ⓑ ⓒ ⓓ ⓔ	25. ⓐ ⓑ ⓒ ⓓ ⓔ	45. ⓐ ⓑ ⓒ ⓓ ⓔ
6. ⓐ ⓑ ⓒ ⓓ ⓔ	26. ⓐ ⓑ ⓒ ⓓ ⓔ	46. ⓐ ⓑ ⓒ ⓓ ⓔ
7. ⓐ ⓑ ⓒ ⓓ ⓔ	27. ⓐ ⓑ ⓒ ⓓ ⓔ	47. ⓐ ⓑ ⓒ ⓓ ⓔ
8. ⓐ ⓑ ⓒ ⓓ ⓔ	28. ⓐ ⓑ ⓒ ⓓ ⓔ	48. ⓐ ⓑ ⓒ ⓓ ⓔ
9. ⓐ ⓑ ⓒ ⓓ ⓔ	29. ⓐ ⓑ ⓒ ⓓ ⓔ	49. ⓐ ⓑ ⓒ ⓓ ⓔ
10. ⓐ ⓑ ⓒ ⓓ ⓔ	30. ⓐ ⓑ ⓒ ⓓ ⓔ	50. ⓐ ⓑ ⓒ ⓓ ⓔ
11. ⓐ ⓑ ⓒ ⓓ ⓔ	31. ⓐ ⓑ ⓒ ⓓ ⓔ	
12. ⓐ ⓑ ⓒ ⓓ ⓔ	32. ⓐ ⓑ ⓒ ⓓ ⓔ	
13. ⓐ ⓑ ⓒ ⓓ ⓔ	33. ⓐ ⓑ ⓒ ⓓ ⓔ	
14. ⓐ ⓑ ⓒ ⓓ ⓔ	34. ⓐ ⓑ ⓒ ⓓ ⓔ	
15. ⓐ ⓑ ⓒ ⓓ ⓔ	35. ⓐ ⓑ ⓒ ⓓ ⓔ	
16. ⓐ ⓑ ⓒ ⓓ ⓔ	36. ⓐ ⓑ ⓒ ⓓ ⓔ	
17. ⓐ ⓑ ⓒ ⓓ ⓔ	37. ⓐ ⓑ ⓒ ⓓ ⓔ	
18. ⓐ ⓑ ⓒ ⓓ ⓔ	38. ⓐ ⓑ ⓒ ⓓ ⓔ	
19. ⓐ ⓑ ⓒ ⓓ ⓔ	39. ⓐ ⓑ ⓒ ⓓ ⓔ	
20. ⓐ ⓑ ⓒ ⓓ ⓔ	40. ⓐ ⓑ ⓒ ⓓ ⓔ	

Section 1: Reading Comprehension

Use the excerpt below from an index to answer the two questions that follow.

> Baby, newborn
>   Apgar scores of, 13–15
>   appearance at birth, 8–9
>   bonding with, 19–29
>   activities, 19–20
>   as father, 21–22
>   breast-feeding, 23–25
>   rooming in, 26–27
>   skin on skin, 28–29
>   bringing home, 30
>   hair, 10, 13
>   and heartburn, 10
>   lanugo, 13
> Baby blues, 40–44
>   caring for baby during, 40–41
>   father's, 42
>   lack of, 43
>   mother's 44
>   see also Postpartum depression

1. On which page(s) would one look to find games that stimulate a newborn?
   a. 19–29
   b. 19–20
   c. 30
   d. 28–29
   e. 40–41

2. Which of the following best describes what the book from which this index was taken is most likely about?
   a. how to stimulate a baby
   b. the process of giving birth
   c. experiences of parents of newborns
   d. all about postpartum depression
   e. all about newborns

Read the passage below; then answer the three questions that follow.

When you hear the name Harlem Globetrotters, a familiar whistled tune may immediately come to mind. Now, the team is world famous for putting on a show while playing good basketball. But did you know they started out as an ordinary basketball team? In fact, they're not even from Harlem—or New York!

In 1926, Abe Saperstein organized a group of five players in Chicago. Saperstein took his team on the road, offering anyone the chance to play against them. _____ They wore uniforms with "New York" written on them, and eventually became known as the Harlem Globetrotters.

It wasn't until 1939 that the team began to perform as they played. During a game against a small team, they had secured a 112–3 lead. One of the players began clowning around with the ball, doing tricks. The audience <u>went wild</u>. Saperstein encouraged his team to play the comedy card, as long as they were winning. Their fame continued to grow, and in 1948, they decided they needed a theme song. "Sweet Georgia Brown," the whistled tune everyone has come to know so well, was it. In the 1950s, their careers really took off. While in Peru, two warring armies halted their battle for a few days so the Globetrotters could play. When they left, the war resumed. Even Pope John XXIII requested the Globetrotters play for him in the Vatican.

Since then, many of the players signed to the Globetrotters have been honored with various awards for their sportsmanship. The team is still performing in countries all around the world.

3. Which sentence, if inserted into the blank line in the second paragraph, would be most consistent with the writer's purpose and intended audience?
   a. They traveled everywhere from Chicago to Minnesota to Washington state.
   b. They were from Chicago.
   c. Basketball should be played as a serious sport.
   d. The Harlem Globetrotters never left Chicago.
   e. The Harlem Globetrotters changed people's view of Harlem.

4. Which is the best meaning of the phrase *went wild* as it is used in the third paragraph?
   a. began looting and rioting
   b. became insane
   c. cheered and laughed
   d. became primitive people
   e. brought animals to the games

5. Which of the following best organizes the main ideas in this passage?
   a. I. Unknown facts about the Harlem Globetrotters
      II. The origins of the Harlem Globetrotters
      III. How the Harlem Globetrotters became famous
      IV. The Harlem Globetrotters today
   b. I. The Harlem Globetrotters effect on history
      II. How the Harlem Globetrotters came from New York
      III. How the Harlem Globetrotters stopped a war
      IV. The Harlem Globetrotters today
   c. I. The Harlem Globetrotters are basketball players
      II. Abe Saperstein's biography
      III. Why the Pope likes the Globetrotters
      IV. What happened to the Harlem Globetrotters
   d. I. The Harlem Globetrotters are not from New York
      II. The Harlem Globetrotters had neat uniforms
      III. Why the Harlem Globetrotters chose "Sweet Georgia Brown" as a theme song
      IV. Different famous members of the Globetrotters
   e. I. How the Harlem Globetrotters got their name
      II. Abe Saperstein learned to play basketball
      III. The contest for the theme song of the team
      IV. How to try out for the team

Read the passage below, then answer the three questions that follow.

Finding alternative fuel sources should be a priority on the national agenda. It is one topic on which both parties should agree. Environmentalists should be concerned about disasters caused by transporting oil, such as the Exxon Valdez spill or the BP oil leak.

_____

Even those for whom the environment is not a priority have reason to be involved. They should care that our dependence on foreign sources of oil keeps our country involved with countries whose governments support terrorism. Whatever the reason, the fact is clear: alternative energy sources need to be developed.

6. Which sentence, if inserted into the blank line in the passage, would best develop the passage using the writer's tone?
   a. They should care that such catastrophic damage to wildlife is not worth any risk.
   b. Not everyone cares about oil, but they really should.
   c. There have been many other such disasters, though.
   d. People protest some wars by chanting, "No blood for oil!"
   e. Businesses that develop green energy are costing oil companies money.

7. The writer is most likely arguing her point to an audience of
   a. environmentalists.
   b. warmongers.
   c. pacifists.
   d. Americans.
   e. businesspeople.

8. What assumption might the author have made that inspired her to write this argument?
   a. The world is interested in alternative fuel sources.
   b. The United States government is not working hard enough to find alternative fuel sources.
   c. The United States government does research better than privately funded companies.
   d. Most Americans do not care about their environment at all.
   e. Environmentally friendly energy choices should be more affordable.

Use the graph below to answer the question that follows.

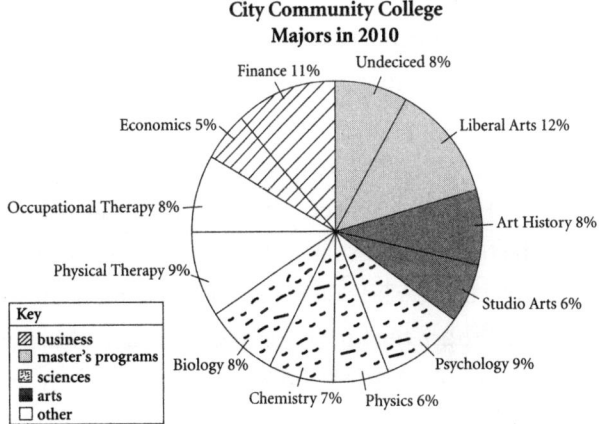

9. In 2010, which area of study was the most popular at City Community College?
   a. other
   b. master's programs
   c. sciences
   d. arts
   e. business

Read the passage below, then answer the three questions that follow.

Maintaining the proper habitat for a red-eared slider is no easy matter. First, a slider must be purchased at a reputable shop. It is illegal to sell sliders less than 2 inches long because of possible salmonella infection. _____ select the largest tank your budget will allow. Eventually, sliders grow to be 11 inches. They will need ten gallons of water per inch. Add distilled water to the tank. Place an aquarium heater in it and allow the water to heat to 75°. This temperature should be maintained constantly. If you are <u>up to it</u>, place freshwater plants, such as anacharis or water lilies, in the enclosure. Turtles need a varied diet of vegetation, and these are two of their favorites. Next, place the filter in the water and allow it to run for about a half an hour. _____ it runs, place a basking dock at a height so that the turtle can swim up a ramp and dry out completely. Above the dock, add a heat lamp so the turtle can bask in a temperature even warmer than its tank. A lid will make sure the lamp will not fall in or burn the turtle—and that the turtle will not climb out. You should also have a UVB light near the basking dock. Finally, add your turtle to the tank, and watch as he checks out his new digs! If you'd like, you can also add hiding spots, such as a mug covered with plant matter or fake plants floating atop the water. Turtles enjoy hiding!

10. If inserted *in order* into the blanks above, which words would help the reader understand the sequence of the writer's ideas?
   a. First; Since
   b. Meanwhile; As
   c. First; Finally
   d. Next; Since
   e. Next; While

11. Which is the best meaning of the phrase *up to it* in the passage?
   a. buried to that point
   b. having reached a certain point
   c. able to perform a task
   d. in the area of a certain point
   e. elevated to a certain height

12. According to the passage, what should a turtle owner do while running the filter?
   a. add hiding spots
   b. place a water heater in the tank
   c. add a basking dock
   d. change the UVB bulb
   e. provide an additional water source

Read the passage below, then answer the four questions that follow.

Chivalry is a term used today to refer to the manners of a true gentleman. Its origins are from medieval days, when knights were expected to live within a chivalric code.

In fact, there were ten commandments of chivalry all knights were expected to follow. Most of them revolved around respecting church and country and defending the weak. They also required a knight to be generous, brave, and loyal. While all these rules may sound <u>magnanimous</u>, history is not always as noble as it may seem.

For example, all women—especially those of noble bearing—were considered among the "weak." If a knight perceived a slight against her, he was to insist on protecting her honor, often by fighting his opponent to the death. A woman had no choice in whether or not she was "protected" in such a manner. Chivalry even applied during battles. If a knight captured an opponent or had the chance to kill him, he was supposed to allow him to live—for mercy. In fact, sparing his life gave the knight a chance to make money by ransoming him, or exchanging his life for his land.

Often, the rules of chivalry were twisted for personal gain. For example, a competitor for a woman's hand may be challenged to a fight under false claims, in order to eliminate him. A knight may claim insult to church or country in order to lead a battle and gain personal glory.

13. Which of the following titles best reflects the main idea of this passage?
    a. The True Meaning of Chivalry
    b. The Love Life of Knights and Maidens
    c. How to Lead a Chivalric Life
    d. A Knight in Battle
    e. Where Has Chivalry Gone?

14. According to the passage, what was a knight's secondary motive for sparing an opponent's life in battle?
    a. to gain glory
    b. to ransom him or steal his land
    c. to honor his love
    d. to honor his church and country
    e. to impress the maiden's family

15. What can be inferred from the information in the passage?
    a. Knights still exist today.
    b. The ten commandments of chivalry still apply today.
    c. Not all knights were true gentlemen.
    d. The code of chivalry should still be followed.
    e. Anyone could become a knight with enough money.

16. What is the meaning of the word magnanimous as it is used in the second paragraph?
    a. amazing
    b. true
    c. high-minded
    d. historical
    e. gigantic

Read the passage below, then answer the four questions that follow.

(1) Humans have been searching for the secret of immortality for years—but another species already has it! (2) *Turritopsis nutricula* is a very small jellyfish, just large enough to be seen with the naked eye. (3) It is the most beautiful of all jellyfish. (4) More importantly, it is the only organism on Earth that truly may outlive death.

(5) All jellyfish have two life stages: the first is called the polyp stage. (6) During this time, it is fixed to the sea floor and produces mature jellyfish, or medusas. (7) The medusas are released. (8) The medusa stage is what a person pictures when they think of a jellyfish: a bell-shaped organism with several tentacles, drifting along. (9) They have a graceful style of motility.

(10) During the medusa stage, sexual maturity is reached. (11) Eggs or sperm are released, and new polyps are fertilized where they fall and meet. (12) For most organisms, the life cycle is over sometime after reaching sexual maturity. (13) But this isn't the case with the *Turritopsis nutricula*. (14) They are blessed with very specialized cells that allow them to revert back into their polyp stage, thereby evading death. (15) Scientists consider them biologically immortal—no other species has come close to achieving such a feat.

17. Which sentence in the passage is an opinion, rather than a fact?
   a. sentence 1
   b. sentence 2
   c. sentence 3
   d. sentence 4
   e. sentence 5

18. Which sentence is the least relevant to the main idea of the second paragraph?
   a. sentence 5
   b. sentence 6
   c. sentence 7
   d. sentence 8
   e. sentence 9

19. Which best summarizes the main idea of the passage?
   a. *Turritopsis nutricula* is the only immortal organism on Earth.
   b. Jellyfish have two stages in their life cycles: polyp and medusa.
   c. *Turritopsis nutricula* is a small member of the jellyfish family.
   d. Sexual maturity is the last part of the life cycle for many organisms.
   e. Humans can use their knowledge of jellyfish to cure diseases.

20. According to the passage, *Turritopsis nutricula* has achieved immortality because
   a. it has reverse life cycles.
   b. it does not reproduce or grow.
   c. it experiences a medusa state before the polyp state.
   d. it can return to its polyp state after being in the medusa state.
   e. it reproduces as soon as it starts to die.

Read the passage below, then answer the question that follows.

The standard poodle has historically been a crowd favorite at dog shows, and more importantly, among hunters. Its abilities to retrieve kills from water have been lauded for centuries. In fact, the haircut so famous now originally allowed the dog to swim faster. Hair was left on the chest and joints to keep the dog's muscles and vital organs warm.

21. Which sentence does NOT fit into the pattern of logic the author used to write the above passage?
   a. The standard poodle is a favorite at dog shows.
   b. The standard poodle is a favorite with hunters.
   c. Standard poodles are great swimmers and retrievers.
   d. The haircut poodles wear today had practical origins.
   e. Poodles make great pets for people with allergies.

Read the passage below, then answer the question that follows.

What sport combines skateboarding, snowboarding, and surfing? Kite surfing! It's the best sport in ages. Picture riding a snowboard and holding onto a giant kite while flying over the waves. That's what kite surfing is all about: harnessing the power of the wind and the waves. Experienced kite surfers can work with the wind, reaching high speeds, and flying about 20 feet in the air.

Mark Jones is considered an expert in the sport. He has been kite surfing for five years. "It's a huge rush," he said, "a total thrill." Jones is in top athletic shape and emphasizes the amount of training that goes into the sport. In winter, he practices on sand using a skateboard with modified wheels. "The tricky part is learning how to get the wind in your kite and then steer it to go in the direction you want." Kite surfing is considered an extreme sport, and with good reason. Because of changing wind and water patterns, the risk of losing control is real. Serious injuries are possible. However, those who enjoy the sport say the rewards are worth the risks.

22. Which detail supports the author's statement that kite surfing is an extreme sport?
    a. Kite surfing harnesses the power of the wind and waves.
    b. You have brakes to avoid reaching high speeds.
    c. Kite surfers must be in good shape to steer the kite.
    d. The risk of losing control and getting hurt is real.
    e. Jones is in top athletic shape.

23. Which of the following offers a statement of opinion?
    a. Kite surfing is considered an extreme sport.
    b. It's a risky sport.
    c. It's the best sport in ages.
    d. To kite surf, you must harness the wind to ride the water.
    e. Serious injuries are possible.

24. From the information in the passage, what can you conclude about kite surfing?
    a. It is only popular with surfers.
    b. You do not need to know how to swim to do it.
    c. It has been around for ages.
    d. It should be made illegal for children.
    e. It is a new sport.

25. Which of the following most closely reflects the meaning of the phrase *It's a huge rush* as it is used in the passage?
    a. The kite moves quickly.
    b. The ride is exciting.
    c. There is little time left to join the sport.
    d. The ride is over very quickly.
    e. The waves crash over the surfer.

Read the passage below, then answer the three questions that follow.

Friends who had no brothers felt I was lucky. I felt like I had four very overprotective fathers, instead of three older brothers. It was true my boyfriends were always a bit more <u>deferential</u> to me than they were other girls, but at the same time, they were usually too scared to speak to me. And not because of my stunning looks—because of my brothers. One brother snuck into my high school dance just to make sure I wasn't dancing with any boys. Another brother found out that a crush would be trick-or-treating to our house in eighth grade. When my crush arrived, my brother came from the backyard with a pillow case over his head ... and a chainsaw. Both my brother and the chain saw were running. Did I mention we had just moved to that town? There are countless more examples—that I know about. Needless to say, my reputation preceded me for several years.

26. Which of the following sentences summarizes this passage's main idea?
    a. Growing up with older brothers wasn't easy.
    b. Boys were afraid to speak to the narrator because of her stunning looks.
    c. The narrator's brother once chased a crush away with a chain saw.
    d. The narrator's father was not as overprotective as her brothers.
    e. Having brothers scared away friends for most of the narrator's life.

27. What does the narrator's statement *my reputation preceded me for several years* suggest about her social life?
    a. She was very popular wherever she went.
    b. She probably chose friends who lived far away.
    c. She didn't make friends because she was closed off to many people.
    d. She probably did not have many dates in high school.
    e. She made sure people knew who she was.

28. Which of the following is the best meaning of the word <u>deferential</u> as it is used by the author?
    a. admiring
    b. respectful
    c. untruthful
    d. uncertain
    e. late

Read the passage below, then answer the two questions that follow.

Cleopatra is the most famous female ruler in history. Her beauty was well recorded. However, it was her intelligence and cunning that made her so powerful. Cleopatra spoke nine languages. She came to rule when she was only 18. Although Egypt was facing famine and war when she came to power, she restored it to its former glory. Laws dictated that she rule with a brother or son. Yet Cleopatra survived two attempts by her brothers to oust her from the throne. She made a statement about her power by having coins feature her image, rather than her brother's. No other female ruler had been strong enough to do this. While the rest of the world feared Rome's power, Egypt was secure, as Cleopatra bore Caesar a son. When Caesar was assassinated, she became the lover of Marc Antony, another Roman ruler. When Marc Antony left his wife for Cleopatra and the twins she gave birth to, his wife's brother, Octavio, became enraged. Octavio was a powerful man, and Cleopatra feared for her life. She committed suicide rather than be taken prisoner.

29. In the passage, the writer bases his argument primarily on which idea?
    a. History has not emphasized Cleopatra's leadership qualities.
    b. People haven't heard of the ruler Cleopatra.
    c. Younger rulers make stronger rulers.
    d. Cleopatra had children with Roman rulers because she loved them.
    e. What people know about Cleopatra is mostly myth.

30. According to the information in the passage, what was Cleopatra's first political move?
    a. she married Marc Antony
    b. she married Caesar
    c. she had coins minted with her image
    d. she kicked her brothers out of the palace
    e. she committed suicide

Read the passage below, then answer the three questions that follow.

Separation anxiety in dogs occurs when a dog thinks it is his job to protect his owner. When the owner leaves, the dog becomes crazed, chewing objects or urinating, feeling incredibly uneasy about the owner's absence. To help a dog overcome separation anxiety, there are tactics an owner can use. One of them is to get the dog to remain calm when the owner begins to take steps to leave the house. Most dogs who suffer from this condition will become anxious as soon as they hear keys jingle. Others have memorized the owner's routine and may become nervous as soon as the owner enters the shower, sprays a certain perfume, or puts on a coat. In order to correct the behavior, an owner must first determine what sets the dog off. Suppose the dog becomes nervous when keys are picked up. The owner can pick up his keys and leave the house for short periods of time, such as five minutes. The time for which he leaves should be escalated until the dog no longer reacts to him picking up his keys.

Many owners resort to kenneling their pet in an effort to reduce damage to the home caused by separation anxiety. Kenneling for this reason is the exact wrong move. It will only increase anxiety and lead the dog to self-injury.

31. Based on the information in the passage, a dog is most likely to lick its paws to the point of rash when an owner leaves if
   a. the owner tries to sneak out the door.
   b. the dog is left outside when the owner leaves the house.
   c. the dog is kenneled when the owner leaves the house.
   d. the owner leaves for short periods of time.
   e. the dog is not given an opportunity to go outside first.

32. According to the passage, what is the *first* step in reducing separation anxiety?
   a. escalating the time out of the home
   b. figuring out what lets the dog know the owner is leaving
   c. buying the dog a large-sized kennel
   d. returning home after a very short period of time
   e. spraying perfume or another familiar scent

33. The intended audience for this passage is most likely
   a. veterinarians.
   b. animal behaviorists.
   c. dog owners.
   d. cat owners.
   e. landlords.

Read the passage below, then answer the two questions that follow.

Organic foods are the foods of the future. Studies have shown that organic food has several health benefits. Certain pesticides have been proven to be carcinogenic, or cancer-causing. Organic fruits and vegetables are grown without any of these chemicals. In addition, studies have shown that organic foods lessen the risk of birth defects when consumed by pregnant women. Consuming nonorganic foods is not the only way humans can get sick; chemicals in fertilizers and pesticides can run off into water or on land, leading to water and air pollution. If nonorganic food continues to be the more popular choice, our health and environment will suffer.

34. What persuasive technique does the writer of the passage use?
   a. appealing to feelings
   b. using supportive examples
   c. describing other people with similar feelings
   d. describing counterarguments
   e. citing scientific research

35. Which assumption most influenced the writer's argument?
   a. People care about their health and the environment.
   b. Consumers choose the cheapest option.
   c. Scientific data is unreliable.
   d. Water and air pollution levels decline each year.
   e. Organic foods cost less money than foods grown with chemicals.

Read the passage below, then answer the two questions that follow.

Long before rock stars and activism went hand-in-hand, Bob Geldof was on the forefront of both. A founding member of the band Boomtown Rats, he had already established his reputation in the music world. Then he watched a documentary on BBC that changed his life. He flew to Ethiopia and witnessed starving children and deplorable living conditions. Upon his return, he wrote "Do They Know It's Christmas?" and organized several famous musicians to record it under the name Band Aid. Geldof also organized Live Aid, a rock concert whose profits went to help end hunger. It was the first of its kind. In addition to being nominated for a Nobel Peace Prize for his activism, he was also knighted by Queen Elizabeth.

36. The writer's purpose in writing this passage is to
   a. tell the life story of Bob Geldof.
   b. explain how Live Aid influenced the music world.
   c. inform the reader about Bob Geldof's activism.
   d. compare Geldof to other musicians of his day.
   e. explain Geldof's evolution as a musician.

37. Which of the following conclusions is best supported by information in the passage?
   a. The Boomtown Rats belongs in the Rock and Rock Hall of Fame.
   b. The documentary Geldof watched was about Ethiopia.
   c. Bob Geldof won the Nobel Peace Prize.
   d. Live Aid made Bob Geldof a lot of money.
   e. Geldof is as much a citizen of Ethiopia as of Great Britain.

Use the table of contents below from a book on gems, rocks, and minerals to answer the two questions that follow.

Introduction	1
Part I: Gems and Crystals	
What Is a Gem?	5
Diamond	15
Tourmaline	25
Turquoise	35
Opal	45
Pearls	55
Rare Gems	65
Part II: Rocks and Minerals	
Earth Minerals	67
The Rock Cycle	77
Minerals from Lava	80
Metamorphic Minerals	90
Heat and Pressure on Minerals	100
Biogenic Minerals	110
Rare Minerals	120
Glossary	130
Index	135

38. The mineral benitoite was found in 1907 in California and has not been found anywhere else. In which section might a reader find more information about it?
   a. What Is a Gem?
   b. Rare Gems
   c. Earth Minerals
   d. Biogenic Minerals
   e. Rare Minerals

39. A reader is looking for the scientific definitions for metamorphic rocks. The quickest way to find them is by looking where?
   a. Introduction
   b. Metamorphic Minerals
   c. Glossary
   d. Index
   e. Part I: Gems and Crystals

Read the passage below, then answer the three questions that follow.

> Plants are remarkably well-suited to their environments, with special adaptations that allow them to survive. _____, the image of the saguaro cactus is a familiar one. Its adaptations allow it to live up to 200 years! It may only grow ten inches a year, but a full-grown cactus can have a stem that is 12–18 meters tall. One long root extends deep into the ground to support it. However, the desert is a dry place, and that deep root wouldn't provide such a large plant with enough water. _____, the cactus uses a network of shallow roots just under the ground. These collect water, which is stored in its stem. Folds along the stem allow it to expand, to take in more water during rare summer rains. In fact, when filled with water, a saguaro can weigh several tons.

40. Which words, if inserted *in order* into the blanks in the passage would correspond to the sequence of the writer's ideas?
   a. However; Also
   b. Yet; For instance
   c. For example; Instead
   d. Since; However
   e. While; Yet

41. Which inference can be made using the information in the passage?
   a. In general, cacti do not need water.
   b. Flowers never bloom on the saguaro cactus.
   c. There are no roots on the saguaro cactus.
   d. The saguaro cactus would not survive in a rain forest.
   e. The saguaro cactus is a short-lived plant.

42. Which describes the author's organizational pattern in the passage above?
   a. using examples to explain
   b. sequencing events
   c. problem-solving format
   d. details to support an argument
   e. least important to most important details

Read the passage below, then answer the four questions that follow.

(1) Tae kwon do and karate are the two most popular forms of martial arts in the United States today. (2) However, there are many differences between them. (3) Karate is considered a Japanese style, but is based on a combination of ancient Chinese martial arts dating back to the 16th century. (4) _____. (5) Many of its moves were influenced by karate during the Japanese occupation of that country in the earlier 20th century.

(6) About 60% of karate blocks and strikes are performed with the hands. (7) About 40% involve kicks. (8) In tae kwon do, the opposite is true. (9) Karate focuses more on self-defense and using the entire body as a weapon. (10) Tae kwon do involves many more aerial moves, such as kicking while in the air.

(11) Both forms have in common an emphasis on self-control and discipline. (12) Beginners are assigned white belts, while experts have black belts of varying levels.

43. Which sentence, if inserted as sentence 4, would best fit with the author's purpose?
    a. Karate is better than tae kwon do.
    b. Tae kwon do is much more modern than karate and was developed in Korea.
    c. Tae kwon do schools are everywhere.
    d. Avoid karate classes with American teachers.
    e. Martial arts schools teach both karate and tae kwon do.

44. Based on the passage, which statement best sums up a major difference between karate and tae kwon do?
    a. Karate is more popular than tae kwon do.
    b. Karate incorporates more hand movements, and tae kwon do more leg movements.
    c. Tae kwon do has expert black belts, and karate has expert white belts.
    d. Tae kwon do focuses more on self-defense.
    e. Karate takes longer to learn than tae kwon do.

45. Which statement best assesses the author's preferences for one martial art over another?
    a. The author feels karate is more useful.
    b. The author feels tae kwon do is more useful.
    c. The author does not express an opinion.
    d. The author thinks tae kwon do is more difficult.
    e. The author would like to learn karate.

46. Which of the following best organizes the information in the passage?
    a. I. The history of tae kwon do and karate
       II. Physical differences in tae kwon do and karate
       III. Similarities in tae kwon do and karate
    b. I. The history of all martial arts
       II. The challenges of karate
       III. The challenges of tae kwon do
    c. I. The influence of karate on tae kwon do
       II. The distinction that makes tae kwon do better
       III. The reasons the two are the same sport
    d. I. The geographical differences in tae kwon do and karate
       II. Hands and feet in martial arts
       III. Explanation of belt levels in martial arts
    e. I. The roots of tae kwon do and karate
       II. The popularity of martial arts
       III. Comparing competition

Read the passage below, then answer the four questions that follow.

(1) As far as the eye can see is a brutal landscape, gray and black with smoke swirling and darkening the sky. (2) Apocalyptic remains of fallen trees lie strewn about. (3) A horrendous odor fills the air. (4) Pits of hot, bubbling liquid make crossing these lands treacherous. (5) There are no signs of life. (6) As you step nearer to one pit, you notice the earth changes to the rusty color of dried blood and that the liquid below is an unnatural blue-green.

(7) Is this the site of a far-off planet? (8) Or the aftermath of some chemical disaster? (9) Not quite! (10) In fact, it's one of the most popular tourist destinations in the world! (11) Yellowstone National Park sits atop several calderas, or volcanic craters sunk into the earth. (12) Hawaii is made from several volcanoes, too. (13) The result is geothermal features such as colorful hot springs, bubbling mud pits, and spouting geysers.

(14) The West Thumb area of Yellowstone is well known to travelers for its abundance of such features. (15) _____ (16) The eggy smell of sulfur fills the air as bubbles of it burst out of mud pits. (17) Its vapors cloud the vision. (18) The resulting landscape is bizarre and otherworldly—and incredible to see!

47. Which sentence, if inserted into the blank line in the third paragraph, would be most consistent with the writer's purpose and intended audience?
   a. Other areas of Yellowstone are known for animal sightings.
   b. A nearby lake allows for wonderful fishing opportunities.
   c. A boardwalk through the area allows visitors to safely view many of these super-heated spectacles.
   d. To get there, enter through the northernmost entrance.
   e. Traveling to Yellowstone can be difficult in wintery weather.

48. Which sentence is least relevant to the main idea of the second paragraph?
   a. sentence 8
   b. sentence 9
   c. sentence 10
   d. sentence 11
   e. sentence 12

49. Between the first and second paragraphs, the author's writing style shifts from
   a. descriptive to informative.
   b. informative to descriptive.
   c. cause to effect.
   d. demonstrative to persuasive.
   e. persuasive to informative.

50. Which of the following best summarizes the main idea of the passage?
   a. Yellowstone National Park is a popular tourist destination.
   b. Geothermal features at Yellowstone are unique and intriguing.
   c. Volcanic matter has a terrible smell.
   d. Geysers shoot water incredible distances.
   e. Yellowstone was formed by volcanoes.

Section 2: Mathematics

1. In the spring semester, a student received scores of 96, 88, 73, 90, 81, and 78 on six tests. What was the student's average for the semester?
   a. 73
   b. 84
   c. 85
   d. 96
   e. 504

Use the following table to answer the question below

Section	Total Number of Questions	Number of Questions Correctly Answered
Geometry	30	21
Statistics	20	16
Algebra	25	19

2. The table shows the number of questions a student answered correctly on a math test. What percent of the questions on the test did the student answer correctly?
   a. 20%
   b. 52%
   c. 56%
   d. 75%
   e. 98%

Use the diagram below to answer the question that follows.

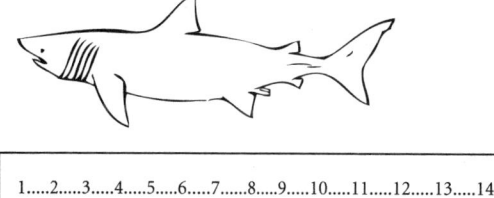

1.....2.....3.....4.....5.....6.....7.....8.....9.....10.....11.....12.....13.....14.....15
UNITS

3. If the shark is actually 4,560 millimeters long, then what is the scale of the diagram of the shark?
   a. 1 unit = 15 millimeters
   b. 1 unit = 100 millimeters
   c. 1 unit = 304 millimeters
   d. 1 unit = 1,000 millimeters
   e. 1 unit = 4,560 millimeters

4. Which unit would you use to express the weight of a paper clip?
   a. pounds
   b. pints
   c. quarts
   d. ounces
   e. inches

5. Mrs. Torpie needs to order twine for a science experiment. There are 47 students in her class. Each will receive a length of twine that is 4 feet 9 inches long. What is the total length of twine Mrs. Torpie needs to order so that each student has enough?
   a. 267 feet 9 inches
   b. 223 feet 3 inches
   c. 223 feet 2 inches
   d. 51 feet 9 inches
   e. 48 feet 9 inches

Answer the following question based on the diagram below.

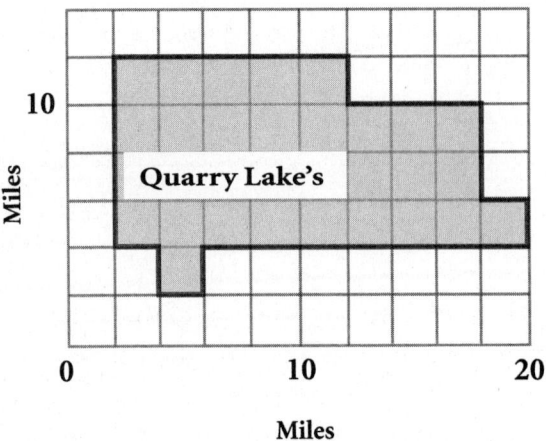

6. How long is Quarry Lake's shore?
   a. 20 miles
   b. 27 miles
   c. 28 miles
   d. 31 miles
   e. 56 miles

Use the diagram below to answer the question that follows.

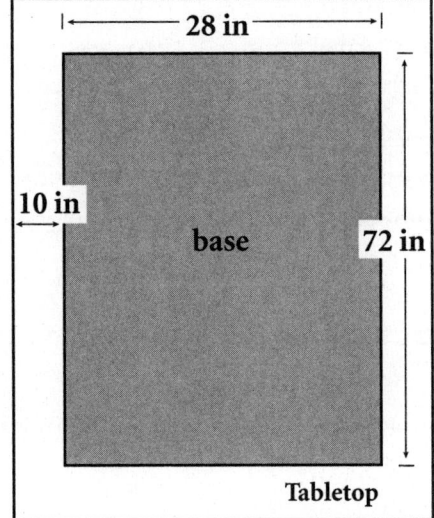

7. The wood shop class is making a table that is supported by a squared tree-trunk base. If the tabletop is 10 inches wider than the base on each side, what is the perimeter of the tabletop?
   a. 20 inches
   b. 110 inches
   c. 200 inches
   d. 220 inches
   e. 2,736 inches

8. Scott uses one bag of dog food every ten days to feed his two dogs. Approximately how many bags of dog food does he use per month?
   a. 1 bag
   b. 3 bags
   c. 5 bags
   d. 30 bags
   e. 31 bags

9. Delaney can run three miles in about 27 minutes. If she continues running at this pace, how long will it take her to run seven miles?
   a. 54 minutes
   b. 56 minutes
   c. 65 minutes
   d. 1 hour 6 minutes
   e. 1 hour 5 minutes

10. Declan has a bag of chewing gum. The bag contains 12 grape, 15 strawberry, 9 bubble gum, and 17 mint flavored pieces. Declan pulls out a grape piece and leaves it on a table. What is the probability that he will next take a mint flavored piece from the bag?
   a. $\frac{187}{27,540}$
   b. $\frac{17}{52}$
   c. $\frac{28}{53}$
   d. $\frac{29}{53}$
   e. $\frac{29}{54}$

11. Approximately 7 out of 10 seniors go to college after graduating from West High School. If there are 340 seniors graduating, how many will be going to college?
   a. 71 seniors
   b. 75 seniors
   c. 107 seniors
   d. 238 seniors
   e. 350 seniors

12. The population of Rosedale City is 938,570 people. Westchester has a population of 1,940,612. Which answer shows the best estimate of how many more people live in Westchester than in Rosedale City?
   a. 1,000 people
   b. 10,000 people
   c. 100,000 people
   d. 900,000 people
   e. 1,000,000 people

13. Which of the following is the best estimate for $5,304 \times 270$?
   a. 1,500,000
   b. 1,000,000
   c. 180,000
   d. 15,000
   e. 5,600

14. The highest score ever on a certain game show was 66,712 points. The lowest a contestant ever left with was −16,038 points. Which of the following is the best estimate of the number of points between the lowest and highest scores in the game show's history?
   a. 49,000 points
   b. 50,000 points
   c. 51,000 points
   d. 66,000 points
   e. 83,000 points

Koda takes a math placement exam, and her scores are below. Use this information to answer question 15.

Raw	Percentile	Stanine	Grade Equivalent
85	91	8	11.5

15. Koda's test scores indicate that
   a. she answered 85 questions correctly.
   b. 91% of the other students scored higher than she did.
   c. she could do the same level of math as a high school junior.
   d. she answered 85% of the questions correctly.
   e. she answered 8 question incorrectly.

16. The expression −234 + (−12) + 56 simplifies to which of the following?
   a. −19
   b. −50
   c. −190
   d. −230
   e. 278

Use the information below to answer the question that follows.

Monday	Tuesday	Wednesday	Thursday	Friday
16°C	6°C	10°C	−4°C	−16°C

17. During a science experiment, a class recorded the temperature at 6:30 A.M. for one week. What was the difference between the highest and lowest morning temperatures that week?
   a. −32°C
   b. −16°C
   c. 0°C
   d. 6°C
   e. 32°C

18. A sponsor brings free beverages to pass out along the course of a long-distance running race. They bring 620 bottles of a sports drink, 1,000 bottles of water, and 380 bottles of juice. If the sponsor divides all the drinks among the 500 participants in the race, how many drinks will each receive?
   a. 2 drinks
   b. 3.4 drinks
   c. 4 drinks
   d. 5 drinks
   e. 40 drinks

19. What is the tens digit in the dividend of the problem below?

$$\begin{array}{r} 5 \text{ R } 28 \\ 30\overline{)1\_8} \end{array}$$

   a. 5
   b. 6
   c. 7
   d. 8
   e. 9

20. Last month, Sean finished $2\frac{4}{5}$ paintings. This month, he finished $10\frac{3}{4}$ paintings. What is the sum of the number of paintings he completed this month and last month?
   a. $12\frac{11}{20}$ paintings
   b. 13 paintings
   c. $13\frac{11}{20}$ paintings
   d. 14 paintaings
   e. $14\frac{1}{20}$ paintings

21. An outdoor store is having a 20% off sale on all tents. If a tent normally costs $299, how much will it now cost, not including tax?
   a. $29.90
   b. $59.80
   c. $180.00
   d. $239.20
   e. $269.10

22. At cheerleader tryouts, half of the people trying out were eliminated during the first cut. Half of the people left were eliminated during the second cut. If 12 students make the squad after that, how many students tried out?
   a. 3 students
   b. 16 students
   c. 24 students
   d. 32 students
   e. 48 students

23. Jane grooms horses 26 hours per week and earns $6.75 per hour. After working at the stables for six months, she gets a raise that increases her weekly gross pay to pay to $201.50. How much more is she making each week?
   a. $7.75
   b. $26.00
   c. $26.50
   d. $33.55
   e. $201.50

Use the diagram below to answer the question that follows.

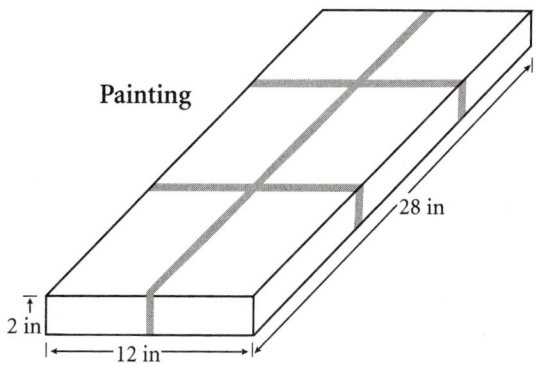

24. Katie ordered a painting from Handsome Galleries but is concerned that it may not fit in the nook where she wants to put it. The nook is two feet three inches high. How does the height of the painting compare to the height of the nook?
   a. They are exactly the same height.
   b. The nook is one inch shorter than the painting.
   c. The nook is three inches shorter than the painting.
   d. The nook is one inch taller than the painting.
   e. The nook is three inches taller than the painting.

25. Penny is taking a road trip. At 12:00, she sees the following sign.

Long Beach	32 miles
Manhattan Beach	25 miles
Santa Barbara	95 miles
Pismo Beach	176 miles

If Penny drives steadily at 60 miles per hour, how far from Pismo Beach will she be at 1:30?

a. 60 miles
b. 86 miles
c. 110 miles
d. 116 miles
e. 170 miles

26. Lara and her sister Anna both collect jewelry. Anna has 26 more bracelets than Lara. If both sisters have a total of 68 bracelets, how many bracelets does Lara have?

a. 21 bracelets
b. 26 bracelets
c. 42 bracelets
d. 48 bracelets
e. 68 bracelets

27. Solve for y.

$4y + 1 - 2y = 19$

a. 5
b. 6
c. 7
d. 8
e. 9

The following article appeared in the school newspaper. Use it to answer the question below.

> The school library is selling off 100 books to raise money. There are 21 biographies, 17 true crime cases, 15 mysteries, and 47 literary novels. By the end of the sale, 82 of the books have been sold.

28. Which of the following facts can be determined from the information given above?

a. the number of true crime stories sold
b. the best-selling genre
c. the number of books that remain after the sale
d. the amount of money raised by the sale
e. the number of books they can buy with the earnings

29. Nick and Alex are going on spring break. They have budgeted $750 for their trip. Their hotel offers three meals a day for about $10 each. What additional information is necessary in order to find out how much they should budget for food on this trip?

a. the kind of food they plan on ordering
b. the number of days in their vacation
c. the number of meals they will eat on the trip
d. which three meals the hotel provides
e. how much gas is needed to get to the hotel

30. Amy left her home at 7:00 A.M. and biked 4 miles to a national park. She completed a mountain biking trail there, then rode home, for a total distance of 16 miles. What additional information would you need in order to find Amy's average riding speed?
   a. the time she arrived home
   b. the time she arrived at the park
   c. the number of times she stopped and rested
   d. the distance of the trail
   e. whether the course was on a hill or not

31. DJ buys five shirts for $10.50 each. The next day he returns the T-shirts, but four of them have been marked down to $8.99 each. The store will only refund the current price of the shirts. He uses the following expression to figure out how much less money he will get back:

$(5 \times \$10.50) - (4 \times \$8.99)$

Which of the following expressions would also have worked for DJ?
   a. $10.50 − $8.99
   b. 4($10.50 − $8.99) + $10.50
   c. (5 × $10.50) − $8.99
   d. (5 × 4) − ($10.50 × $8.99)
   e. 4($10.50 + $8.99)

32. Patty wants to buy a dress that is 15% of $75. To see how much money she will save, she computes 15% of 75 in the following way:

$75 \times \frac{15}{100}$

How else could she have figured it out?
   a. $\frac{15}{(100-75)}$
   b. 75 ÷ 15
   c. $\frac{15}{75} \times 100$
   d. 75 × 0.15
   e. 15 ÷ 75

The table below shows Frank's averages for the semester

Quiz Average	Test Average	Final Average
92%	85%	87%

For his overall average, the test average counts twice as much as the quiz average, and the final exam counts twice as much as the test average. Frank uses the following expression to figure out what his grade will be:

$(92 + 85 + 85 + 87 + 87 + 87 + 87) \div 7$

33. Which of the following expressions also would have worked to find his overall average?
   a. $92 + \frac{2(85)}{7} + \frac{4(87)}{7}$
   b. 92 + 0.2(85) + 0.4(87)
   c. $[92 + 2(85) + 4(87)] \div 0.7$
   d. $[92 + 2(85) + 4(87)] \times 7$
   e. $[92 + 2(85) + 4(87)] \times \frac{1}{7}$

The following article appeared in the school newspaper. Use it to answer the question below.

X	Y
1	4
1.5	6
2	8
2.5	
3	12
3.5	14

34. What is the missing value of Y?
   a. 4
   b. 6
   c. 8.5
   d. 9
   e. 10

35. Sands Central School District is considering a 5% decrease in the number of days in the school year. Currently, there are 180 days in the school year. How long would it be with the proposed decrease?
   a. 18 days
   b. 171 days
   c. 176 days
   d. 181 days
   e. 190 days

36. Which of the following mathematical statements is true?
   a. $5\frac{3}{7} > 5\frac{2}{7} > 4\frac{3}{7}$
   b. $5\frac{3}{7} > 4\frac{3}{7} > 5\frac{2}{7}$
   c. $5\frac{2}{7} > 5\frac{3}{7} > 4\frac{3}{7}$
   d. $5\frac{2}{7} < 5\frac{3}{7} < 4\frac{3}{7}$
   e. $4\frac{3}{7} < 5\frac{3}{7} < 5\frac{2}{7}$

Use the mathematical statement below to answer the question that follows.

$$\frac{4}{8} < \underline{} < \frac{9}{12}$$

37. Which of the following values could be placed in the blank to make the above statement true?
   a. $\frac{1}{4}$
   b. $\frac{1}{2}$
   c. $\frac{2}{3}$
   d. $\frac{3}{4}$
   e. $\frac{7}{8}$

38. Which of the following mathematical expressions is equivalent to $\frac{1}{4}(kw)$?
   a. $\frac{k}{4} \times \frac{w}{4}$
   b. $\frac{kw}{4}$
   c. $\frac{k}{4} + \frac{w}{4}$
   d. $4(k \times w)$
   e. $4(k + w)$

39. Which of the following numbers is between 7,658,500 and 7,896,300?
   a. 7,986,400
   b. 7,689,500
   c. 7,568,900
   d. 7,658,300
   e. 7,653,800

40. If the value of m is between 0.0075 and 0.032, which of the following could be m?
   a. 0.0069
   b. 0.00725
   c. 0.0267
   d. 0.075
   e. 0.0761

41. Richie takes the bus 14 miles round trip between home and school each day, Monday through Friday. If his daily round trip is rounded to the nearest 5 miles, which is the best estimate of the total number of miles he travels in one school week?
   a. 50 miles
   b. 75 miles
   c. 100 miles
   d. 110 miles
   e. 150 miles

42. Mary Elizabeth swam the 50-meter freestyle at five different meets. Her times were 24.53 seconds, 25.32 seconds, 27.06 seconds, 26.39 seconds, and 23.24 seconds. If each time is rounded to the nearest one-tenth of a second, what is the best estimate of Mary Elizabeth's total time for all five races?
   a. 125 seconds
   b. 126 seconds
   c. 126.5 seconds
   d. 129 seconds
   e. 129.5 seconds

Use the information below to answer the question that follows.

- The library is located seven miles from the town pool.
- The town pool is located five miles from the mall.

43. Which of the following conclusions can be made based on this information?
   a. The library is no more than 12 miles away from the mall.
   b. The library is no more than 2 miles away from the mall.
   c. The library is no more than 5 miles away from the mall.
   d. The library is exactly 5 miles from the mall.
   e. The library is between the town pool and the mall.

Tim has a day off and is deciding what to do. His options are shown below. Use them to answer the question that follows.

- If the temperature is over 85°, Tim will go to the beach.
- If the temperature is between 60° and 84°, Tim will go to the stadium and watch a ball game.
- If the temperature is less than 59°, Tim will go see a new movie.

44. If Tim watched the Dodgers play against the Angels, which of the following statements could be true?
  a. the temperature is 40°
  b. the temperature is 59°
  c. the temperature is 75°
  d. the temperature is 85°
  e. the temperature is 90°

A section of Summer's cheerleading practice schedule is shown below. Use it to answer the question that follows.

There will be cheerleading practice every Monday, Wednesday, and Friday throughout the season with the following exceptions:

- On half-days, practice will be canceled.
- There is no practice on the first Friday of each month.

45. If it is Friday but there is no softball practice, then it must be true that
  a. it is a half-day.
  b. it is the first Friday of the month.
  c. it is a half-day and it is the first Friday of the month.
  d. it is a half-day or it is the first Friday of the month.
  e. this Friday is a half-day.

The partial school schedule below shows the start and end times of class periods. Use this information to answer the question below.

Middle School Bell Schedule		
Class Period	Start Time	End Time
Second	8:30 A.M.	9:25 A.M.
Third	9:30 A.M.	10:25 A.M.
Fourth	10:30 A.M.	11:25 A.M.
Lunch	11:30 A.M.	12:10 P.M.
Fifth		1:10 P.M.

46. Except for lunch, all the periods are the same length. What is the missing start time for fifth period?
  a. 12:15 A.M.
  b. 12:15 P.M.
  c. 12:25 P.M.
  d. 12:30 P.M.
  e. 2:05 P.M.

In an effort to reduce waste, the county has been keeping track of how much paper waste is produced by various schools within the Orange County limits. The chart below shows this information over the course of 20 years. Use it to answer the question that follows.

Paper Waste per Metric Ton		
Year	PS 207	Orange County
1990	100	560
1995	125	692
2000	133	730
2005	103	803
2010	112	858

47. How many metric tons of waste were produced by county schools other than PS 207 in 2000?
    a. 132 metric tons
    b. 597 metric tons
    c. 730 metric tons
    d. 862 metric tons
    e. 970 metric tons

The L'il Luv Animal Shelter is studying the success of their mobile adoption program. The graph below shows how many pets they've adopted out over a 50 year period through mobile adoption fairs. Use the information in the graph to answer the question that follows.

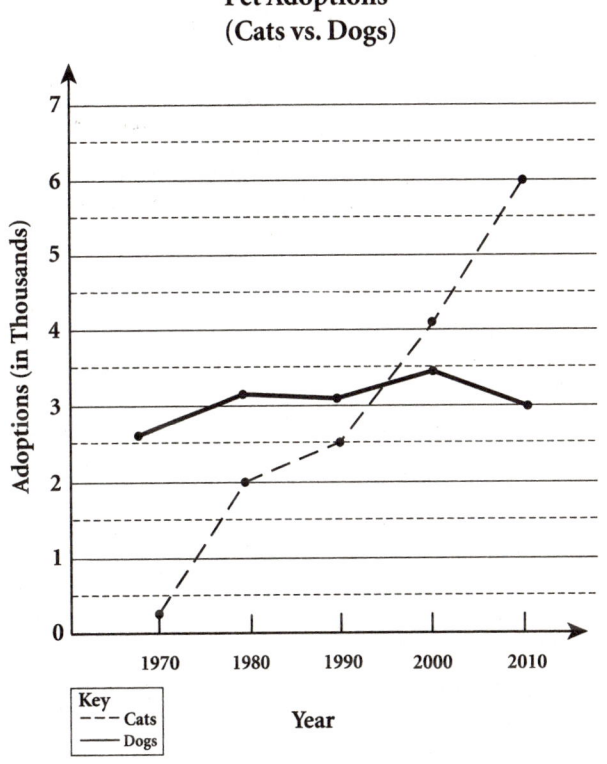

48. What was the maximum difference between the number of adoptions of cats and dogs in any one of the years shown?
    a. 2,000 more dogs
    b. 2,000 more cats
    c. 3,000 more dogs
    d. 3,000 more cats
    e. 6,200 more cats

Use the chart below to answer the question that follows.

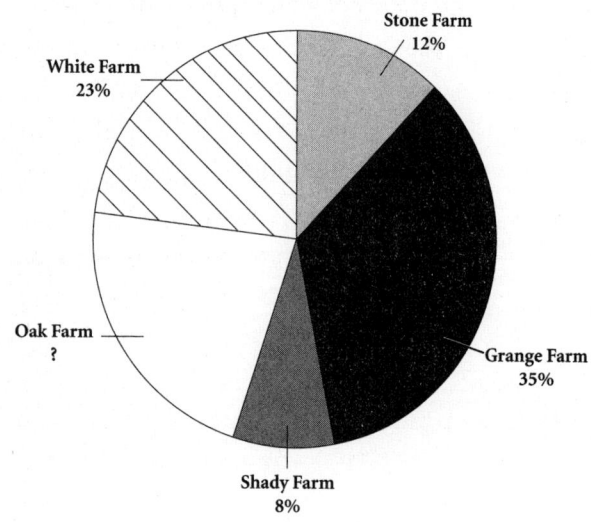

Percent of Total Wheat Crop Yield in 2010

The graph below shows the sales of a certain candy bar over a 50-year period. Use it to answer the question that follows.

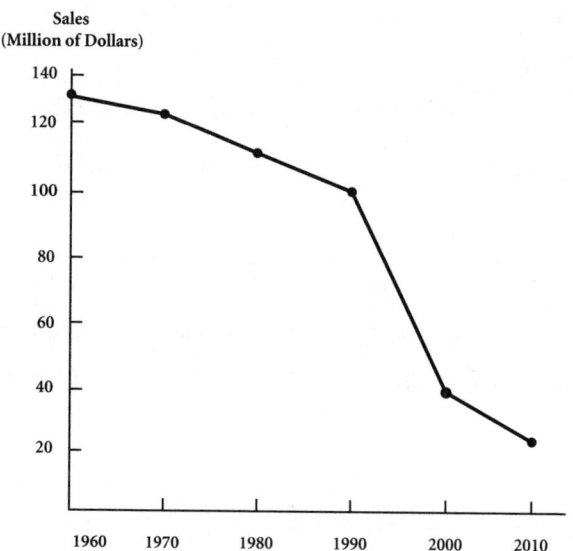

49. What percent of the total crop yield did the Oak Farm generate in 2010?
   a. 15%
   b. 22%
   c. 30%
   d. 50%
   e. 88%

50. Between what years did sales decrease by the greatest amount?
   a. between 1960 and 1970
   b. between 1970 and 1980
   c. between 1980 and 1990
   d. between 1990 and 2000
   e. between 2000 and 2010

Section 3: Essay Writing

Carefully read the two essay-writing topics that follow. Plan and write two essays, one on each topic. Be sure to address all points in the topic. Allow about 30 minutes for each essay.

Topic 1

William Saroyan once observed, "Good people are good because they've come to wisdom through failure." In an essay to be read by an audience of educated adults, state whether you agree or disagree with Saroyan's comment. Use logic to argue your position, and support it with specific examples.

Topic 2

At some point in their academic careers, most students encounter conflict with another student or teacher. Students may have to deal with bullies or being pressured by other students. Conflicts between teachers and students may stem from different ways of thinking or personality clashes. In an essay to be read by an audience of educated adults, describe an example of a conflict you faced, and explain how you handled the situation. Your example can come from your time as either a student or a teacher.

Answer Key

Section 1: Reading Comprehension

1. **b.** Pages 19–20 contain information about activities. Games that stimulate a newborn would fall into this category.
2. **e.** The index shows information on giving birth, stimulating a baby, and postpartum depression, among other topics involving newborns.
3. **a.** This statement fits contextually with those before and after it.
4. **c.** The team was encouraged to continue, so it would make sense that the crowd liked it and cheered.
5. **a.** The correct answer choice shows the main idea of each paragraph in the passage.
6. **a.** The author is writing about environmentalists, and the answer choice describes an environmental concern.
7. **d.** The author mentions *our country* and *the national agenda* in the passage.
8. **b.** The passage provides reasons why the issue should be of greater importance on the national agenda. The other answer choices are not supported by the passage at all.
9. **c.** A full 30% of the class chose a major in the sciences.
10. **e.** The words correctly fit with the timeline used by the author.
11. **c.** This is the meaning of the phrase *up to it*.
12. **c.** The sentence immediately following the instruction to run the filter tells the reader to place a basking dock in the tank.
13. **a.** The passage describes chivalry's origins and how its ideals were carried out in different arenas.
14. **b.** The chivalric notion was mercy, but the author provides money as a second motive.
15. **c.** The author provides realistic, and not too flattering, examples of chivalry in action.
16. **c.** The author used the word to describe the positive way the commandments of chivalry appear, before dispelling that idea.
17. **c.** That Turritopsis nutricula is "the most beautiful" jellyfish cannot be proven, so this is only an opinion.
18. **e.** Their method of movement is off the main topic, which is their immortality.
19. **a.** The author states the main idea in the first paragraph and backs it up with supporting scientific details.
20. **d.** This tests comprehension, as this is the most important detail to understanding the passage.
21. **e.** The passage is about the poodle's sporting ability and history, and it does not mention allergies.
22. **d.** This choice is the only one that lists a fact about kite surfing's risks.
23. **c.** It cannot be proven that kite surfing is the best sport, so that is an opinion.
24. **e.** It is described as being a combination of many sports, including the modern snowboarding. The expert has only been involved in it for five years.
25. **b.** The answer choice is supported by the interviewee's next comment, describing it as a thrill.
26. **a.** The other answer choices are details and are not all accurate.
27. **d.** This can be inferred by the placement of the sentence, directly following the anecdote about her brother and the chain saw incident.
28. **b.** The answer choice is a synonym and would make sense if used in the passage instead of the underlined word.
29. **a.** The use of the word *However* in the third sentence hints that the author is about to argue a lesser-known point about Cleopatra.
30. **c.** Sequentially, the coins came before her marriages to the Roman rulers.

31. c. The passage states that kenneled dogs with separation anxiety may injure themselves.

32. b. The sentence that reveals the answer contains the clue word *first*.

33. c. The passage offers advice to dog owners.

34. e. The author cites scientific research about personal and environmental effects of chemicals used in nonorganic farming.

35. a. The author's argument is about the environment and health. A person must care about these issues to buy the author's argument.

36. c. The author provides more information on Geldof's activism than on his life or music.

37. b. Shortly after seeing the documentary, he began working to end world hunger and started with Ethiopia.

38. e. Benitoite is a mineral found in only once place at one time. It would fall under the Rare Minerals category.

39. c. A glossary is always the quickest way to find a definition.

40. c. These words fit best within the passage.

41. d. The passage is about adaptations to environments. It describes the cactus's specialized stem that allows it to store water. The reader can infer that too much water would drown it.

42. a. The author provides details to support the main idea.

43. b. The correct choice provides a segue between the history of karate and tae kwon do. The passage mentions the influence of karate, which is a clue that the missing sentence is about tae kwon do.

44. b. The other answer choices are not accurate or supported by the passage.

45. c. The passage is strictly informational.

46. a. The correct answer choice shows the main idea of each paragraph in the passage.

47. c. The other choices do not support the author's purpose, which is to describe geothermal features of Yellowstone.

48. e. The passage is about Yellowstone, not other volcanic landforms.

49. a. The author provides a description of the landscape before switching to explain what it is and how it occurs.

50. b. The other responses are details, not main ideas.

Section 2: Mathematics

1. b. Add all six values and divide by 6. $(96 + 88 + 73 + 90 + 81 + 78) \div 6 = 84$

2. d. Find the total number of questions and the total number of questions answered correctly. Divide the total number answered correctly by the total number of questions. $56 \div 75 = 74.6\%$. Round up to 75%.

3. a. Divide the total number of millimeters by the number of units the shark measures. $4,560 \div 15 = 304$.

4. d. A pound would be too large to measure a paper clip's weight. Pints and quarts measure volume, and inches measure length.

5. b. Determine how many inches of twine each student needs by dividing the number of feet by 12 and adding the number of inches (4 feet 9 inches = 57 inches). Multiply 57 inches by the number of students in the class to find the total length of twine in inches ($57 \times 47 = 2,679$). Convert to feet by dividing 2,679 by 12 to get 223 feet and 3 inches.

6. e. Count the distance around the lake, which is 28 units. The scale indicates that each square is two miles long, so multiply 28×2, which is 56.

7. d. Add 10 inches to the width of the base of 28 inches. Then use the perimeter formula: $2L + 2W = P$. $2(72) + 2(38) = 220$ inches

8. **b.** Divide 30 days by the number of days it takes Scott to use up a bag. $30 \div 10 = 3$
9. **b.** Find her pace per mile by dividing $27 \div 3 = 9$ minute miles. Multiply that rate by the total distance run to find how long it will take ($9 \times 7 = 56$ minutes).
10. **b.** The numerator of the fraction is the total number of mint flavored pieces (17). The denominator of the fraction is the total number of pieces of gum left after Declan pulls out a grape piece. Therefore, the correct answer is choice **b**.
11. **d.** Set up a ratio, then solve for x by cross multiplying and dividing. $\frac{7}{10} = \frac{x}{340}$, $x = 238$
12. **e.** Round each to the nearest hundred thousand, then subtract. $1{,}900{,}000 - 900{,}000 = 1{,}000{,}000$
13. **a.** Round 5,304 to the nearest thousand and 270 to the nearest hundred, then multiply. $5{,}000 \times 300 = 1{,}500{,}000$
14. **e.** Round each score to the nearest ten thousand. Find the difference between them. $67{,}000 - (-16{,}000) = 83{,}000$
15. **a.** She answered 85 questions correctly as indicated by her raw score.
16. **c.** Subtract 12 from -234, then add 56.
17. **e.** Find the difference between -16 and 16. $16 - (-16) = 32$
18. **c.** Add to find the total number of bottles, and divide by the number of participants. $620 + 1{,}000 + 380 = 2{,}000 \div 500 = 4$
19. **c.** Multiply 30 by 5, then add 28 to find the dividend. $30 \times 5 = 150 + 28 = 178$
20. **c.** Turn the mixed numbers into improper fractions. Find a common denominator, and add them. Simplify the answer. $\frac{14}{5} + \frac{43}{4} = \frac{56}{20} + \frac{215}{20} = \frac{271}{20} = 13\frac{11}{20}$
21. **d.** Multiply $299 by 0.20, and subtract the answer from $299. $299 \times .20 = 59.8$; $299 - 59.80 = 239.20$
22. **e.** Multiply 12 by 2 to find out how many students remained after the first cut (24); multiply that number by 2 to find out how many tried out (48).
23. **b.** Multiply hours and hourly wage to determine how much Jane was making before her raise; subtract that amount from her new earnings. $26 \times 6.75 = 175.50$; $201.50 - 175.50 = 26$
24. **b.** Change the measurement of the nook to inches so it can be compared to the painting. Two feet = 24 inches, so two feet three inches is $24 + 3 = 27$ inches. Twenty-seven is one less than 28, so the nook is one inch shorter than the painting.
25. **b.** Subtract 60 miles from 176 for the distance traveled between 12:00 to 1:00 to get 116. Then, subtract half of 60 (30) for the distance traveled in a half an hour. $116 - 30 = 86$
26. **a.** Set up an equation and solve for x. $(x + (26 + x)) = 68$; $x = 21$
27. **e.** Simplify by combining y values before solving the equation. $(2y + 1 = 19)$; $y = 9$
28. **c.** To find the number of books remaining, the amount sold can be subtracted from the total for sale ($100 - 82$).
29. **b.** The other choices do not contain essential information.
30. **a.** The other choices do not contain essential information.
31. **b.** The other answer choices do not yield the same answer as the expression DJ used.
32. **d.** The other answer choices do not yield the same answer as the expression Patty used. 0.15 and 15% are equivalent.

33. e. The other answer choices do not yield the same answer as the expression Frank used.

34. e. The relationship established is that $Y = 4(X)$, so $4(2.5) = 10$.

35. b. Find 5% of 180 by multiplying $180 \times 0.05 = 9$. Subtract 9 from 180 to get 171.

36. a. The correct answer shows the fractions from largest to smallest.

37. c. Find the least common multiple for the fractions in the statement and the denominators in the answer choices (24). Convert each answer choice to an equivalent fraction with a denominator of 24. Then look at the numerators to find one that is larger than $\frac{12}{24}$ but smaller than $\frac{18}{24}$.

38. b. Following the correct order of operations, the given expression can be simplified to $\frac{kw}{4}$.

39. b. The first answer choice is greater than both numbers, and the last three are less than both numbers.

40. c. Placing the choices on a number line will make it clear that the other choices do not fall between the two given numbers.

41. b. Round 14 miles to 15. Multiply 15 by 5.

42. c. Round each time to the nearest one-tenth. Add them together. $24.5 + 25.3 + 27.1 + 26.4 + 23.2 = 126.5$

43. a. Add the distances from the library to the pool and the pool to the mall. No matter which direction the library is in, it cannot be farther away than this sum. $5 + 7 = 12$

44. c. The only temperature between 60° and 84° is 75°.

45. d. There is not enough information to determine which of the statements is true, and either one can be.

46. b. All the classes with the exception of lunch are 55 minutes long. Subtract 55 minutes from the end time of the fifth period to determine its start time. $1:10 - 55 = 12:15$

47. b. Subtract the amount of waste produced by PS 207 from the total amount of waste in Orange County. $730 - 133 = 597$

48. d. In 2010, there were 3,000 dogs adopted and 6,000 cats adopted. The difference between the values is 3,000.

49. b. To set up the equation, subtract the sum of the other parts from 100. Solve for x. $100 - (23 + 12 + 35 + 8) = x; x = 22$

50. d. Between 1990 and 2000, sales decreased by $60 million from $100 to $40 million. This is a larger decline than any other period shown on the graph.

Section 3: Essay Writing

Following are the criteria for scoring CBEST essays.

An essay with a score of 4 is a coherent writing sample that addresses the assigned topic and is aimed at a specific audience. Additionally, it has the following characteristics:

- a main idea and/or a central point of view that is focused, with sound reasoning
- points of discussion that are clear and arranged logically
- assertions supported with specific, relevant details
- word choice and usage that is accurate and precise
- sentences that have complexity and variety, with clear syntax; paragraphs that are coherent (minor mechanical flaws are acceptable)
- style and language appropriate to the assigned audience and purpose

An essay with a score of 3 is an adequate writing sample that generally addresses the assigned topic but neglects or only vaguely addresses one of the assigned tasks; it is aimed at a specific audience. Generally, it has the following additional characteristics:

- a main idea and/or a central point of view and adequate reasoning
- effective organization of ideas, with clear meanings
- generalizations that are adequately, though unevenly, supported
- word choice and language usage that are adequate; mistakes exist but do not interfere with meaning
- some errors in sentence and paragraph structure, but not so many as to be confusing
- word choice and style appropriate to a given audience

An essay with a score of 2 is a writing sample that attempts to address the topic and to communicate a message to the assigned audience but is generally incomplete or inappropriate. It has the following additional characteristics:

- a main point, but one which loses focus; reasoning that is simplistic
- ineffective organization that causes the response to lack clarity
- generalizations that are only partially supported; supporting details that are irrelevant or unclear
- imprecise language usage; word choice that distracts the reader
- errors in mechanics, syntax, and paragraphing
- style that is monotonous or choppy

An essay with a score of 1 is an inadequately formed writing sample that only marginally addresses the topic and fails to communicate its message to a specific audience. Additionally, it has the following characteristics:

- general incoherence and inadequate focus, lack of a main idea or consistent point of view, and illogical reasoning
- ineffective organization and unclear meaning throughout
- unsupported generalizations and assertions; details that are irrelevant or inappropriate and presented in a confusing manner
- language use that is imprecise, with serious and distracting errors
- many serious errors in mechanics, syntax, and paragraphing

Following are examples of scored essays for Topics 1 and 2. (There are some deliberate errors in all of the essays so that you can tell how much latitude you have.)

Topic 1

Pass—Score = 4

I disagree with Saroyan's sentiment. In my opinion, it implies that moral goodness is directly correlated to the amount of failure one experiences. In other words, those who were born into fortunate circumstance, or are successful in their endeavors cannot achieve goodness, no matter how philanthropic their intentions may be. By another token, a person who is severely developmentally disabled may not be able to recognize failure in his or her own life; Saroyan seems to indicate that they must, then, all be "bad" people.

My own aunt was born with Down Syndrome. She was kind, altruistic, and heartbreakingly naive. I remember one incident in particular, when we visited an amusement park with my little brothers. My aunt was approached by a mascot who extended his hand for a shake. My brothers immediately began mocking him, pointing out that he was not real and that they could see his hair under his costume zipper. My aunt was so upset, she refused to speak to them for the rest of the day. Before we left, we bumped into the mascot again (or at least, someone wearing that costume). My aunt ran back and tearfully apologized for my brothers' behavior. Such tenderness can only come from someone "good." Yet her family and school made sure she was shielded from any overarching feelings of failure.

Some people seem born with an innate goodness: Mother Teresa, a winner of the Nobel Prize for Peace, knew she wanted to dedicate her life to missionary work when she was only a young girl. According to the Buddhist religion, Siddhartha was born as a royal prince who never knew of suffering until he observed it—not experienced it—when he left his palace for the first time as a young man. He is now more commonly known as Buddha.

It is true that great suffering or failure can bring about wisdom and therefore goodness. People such as Mahatma Gandhi, or Nelson Mandela embody such an idea. However, I cannot abide by the notion that only through failure can one become "good."

Marginal Pass—Score = 3

I disagree with Saroyan's statement that goodness comes from failure. It means that a person cannot be considered good if they haven't failed. I don't think it is fair to punish people for being successful. Not all successful people are bad.

A person who is born into a family with a lot of money could not experience failure all his life. Maybe he's wise enough to run his familie's investments and turn millions into billions. Then maybe he could one day give the family fortune all away to charity.

Also, children haven't lived long enough to experience the type of failure that I think Saroyan is describing. So by his logic, would he then say that all children are "bad?" While some seem that way, certainly not all of them are!

Some people may be successful all their lives because they are wise. Some people may have huge failures and become mean because of them instead of becoming wiser and kinder. For these reasons, I disagree with Saroyan.

Marginal Fail—Score = 2

You can't be a good person if you aren't wise. You can't be a wise person if you aren't good. I agree with Saroyan when he says, "Good people are good because they've come to wisdom through failure."

If you don't fail at all, you wont learn from your mistakes. Learning from mistakes is what makes people wise. Wise people get wisdom and then you can become successful. Only people who became successful this way are good.

I don't think that people who have it easy all their lives are good people. They don't know what it's like not to have everything.

When people fail, they gain wisdom. Wisdom helps make people better. Therefore, I agree with failure making people good.

Fail—Score = 1

I believe that you can be a good person because you failed. Not everyone fails because they are bad people and everyone who is bad doesn't always fail. A wise person nows the differences between good and bad. You cant be wise and not be good. But you can be wise and fail. So you can fail and be food.

Topic 2
Pass—Score = 4

In an attempt to fulfill my science core without having to challenge myself, I enrolled in a class called "The Physics of Music and Sound." I liked music; the catalog described the course in a way that had me envisioning musical instruments of all kinds, and, oddly enough, a laser light show. As I soon found out, the physics of music and sound were not easy, nor were they fun to learn about.

I was a creative writing major, and veered away from anything remotely scientific. Having Dr. Ejnes as a teacher didn't help the cause. He was a brilliant man, the kind of genius who often showed up late in a stained shirt, with his hair askew; his mind was simply operating at a level too high to be concerned with the minutiae of his daily appearance. He was socially inept, but an incredible physicist. Shortly after my class he was recruited by a much better school to supervise some sort of research. He was also a terrible teacher.

Physics came easily to Dr. Ejnes. In the beginning of the semester, I asked questions constantly. At first he would stop his lecture, only to stare blankly at me, and, after hearing my question, repeat verbatim what he had just said. Sometimes, he would shake his head in confusion and say, "I don't know how to answer that. I don't understand what you don't get. I can't make it any simpler." As the semester went on, he simply turned his head away from any student who had their hand raised.

Some of the more analytic students were fine with this. But there were plenty of us who were not. One malcontent suggested we all talk to the dean. Instead, I decided to speak to the professor. I knew that we processed things very differently. I wasn't sure we could even communicate. However, I suspected he would relate to my frustration at not being able to understand something, no matter how many angles I approached it from. Using that as my lead, I approached him.

During our conversation, I learned that Dr. Ejnes was attempting to write a textbook. We worked out a deal: for extra credit, I could provide feedback on each of the chapters as he wrote it. My point of view, it turned out, was exactly what he needed—I was his audience. And, as he learned, he had no idea how to write for it. I told him that the more feedback he received, the better off he would be in the end. As a result, he offered the same deal to other students in the class. Some students who, like me, signed up for the class as a way to meet a science core, quickly jumped at the chance to avoid failing.

As it turned out, physics was fun. I learned more about the nature of sound reviewing that book that I did from the semester that I paid for. I also learned that no matter how different two people are, a compromise can always be reached.

Marginal Pass—Score = 3

I was excited when I learned that my roommate in college would be studying psychology, too. We could study together. We could sign up for the same classes! What a great luck to be put together! However, as time whent on, it turned out that my roommate and I weren't to be friends.

She was a 4.0 student and I was not. But I had good grades in psych classes because I was interested. But before every test I asked if she wanted to study together. She always had somewhere else to go. She always had some reason our schedules wouldn't mesh and that's why we couldn't study together. It took me longer than I'd like to admit, but I figured out she was competitive about grades. And friends. And guys. And the list goes on.

After each exam she wanted to know what's my grade? She never volunteered hers, and I stopped asking. Apparently my grades were actually just as good as hers. I was as shocked as she was! Twice she asked me for my notes, and I gave them to her in hopes that she would see we could work together. But when I asked for her notes once, she claimed she hadn't gone to that class. I knew she did.

Everything came to a head a week before finals, when my notebook went missing. I moped, but figured I was just careless. But the day before our final, I skipped out on work to cram. So I was home earlier than I said I'd be. My roommate was in the bathroom. And my notebook was on the table next to hers. For a split second, I nearly yelled "hey, I found my notebook!" before I realized the situation. She took it so I couldn't study, I was stunned, and hurt. My first thought was to steal hers before she got out of the bathroom and run away and take it with me. But I just took mine and went into my bedroom and stewed. I barely even studied.

I never mentioned it to her. I made sure she saw that I had it, which I knew was embarrassing enough for her. It took that for me to see she was really sad and pathetic. Still. When she asked what I got on the exam, I may have lied. A person can only be so good.

Marginal Fail-Score = 2

I have had many conflicts. One conflict one time was with a student I had. She had a bad attitude. She liked to show off and be fresh. This led to many conflicts between she and me.

I called her parents to talk to them. I told her parents that she was very fresh and distractive in class. I told them that she didn't do her homework and was being a bad influence on other students.

They said they would talk to her. They said she isn't like that at home at all. The next day I asked the student if her parents talked to her. She told me that they grounded her for a month. I felt bad about it, but not really.

She stopped showing off and being mean to me. I think she actually began to like the class after, to.

Fail-Score = 1

Conflicts are like arguments or fights. People get in conflicts about things like money or things they say. Teachers get into conflicts with students who are rude all the time. And students don't like teachers who are too strict or don't make sense. Students have conflices with each other too. Some students don't like each other and are mean to each other. They have to solve these conflicts.

GLOSSARY

Reading Terms

analyze: to examine information for deeper understanding

author's purpose: the reason an author writes: to entertain, inform, explain, or persuade

context clues: information from surrounding text that helps clarify meaning

generalize: making an inference based on the information in a passage

graphic features: features that illustrate information in text, such as graphs, charts, maps, diagrams, and tables

index: a list of words or phrases with corresponding page numbers indicating where that word or phrase can be found in a document

infer: to arrive at an idea by reasoning with facts from a passage

main idea: the central thought of a passage

scan: to look over text quickly for a specific purpose

summarize: to briefly describe the general idea of a passage

table of contents: the list of the chapters or sections in a book with the corresponding page numbers

text features: headings, key words and phrases, illustrations and photos, graphics, and text organizers theme: a topic; the unifying idea of a piece of writing

GLOSSARY

Writing Terms

active voice: a sentence style in which the subject performs the action agreement: the rule that a singular noun or pronoun must take a singular verb, and a plural noun or pronoun must take a plural verb

brainstorm: to list all of the possible ideas that you can write about

conclusion: a closing paragraph that reemphasizes the main points

draft: a first copy of your writing

edit: to prepare a written piece for its final copy by checking it over and correcting all mistakes

elaborate: to add details to written work to support an idea

fluency: the smooth flow of ideas that helps the reader understand a piece of writing

graphic organizer: a chart or graphic that organizes and records thoughts about a topic

introduction: an opening paragraph that includes a thesis statement

outline: a logically organized plan setting out the structure of a piece of writing

paragraph: a group of sentences written to tell about a central idea

parallel construction: a sentence construction where equal parts are expressed using similar grammatical forms

passive voice: a sentence style in which the action is performed on the subject; usually inferior to the active voice unless specifically called for

proofread: to read a written piece in order to make edits

revise: making changes to writing in order to improve it

sentence: a group of words that tell a complete thought; it includes a subject and predicate

thesis: a sentence that states what the writer believes or intends to prove

topic sentence: a sentence that tells the main idea of a paragraph

Math Terms

addend: a number that is added to another number

algebra: a branch of mathematics that substitutes letters for numbers

arithmetic: a branch of mathematics concerned with the computation of numbers

average: the middle or most common in a set of data, usually found by the mean, the median, or the mode

calculate: to compute

calculator: a machine used for computation

capacity: the amount a container holds

Celsius: a temperature scale in which water freezes at 0° and boils at 100°

circle: the set of points in a plane that are a fixed distance from a given point called the center

GLOSSARY

circle graph: a graph in the form of a circle divided into sectors, with each sector representing a part of a set of data

circumference: the distance around a circle

common denominator: a denominator shared by two or more fractions

common factor: a factor of two or more numbers

common multiple: a multiple of two or more numbers

cross product: a product found by multiplying the numerator of one fraction by the denominator of another fraction and the denominator of the first fraction by the numerator of the second

cube: a solid figure with six square faces

data: gathered information

decimal number: numbers with one or more places to the right of a decimal point

decimal point: a period used to separate the whole number part from the decimal part

denominator: the bottom part of a fraction that represents the size of the parts

difference: the result of subtracting two numbers

digit: the ten symbols 0, 1, 2, 3, 4, 5, 6, 7, 8, and 9

distance: length, as between two points

division: the process of partitioning an amount into groups

equal: to have the same value; the symbol is =

equation: a mathematical statement that says two expressions have the same value; a number sentence with an equal sign, =

equivalent: two or more expressions that have the same value

equivalent fractions: fractions that reduce to the same number

estimate: an approximate calculation of a value

exponent: a number that indicates the operation of repeated multiplication

expression: a combination of mathematical symbols representing a value or relation

factor: one of two or more expressions that are multiplied together to get a product

factoring: to break a number into its factors

Fahrenheit: temperature scale in which water boils at 212° and freezes at 32°

formula: an equation that states a rule or a fact

fraction: a number used to name a part of a group or a whole

graph: a visual representation of data

greatest common factor: the largest number that divides into two or more numbers evenly, also called GCF

height: the dimension used to describe the length from lowest point to highest point; how tall something is

improper fraction: a fraction with a numerator that is greater than the denominator

GLOSSARY

inequality: a mathematical expression which shows that two quantities are not equal using symbols such as > or <

integer: a number in the set of numbers containing zero and positive and negative whole numbers

inverse operations: two operations that have the opposite effect, such as addition and subtraction

least common denominator: the smallest multiple of the denominators of two or more fractions

least common multiple: the smallest nonzero number that is a multiple of two or more numbers

length: measure of distance; a dimension of a solid or rectangle

like fractions: fractions that have the same denominator

lowest terms: simplest form; when the GFC of the numerator and the denominator of a fraction is 1

mean: in a data set, the sum of all numbers divided by the number of data points; the average

median: the middle number in a data set when the numbers are put in order

minus: subtract or decrease by; the symbol is −

mixed number: a number written as a whole number and a fraction

mode: the value that occurs the most frequently in a data set

multiple: the product of a number and any other whole number

multiplication: the process of repeating additions of the same number

multiply: to compute a product; to perform multiplication

negative number: a real number that is less than zero

number line: a line on which every point represents a real number, usually increasing in value from left to right

numeral: a written symbol referring to a number

numerator: the top part of a fraction describing the number of parts in a whole

odds: the ratio of the probability that an event will occur compared with the probability that it will not occur

operation: addition, subtraction, multiplication, and division are the basic arithmetic operations

order of operations: the mathematical rules that determine the correct order for solving any sequence of math operations; powers and roots are solved before multiplication and division, which in turn are solved before addition and subtraction

percent: a fraction or ratio in which the denominator is assumed to be 100; the symbol is %

percentile: a score location below which a specified percentage of the population falls

perimeter: the sum of the lengths of the sides of a polygon

pi: the ratio of the circumference of a circle to its diameter equaling 3.1415926…; the symbol is π

plus: add or increase by; the symbol is +

polygon: a closed figure made up of several line segments that are joined together

positive number: a number greater than zero

power: an exponent; a number that indicates the operation of repeated multiplication

GLOSSARY

probability: for an experiment, the total number of successful events divided by the total number of possible events

product: the result of two numbers being multiplied together

proper fraction: a fraction whose numerator is less than its denominator

proportion: an equation of fractions in the form $\frac{a}{b} = \frac{c}{d}$

proportional: a statement of equality in which each member is a fraction

quotient: the answer to a division problem

radius: the distance from the center to a point on a circle

range: the difference between the largest and the smallest numbers in a data set

rate: a ratio that compares different kinds of units

ratio: a pair of numbers that compares different types of units

reciprocal: the number which, when multiplied times a particular fraction, gives a result of 1

remainder: the portion of the dividend that is not evenly divisible by the divisor

sequence: a set of numbers, called terms, arranged in some particular order

simplest form: a fraction is in simplest form if both its numerator and denominator are whole numbers and their only common factor is 1

simplified fraction: a fraction in simplest form

simplify: to reduce to lowest terms

stanine: standardized student score ranging from 1 to 9; stanines of 1 to 3 are considered below average, stanines of 4 to 6 are considered average, and stanines of 7 to 9 are considered above average

subtraction: the process of finding the difference between two or more numbers or expressions

sum: the result of adding numbers or expressions

unit: a standard quantity used in measurement

variable: a letter used to represent a number value in an expression or equation

Venn diagram: a diagram that uses circles to represent mathematical or logical sets pictorially; elements common to more than one set are represented by intersections of the circles

volume: a measurement of space, or capacity

weight: a measure of how heavy something is

width: measure of a (usually horizontal) distance

ADDITIONAL ONLINE PRACTICE

Whether you need help building basic skills or preparing for an exam, visit the LearningExpress Practice Center! On this site, you can access additional practice materials. Using the code below, you'll be able to log in and take an additional full-length CBEST practice exam. This online practice exam will also provide you with:

- **Immediate Scoring**
- **Detailed answer explanations**
- **Personalized recommendations for further practice and study**

Log on to the LearningExpress Practice Center by using the URL: **www.learnatest.com/practice**

This is your Access Code: **7595**

Follow the steps online to redeem your access code. After you've used your access code to register with the site, you will be prompted to create a username and password. For easy reference, record them here:

Username: _____ **Password:** _____

With your username and password, you can log in and answer these practice questions as many times as you like. If you have any questions or problems, please contact LearningExpress customer service at 1-800-295-9556 ext. 2, or e-mail us at **customerservice@learningexpressllc.com**

LB 3060.33 .C34 C24 2011

CBEST